MONEY, WEALTH, AND ECONOMIC THEORY

MONEY, WEALTH, AND ECONOMIC THEORY

BORIS P. PESEK
MICHIGAN STATE UNIVERSITY

THOMAS R. SAVING
MICHIGAN STATE UNIVERSITY

THE MACMILLAN COMPANY · NEW YORK
COLLIER-MACMILLAN LIMITED · LONDON

First Printing

Library of Congress catalog card number: 67-11626

THE MACMILLAN COMPANY, NEW YORK
COLLIER-MACMILLAN CANADA, LTD., TORONTO, ONTARIO

Printed in the United States of America

Acknowledgments

Appreciation is hereby expressed to the following for permission to quote extensively:

Harper and Row, Publishers:
From Don Patinkin, *Money, Interest, and Prices*, First Edition (New York: 1956); Don Patinkin, *Money, Interest, and Prices*, Second Edition (New York: Harper & Row, Publishers, Inc., 1956, 1965).

Harcourt, Brace & World, Inc., Macmillan & Co., Ltd., and the Trustees of the Estate of Lord Keynes:
From John Maynard Keynes, *The General Theory of Employment, Interest, and Money* (New York: Harcourt, Brace & Co., 1936; London: Macmillan & Co., Ltd., 1936).

The Brookings Institution:
From John G. Gurley and Edward S. Shaw, *Money in a Theory of Finance* (Washington, D.C.: The Brookings Institution, 1960).

TO MILENA *AND TO* BARBARA

Preface

This book owes its existence to the numerous discussions of wealth, the wealth effect, and monetary theory that have appeared in the professional literature in the past decade. The most direct impetus was provided by Harry G. Johnson's review of monetary theory and policy, in which he pinpointed with great clarity some of the basic difficulties facing monetary theory, and in which he asked whether the present state of that theory is really the best that can be achieved. We resolved to try to do better.

Trying to do better, we discovered, meant not only building upon the foundations provided by our predecessors but also, especially in the case of monetary theory, disagreeing with them on some quite fundamental issues. In view of this disagreement and the intricacy of some of the arguments, we decided not to incur the risks associated with a paraphrasing of what others have said. Direct quotes appeared to increase the likelihood that we shall present the currently dominant monetary theory fairly and that we shall be able to demonstrate the precise character of the opposing viewpoints. As a result, our book contains more than a normal share of direct quotations; we are grateful for all permissions to quote directly.

This book is fully a joint effort. While each of us wrote some of the first rough drafts of various chapters, these first drafts were passed back and forth, discussed, and rewritten so many times that any allocation of responsibility for the end product between the two

vii

of us appears impossible. In addition, we received much helpful advice. Our colleagues Karl Brunner, Victor E. Smith, and William Russell read several versions of the manuscript; Jan Kmenta and Jack R. Vernon read parts of it. To all of them we wish to express our gratitude.

Our work was greatly facilitated by several grants of time free from teaching responsibilities, and of financial aids of various kinds provided by Michigan State University. The last part of the book was written while one of the authors (Boris P. Pesek) was a recipient of a Ford Foundation Faculty Research Fellowship. The chairman of our department, Robert F. Lanzillotti, could not have been more helpful in obtaining for us some of the above aids, and in providing us with all the technical resources needed for the completion of our work. We are grateful to all those who helped us in this manner. As is customary and required, let us state that none of the institutions named above is in any manner responsible for the views expressed in this book.

Mr. Jeffrey A. Roth checked all our quotations and bibliographical references for accuracy. Mrs. Alice Semrau typed all the various drafts and made numerous editorial decisions. Her competency, efficiency, and dedication to this task could not be appreciated more by either one of us.

B. P. P.
T. R. S.

Michigan State University
East Lansing

Contents

There can be no doubt, however, that the theory of the "Keynes effect," the "Pigou effect," or more generally the "wealth-saving relations" constitute a permanent enrichment to our analytical apparatus: this we largely owe to the stimulus provided by the *General Theory*. Keynes forced the classical writers to rethink, restate, and to refine their theories.

—GOTTFRIED HABERLER,
"Sixteen Years Later" in Robert Lekachman (ed.), *Keynes' General Theory* (New York, 1964), p. 292.

PART I

THE ORIGINS OF THE
WEALTH EFFECT

In general, the concept of the relationship between the wealth
of the consumer and his economic behavior has long been
acknowledged. Adam Smith recognized the relationship when
he wrote that "The prodigal perverts it [i.e., the proper desti-
nation of capital] in this manner. By not confining his expenses
within his income, he encroaches upon his capital."[1] Alfred
Marshall, when discussing the determinants of demand for
goods, mentions the real quantity of money as one determinant and the quantity of real wealth as another.[2] However,

[1] Adam Smith, *The Wealth of Nations* (New York: Random House, 1937),
p. 322.
[2] Alfred Marshall, *Principles of Economics* (New York: The Macmillan Co.,
1949), pp. 109–110.

all these statements were mere precursors of the concept of the wealth effect as we know it today. Systematic incorporation of wealth into the main body of economic theory occurred only in response to the serious challenge that *The General Theory of Employment Interest and Money* posed to the profession. Prior to the publication of this book, economic theory asserted that a fully competitive economic model, containing the necessary wage and price flexibilities, would have an automatic tendency towards a full equilibrium in *all* markets. However, John Maynard Keynes had constructed a new macroeconomic model that combined all the major macroeconomic variables. On the basis of this model he showed that under certain conditions, the existence of which cannot be ruled out—however unlikely they may be—even a perfectly competitive model may yield a stable solution whereby all but one market are cleared. The possibility that we might have a "general" equilibrium in which one market is out of equilibrium represented a serious challenge to economic theory. Moreover, the problem posed was of more than just theoretical interest because the sole exception was a market of overwhelming social importance— the labor market. Finally, inherent in the less-than-full-employment-equilibrium case was the conclusion that the correction, which only a government may provide, must not be based on monetary policy but only on fiscal policy. This aspect of the problem raised by Keynes was, obviously, of great interest to the policy maker.

It was in response to these problems posed by the Keynesian analysis that wealth was formally introduced into the body of economic analysis by Haberler, Scitovsky, Pigou, and Hicks. Subsequent analysis of the fundamentally simple concept of the wealth-consumption relationship by many economists revealed that the apparent simplicity actually hides a relationship that is very subtle and complex. In Part I of this book, we shall first trace the birth of the wealth effect and then outline the many-faceted criticism to which it has been subjected.

CHAPTER 1

The Birth of the Wealth Effect

Wealth was introduced into economic analysis in response to the challenge posed to the economic theorist and to the policy maker by the Keynesian less-than-full-employment-equilibrium case. Because an answer may be more readily explained and understood if the problem to be answered is stated first, we shall outline, in some detail, the less-than-full-employment case and then outline the role the wealth effect plays in it. We shall employ a macroeconomic model that is only as complex as is absolutely necessary.

Basic Keynesian Model

Keynes' macroeconomic model[1] divides the forces in the economy on the traditional lines of supply for goods and services and demand for goods and services. The aggregate demand subset that is used to yield the aggregate demand function contains two parts: the commodity market and the money market. We shall discuss each

[1] John Maynard Keynes, *The General Theory of Employment Interest and Money* (New York: Harcourt, Brace & World, 1936), pp. 304–306.

3

component of the model first; then we shall indicate the way in which all the components participate in the determination of the equilibrium of the system as a whole.

AGGREGATE DEMAND. Equilibrium in the commodity market requires that the demand for consumption goods plus the demand for investment goods be equal to the total supply of goods. If, for the sake of convenience, we wish to base our discussion not on the consumption function but on the saving function, we may restate the equilibrium condition: saving (s), which depends on the level of real income (y), must equal investment (i), which depends on the rate of interest (r):

$$s = s(y) \qquad [1.1]$$

$$i = i(r) \qquad [1.2]$$

$$s = i \qquad [1.3]$$

Since, for expository purposes, it is useful to employ a geometric interpretation of the model, in Figure 1–1 we have placed the investment function in the northwest quadrant and the saving function in the southwest quadrant. By the use of a 45° line that converts vertical measurements into horizontal ones, we may construct the Hicksian *IS* function that (utilizing the equilibrium condition [1.3] attached to the two behavior relations [1.1] and [1.2]) shows all the pairs of the rate of interest and income consistent with equilibrium in the commodity market.

In the money market, equilibrium requires that the demand for real money for transaction purposes m_t, which depends on the level of income, plus the demand for money for asset purposes m_a, which depends on the rate of interest, be equal to the real money supply m_s.[2] This real money supply is definitionally equal to the nominal money supply M_s deflated by the price level P:

---

[2] We shall discuss the meaning of this dichotomy, or rather the lack of it, in detail in Chapter 14.

$$m_t = m_t(y) \qquad [1.4]$$

$$m_a = m_a(r) \qquad [1.5]$$

$$m_s = m_a + m_t \qquad [1.6]$$

$$m_s = \frac{M}{P} \qquad [1.7]$$

$$M_s = \overline{M}_s \qquad [1.8]$$

The nominal money supply is assumed, for simplicity, to be determined by the government and therefore is exogenous. The price level is one of the endogenous variables, the level of which we must determine. For the time being, we shall assume some arbitrary level of prices, such as

$$P = P_1 \qquad [1.9]$$

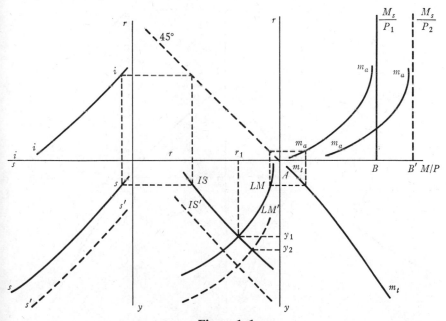

Figure 1–1
The Demand Subset

On the horizontal axis in the eastern panel of Figure 1–1, we place the real money supply (distance AB), and at point B we erect another vertical axis. With point B serving as the origin, we place in the northern quadrant the asset demand for money (equation [1.5]); with point A serving as the origin, we place in the southern quadrant the transaction demand for money (equation [1.4]). Again using the

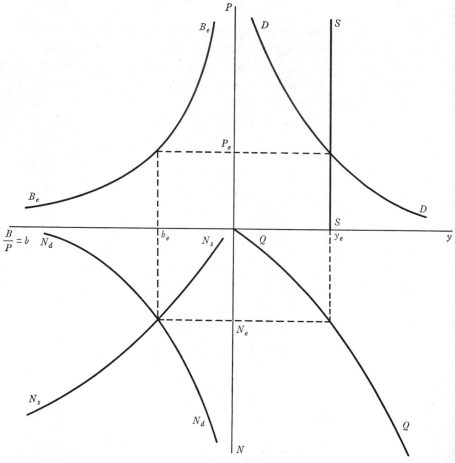

Figure 1–2
The Full-employment Case

45° line we construct the Hicksian LM function that, utilizing the equilibrium condition [1.6], shows all the pairs of the rate of interest and income consistent with equilibrium in the money market.

The intersection of the IS and LM functions gives the output that will be demanded (y_1) if the general price level is, as assumed, P_1. If we assume a different level of prices, say, P_2, the real money supply will change, and thus point B will shift to B'. Since this point serves as the origin for the $m_a m_a$ function, this function moves along with it. As a result of these changes, we get a new LM function (LM') and a new intersection of the IS and LM functions. This intersection indicates another equilibrium pair of the level of output (y_2) and the price level (P_2). By repeating this procedure and by plotting the resulting equilibrium pairs of y and P in the northeast corner of Figure 1–2, we obtain the aggregate demand function.

AGGREGATE SUPPLY. In the supply subset Keynes assumed a production function that, with capital in the short run given, relates employment (N) to the real income produced. Both the demand for labor (N_d) and the supply of labor (N_s) depend on the real wage b.[3] In equilibrium, they will be equal. Real wage, of course, is definitionally equal to the money wage (B) deflated by the price level:

$$y = y(N) \qquad [1.10]$$

$$N_d = N_d(b) \qquad [1.11]$$

$$N_s = N_s(b) \qquad [1.12]$$

$$N_s = N_d \qquad [1.13]$$

$$b = \frac{B}{P} \qquad [1.14]$$

[3] We apologize for using the unusual symbol b and B for real and money wages. Our excuse is that all other symbols with mnemonic connotations have been reserved for variables that are discussed much more frequently than are wages in this book. It might be useful, at this point, to draw the reader's attention to the fact that at the end of this book there is a *List Of Symbols Used* that might be consulted in case of need.

To obtain a geometric interpretation of this model we may place the production function QQ (equation [1.10]) in the southeast corner of Figure 1–2 and the supply and demand for labor (equations [1.11] and [1.12]) in the southwest corner. The intersection of the labor supply and demand functions determine the equilibrium level of employment N_e, real wage b_e, and the full-employment level of income y_e. Price level plays no role in this case: the aggregate supply function SS is perfectly inelastic. Its intersection with the aggregate demand function DD determines the equilibrium level of income y_e, of prices P_e, and, in the northwest quadrant, the equilibrium level of money wages B_e. By substituting the equilibrium price level and real income in Figure 1–1, we may also find the equilibrium rate of interest. If the aggregate demand function should fall to $D'D'$ (Figure 1–3), income will stay the same, and only the price level will change (falling from P_1 to P_2).

LESS-THAN-FULL-EMPLOYMENT EQUILIBRIUM. This framework gives us all the tools we need to demonstrate the Keynesian assertion that under certain conditions even a fully competitive model may find itself in a less-than-full-employment equilibrium. Suppose that the aggregate demand function falls to, say, $D'D'$ in Figure 1–3 and that there are forces that prevent the money wage B_e from falling and reaching the new equilibrium level B'_e. This makes it impossible for the rectangular hyperbola (expressing, in the northwest corner, equation [1.14]) to fall from B_eB_e to $B'_eB'_e$; the new real wage-price relationship *must* be found somewhere along the old function B_eB_e that is constructed for the old money wage B_e:

$$N_s = N_d \quad \text{if} \quad B = B'_e$$
$$N = N_d \quad \text{if} \quad B > B'_e \qquad [1.13a]$$

and

$$B = B_e \qquad [1.15]$$

With money wages constant, the function B_eB_e remains unchanged so that the above specified drop in aggregate demand and subsequent

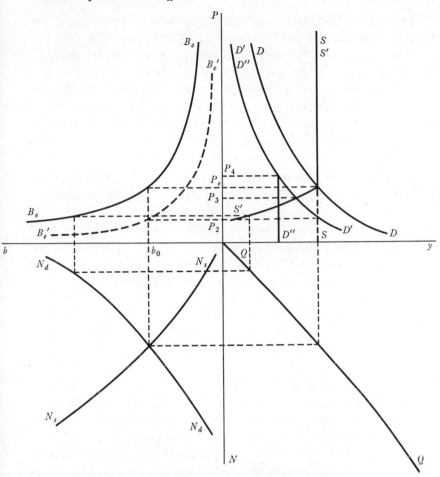

Figure 1–3
The Less-than-full-employment Case

price level reduction increases real wages. At this new higher real wage rate, employers employ fewer workers and output supplied falls. Thus, price changes now affect the aggregate supply function, giving it a positively sloping segment; the original SS function is replaced with the $S'S'$ function (Figure 1–3). A new equilibrium, at

less than full employment, is established at price level P_3 given by
the intersection of the $D'D'$ function with the new $S'S'$ function.
This result is, as yet, in no conflict with the classical analysis:
with rigid money wages we obtain unemployment.

What can we say, however, about the classical cure for this unemployment: a fall in money wages? To discuss this question we need
to return to the demand subset, where the real difference between
Keynes and the classicists lies:

1. If the investment function *ii* is perfectly inelastic with respect
   to the rate of interest at low levels of the rate, the *IS* function also
   will be perfectly inelastic within this range.
2. If the investment function *ii* has a negative slope throughout
   but intersects the investment axis at a point that does not yield
   a full-employment level of investment, the *IS* function will
   intersect the income axis at a less-than-full-employment level of
   income.
3. If the asset demand for money $m_a m_a$ is perfectly elastic at low
   levels of the rate of interest, the *LM* function will also be perfectly
   elastic at these low rates.

As long as none of these conditions prevails, a decrease in the level
of prices will cause the intersection of the *IS* and the *LM* functions
to shift to a higher and higher level of income: the aggregate demand
function will have a negative slope. The moment any one of these
conditions becomes operative, decreases in the level of prices cannot
result in any additional increase in the aggregate demand for goods
and services: the aggregate demand function becomes perfectly inelastic whenever one of the above three special conditions becomes
operative and will have a shape as shown by the function $D''D''$ in
Figure 1–3. Regardless of the aggregate supply function, the maximum level of output that can be sold at the price level P_4 or at any
lower one is fixed and is determined solely by the inelastic portion of
the aggregate demand function, resulting in a less-than-full-employment equilibrium.

True enough, we have this equilibrium with wage rigidities, but a removal of these rigidities cannot change the level of income; it will merely cause a proportionate decrease in the general price level. Indeed, should the rigidities with respect to money wages disappear, the aggregate supply function would become perfectly inelastic as in Figure 1–2, it would not intersect the aggregate demand function $D''D''$, and there would be no equilibrium at all. Rigid wages, in this case, are all that stand between us and chaos. Without them, as Gottfried Haberler put it, "the system would collapse."[4] The economy is in a situation from which it cannot be extricated by any automatic mechanism, the government must come to the rescue, and this rescue must have a specific form. Even though increases in the nominal money supply will shift the negatively sloping segment of the aggregate demand function upwards, the perfectly inelastic segment of this demand function cannot be shifted to the left for precisely the same reason that we have the inelastic segment. That is, changes in the real quantity of money, regardless of whether they are brought about through changes in the numerator or the denominator, nominal money supply, or the price level, either cannot decrease (item 3 above) the rate of interest or, even if they do, such a decrease cannot cause the level of investment to increase (items 1 and 2 above). Aggregate demand remains unchanged. Therefore, while the government is the only agency that is able to restore full employment, any attempt to achieve this by the use of monetary policy must fail. The only effective tool is a fiscal policy that either increases the demand for goods and services by the government, or, by decreasing taxes, increases private demand.

Birth of the Wealth Effect

This analysis, making even a perfectly competitive model with full price and wage flexibilities unable to reach full employment, proved

---

[4] Gottfried Haberler, *Prosperity and Depression* (Geneva: League of Nations, 1941), p. 500, footnote 2.

disturbing to many economists. Is it conceivable that a simple economy, in which there is no government, could not right itself and reach full employment? Even in a complex system, many are ready to concede, a government may make adjustments easier and more efficient. But is government's intervention *a conditio sine qua non*? This is intellectually as dissatisfying as would be an astronomical theory that explains the position of all planets, but asserts that the position of the sun is determined each day by the Lord. A solution to this dilemma was not long in coming. A year after the publication of the *General Theory*, Gottfried Haberler published his *Prosperity and Depression*, and the wealth effect was born.

PRICE-INDUCED WEALTH EFFECT.   At first, the reply was based on the fall in prices which, as we have seen, must accompany a fall in money wages. Gottfried Haberler wrote:

> The magnitude of these [money] hoards will increase . . . : it increases still faster, owing to the fall in prices, in terms of real purchasing power. These hoards will grow in relation to real income as well as in relation to real wealth. . . . After liquid resources have reached a certain high proportion of wealth, the need for liquidity will eventually become satisfied and people will stop adding to their hoards. . . . One or both of two things will then happen. Either more money will be lent out on the capital market, with the result that interest will be forced down . . . ; or . . . people will become less disposed to save—in Mr. Keynes' terminology, the propensity to consume will rise in addition to the decrease in the liquidity preference—and the demand for consumers' goods will cease to fall, or may even rise.[5]

Thus Haberler pointed out that the propensity to consume depends not only on the level of income received by each individual but also on his holdings of wealth (w), both real (w_{nm}) and monetary $\left(\dfrac{M}{P}\right)$. In our notation, he revised the Keynesian saving function to read:

$$s = s\left(y, w_{nm} + \frac{M}{P}\right) \qquad\qquad [1.1a]$$

[5] Gottfried Haberler, pp. 388–389.

The Birth of the Wealth Effect

Concentrating on monetary wealth, he pointed out that as money wages fall, prices also fall; and as prices fall, holdings of real money balances increase. This makes people wealthier and, as a result, their consumption increases.

INTEREST-INDUCED WEALTH EFFECT. Much later, in 1951, Lloyd A. Metzler let the other shoe drop. He wrote:

... we may say that the real value of the given common stock [in Metzler's terminology *all* real nonhuman wealth is measured by the quantity of "common stock"] is inversely related to the prevailing rate of interest. The higher the rate of interest, the lower the real value of common-stock holdings and conversely.[6]

In our notation, real wealth yields a stream of income y. The value of the real wealth is simply the capitalized value of this stream:

$$w = \frac{y}{r} \qquad [1.16]$$

If, as Haberler claimed, in a depression not only the price level but also the interest rate falls, this fall in the rate will cause the discounted value of streams of income yielded by wealth to increase. Again, individuals will be wealthier and the propensity to save will fall.

WEALTH EFFECT IN THE KEYNESIAN MODEL. If we now return to the aggregate demand subset, we may trace the consequences of the two parts of the wealth effect: Haberler's price-induced wealth effect and Metzler's interest-induced wealth effect. In the simple Keynesian model, a fall in prices shifts the *LM* function to $L'M'$ (Figure 1-1) and causes an increase in the income demanded. However, once one of the three conditions specified earlier becomes operative, the shift in the *LM* function becomes ineffective in that it is unable to increase the demand for goods and services. With the price and interest rate wealth effects, a decrease in either the price level, or the interest rate, or both, increases the value of wealth and thus causes a shift of the saving function to $s's'$. Therefore, in addition

[6] Lloyd A. Metzler, "Wealth, Saving, and the Rate of Interest," *Journal of Political Economy*, LIX (April, 1951), p. 101.

to the shift of *LM* to *LM'* there is also a shift of *IS* to *IS'*.[7] This makes it certain that the aggregate demand function has a negative slope throughout; the inelastic segment of it (due to the three possibilities outlined above) on which the less-than-full-employment model rests cannot exist. While rigorous proof must wait, it is enough to point out that if the price level approached zero, or if the interest rate approached zero, or both, the value of wealth would approach infinity. With infinitely great wealth, consumption would also become infinitely great: the aggregate demand function is negatively sloping throughout and asymptotic to the output axis. But then a less-than-full-employment equilibrium in a competitive economy without price and wage rigidities is impossible. If, in any specific economy, such rigidities do exist, a removal of unemployment may again be accomplished either by the removal of them or by the application of government fiscal *or* monetary policy. Actually, it might be more expeditious to employ the powers of the government to neutralize price and wage rigidities rather than to attempt to achieve perfection by combatting these rigidities. But no matter how convenient a tool the government may be, once the wealth effect is brought into economic analysis we do not *have* to have the government, as a *deus ex machina*, to rescue us. In addition, the government once again has all the traditional policy tools at its disposal: it may still use fiscal policy, but it may also use monetary policy. Even if increases in the quantity of money do not lower the rate of interest through the *LM* function, they do increase the aggregate demand by shifting the saving function and hence the *IS* function.

REACTIONS TO THE WEALTH EFFECT.   A. C. Pigou, in the same article in which he offered his answer to the problem posed by Keynes, supplied those followers of Keynes who became committed to the less-than-full-employment model and to the policy implications

---

[7] Whereas the effects of changes in prices on the *IS* function are obvious, the effects of changes in the rate of interest are more complex. It would not be profitable at this point to attempt to be too rigorous in that respect, however, because price changes will suffice to bring about the consequences just outlined.

of this model with a rebuttal that they have used vigorously ever since. After presenting his price-induced wealth effect and demonstrating that it destroys the less-than-full-employment equilibrium case, he pointed out the empirical difficulties associated with the necessary price flexibilities and concluded:

> Thus the puzzles we have been considering in the last section are academic exercises, of some slight use perhaps in clarifying thought, but with very little chance for ever being posed on the checker board of actual life.[8]

Similarly, J. R. Hicks wrote that he has "no doubt that it [the price-induced wealth effect] is valid theoretically and in principle it ought to be allowed for," but stated that he "cannot . . . attach much practical importance to it."[9] Ever since, the moderate disciples of Keynes admit that Keynes overlooked the wealth effect, but excuse him on the grounds of justifiable neglect.[10] His less moderate disciples even claim that Keynes surely must have considered the effect only to discard it after reaching a conclusion that in view of the existing price and wage rigidities it has no empirical significance.[11] We cannot help but feel that introspection in general, and introspection into somebody else's mind in particular, places any debate

---

[8] A. C. Pigou, "Economic Progress in a Stable Environment," in F. A. Lutz and Lloyd W. Mints (ed.), *Readings in Monetary Theory* (New York: The Blackiston Co., 1951), p. 251.

[9] J. R. Hicks, *Value and Capital* (Oxford, Eng.: Oxford University Press, 1948), p. 335.

[10] Cf. D. C. Champernowne, "Expectations and the Links Between the Economic Future and the Present," in Robert Lekachman (ed.), *Keynes' General Theory* (New York: St. Martin's Press, 1964), p. 191: "One theoretically possible effect which he did not find worthwhile to mention was [the wealth effect] . . . But there seems to be no good evidence on which to doubt Keynes' good judgment in ignoring this effect as being of no practical importance."

[11] Cf. Abba P. Lerner, "The General Theory After Twenty-Five Years: Discussion," *American Economic Review, LI* (May, 1961), p. 22: "Keynes was an impatient man and had no use for academic philosophizing about impossible degree of flexibility, and I am convinced that it was this impatience and not a failure to consider the theoretical possibility that is responsible for his not mentioning the 'wealth effect.'"

on quite slippery ground: a hypothesis based on introspection is normally nondebatable. Fortunately, in the case of John Maynard Keynes very few things are normal.

Keynes: Father of the Wealth Effect

In view of the general agreement of friend and foe that Keynes in his *General Theory* either overlooked or decided not to consider the wealth effect we were startled indeed when, upon rereading the *General Theory*, we realized that in it Keynes:

1. Has an excellent statement of the interest-induced wealth effect.
2. Has a rudimentary but still adequate statement of the price-induced wealth effect.
3. Repeatedly and emphatically declares these two effects to be empirically very important.
4. After stating all this, forgets all about it, but—indirectly—provides a likely explanation for this lapse.

In his Chapter 8, "The Propensity to Consume," Keynes states:

> The amount that the community spends on consumption obviously depends:
>   (i) partly on the amount of its income,
> (ii) partly on the other objective attendant circumstances, and
> (iii) partly on the subjective needs . . . propensities . . . habits . . . principles on which income is divided. . . .[12]

He asserts that the subjective factors (item iii), though not unalterable, are unlikely to undergo a material change over a short period of time and that, therefore, he will take them as given. This, by indirection, is equivalent to an assertion that the objective factors (item ii) are not constant in the short run and, indeed, he does state that he will assume the propensity to consume [or, what is saying

[12] John Maynard Keynes, *The General Theory of Employment Interest and Money* (New York: Harcourt, Brace & World, 1936), pp. 90–91. Reprinted by permission of Harcourt, Brace & World, Inc. Also by permission of Macmillan & Co. Ltd. and the Trustees of the Estate of Lord Keynes.

the same thing, the relationship between income and consumption (item i)] to depend only on changes in the objective factors (item ii). As we shall show next, two of these objective factors turn out to be what we now call the price-induced wealth effect and the interest-induced wealth effect.

INTEREST-INDUCED WEALTH EFFECT. Among the "principal objective factors" (despite the shift in terminology, this is the item (ii) above) Keynes lists the rate of interest, discusses the numerous ways in which it might affect consumption, and discards all but one as of "secondary importance." About the exception he writes:

> Perhaps the most important influence, operating through changes in the rate of interest, on the readiness to spend out of a given income [i.e., the propensity to consume], depends on the effect of these changes on the appreciation or depreciation in the price of securities and other assets. For if a man is enjoying a windfall increment in the value of his capital, it is natural that his motives towards current spending should be strengthened, even though in terms of income his capital is worth no more than before; and weakened if he is suffering capital losses.[13]

This is one of the most concise descriptions of the interest rate-induced wealth effect. Lloyd A. Metzler in his pioneering article in 1951, fifteen years after the appearance of the *General Theory*, does not have a better one. Keynes goes on to point out that this particular interest effect really belongs in his third group of objective factors (item ii) determining consumption; a group called by him "(3) Windfall changes in capital-values not allowed for in calculating net income."

PRICE-INDUCED WEALTH EFFECT. In discussing this third group of objective factors, Keynes states:

> The consumption of the wealth-owning class may be extremely susceptible to unforeseen changes in the money-value of its wealth.[14]

[13] Keynes, *ibid.*, p. 94.
[14] Keynes, *ibid.*, pp. 92–93.

When compared with Keynes' crystal-clear description of the interest-induced wealth effect, this description of what appears to be the price-induced wealth effect is much less adequate. Before we can be sure that that effect is what Keynes meant, we have to explore his terminology and his justification for the inclusion of these two effects in his analysis.

1. Does Keynes' definition of wealth include money? Unless it does, the above statement cannot refer to the price-induced wealth effect. Keynes' terminology was not entirely consistent, but in other places he makes it clear that his definition of wealth does include money. He speaks about "the owner of wealth" who holds "capital-assets"—a term employed in the heading of the section quoted above. A few paragraphs later he defines capital-assets as "real capital assets" and "*money*"[15] [emphasis ours].

2. The expression "changes in the money-value" is a curious one. The price-induced wealth effect, as modern theorists would say, results in changing real value of monetary wealth, given a constant money value of it; however, this discrepancy is purely terminological. This is well illustrated in the following passage:

> . . . a reduction in the wage-unit will release cash from its other uses for the satisfaction of the liquidity-motive; . . . in addition to this, as money-values fall, the stock of money will bear a higher proportion to the total wealth of the community.[16]

These two clarifications demonstrate that Keynes, in the above quoted statement, really did state the price-induced wealth effect.

To clinch the argument, we might point out that Keynes not only correctly stated both halves of the wealth effect under a single heading but also used the same reasoning as our modern economic theory does to justify the incorporation of wealth as an independent determinant of consumption. Wealth is at present included as a separate determinant of consumption, in addition to income,

[15] Keynes, *ibid.*, p. 212.
[16] Keynes, *ibid.*, p. 232.

because changes in income are not a good index of changes in wealth. Income may, for example, fall, and prices may either increase if aggregate supply is causing the fall, or decrease if aggregate demand is responsible. But that means that with income falling, the real value of one part of wealth, money, may either fall *or* rise. Similarly income, for example, may fall while the interest rate may increase if the drop in demand originates in the money market; or decrease if it originates in the commodity market. But this means that with income falling, the value of nonmonetary wealth may either decrease *or* increase. Both in the case of changes in prices and in the case of changes in the rate of interest, income cannot serve as a proxy for wealth; and hence both income and wealth must be said to determine consumption. But this is precisely how Keynes justified his inclusion of wealth among the determinants of consumption, in addition to income. He says that changes in wealth "are of much more importance in modifying [consumption], since they will bear no stable or regular relationship to the amount of income." [17] In view of all this there cannot be the slightest doubt that Keynes described accurately the two parts of the wealth effect and justified correctly his inclusion of wealth as a determinant of consumption in addition to income.

KEYNES' ESTIMATE OF EMPIRICAL SIGNIFICANCE OF THE WEALTH EFFECT. Keynes could hardly be more emphatic about his belief that the consequences of these two changes in capital-values on consumption are of great importance. About the interest-induced wealth effect he states:

> Perhaps the most important influence, operating through changes in the rate of interest . . . depends on the effect of these changes on the appreciation or depreciation in the price of securities and other assets. . . . *Apart* [emphasis ours] from this, the main conclusion suggested by experience is, I think, that the short-period influence of the rate of interest on individual spending . . . is

[17] Keynes, *ibid.*, p. 92.

secondary and relatively unimportant, except, perhaps, where unusually large changes are in question.[18]

About both effects combined he speaks, again, in the most vigorous terms: "These are of much more importance in modifying the propensity to consume..."; "the consumption of the wealth-owning class may be extremely susceptible" to them. "This should be classified amongst the major factors capable of causing short-period changes in the propensity to consume." "Windfall changes in capital-values will be capable of changing the propensity to consume...; but the other objective factors which might affect it, whilst they must not be overlooked, are not likely to be important in ordinary circumstances;"[19] thus again, by the use of his favorite method of indirection, he is saying that changes in capital-values *are* "likely to be important in ordinary circumstances."

POSSIBLE REASONS FOR KEYNES' SUBSEQUENT NEGLECT OF THE WEALTH EFFECT.   Why did Keynes, after stating the nature of both parts of the wealth effect, after explaining the analytical reasons for their addition to income as separate determinants of consumption, and after repeatedly emphasizing the empirical importance of the two wealth effects, retrogress and forget all about them in his *General Theory*? Why did he give an excellent verbal explanation of the determinants of consumption only to reduce it, in his mathematical symbols,[20] to a function of a single variable, income,

$$C_w = \mathsf{X}(Y_w) \qquad\qquad [1.17]$$

and in the rest of his book develop his model on this narrow basis?

[18] Keynes, *ibid.*, p. 94. In this quotation we emphasized the word "*apart*," since Keynes' followers frequently completely reverse Keynes' evaluation of the importance of the rate of interest by overlooking this word and by concentrating only on the remainder of the sentence. E.g., Alvin Hansen in his *Guide to Keynes* (New York: McGraw-Hill, 1953), p. 84, writes: "The *net* [emphasis ours] conclusion with respect to the rate of interest is that short-period changes are likely to be of secondary importance."
[19] Keynes, *ibid.*, pp. 92–93, 95–96.
[20] Keynes, *ibid.*, p. 90.

Mind reading, as we have just seen, is a treacherous business. However, Keynes himself, while criticizing Professor Pigou, appears to provide an excellent explanation of his own failure:

> The pitfalls of a pseudo-mathematical method, which can make no progress except by making everything a function of a single variable . . . could not be better illustrated. For it is no good to admit later on that there are in fact other variables, and yet to proceed without re-writing everything that has been written up to that point.[21]

Conclusion

The history of the wealth effect is one of the most ironic ones in economics. Keynes stated both parts of the wealth effect, emphasized their importance, and then let wealth slip through his fingers by his failure to build it into his analysis. His critics rediscovered one effect but, except for Gottfried Haberler, minimized its empirical relevance. His supporters admitted that Keynes did not consider it—which he did—but excused his alleged failure by arguing that he must have considered it unimportant—which he did not. Both sides, in general, ignored the problems connected with the wealth effect for more than a decade: twelve years after the appearance of the *General Theory* a memorial to Keynes was published and in the whole volume there is but one passage mentioning the wealth effect and that passage rejects it out of hand simply as

> . . . a modern recrudescence of an excessive pre-occupation with the mere quantity of money—a pre-occupation no less defensible than the old.[22]

Don Patinkin in his Second Edition compiled a whole list of postwar

---

[21] Keynes, *ibid.*, pp. 275–276. Cf. an identical statement in Keynes, pp. 297–298.

[22] Alvin H. Hansen, "The General Theory (2)" in Seymour E. Harris (ed.), *The New Economics* (New York: Alfred A. Knopf, 1948), p. 142.

writings in which the price-induced wealth effect is being ignored;[23] we may merely add some spice to it by pointing out that Don Patinkin himself, even now, keeps ignoring the interest-induced wealth effect.[24]

The explanations for all this neglect are likely to be numerous and only the few most readily apparent may be mentioned here. First, the wealth effect, by depriving the Keynesian analysis of the very striking and truly distinctive feature of a fully competitive equilibrium in which one market is out of equilibrium, was taken as an attack on Keynes, for whose teachings many economists had formed an attachment. The intense emotional pitch of those times, so hard to grasp a mere three decades later, was well transmitted to us by Paul A. Samuelson:

> It is quite impossible for modern students to realize the full effect of what has been advisably called "The Keynesian Revolution" upon those of us brought up in the orthodox tradition. . . . To have been born as an economist before 1936 was a boon—yes. But not to have been born too long before!
> Bliss was it in that dawn to be alive,
> But to be young was very heaven![25]

The second reason, probably a consequence of such an emotional involvement of Keynes' disciples, was recently suggested by Milton Friedman and David Meiselman when they wrote about another controversy, also stimulated by "The Keynesian Revolution":

> The striking thing about the intellectual history of economics in the past three or four decades, and it strongly suggests the flabbiness of the profession, is that so large a fraction of the profession

---

[23] Don Patinkin, *Money, Interest, and Prices*, 2d ed. (New York: Harper & Row, 1965), p. 637.

[24] Patinkin, *ibid.*, p. 295. Patinkin's definition of wealth contains tangible assets A that "are assumed constant" and "hence ignored" regardless of what happens to the rate of interest.

[25] Paul A. Samuelson, "A Brief Survey of Post-Keynesian Development," in Lekachman, *op. cit.*, p. 315.

shifted from one side to the other of this issue on the basis of essentially no evidence.[26]

The third reason for the startling neglect of the wealth effect might have been the preference of many economists for certain public policies. As long as the less-than-full-employment-equilibrium analysis remained intact, there was an objective, scientific case in favor of fiscal policy as the only suitable tool for the maintenance of full employment; a policy that cannot help but be selective in its effects and is therefore well suited to the purposes of social reform. A weakening of the analysis asserting the possibility of a less-than-full-employment equilibrium would have brought in its wake a rehabilitation of monetary policy, relatively poorly suited for governmental attempts to influence the structure and allocation of output. Social reform would have had to depend, once again, on its own merits.

Be that as it may, it is difficult not to speculate how different the history of economic thought would have been in the last thirty years if all this confusion had not occurred. Had Keynes incorporated wealth into his final analysis, he would not have reached the conclusion, so provocative to the classicists, that a less-than-full-employment equilibrium in a perfectly competitive model is possible; the bitter controversy surrounding this claim could have been avoided. More importantly still, his general theory of money would not have been turned, as Harry G. Johnson stated, "into the theory that money is unimportant" and would not have "diverted attention from the influence of money and of price expectations on spending"[27] in a period that required the policy maker to use *all* available tools: first, to fight a depression and, shortly afterwards, to fight inflation. Conversely, had the classicists at least noticed that they were just

[26] Milton Friedman and David Meiselman, "The Relative Stability of Monetary Velocity and the Investment Multiplier in the United States, 1897–1958," in Bertrand Fox and Eli Shapiro (ed.), *Stabilization Policies* (Englewood Cliffs, N.J.: Prentice-Hall, 1963), p. 169.

[27] Harry G. Johnson, "The General Theory After Twenty-Five Years," *American Economic Review, LI* (May, 1961), p. 15.

reminding Keynes of the wealth effect about which he knew and which he stated more fully than they, they might not have awakened the defensive mechanism of Keynes' followers and might have achieved quick settlement of these spurious issues. In the absence of the needless and divisive controversy, the profession could have concentrated fully on the "many genuine and ingenious innovations, both in substance and in emphasis"[28] that Keynes did present in his *General Theory*.

Surely an element in micro- and macroeconomic analysis that has a history as fascinating as the wealth effect does merit detailed scrutiny. This it shall be given in the remainder of this book.

---

[28] Gottfried Haberler, "The General Theory After Ten Years," in Robert Lekachman, *op. cit.*, p. 288.

CHAPTER 2

Criticism of the Wealth Effect

Since the introduction of wealth into macroeconomic analysis, numerous objections have been raised. In this chapter we shall briefly review the major ones. Some of them will be disposed of, we hope, here and now. Others, based on empirical evidence, cannot be dismissed in a book devoted to economic analysis; yet, arguments will be offered suggesting that the sweeping scope assigned to this evidence is, analytically, unwarranted. Finally, several purely analytical objections of great importance are so intricate that we can only outline them in this chapter. Their discussion and—we hope—resolution will come in Parts II through V of this book.

Is the Wealth Effect an Argument over Semantics?

The first point we wish to discuss has not been raised as an objection to the inclusion of wealth in a macroeconomic model; however, it gives the appearance that it disposes of the effect of wealth completely. In some economic analyses,[1] a system that, at the

[1] Lawrence R. Klein, *The Keynesian Revolution* (New York: The Macmillan Co., 1950), p. 195.

outset, makes the behavior of the consumer depend on the stock
of wealth and on the flow of income is, in the course of the analysis,
transformed into a system that makes this behavior depend only on
the flow of income. Such a transformation may be accomplished
because wealth (w) is a stock from which a flow of goods or services
(y) emanates at the rate of (r) per year, where r is the rate of interest.
Therefore we may define wealth in the following manner:

$$w = \frac{y}{r} \qquad [2.1]$$

If we substitute equation [2.1] for wealth whenever it appears in the
system, we will have disposed of any overt mention of wealth as a
determinant of consumer behavior. However, unless the assumptions
on which such a transformation is based are carefully spelled out,
an erroneous conclusion may easily be reached that by disposing of
any overt mention of wealth, we dispose of the effect of wealth.

Specifically, the concept of income that must be used to make
equation [2.1] express fully the variables determining consumer
behavior includes all nonmarket incomes as well as those that pass
through the marketplace. These nonmarket incomes, in turn, must
include the imputed incomes yielded by real wealth owned by the
final consumer and not used for commercial purposes, the imputed
income yielded by money, and the imputed income yielded by the
ownership of those items of wealth that not only produce a certain
pattern of income streams but that also, by virtue of their market-
ability, enable the owner to rearrange his consumption of these
income streams in any pattern he deems desirable; we denote this
part of the wealth as "calls on present or future resources of the
community."[2] Given the differences between income concepts employed in equation [2.1] and the usual national income accounting
concept, we may now ask how our analysis of the effect of wealth
is affected by the use of the transformation indicated in equation
[2.1]. Let us first consider the price-induced wealth effect. If the

---

[2] The reasons for the calls on the present and future resources of the community yielding an imputed income stream will be discussed in Chapter 10.

general price level doubles, the nominal value of all nonmoney incomes and of all nonmoney wealth doubles, but their real values remain unchanged. In contrast, the real value of a constant stock of nominal money will be halved.

Without the transformation indicated by equation [2.1], this will affect the behavior of the consumer through a change in his wealth— in this case a reduction. With such a transformation, the real value of all the flows of goods and services yielded by nonmonetary wealth (including the imputed flows yielded by calls on present or future resources of the community) remains unchanged as the price level doubles. However, the purchasing power of money falls by one half and thus the real income yielded by money to the owners of money (measured by the value of the command over goods of certain value) also falls by one half. Therefore the *total* real income, market-produced and imputed, declines, and we must expect an appropriate reaction by consumers. In the case we are discussing, we must expect a fall in consumption. We obtain a (general) price-induced income effect. By the use of the transformation of all stocks into flows, we have simply transformed a price-induced wealth effect into a price-induced income effect. This is surely what we would expect to happen, because a mere transformation of stocks into flows or vice versa cannot affect economic analysis and cannot result in a disappearance of any particular mode of consumer response to a given economic stimulus.

The interest-induced wealth effect is more complex and requires us to consider an element in the analysis that was unnecessary for the price induced case. For the very existence of the rate of interest implies that the consumers consider future as well as present flows of income. Hence, every receiver of income is by virtue of his ownership of the source of this income a producer of income. Since the inverse of the rate of interest represents the price of future income streams in terms of present output, any increase in the interest rate will reduce the value of these future income streams. Therefore, this increase in the rate of interest reduces the command over present resources enjoyed by the holder of an income stream and consequently reduces the imputed flow of services from the wealth associated with it. This results in a decline in the consumer's income and a consequent decline in his consumption. In the case of a system that contains both stocks and flows, the increase in the rate of interest will simply reduce the value of the consumer's wealth and hence, his consumption.

Therefore, the transformation of a system that includes both the flows of income and the stocks from which these flows emanate to a system that contains only flows, does not remove the wealth effect but simply makes it an income effect. Consequently, it is perfectly legitimate to construct a macroeconomic system on a purely flow basis or, for that matter, on a purely stock basis. For empirical work, however, income flows cannot be freely transformed into wealth because the income figures available to us exclude a sizeable portion of income yielded by monetary wealth, by real wealth—the income from which is consumed by the owner—and by real wealth owned by the government. Keynes expressed all these considerations succinctly when he wrote that in the consumption function we must account for, in addition to income, "changes in capital-values not allowed for in calculating net income," and for changes that "bear no stable or regular relationship to the amount of income."[3]

Price Rigidities and the Wealth Effect

Even at its inception the wealth effect was termed useless because of the downward rigidities of prices and wages. As we have already stated, A. C. Pigou claimed that the wealth effect (as well as the Keynesian less-than-full-employment case) are "academic exercises, of some slight use for clarifying thought, but with little chance of ever being posed on the checker board of actual life."[4] The reason

[3] John Maynard Keynes, *The General Theory of Employment Interest and Money* (New York: Harcourt, Brace & World, 1936), p. 92.
[4] A. C. Pigou, "Economic Progress in a Stable Environment," in F. A. Lutz and Lloyd W. Mints (ed.), *Readings in Monetary Theory* (New York: The Blackiston Co., 1951), p. 251.

for his rejection of the wealth effect's empirical relevance he stated as follows:

> ... it is ridiculous to suppose that the public authorities would stand passive in the case of catastrophic disturbances. If a situation arose in which money income was being driven inexorably downwards ... no government would allow money wage rates to rush downwards very far; legal minimum rates would inevitably be established. This would very likely be done soon enough to prevent [full-employment] equilibrium from emerging.[5]

Many of the followers of Keynes, while ignoring an accompanying stricture by Pigou against the relevance of the less-than-full-employment-equilibrium case, reject the wealth effect precisely on the basis outlined by A. C. Pigou. Thus Abba P. Lerner rejects the wealth effect as "academic theorizing" because

> Any monetary system that permitted third or fourth order [price] flexibility would go the way of the moneys that were driven out by better moneys when they lost their stability in hyperinflations.[6]

Others, although not assuming that the government would act in a way that would make prices and wages inflexible, simply assert that they are. For example, Paul A. Samuelson rejects the arguments based on the wealth effect by stating:

> Had Keynes begun his first few chapters with the simple statement that he found it realistic to assume that modern capitalistic societies had money wage rates that were sticky and resistant to downward

---

[5] A. C. Pigou, *loc. cit.*

[6] Abba P. Lerner, "The General Theory After Twenty-Five Years: Discussion," *American Economic Review, LI* (May, 1961), p. 22. (Understanding may be facilitated by pointing out that Lerner uses the term "n-th order" not in the technical meaning of it but merely for purposes of enumeration.) For a restatement of the above quotation, see also Abba P. Lerner, "A Program for Monetary Stability," in Marshall D. Ketchum and Leon T. Kendall (ed.), *Conference on Savings and Residential Financing* (Chicago: The United States Savings and Loan League, 1962), p. 39.

movements, most of his insights would have remained just as valid.[7]

We should remember that there are two possible reasons for rejecting a theoretical variable as having no empirical relevance: (1) the variable does not affect the economic behavior of consumers or producers, and (2) the variable under discussion does not change or is prevented from changing by some institutional characteristic in our economy. It is extremely important to recognize that these two arguments are based on a very different footing. It is unfortunate that the rejection of the wealth effect, although based on the second argument, has been interpreted by many to imply the first one. The theoretical and empirical justification for the argument based on downward price and wage rigidity is fragmentary at best. However, even if we were to stipulate merely for the sake of argument that prices and wages are inflexible downwards, we still would not have any reason to reject the wealth effect as unimportant. Let us briefly enumerate all the parts of the wealth effect that are untouched by the argument based on downward rigidities:

1. Although price and wage rigidities discussed above make the automatic operation of the price-induced wealth effect inoperative in depressions and recessions, they do not affect its importance during inflationary periods. To eliminate the wealth effect as a topic worthy of economic analysis, the critics would have to make a stronger claim. They would have to assert that wages and prices are rigid in both directions.
2. Even in depressions or recessions, whatever the price and wage reductions cannot accomplish, a policy-determined increase in the nominal quantity of money can. Before wealth was introduced into macroeconomic analysis, monetary policy was said to affect the aggregate demand for goods and services only through the money market, and there it could have been rendered

---

[7] Paul A. Samuelson, "A Brief Survey of Post-Keynesian Developments," in Robert Lekachman (ed.), *Keynes' General Theory* (New York: St. Martin's Press, 1964), p. 332.

impotent by the less-than-full-employment case. With wealth incorporated into the analysis, monetary policy is shown to affect the behavior of the consumer not only through the money market but also through the commodity market, and this influence persists regardless of whether or not we face the less-than-full-employment case and regardless of whether or not price flexibilities do exist.

3. But the above two points indicate that the argument based on price and wage rigidities poses a dilemma for those who make it. If wage and price rigidities are absent, the wealth effect may be unleashed endogenously through price changes. If wage and price rigidities are present, the endogenous operation of the wealth effect is impaired but, in return, the exogenous—policy-induced—wealth effect is strengthened. The more rigid the prices, the greater the effect of a change of money supply on income demanded and the smaller the dissipation of such an increase in the money supply through price changes. Thus, the more flexible are prices, the more important is the wealth effect as an automatic stabilizer; the more rigid are prices, the more important is the wealth effect as a tool of the policy maker.

4. In addition to the effect of changes in wealth as a result of changes in the real quantity of money, the introduction of wealth into macroeconomic analysis brings into play other wealth effects that are not based on changes in prices and that are, therefore, completely unaffected by the argument of price and wage rigidities. One of them is the interest-induced wealth effect.

5. Finally, if we are discussing an economy other than one based on a pure slave society (and even in this case we must restrict ourselves to one in which all investment in human capital is made in the slaves), the capitalization rates (interest rates) applicable to human and nonhuman income will differ.[8] Consequently, a redistribution of income between human and nonhuman income will change wealth and result in still another type of wealth effect.

---

[8] The reason for the discount rates being different for human and nonhuman income streams will be discussed thoroughly in Chapter 10.

In conclusion we might say that the argument based on price rigidities allegedly grants the theoretical and denies the practical relevance of the wealth effect. Actually, scrutiny indicates that it accomplishes precisely the opposite, insofar as it is relevant at all. If imperfections make prices rigid, the automatic equilibrating mechanism based on price changes is weakened; simultaneously, however, the contribution of the wealth effect to the powers of the policy maker—and thus its practical importance—is not weakened, but strengthened. Finally, that part of the wealth effect that rests not on monetary but on nonmonetary wealth is left completely untouched. It is, therefore, extremely curious that the criticism based on wage and price rigidities has received such widespread currency, because a less potent argument is most difficult to imagine.

Is the Wealth Effect Empirically Irrelevant?

Even after the general acceptance of the theoretical relevance of the wealth effect, economists with Keynesian predilections have persisted in the belief that empirically its influence must be of a second order of magnitude. Thus L. R. Klein writes:

> My theoretical predilections are very much in favor of a theory of the *real* economy. The monetary economy, if in good housekeeping order, will not have a dominant influence on real affairs. Nevertheless, I have tried hard over the years, in several models, to give the benefit of every doubt to money and interest rates when making statistical estimates. My empirical verdict, thus far, is that little evidence can be found for the actual influence of money or interest on real activity.[9]

Such a strong statement must be supported by considerable evidence, and indeed it is. However, there is also considerable evidence to the contrary. Ta-Chung Liu, in his recent econometric model of the

---

[9] Lawrence R. Klein, "A Postwar Quarterly Model: Description and Application," in *Studies in Income and Wealth*, Vol. 28 (Princeton, N.J.: Princeton University Press, 1964), p. 56.

demand subset found a wealth effect—really, a real-balance effect—of significant strength.[10] Thus, the researcher in this area is struck by the diversity of the estimates of the strength of the wealth effect. One wonders why this economic variable yields such contradictory results when subjected to empirical analysis. We believe that these results, whether they indicate a strong or a weak wealth effect, do not at the present time rest on adequate analytical foundations. As the next section ("Is the Wealth Effect an Illusion?") will indicate, there is at present a serious controversy over whether such items as real balances or public debt affect wealth at all, or whether changes in them simply make one part of society better off and another part worse off. In all the empirical studies with which we are familiar, attention has been focused solely on the real quantity of money; the effect of wealth as a whole has never been considered. Consequently, the diversity of results of the empirical relevance of wealth may be due merely to a mis-specification of the wealth variable and, in some cases, even to a failure to recognize a legitimate wealth variable when it is used. One example that documents this statement is furnished by the often quoted article by Thomas Mayer.[11] He tests the wealth effect by claiming to test the real balance effect. Actually, he is not even testing the real balance effect: because his independent variable contains both money and government interest-bearing debt, he is testing what has been called recently by Don Patinkin[12] the real financial asset effect. However, not the entire real financial asset effect is given consideration: only the income effect of a change in real financial assets is quantified, and the portfolio effect of this change is neglected.[13] Another example may be found in one of the

[10] Ta-Chung Liu, "An Exploratory Quarterly Econometric Model of Effective Demand in the Postwar U.S. Economy," *Econometrica*, *31* (July, 1963), pp. 310–348 and especially pp. 331–332. See also J. S. Duesenberry *et al.*, *Econometric Model of the United States* (Chicago: Rand McNally, 1965), pp. 208–209 and 684.

[11] Thomas Mayer, "The Empirical Significance of the Real Balance Effect," *Quarterly Journal of Economics*, *LXXIII* (May, 1959), 275–291.

[12] Don Patinkin, *Money, Interest, and Prices*, 2d ed. (New York: Harper & Row, 1965), p. 290.

[13] We discuss this in detail in Chapter 13.

recent econometric models of Lawrence R. Klein. In this model, Klein uses as one of the determinants of the consumption function the ratio of nonwage to wage income. He claims that this relation is "purely empirical,"[14] by which we understand him to mean that it has been included on the basis of no analytical justification, but simply because it happened to improve the estimates of the consumption function. It is, however, a curious relationship in terms of the standard analysis (based on the notion of diminishing marginal propensity to consume), because it yields, in those terms, three "wrong" signs. As we will show later (Chapters 10 and 11), this variable is a part of the wealth effect. As long as the capitalization rate on human income exceeds the capitalization rate on nonhuman income, a redistribution of income in favor of nonwage income will increase the net wealth of the community, and hence will lead to an increase in consumption. In support of *this* position, we might point out that L. R. Klein's three estimates of the effect of this variable yield, in this interpretation, a "right" sign in all cases.

All this suggests that as long as our economic analysis of the wealth effect is so rudimentary that what appears as an excellent index of one part of the wealth effect may be taken for a purely empirical variable that is based on no analytical explanation and is included merely because it works, the allegations that the empirical evidence reveals that the wealth effect is absent should not be given undue weight. Testing might be much more fruitful after a serious analytical investigation of which are the relevant wealth variables.

Is the Wealth Effect an Illusion?

There is a third group of criticisms that, although not denying the relevance of wealth as a determinant of consumer behavior, asserts that a correct definition of wealth makes it impossible for the wealth effect to be operative either as a force that will be unchained automatically, in a perfectly competitive model, or as a force resulting

---

[14] Lawrence R. Klein, *op. cit.*, p. 22.

from the actions of the policy maker, the government. At this point, we shall simply state—without any documentation—the substance of the main arguments; in Parts II through IV we shall document and discuss, in detail, each single argument listed here. For the sake of argument, say the critics, let us grant the existence of the wealth effect and let us grant that it has sufficient empirical strength to make it analytically relevant:

$$s = s(w) \qquad [2.2]$$

and

$$\frac{\partial s}{\partial w} < 0 \, (!) \qquad [2.3]$$

Let us then consider the definition of wealth to discover whether wealth can actually change and thus give rise to the economic effects just stipulated:

$$w = \frac{M}{P} + \frac{M_D}{P} - \frac{D}{P} + \frac{y_h - t_h}{r_h} + \frac{y_n - t_n}{r_n} + \frac{g}{r_g} \qquad [2.4]$$

The symbols are defined as follows:

w = real wealth
M = nominal commodity money supply
M_D = nominal credit money supply
D = nominal debt of money producers
P = price level
y_h = real human income
y_n = real nonhuman income
g = real government interest payments
t_h = real taxes on human income
t_n = real taxes on nonhuman income
r = capitalization rates applicable to the various income
  streams (r_h to y_h, r_n to y_n, etc.)

A CHANGE IN THE PRICE OF "HARD" MONEY DOES NOT CHANGE WEALTH. A change in the price of any commodity in one direction is simply a change in the price of all other commodities in the other direction. Thus, if commodity money (first term in equation [2.4]) increases in price, the holders of it gain. By the very same token, this is identical to saying that all other goods have decreased in price (the fourth and fifth terms in equation [2.4]) and the holders of these goods lose. A price-induced wealth effect in the case of commodity money may be obtained only if we pay attention to the gain of the former and ignore the loss of the latter.

A CHANGE IN THE PRICE OR QUANTITY OF "CREDIT" MONEY DOES NOT CHANGE WEALTH.   Most of modern money is said to be, however, "credit" money. This money is an asset of the individual who holds it (the second term in equation [2.4]); however, it is simultaneously a debt of the agency that created this money (the third term in equation [2.4]). This agency may be either a private individual or firm or the representative of all individuals and firms, the government. If this is the case, a change in the level of prices cannot change the level of wealth because the second, positive, and the third, negative, term change by precisely the same, offsetting amounts. The price-induced wealth effect is then an optical illusion. If any effect is left, it must be due to assumptions that have no place in a truly general economic analysis; e.g., the government or the public it represents is irrational in that they respond to a change in assets, but do not respond to a simultaneous, offsetting change in debt.

PUBLIC DEBT CANCELS.   As long as we assume that, in a world of reasonable certainty, all the discount rates appearing in equation [2.4] are the same, changes in the level of public debt will cancel because increases in the public debt force simultaneous increases in taxes necessary to pay the interest charges associated with the public debt. In our wealth equation,

$$dg = -dt \qquad\qquad [2.5]$$

and, consequently,

$$\frac{dw}{dg} = 0 \qquad\qquad [2.6]$$

If these three arguments are correct, then the government does not have any tool that enables it to change the wealth of society. Since the price-induced wealth effect is already disposed of, the only possible unleashing of the wealth effect may come through the following two influences:

CHANGES IN REAL INCOME EXIST, BUT THESE CAUSE A PERVERSE EFFECT. As far as changes that originate within the automatically operating mechanism are concerned, changes in real income will reinforce rather than mitigate the explosive nature of the system; the wealth effect is present, but it is perverse in its operation. A decrease in real income diminishes wealth and hence increases saving; the increase in saving results in a further contraction of income.

INTEREST-INDUCED WEALTH EFFECT EXISTS, BUT IT IS INOPERATIVE. As we have already seen, the wealth effect was designed to remove from the Keynesian model the perfectly inelastic aggregate demand function, one of the reasons for which may be the perfectly elastic demand for money function. But if this function is perfectly elastic, the interest-induced wealth effect cannot become operative at that level of interest.

Conclusion

The first argument presented in this chapter, suggesting that the wealth effect may be the result of a semantic confusion, we could show to be unimportant: as long as a given economic stimulus results in a give action on the side of the consumer, it matters not what name we give to this chain of cause and effect. However, national income accounting methods that a researcher may consider as given speak strongly in favor of following the path of the wealth effect rather than making an effort to recompute the national income accounts so as to obtain a definition of income that would lend itself to the expression of all the economic phenomena in terms of flows. The second argument based on the assertion of wage and price rigidities is of no importance because it does not affect the analytical relevance of the monetary wealth effect and enhances, rather than diminishes, its practical relevance. In addition, price and wage rigidities leave completely unaffected the effect of nonmonetary wealth changes. The third argument—employing empirical evidence to show that the response of consumers to changes in wealth is either small or nonexistent—cannot be given much weight, since the evidence is, at present, too fragmentary and even contradictory. In addition, it is based—as the fourth argument shows—on an extremely imperfect analytical foundation. Before we are certain as to what we want to measure, the magnitudes of what we do measure are of little relevance.

On the other hand, the group of criticisms summarized in the last section (Is the Wealth Effect an Illusion?) is an extremely weighty one. If correct, it enables economists to eliminate the effect of wealth from economic analysis without forcing them to pay the heavy price that a denial of the existence of the wealth effect would exact. The consumer, according to this argument, may be behaving rationally and be affected in his saving and consumption decisions by the level of wealth he already has. However, even if all this is granted, a correct definition of the wealth variable is said to show that neither the endogenous nor the exogenous changes have the power, in the short run, to affect wealth and thus to make the wealth effect operational. Not only is this argument weighty, it is also subtle and intricate. We shall discuss it at length in Parts II and III.

PART II

MONEY AND WEALTH

Having completed our survey of the early history of the wealth effect, we shall now present a rigorous analysis of the nature of wealth and of the role it plays in economic theory. Obviously, one cannot analyze the *role* of wealth in the behavior of the consumer without having a precise idea of the *definition* of wealth. Moreover, discussion of "Is the Wealth Effect an Illusion?" in the latter part of our preceding chapter has shown that an inquiry into whether wealth does or does not affect economic behavior may be rendered senseless, regardless of the results obtained, by the inquiry into the proper definition of wealth. One might freely stipulate that there is a relationship between wealth and behavior and, in the next breath, deny any relevance to this discovery by pointing out that neither changes in the endogenous variables (interest and prices) nor changes in the exogenous policy-controlled variables (money and public debt) are able to change wealth and thus unleash the wealth effect. Such a denial, as we have seen, is based on a definition of wealth that implies that all the just-mentioned changes that increase wealth have negative, offsetting counterparts. Given this state of affairs, it appears imperative that we first establish a definition of wealth that will withstand analytical scrutiny. Only if it can be shown that the relevant endogenous and exogenous changes in the variables affecting wealth are not self-canceling will it become profitable to inquire as to whether the changes in wealth that have survived the definitional hurdle, if any, do or do not affect the behavior of the economic decision maker.

In our discussion of the wealth equation, money is our first concern. The problem of money is intricate, and the literature dealing with this topic voluminous. In an attempt to establish whether or not money is a part of net wealth, we encounter problems that have much broader ramifications for economic theory in general and for monetary theory in particular. A satisfactory solution of the more limited problem of the role money plays in the wealth equation is, as we shall see, impossible without a more formal treatment of the broader question of the role of money in the economy and of the relationship between general economic theory and monetary theory. For this reason, we have found it useful to discuss the problem of money in the following, separate, part of our book.

CHAPTER 3

Barter and Money Economy

There is considerable support for the view that money, an asset of the holders, is simultaneously a debt of the issuer. Hence, a consolidation of the balance sheets of all economic units must result in the cancellation of money as an item of the net wealth of the community. It then follows that if the response of all the decision-making units in society to a given change in their assets is identical, then a change in the quantity of money—being offset by changes in debt of precisely the same magnitude—cannot have any net economic consequences. But, if this is so, then the existence of empirical evidence, suggesting that changes in the quantity of money do have economic consequences, must have some explanation other than that of a change in the net wealth of the community. The explanation to which many economists have attached themselves, as we shall discuss and document in detail in Chapter 8, is that the issuer of money is unaffected by changes in the value of his outstanding debts. Thus, the only effect of a change in the quantity of money is the effect of the increase in assets of the holders of money. This analysis reduces the wealth effect to a distribution effect and places monetary theory in the rather precarious position of being "awkwardly dependent on adventitious institutional or historical details"[1]—on the assertion that the issuer of money, the government, does not worry or does not have to worry about the size of its debts. The implication is then inescapable that in an economy in which the issuer of money behaves like any other economic decision-making unit (for example, in an economy in which the issuer of money is a private individual rather than the government), the wealth effect of a change in money is nonexistent, and monetary theory itself irrelevant. We think that the view that money is an asset that is offset by a debt of the same magnitude has been accepted too readily. We intend to show that money is a genuine part of net wealth and that the current view of money as an asset of the owner that is offset by a debt, of equal magnitude, of the issuer is erroneous. For the sake of an orderly presentation, we shall separate the discussion into four main parts: (1) consideration of a moneyless economy, (2) consideration of an economy with commodity money, (3) consideration of an economy with a pure fiat money, (4) consideration of an economy with bank money.

Wealth in a Barter Economy

Consider the case of a pure barter economy in which no good has any attribute that makes it preferable to any other for use as a medium of exchange.

Definition of Wealth

Assume a community in which stocks of capital goods C_i ($i = 1$, ..., n) exist and assume that each unit of (C_i) emanates a perpetual flow of services (y_i). The wealth of this community may then be expressed as the weighted sum of the stocks of each capital good,

[1] Harry G. Johnson, "Monetary Theory and Policy," *American Economic Review, LII* (June, 1962), p. 342.

where the weight for the stock of the (i-th) capital good is the rate of exchange of the base capital good (C_B) for the (i-th) capital good. (A unit of the base capital good is usually called the *numéraire*.) If we let (P_i) represent the price of a unit of (C_i) in terms of (C_B), i.e., the number of units of (C_B) which will exchange for a unit of (C_i), then wealth (w) may be expressed as follows:

$$w = \sum P_i C_i; \quad i = 1, \ldots, n \qquad [3.1]$$

Equation [3.1] yields a measure of wealth in units of the base capital good. Since any one of the (n) capital goods could have served equally well as the base capital good, the measure of wealth is an arbitrary one. In other words, the numerical expression of the value of wealth is not independent of the capital good that is chosen as the base. However, with a fixed set of exchange rates, any one of these nominal values of wealth could be converted to any other.[2]

Consumer equilibrium in the community under discussion will require that for every capital good (C_i), the following relationship must hold:

$$\frac{p_i y_i}{p_j y_j} = \frac{P_i}{P_j} \quad \text{for all } i \text{ and } j \qquad [3.2]$$

where p_i represents the exchange rate of (C_B) per unit of (y_i). Equation [3.2] implies that the value of the permanent flow (y_i) from a unit of capital good (C_i) relative to the value of the permanent flow (y_j) from a unit of capital good (C_j) must equal the relative

[2] Measures of wealth such as the above have the problem that the prices used represent marginal values and only in the case of wealth functions which are homogeneous of degree one will the relevant measure of wealth be obtained. Consider the following example: Assume that two communities are identical in tastes and capital good endowments except for a single capital good, (C_n). Assume additionally that the quantity of (C_n) available in the first of the two communities results in a zero marginal valuation for it. Under such conditions, wealth equation [3.1] computed for the first community will give to the stock of capital good (C_n) a zero value. On the other hand, since in the second community the greater scarcity of the capital good (C_n) gave this good a positive marginal value, this second community will be shown to have a positive value of the good (C_n) and, as a result, will have a higher measured total wealth than the first community.

prices of the capital goods from which they emanate. Or, alternatively, we may write [3.2] as

$$\frac{p_i y_i}{P_i} = \frac{p_j y_j}{P_j} \qquad \text{for all } i \text{ and } j \qquad [3.3]$$

indicating that the ratio of the value of the permanent flows per unit of a capital good to the price of that capital good must be equal for all capital goods.[3]

Let us assume for simplicity that the consumers' utility functions are functions of the (y_i) only and that barter may take place in either the capital goods (C_i) or the services of these capital goods (y_i). Note that as long as equation [3.2] holds, it is not necessary to restrict barter to capital goods. In fact, under these conditions, we would expect some equilibrium amount of trading in services to occur.[4]

Effects of Changes in Relative Prices

Let us now consider an increase in the price of one of our capital goods relative to all others. Since the choice of the base capital good is an arbitrary one, no loss in generality will be involved if we assume that the good whose price has changed is the base capital good. As equation [3.2] shows, an increase in price implies that any constant flow of services from the base capital good will now exchange for a larger flow of services from any other capital good. Therefore, the

---

[3] The ratio $\frac{p_i y_i}{P_i}$ will equal the rate of interest, since it represents the value of the flow of services foregone per unit of (C_B) loaned.

[4] This will be especially true if the flow of services from any one capital good is affected by the amount of another capital good owned, or if two or more capital goods are being combined to produce a flow of services different from that which is available without such a combination. In addition, this equilibrium will insure an economically efficient production sector, i.e., the distribution of the capital goods among consumers will be such that no trading in capital goods can occur that will increase the output of one service without decreasing the output of another.

net-holders[5] of the base capital good will be better off than they would have been in the absence of the price increase because they may continue to consume the same amount of services (y_B) of the good (C_B) and more of all other services. At the same time, the non-net-holders of (C_B) (the net-holders of other capital goods) are now worse off, for in order to consume the same amount of (y_B) they must reduce their consumption of all other services.[6] Note that this evaluation of the effects of a price change on the welfare of the two groups of consumers is independent of the reason for the price change even though the reason for the price change, by itself, will have additional effects. For example, a general increase in the supplies of all other goods will make *all* consumers as a group better off but if, in addition, it gives rise to the above-discussed price change, it will also have the consequences we have specified above. Or, as another example, there may be a change in price due to a change in tastes in favor of the base good by some or all consumers. Now, with the new set of tastes and the old set of prices and stock-holdings as a datum, all those consumers whose new utility maximizing position would leave them as net-holders of (C_B) will be made better off by the resulting increase in the price of (C_B), and all those consumers whose utility maximizing position leaves them as non-net-holders of (C_B) will be made worse off by the price increase that will occur.[7]

At this point, the argument is sometimes made that the amount by which the net-holders of the base capital good (C_B) are better off is exactly matched by the amount that the non-net-holders of (C_B)

[5] A consumer will be said to be a net-holder of the (i-th) capital good if in equilibrium he is trading a positive quantity of the flow of services (y_i) of the (i-th) capital good (C_i), i.e., his excess supply for (y_i) is positive.

[6] The consumer who is self-sufficient in (C_B) is affected by this change only through the substitution effect and would tend to be better off.

[7] By "better off," we mean that the individual will be able, for the new tastes, to reach a higher indifference curve than he would have been able to reach in the absence of the price increase. Note that for the community the price increase must on balance, again for the new tastes, make consumers worse off, since they expected to be able to act with no change in prices, but actually faced rising prices.

are worse off.[8] However, this is only true in the following sense: if we calculate the value of the increase in flow of services that could be consumed by the net-holders of (C_B) valued in terms of units of (C_B) on the assumption that they consume the same amount of (y_B) after the price change as they did before the price change, then this value, simply by an accounting necessity, will be precisely equal to the value of the decrease in the flows of services that could be consumed by the non-net-holders of (C_B) if they continued to consume the same quantity of (y_B) after the price change. But, we expect both the net-holders and the non-net-holders of (C_B) to reduce their desired consumption of (y_B) after the price change. Indeed, stability of equilibrium requires this, since increases in prices must reduce excess demand in order to reach a new equilibrium set of relative prices in which all excess demands are zero.   Therefore, these changes due to prices will only be offsetting if the consumers continue to consume the same bundle of services after the change in prices, i.e., they do not react to the change in prices.[9]

Effects of Changes in the Stock of One of the Capital Goods

Consider an increase in the stock of one of the capital goods, say, C_K. Such a change may be expected to affect the equilibrium set of relative prices existing before the change. Given that relative prices will be affected, what is the mechanism by which the new set of relative prices comes about? First, the increase in the stock of capital good C_K increases the wealth of those consumers whose stocks are increased. For simplicity, we assume that no consumer's stock of C_K is decreased so that, at the new level of the stock of C_K and the old equilibrium prices P_i, wealth is greater than its original

[8] Syed Ahmad, "The Saving-Wealth Relation and the Measure of Real Value of Assets," *The Journal of Political Economy*, LXX (June, 1962), pp. 287–293.

[9] Note that this problem is identical to the bias in the cost of living index. For the cost of living index correctly measures the amount by which the consumer is poorer or richer in income terms whenever the consumer fails to react to the change in price.

value. Since we, in analyzing problems such as this one usually make the assumption that the consumers behave as if their own actions have no effect on prices, the initial change in the wealth as viewed by each consumer is simply the initial change in his stock of C_K times its original equilibrium price P_K. The subsequent changes in prices are due to this increase in wealth whereby the consumers become oversupplied with C_K or, looking at the same thing from the opposite side, undersupplied with all other capital goods. Thus, to reach an equilibrium with the same stock of all other capital goods and an increased stock of C_K, the price of C_K in terms of other capital goods in general must fall. This equilibrating change results from a combination of the wealth effect and the portfolio effect. That is, at the original prices and the new large inventory of C_K, the consumers' wealth is greater so that consumers desire to increase consumption of *all* goods and services. To do so, they must decrease their stock of C_K (or, alternatively, increase their net supply of y_K) since the only change which at first occurred is an increase in the flow of services from C_K. Thus, the initial specialized change in the consumers' wealth portfolios distributes itself throughout the portfolio.

Wealth in an Economy with Commodity Money

Bartering is costly in ways too numerous to discuss. Among others, bartering requires an expenditure of time and the use of specialized skills necessary for judging the commodities that are being exchanged. The more advanced the specialization in production and the more complex the economy, the costlier it will be to undertake all the transactions necessary to make any given good reach its ultimate user by using barter. Let us now assume that there is one commodity that is preferable to all others for use as a medium of exchange. For simplicity, we may assume that this commodity has no other use.[10] Such a commodity will come into use whenever the

[10] We could have assumed that some change has occurred in one of the existing capital goods, which allowed it to play this role. However, this would complicate some of the succeeding analysis without adding anything to the main analytical result obtained.

cost of producing it becomes smaller than—and in final equilibrium, equal to—the cost, at the margin, of the time used up and the skills necessary for barter.[11]

Commodity Money Is a Part of Net Wealth

After this good that we call commodity money becomes used, the consumers are able to consume the same quantity of the flows of all services as before and increase their consumption of leisure. We would then expect that they will utilize some of this increase in leisure for the production of some nonmoney capital good, thus increasing the flow of services of some good without decreasing the flow of any other. But, if this is the case, then the introduction of a good that serves no function other than that of facilitating exchange must have increased wealth. In addition, the value of the money commodity itself is a part of the wealth of the community, because it yields a positive income stream to the users of it *which is not offset* by a negative income stream to the nonusers. Although this income stream yielded by money is not directly an argument of the consumers' utility functions, it can be instantly converted into an argument of the utility function because the flow of services of the money commodity is the saving of time in barter transactions. This time may be used either for leisure or for the production of capital goods. In view of the above, we conclude that our money commodity, which—as any other commodity—yields a positive flow of services to the user and no negative flow of services to the nonusers must be part of the net wealth of the community.

After establishing that the money commodity is net wealth we must, as in the barter case, inquire into the consequences of a change

---

[11] An excellent discussion of the manner in which money accomplishes this task may be found in Ludwig von Mises, *The Theory of Money and Credit* (New Haven, Conn.: Yale University Press, 1953), pp. 30–34. Or, for a still earlier treatment that leaves nothing to be desired, see Carl Menger, *Principles of Economics* (New York: Free Press of Glencoe, 1950), pp. 254–261.

in the price of *this* commodity on wealth. Before we do so, however, it appears necessary to consider explicitly two objections that may be raised against the conclusion that money is net wealth.

OBJECTION I: MONEY AS A DEBT IS NOT NET WEALTH. As we have seen in Chapter 2, the conclusion that commodity money is net wealth conflicts with the opinion expressed by some economists. Harry G. Johnson summarized this view concisely when he wrote:

> If this logic applies to interest-bearing government debt, why should it not apply to the limiting case of non-interest-bearing government debt, which is equally a debt of the public to itself, and to *commodity moneys* [emphasis ours], which are the same thing though based on custom rather than law?[12]

This statement contains two basic ideas: that money is a debt and that a noninterest-bearing debt is the same thing as the interest-bearing debt. Let us consider each idea in turn. Because commodity money yields a positive flow of services to the user and no negative flow of services to the nonusers, it is in this respect indistinguishable from all other capital goods and cannot be shown to be a debt of the society to itself. On this basis, it cannot be denied net existence as a part of wealth. Thus, the only remaining way in which the money commodity can be a debt is if it can be shown to be a debt of the producer. However, once the producer has sold his money commodity for other capital goods, he is in the same position as any producer of any nonmoney commodity and, hence, the money commodity can only be considered a debt of the producer if all nonmoney commodities are also considered to be debts of their producers. But such a definition of debt would reduce wealth in the society to zero. In addition, a change in the value of the existing stock of the money commodity can in no way be construed to affect the flow of services that can be consumed by the producer of the money

[12] Harry H. Johnson, *op. cit.*, p. 343.

commodity any differently than any other consumer. Namely, he is affected only to the extent that he holds the money commodity. Therefore, the money commodity cannot be shown to be a debt of anyone.

The second part of the statement quoted above consists of a claim that money as a noninterest-bearing debt is the same thing as interest-bearing debt "in the limit."[13] Not only does Johnson's statement concisely present the argument, albeit in terms of a question, but it brings out the basic erroneous underlying assumption on which the analysis depends. This basic assumption, and it *is* an assumption because the above analysis will not support it, is that money is simply the limiting case of interest-bearing debt; namely, that it is noninterest-bearing debt. This conclusion must be reached through some misapplied logic such as: (1) The limiting case of an interest-bearing debt is a noninterest-bearing debt; (2) money does not bear interest; (3) therefore, money is the limiting case of interest-bearing debt. Obviously this is a logically fallacious argument because all we can conclude about money from (1) and (2) above is that money is noninterest-bearing money. An example may help make this important point clearer. Suppose that refrigerators were suddenly to become the money commodity. Refrigerators would now have two flows of services emanating from them: (1) refrigeration; (2) time saved in barter transactions. However, nothing here indicates that refrigerators, even that part of their value that is due to their being the money commodity, comprise a debt of the public to itself and, certainly, nothing here indicates that they are a debt of their producer. Indeed, this money commodity is no more a debt of the public to itself than is *any other item of wealth* in the community, say, automobiles. True enough, the money commodity *and* every other piece of wealth in the community does measure the power of the holders of this wealth to call upon the resources owned by others. However,

---

[13] We return to the issue of whether each and every money is a noninterest-bearing debt in Chapter 7 in the section "Money as the Limiting Case of Interest-bearing Debt." Here we limit our attention to that type of money we are discussing; namely the commodity money.

only if these other holders view their holdings as being owed to other holders of capital goods who might want to barter some of their wealth will the money commodity be an asset that is offset by a debt of the same magnitude. But, in this instance, *all* other wealth is also an asset that is offset by a debt of the same magnitude so that the net wealth of the community is zero. Such a definition of debt is clearly not a useful one.

Let us pursue somewhat further the question of the relationship of money to the limiting case of interest-bearing debt, noninterest-bearing debt. Assume that this producer of money would like to increase his present consumption of the flow of services of other capital goods. He can accomplish this in two ways: (1) he can *borrow* resources from others; (2) he may *produce* more refrigerator money and *sell* it at the going market price. If he chooses to borrow re-sources, this is indeed a debt, interest-bearing or noninterest-bearing, depending on whether or not the lender requires him to pay interest. If the lender does not require interest payments, then the transaction is equivalent to a loan of resources, coupled with a gift of the flow of services of those resources. Certainly, such borrowing of resources does not affect the money supply; it does not affect the stock of refrigerators in existence. Whether the debt is interest-bearing or noninterest-bearing has no bearing on this issue. If, on the other hand, our producer of refrigerator money chooses to produce and sell additional units of refrigerators, this will increase the stock of refrigerator money in existence, but it does not represent a debt of anyone. The sale, as the sale of any other good, is final and the buyer of the refrigerator has no call on the resources of the producer of refrigerators precisely as the buyer of any other good has no call on the resources of the producer of that good: commodity money is not a debt of the producer. Buyers of refrigerator money have the same right as do buyers of any other capital good: they can go on the market and sell the goods they own, at the going market price, for other goods. Thus commodity money is not a debt of the society. But, since it is wealth for the owner and it is not a debt of either the producer or society, money must be net wealth.

OBJECTION II: IF MONEY IS A PRODUCER'S GOOD, IT IS NOT WEALTH. We have just rejected on analytical grounds the view that commodity money, merely because it performs the same task as fiat money or bank money, is to be considered a debt and therefore not a part of the net wealth of the community. In our discussion we did not find it necessary to consider the classification of money as a producer's good or as a consumer's good. However, Don Patinkin considers this classification carefully, and even though he seems to be supporting the conclusion that the classification of money makes no difference, his phrasing is such that it might cause an unwary reader to be misled and reach the conclusion that money is net wealth if it is a consumer good, and money is not net wealth if it is a producer good. In particular, Patinkin reaches the following conclusions:

1. Either approach yields the same demand function for money and thus these two approaches to money are operationally equivalent: they cannot be identified, in the econometric sense of the term.
2. If money is a consumer good, the services it yields are final product and hence an independent part of national income; if money is a producer's good, these services are already counted in final output and it would be double counting to count them again.
3. Finally, and since this is a point to which we want to address ourselves in some detail, we quote:

   This is the meaning of our representing the services of money balances as a deduction from total wealth on the right-hand side of equation (5), and not as an addition to consumption on its left-hand side.[14]

We fully agree with *all* three points. Yet, the phrasing of the last point is so terse that an unwary reader might conclude that a decision that money is a producer good, by forcing subtraction of money from wealth, signifies an analytical conclusion that money is not

---

[14] From Don Patinkin, *Money, Interest, and Prices*, 2d ed. (New York: Harper & Row, 1965), p. 161.

wealth. Such a conclusion would be a *non sequitur* as is best manifested by a realization that, if correct, it would force removal from wealth of a huge part of it yielding intermediate rather than final goods and services.

In point 2, above, the correct proposition is made that if we change our minds about the nature of money in favor of the producer's good hypothesis we must, on *the use side of national income accounts*, remove the services of money as a final good. Since these services merely facilitate the production of other goods, they are contained in the value of the other goods produced; to list them separately is double counting. To illustrate this point, suppose that money is really a producer's good that we have erroneously classified as a consumer's good in our measure of the wealth of society. Then the services of money as a producer's good are reflected in the value of the other final goods produced. However, since we have been erroneously treating money as a consumer good, the value of the services of money *also* appears as a separate final good produced. Thus, money services have been double counted. Since wealth, if we base the computation of it on the *use* side of the T-accounts, is the capitalized value of the final goods and services yielded by wealth, monetary wealth has been doubly counted because its output has been doubly counted. When, after deciding that money is really a producer good, we subtract money from wealth (cf. Patinkin's point 3 above), we are not expressing the opinion that money is not wealth and does not belong in our measure of wealth. We are merely giving expression to a decision that it does not belong in our measure of wealth twice.

We might look at the same problem from the other side. Since T-accounts must balance, a correction of the T-accounts on the *origin side of national income* is also necessary. By deciding that our original decision that money services are a final good has been wrong and by deciding that money is really a producer's good, we have decided that the net contribution of means of production other than money (of human capital and nonmoney nonhuman capital) to output, as we have originally shown it on the origin side of the T-accounts, is overstated. These nonmoney capital goods were initially credited with the production of final goods and services other than money services, whereas the money capital good was credited with the separate production of money services. However, if money is a producer good, it participated with the other capital goods in the production of final goods and services other than money services; but then, our original accounts double counted the output of money capital. Therefore, the value of money services must again be subtracted, not because money would not yield a service but because the one service that it does yield has been counted twice. Since wealth, computed on the basis of the *origin* side of the T-accounts, is the capitalized value of the net contributions of various capital goods to output, the contribution of monetary wealth has been doubly counted because its net contribution to output has been doubly counted. When, after deciding that money is a producer's good, we subtract money from wealth (cf., again, Patinkin's point 3 above) we are not expressing the opinion that money is not wealth and does not belong in our measure of wealth. We are merely giving expression to a decision that it does not belong in our measure of wealth twice.

There is one additional fringe benefit that results from the necessity to clarify the statement by Don Patinkin quoted above—a benefit that will become especially important when we discuss not commodity money, but fiat money and bank money. In the above analysis, Patinkin makes no distinction and speaks simply about money. Yet, point 2 in his analysis clearly indicates that in Part I of his book he is not considering money as mere evidences of debt, but as means of production of either final or intermediate services and therefore as net wealth. He still views money not as a debt that yields income to one sector merely by yielding negative income to some other sector, thus washing out of national income accounts and, consequently, out of the net wealth account; he views money as a capital good that yields income as any other capital good, and merely considers the problem of whether this income is final income (whether money is a consumer's good) or whether this income is intermediate income that becomes in the course of production embedded in a final good (whether money is a producer's good). This treatment of money as net wealth that, in one form or another, yields net income to society continues throughout Part I of his book. Only in Part II does money become merely a debt and thus the income it yields is denied the ability to enter national income accounts either directly as a final good or indirectly as a component of some other final good.

Price of Money Defined

After considering the effects of a change in the quantity of money on wealth, we need to consider the effects of a change in the price of money on wealth. Before we discuss the effects of changes in the price of money, however, it appears highly advisable to discuss the meaning of the variable that is being changed—the meaning of the concept "price of money." The simplest answer is that by the price of money we mean precisely the same thing that, in the preceding section dealing with a barter economy, we meant by the price of any other good. Yet, this simple answer would gloss over some issues that we consider of substantial importance.

In the preceding section we expressed the price of a good by noting its exchange value relative to some other good referred to as the base good. Using this formulation, we find that the price of the base good is then identically equal to one. How then can we express the idea of a base good changing in price? One approach that immediately suggests itself is looking at the amounts of other goods that must be given up to get a unit of the base good. If, for example, more of every good must be given up to get a unit of the base good, then we can say unambiguously that the price of the base good has increased; that is, if

$$\left(\frac{1}{P_i}\right)_1 > \left(\frac{1}{P_i}\right)_0 \qquad \text{for all } i \neq B \qquad [3.4]$$

then

$$P_{B_1} > P_{B_0} \qquad [3.5]$$

However, the internal structure of relative prices of all the nonbase goods is unlikely to remain constant over time, so that it is unlikely that all $\left(\dfrac{1}{P_i}\right)$ will move in the same direction. All we can say then is that *the relative price* of the base good increased with respect to some of the goods and decreased with respect to the remaining goods. If we want to obtain a unique answer, nevertheless, we must construct an index that tells us what has happened to the *average relative price* $(\bar{P}_B)$ of the base good. Normally, this is done by weighting each $\left(\dfrac{1}{P_i}\right)$ by the share of (C_i) in the total wealth of the community, excluding the base good. Hence

$$\bar{P}_B = \frac{\sum C_i\left(\dfrac{1}{P_i}\right)}{\sum C_i} \qquad \text{for all } i \neq B \qquad\qquad [3.6]$$

The existence of the average relative price of the base commodity depends on the existence of each of the individual relative prices $\left(\dfrac{1}{P_i}\right)$ of the base commodity. For example, if (C_B) were a good that could be had for the wishing, then each (P_i) would be infinite and all the individual relative prices, and the average relative price, of the base good would be zero. That is, no one would be willing to give up any good to get the base good. Of course, in this case a different base good would be chosen, since the relative price of the desired good could be no longer obtained from the price of this good relative to the base good.

What will be the effect of an increase in the quantity of the base good on the set of relative prices prevailing in the community? First, such a change can be expected to decrease the price of the base good relative to each of the other goods; the average relative price of the base good will fall. Second, the increase in the quantity of the base good may disturb the prices relating all the other goods to each other, since some of the goods will be substitutes for and some complements to the base good. Thus, the increase in the quantity of the base good will reduce the price of the base good and may change the relative prices of all other goods. It is, of course, possible that the relative prices of all other goods will remain undisturbed; this will be the case, e.g., if the supply functions governing the production of all other goods are perfectly elastic. However, it is not likely.

As we pointed out in the section dealing with barter, *any* good may be selected to be a base good. Suppose that the base good selected happens to be money. Nothing has changed when we make this decision, since money is simply a commodity that people desire to have and are willing to pay for. However, quite often when this transition is made, economists suddenly begin to treat the relative price of money and, especially, *the average relative price of money* differently than they treat the relative prices of all other commodities. They begin to feel that there is some fundamental difference between the relative prices of nonmoney goods and the relative price of money or between the average relative price of nonmoney goods and the average relative price of money. This feeling that there is a fundamental difference becomes further enhanced by the habitual terminology employed in discussions; instead of speaking about the average relative price of money, we tend to speak about the reciprocal of this variable, about "the general price level." It is then extremely easy to lose sight of the fact that there is no analytical difference between the price of cheese and the price of money. As Don Patinkin points out, there is "the intuitive feeling that in some sense, value theory is connected with the determination of relative prices and monetary theory with the determination of absolute prices."[15] In one sense, the point that "*the general price level*" is but the reciprocal of the *average relative price* of one good in the economy is almost too obvious to be stated. Yet, in another sense, it appears extremely important to state it since it greatly facilitates our understanding of some extremely involved discussions of various issues in economics. Let us suggest a few examples to establish the validity of this claim:

1. Consider the issue as to whether some economic model does or

[15] Don Patinkin, *ibid.*, p. 182.

does not yield a determinate price level. After extensive and complex discussion of one such problem, Don Patinkin concludes his analysis by the following statement:

> Indeed, what we have here is the indeterminacy of Wicksell's "pure credit" economy in which all transactions are carried out by checks, while banks hold no reserves. The economic interpretation of this indeterminacy is straightforward: In order for the absolute price level to be determined by market-equilibrating forces, changes in it must impinge on *real* behavior in *some* market—i.e., must create excess demands in some market.[16]

Yet, with the realization that the general price level is the reciprocal of the average relative price of money, the answer to this problem is fully stated by the phrase "pure credit economy." In an economy in which money does not exist, it cannot have a relative price or an average relative price; since the price level is a reciprocal of the latter, the economy does not have a general price level. If we so choose, we may say that the price level is indeterminate.

2. Or, consider the lengthy discussion of the subject of the "Invalid Dichotomy" in Don Patinkin's Second Edition that causes the author to castigate numerous authors for serious analytical errors and that results in the author's claim that

> In particular, . . . , it is fatal to succumb to the temptation to say that relative prices are determined in the commodity market and absolute prices in the money market.[17]

Yet, once we view the "absolute price level" as the reciprocal of the average relative price of money, the whole issue reduces to an elementary problem of value theory: If a *new* good is introduced among *old* goods, (a) relative prices $\left(\dfrac{1}{P_i}\right)$ and the average relative price

---

[16] Don Patinkin, *ibid.*, p. 303.

[17] Don Patinkin, *ibid.*, p. 181. For other examples, see Chapter 5, Appendix on Banking Theory, of the present book; also, the discussion of the issue of price determinacy in George Horwich, *Money, Capital, and Prices* (Homewood, Ill.: Irwin, 1964), chapter X.

$\bar{P}_B$ must be found relating this new good to all the old goods singly and collectively, respectively. In addition, (b) it is *likely* that in the course of the adjustment to the new goods the relative prices (P_i) relating the old goods to each other will be disturbed and displaced, the extent of the adjustment depending on the substitutability and complementarity of some of the old goods to the new one and on the supply of and demand for each of the old goods. Note that all that value theory can tell us in this case is that the disturbance of the relative prices relating the old goods is likely—not that it is certain. If we could say that it is certain, we would *know* that the dichotomy referred to by Patinkin as the "Invalid Dichotomy" is, indeed, invalid. Since we can merely say that it is likely, all we can be sure of is that the dichotomy may be invalid or is likely to be invalid.

Perhaps these two examples demonstrate sufficiently that there is merit in remembering that the absolute price level is merely the reciprocal of the average relative price of one good in the economy; we cannot consider this relative price to be outside of the scope of value theory. Needless to say, however, the concept of a general price level is so useful, especially for policy discussions, that we have no intention of giving it up completely, even though in most connections we shall not prefer to divorce ourselves, even terminologically, from value theory. That is, we shall prefer to phrase our discussion in terms of the variable of which the price level is the reciprocal: in terms of the relative price of money.

Effects of Changes in the Relative Price of Commodity Money

A unit of commodity money, serving as a medium of exchange, cannot help but be, in between transactions, a store of value. It yields, as does any other good, a flow of services. Concentrating on the medium of exchange role, we may measure this flow in terms of the value of the transaction that a unit of the money commodity will support. Alternatively but identically, if we concentrate on the store of value role, this flow of income may be measured by the size of the flows of incomes yielded by other goods that a unit of money will purchase. Let us now consider a change in the price of one of our capital goods, namely money, relative to all others. (The reader might note that the preceding sentence is a verbatim repetition of a sentence that we used to consider an effect of a price change in a barter economy. This verbatim repetition is deliberate because we want to stress that the dichotomy between "relative" prices of a barter economy and "absolute" prices in an economy containing money is purely artificial.) If the price of a unit of the money commodity increases, *the nonholders* of money are completely un- affected. For instance, consider an individual who desires enough money to undertake a given transaction, say, a transaction in the course of which a sedan will be exchanged for a convertible. A doubling of the price of a unit of money will not affect the cost of obtaining the number of units of the money commodity that are necessary to effectuate this transaction, simply because the individual now needs to purchase, at a price twice as high as before, only half as many units of the money commodity as before. On the other hand, *the holders* of money will be made better off by the same change in the price because the flow of services yielded by a unit of money will have increased. A unit of their money will now support a higher valued transaction than before, or, saying the same thing in a way that appears more relevant for the holder of money, a unit of money will purchase a greater flow of services yielded by other goods than before; it will purchase more goods than before. Note that the increase in the total value of the services yielded by money to the holder of it has occurred through an increase in the size of the flow of the real services emanating from a unit of money rather than through a change in the price of these services. It is now clear that the assumed increase in the price of the money commodity makes the holders of money better off without making anyone else worse off. The same thing would occur in the case of any other good that might have the peculiar technical property by which a physical unit of that good would also yield physical income, the size of which would be perfectly proportional to the price of this commodity in terms of other commodities. With this special technical property, a change in the *price* of this good is indistinguishable from the change in the physical *quantity* of the good. But then, since the latter represents, indubitably, a change in wealth, the former must also do so.

This special technical property of money furnishes the key distinction between money and other goods and is of extreme importance for our entire analysis. Let us, therefore, spell out the above conclusions in additional detail. All nonmoney goods have the technical property of yielding output that is independent of the price of these goods. A given physical quantity of apple trees yields a given quantity of apples irrespective of the price of apple trees; if we want more apples, we must have more apple trees (or use more resources such as fertilizers that cooperate with apple trees in the production of apples). A given physical quantity of cranes has a given lifting capacity irrespective of the price of cranes; if we want more lifting capacity, we must have more cranes (or more resources cooperating with cranes in lifting loads). Only money has the special technical property of yielding a higher output (of being able to transfer more of other goods from one person to another) if the price of this resource increases, even if the physical quantity of this resource remains unchanged.[18] Apple trees would have this technical property if they would yield, *ceteris paribus*, 10 per cent more apples if the price of apple trees increases by 10 per cent; cranes would have this technical property if a crane with the lifting capacity of, say, 50 tons would become able to lift, *ceteris paribus*, 55 tons if the price of cranes increases by 10 per cent.

Just as the conclusion that nonmoney goods do not have this special technical property is independent of the reason for the increase in the price of these nonmoney goods, so the conclusion that money has this special technical property is independent of the reason for the increase in the price of the money resource. For example,

---

[18] This statement of a purely *technical* property of money is deceptively similar to the *analytical* propositions contained in the Quantity Theory of Money. We shall show in Chapter 9 that the validity of the former is completely independent of the validity of the latter (but not vice versa).

consider a change in the tastes of the members of the community in favor of the services of money. Such a change may have occurred because of an increase in the subjective valuation of leisure that must be sacrificed for barter. This change in tastes will, at the old price of money, lead to excess demand for the services of money and hence to a higher price for money. This higher price of money will make the holders of money better off and will not affect the nonholders. Note that the original change in tastes made excess supply of all nonmoney capital goods positive, and it is the subsequent change in the price of money and the resulting wealth effect that brings the goods market back to a position of zero excess supply. Thus we see from the above that money presents a rare case of a good that yields a service, the *demand for which creates its own supply*. If the demand for money increases, the price of money increases and this causes a proportionate increase in the flow of services yielded by the existing stock of money. Unfortunately, in the case of competitively produced money, the working of the market dissipates this gain. If the money commodity is produced freely, an increase in the price of money will make each unit of money yield a higher income than before. Therefore, the increase in the price of money will result in an increased output of new money, and this will, in turn, cause an eventual reduction of the price of money. Although *originally* the increased demand was met through an increase in the flow of services yielded by a given number of physical units of money, the operation of the market under the conditions just specified would ultimately cause an increase in the number of units of money accompanied by a decrease in the flow of physical services yielded by each unit. After all these adjustments are concluded, there will be more units of money, with each unit yielding a real income lower than the one it yielded before the change in quantity took place. How much lower this income will be depends, on the one hand, on the demand for money and, on the other hand, on the increase in the quantity. This increase in quantity depends on the production conditions under which the money industry operates. Should it, for instance, operate under constant cost conditions, the income yielded by each unit of money will return to the level that existed before the change in demand. The entire increase in demand will be satisfied by an increase in the quantity of units of money in existence; no part of it will be satisfied by an increase in the real income yielded by a unit of money.

Effects of Changes in the Quantity of the Money Good

In the preceding we have shown that there is a basic difference in the relationship between the price of a good and the flow of services yielded by this good depending on whether the good in question is a money good or a nonmoney good. Money goods yield flows of services that are proportionate to their price per unit while non-money goods yield flows of services that are independent of their price per unit. Thus, a change in the quantity of nonmoney goods result in a constant and permanent (i.e., initial, intermediate, and ultimate) change in the flow of services of these goods irrespective of what happens to the price of these goods in the course of the adjustment to the change in their quantity. In contrast, a change in the flow of services of money goods resulting from a change in the quantity of these goods will, ultimately, be co-determined by the subsequent change in price per unit of these goods, if any. As a result, analysis of the effects of changes in the quantity of money on wealth is more complex since the ultimate effect of the initial change in the quantity of the money good on wealth is indeterminate without further specification of the behavior relationships in the economy. Another result is that in an economy containing a good with the special technical property that a money good has (i.e., in a monetary economy), a change in the quantity of *any* good brings into operation not one but two economic mechanisms. As in a barter economy, a change in the quantity of any good leads to the combined wealth and portfolio effects described above in our discussion of the Barter Economy. In addition, as the wealth and portfolio effects, in response to the initial disturbance, change the relative prices of all goods, they are likely to change the average relative price of money. This changes the flow of services yielded by money and thus, in the course of adjustment to the initial disturbance in wealth, there is created another disturbance in wealth, usually called the real balance effect. Equilibrium in a monetary economy cannot be reestablished before both the initial change in wealth and the additional change in wealth created in the process of adjustment to the initial change are both disposed of.

Before we consider these two mechanisms, let us say a few words about the problem of the valuation of the increase in stock. For purposes of an abstract analysis, we do not need any valuation at all: all we need to do is to specify that the capital endowment of the consumers is increased by, say, a thousand units of wheat, steel, or gold pieces. However, when we later attempt to relate analysis to empirical facts, it is convenient to express this change in value terms and specify that the wealth of the consumers increased by a stock of goods worth x number of dollars. What price are we then to assign to the increase? The one that exists at the moment, the one that will exist after the equilibrating processes have had a chance to work themselves out, or some other one? This is not an important decision since all that matters is the increase in the stock, not the value that we decide to assign to it. In what follows, however, we shall follow the economic literature and make the assumption that consumers—considered to be fully competitive—behave as if their actions had no effect on prices so that they value any increment to their endowment as the increment to the stock times the existing price per unit of this stock.

Let us now return to our discussion of substantive issues. The result of a change in the stock of the capital good C_B (that we express in value terms as the change in this stock ΔC_B times the existing price P_B) is that the consumers are now oversupplied with C_B or, looking at this from the opposite side, undersupplied with all other goods. To reach an equilibrium, the price of C_B must fall; that is, the prices of other goods (not necessarily all) must rise. This equilibrating change results from a combination of the wealth and portfolio effects: at the original prices and the new, larger inventory of C_B the consumers' wealth is greater so that they desire to increase consumption of all goods and services. To do so, they must decrease their stock of C_B (or, alternatively, increase their net supply of y_B) since the only change that initially occurred is an increase in the stock of C_B which increases the flow of services of C_B, i.e., increases y_B. Thus, the initial specialized change in the consumers wealth portfolio distributes itself throughout the portfolio.

However, as the initial equilibrium price of C_B becomes reduced in the process of adjustment to the increased quantity of C_B, the flow of services yielded by the money good C_B is reduced by virtue of this flow being proportionate to the price of money. Thus, the equilibrating mechanism that operates in a barter economy becomes joined, in a monetary economy, by another one. Since the subject of money is so difficult, an analogy might be useful at this point. Consider an increase in a nonmoney good in a barter economy in which, however, the government has the policy of impounding one per cent of a certain capital good C_K whenever the price of this capital good falls by one per cent. In that case, too, the equilibrating process that leads to an adjustment to a change in the quantity of the capital good C_K or of any other good C_i (as we described it in the Barter Economy section of this chapter) would become more complex: the wealth and portfolio effects would be joined by an artificial "government effect" akin to the real balance effect. What in a barter economy would occur only on the basis of a policy decision of some governing body, in a monetary economy occurs automatically by virtue of the special technical property of the money good. Thus, in a monetary economy the automatic economic mechanism based on the wealth and portfolio effect becomes joined by another automatic mechanism based on what is in the literature called the real balance effect. If the quantity of the money good is increased, the economy adjusts to this disturbance through the wealth and portfolio effect and, in the course of this adjustment, the real balance effect comes into operation, reduces the size of the initial disturbance, and thus speeds up the equilibrating process.

Notice that in an economy that contains a money good, in a

monetary economy, the same two mechanisms become operative even when the quantity of some *nonmoney* good is changed. In this respect, the analysis of the effects of a change in a money good as presented in the above section dealing with Barter Economy is incomplete and must now be supplemented. In that section we have seen that the combined wealth and portfolio effects respond to a change in the nonmoney capital good C_K by reducing the price P_K relative to the prices of all other goods and thus restore equilibrium. However, in a monetary economy one of these "other" goods is the good C_B, money, that has the technical property described above. The statement that the price P_K of the nonmoney good C_K falls is equivalent to saying that the price P_B of the money good C_B rises; but this means that the flow of services yielded by each unit of the good C_B increases. Therefore, as the combined wealth and portfolio effects keep reducing the price of the nonmoney good C_K to its new equilibrium level they give rise, in a monetary economy, to the real balance effect and create an additional disturbance in the level of consumers' wealth. A new equilibrium will be reached only after both the initial disturbance consisting of an increase in C_K *and* the resulting disturbance consisting of an increase in the productivity of each unit of C_B are both neutralized by an appropriate change in the relative prices. Notice that in the case of a change in the *nonmoney* capital in a monetary economy this additional disturbance is likely but need not occur since it is conceivable that the change in the quantity of the nonmoney capital good C_K will so change the relative prices of nonmoney capital goods so as to leave the average relative price $\bar{P}_B$ of the money good unchanged. Only in this special case will the mechanism that restores equilibrium disturbed by a change in the quantity of a nonmoney good be the same in the case of a barter economy and in the case of a monetary economy.

It would court confusion to analyze simultaneously the forces that are capable of bringing about the initial disturbance (e.g., forces capable of changing the stock of one of the capital goods in the economy), the equilibrating forces that the initial disturbance will unleash (i.e., the wealth, portfolio, and real balance effects), and the ultimate determination of the new equilibrium values of all the variables. As a result, in the remainder of this book we shall divide the whole problem and proceed step by step. *In Part II of this book, we concentrate our attention solely on the production processes that are capable of changing the stock of the money good C_B; that is, we concentrate on the forces that are capable of changing the initial endowment of the consumers with money and that are, therefore, capable of giving rise to the equilibrating adjustments discussed above.* We focus our attention solely on the problem as to which economic units, and in what manner, are capable of causing an initial change in the capital good called money; we leave any consideration of equilibrating adjustments that such change will give rise, to subsequent parts of the book. If a change in the price of various goods, including money, will be discussed nevertheless, it will not be for the purpose of discovering the *new* equilibrium price; it will be merely for the purpose of discovering whether *the possibility* of a change in prices— in whatever direction and in whatever magnitude—represents an additional constraint upon those economic units capable of causing an initial change in the stock of money. In Part IV we then explore the modes of consumer behavior that determine the consumers' responses to the change in the initial stocks of capital goods, both nonmonetary and monetary. Only in Part V do we take the final step and specify various initial changes in the stock of these capital goods, the equilibrating adjustments that these initial changes will bring about, and the new equilibrium values to which these adjustments will lead.

Changing of the Symbols

In the preceding discussions we were most intent on demonstrating that general value theory is equally applicable to all commodities, regardless of whether they perform economic tasks such as yielding fruit, lifting loads, facilitating spacial transfers of persons and goods or whether they perform the economic tasks of facilitating transfers of goods among persons and thus, by so doing, greatly increase efficiency of the economy by making possible specialization of functions. In other words, we were intent on demonstrating that general value theory is equally applicable to nonmoney commodities and to money commodities. In the pursuit of this goal we preferred to avoid separatism even in our notational system and thus we assigned to *all* commodities the symbol C_i, to all relative prices the symbol P_i, and to all average relative prices the symbol $\bar{P}_i$.

Assuming that this goal has been accomplished, it will now be convenient to return to a more customary notation. Therefore the money good previously labelled C_B will hereafter be denoted as M, a symbol with obvious mnemonic advantages. Similarly, in economic literature it is not customary to speak about the relative price of money P_B or about the average relative price of money $\bar{P}_B$ but only about the reciprocal of the latter, the general price level P; we shall adopt this usage. Thus, in the remainder of this book that part of the society's wealth that in the above was labelled ($C_B \times \bar{P}_B$) will be labelled $\left(\dfrac{M}{P}\right)$.

Wealth in an Economy with Fiat Money

We have just seen that the real income yielded by money is independent of the quantity of the money resource in existence, provided that this quantity is fixed either by nature or by law. The real income yielded by a unit of money then becomes proportional to the price of a unit of the money commodity. But if the real income yielded by money can be independent of the physical quantity of the resource yielding this income merely through fixing the quantity of it, it can also be independent of the physical substance of this resource. This opens the gates to all types of substitutes for the money commodity: for cheap substances such as paper and, best of all, for no physical substances whatever, for mere accounting entries. In other words, this technical property of money opens the gates for fiat money and bank money. In the remainder of this chapter, we shall discuss monopolistic production of commodity money and show that the economic principles governing it lead directly to the case of fiat money; next we shall discuss fiat money directly. The bank money case, which is more complex, we reserve for Chapter 4.

All nonmonetary capital goods considered by the theory of value have the technical property that a unit of them yields a constant quantity of physical service (output), regardless of the price of these goods. If the demand for these goods increases, the prices of them increase, but the flow of services (output) yielded by a unit of them remains unchanged. As we have seen, this is not the case with a money capital good; money capital goods have the technical property that a unit of them yields a quantity of physical service (output) that is proportional to the price of money in terms of other goods. Inevitably, the conclusions reached by the theory of value for a good with one technical property need not be the same as the conclusions reached for goods with another technical property. In what follows, we shall point out three key conclusions of value theory that are different when we analyze a money capital good rather than nonmonetary capital goods. In combination, these three conclusions indicate why commodity money as discussed above may be profitably replaced with a perfect substitute represented by fiat money.

MONOPOLIST ECONOMIZES SOCIETY'S RESOURCES BY RESTRICTING OUTPUT. Although it would not be appropriate at this point to restate the conclusions of value theory as to the desirability of competitive production of nonmonetary goods, it is easy to show that competitive production of commodity money is undesirable. We have seen that an increase in demand, with supply given, will increase the price of money and hence will create its own supply of services (output) yielded by this given supply. However, a competitive producer of money will be unable to leave well enough alone. He faces an increased price of his output while his costs of production are unchanged. Inevitably, he will increase his output. From the standpoint of society, the competitive producer of money is wasting resources on output that is unnecessary.

A monopolistic producer of money will produce a smaller output than will a competitive producer. Thus, with monopolistic production, fewer resources will be devoted to the production of the money commodity, and hence more resources will be available for production of nonmonetary commodities. The community, as far as its money wealth is concerned, will be no worse off as a result of these monopolistic practices because the total service (output) that the money supply yields does not depend on the number of units in existence.[19] In all other respects, the community is better off, since the resources that would have gone into the competitive production of money (without increasing the total services yielded by money) are now free to be utilized in the production of nonmoney capital that *will* increase the total flow of services available to the community. If the economy we are discussing is a growing one, then with an increase in the stock of nonmoney goods we can expect an increase in the number of transactions in these goods and hence an increase in demand for money. Also, with increased wealth, people might be more willing than before to let more time lapse between transactions (that is, devote less effort to timing receipts and payments) and, since during this time money serves also as a store of value, this is equivalent to an increase in the demand for money for this purpose. Both these changes in demand will cause the price of money to increase. Under these circumstances, a competitive industry would

---

[19] At least, does not depend on it within very broad limits. What are these limits? Pushing the case to the one extreme, the size of the stock could be so small that it might require a huge price per unit; but then the average-valued transaction would have to be achieved by the use of a quantity of the money resource that is microscopic. Pushing the case to the other extreme, the size of the stock could be so huge as to require a negligible price per unit; but then the average-valued transaction would have to be accomplished by the use of a quantity of the money resource that is macroscopic. Either would be most inconvenient: microscopic quantities can get lost easily; macroscopic are a burden to carry. Once the practical size of the stock is reached, the community is no worse off if the output of the commodity ceases. Within the limits just described, the given quantity can yield any real income desired merely through changes in the price per unit of the money resource.

continue to devote resources to the production of money. In other words, with a competitive money industry, the increase in the flow of services of money is brought about by an increase in the number of units of the money commodity rather than by a simple change in the value of each unit. But, as we have seen above, such a change uses resources that could have been used elsewhere. Since the monopolist will not have increased production by as much as the competitive industry, and since the community has no fewer services than it would have in the competitive case, the monopolist will be more efficient than a competitive industry.[20]

MONOPOLIST ECONOMIZES SOCIETY'S RESOURCES BY USING CHEAP COMMODITY. In the case of money, there is another very important resource-saving advantage of monopoly production. It is to be found in the possibility of using a relatively low-valued commmodity for money. By low-valued we mean, of course, a commodity with lower production costs per unit than would be economically acceptable (cf. footnote 19) in the case of competitively produced money and, if it were economically acceptable, would not lead to any conservation of resources. In the competitive case, if the money commodity were replaced by a cheaper one, output would, as has already been shown, be increased until the cost of production would again equal the price. Although not saving any resources this would, in addition, make money an inefficient medium of exchange due to the vast quantities of money that would be required to carry out even a modest transaction.

---

[20] This argument neglects the possible short-run effects that changes in the price level may have on the level of output. However, it is not apparent that these price level changes would be different under monopoly than under competitive money production even though the absolute level of prices would be lower under monopolistic money production. Thus, the argument that it may be more efficient to increase money proportionately with increases in the demand for money, to keep prices constant, rather than to allow the desired increase in the money supply to come about through general reductions in the price level implies nothing concerning the desirability of competitive production of money.

MONOPOLIST ECONOMIZES SOCIETY'S RESOURCES BY USING LITTLE OF
CHEAP COMMODITY. Finally, the monopolistic producer of money
may carry this advantage even further. He may use the same units
of the money commodity—the same in the sense that they have the
same physical content or size and the same cost of production—and
endow them with different values: a twenty-dollar bill will do the
work of twenty one-dollar bills. This type of differentiation is made
possible by the monopolist's guarantee that he will exchange these
artificially differentiated commodities at the fixed exchange rate
without cost.

These three points make it obvious that the case of monopolistic
output of commodity money provides us with a smooth transition
from pure commodity money into fiat money. When money is produced by a monopolist who takes advantage of the above specified
resource-saving possibilities, the resulting output is not called
"monopolistically produced commodity money" but is usually
called "fiat money." It would be simplest merely to point out that
all the principles arrived at when we discussed commodity money
surely apply when this money is produced monopolistically: specifically, that regardless of its mode of production, money is a part
of net wealth, and that changes in the price of money will change
wealth. However, in view of the fact that—as Chapter 8 will amply
document—the assertion is frequently made that there is a fundamental analytical difference between commodity money ("hard
money") and fiat money ("credit money"), it appears imperative
to discuss the fiat money case in detail.

Fiat Money as Part of Net Wealth

Money, as we have seen earlier, is a part of the net wealth of the
community because it yields services to the owner while it yields no
negative service to the nonowner. The service yielded is based on the
role of money as a medium of exchange or store of value; for the
performance of these roles the physical substance of a unit of money

is of no consequence whatever. But then fiat money is just as much a part of the net wealth of the community as is commodity money. This is most easily shown by pointing out that it could not make any difference if someone would replace, overnight, commodity money with fiat money that would serve the citizens equally well in all respects. Similarly, it would not make any difference in our conclusions if the barter economy skipped the step represented by competitively produced commodity money and shifted directly to a monopolistically produced commodity money or to fiat money. In any case, money—*simply money*—would yield the services that we discussed in detail in connection with commodity money, and would be a part of the total net wealth of the community. It should be pointed out that net wealth surely cannot decrease if fiat money rather than commodity money is used to provide the services that (any) money yields. On the contrary, net wealth will increase. Monopoly production of money will utilize fewer resources than would be utilized under competitive conditions. Thus the community has more resources available for the production of nonmoney capital goods; so it will have, under conditions of monopoly production of money, a greater flow of nonmoney services. Since the flow of money services is independent of the stock of units of money in existence, it will also have the same quantity of money services. Therefore, the wealth of the community is greater when the production of money is undertaken by a monopolist. Parenthetically, we might mention that it obviously makes no difference whether this monopolistic producer of money is a private firm or the government—though the second is, of course, more likely. Moreover, monopoly production gives us the additional advantage of choosing a commodity that has a lower value and lower production costs than one produced by a competitive money industry. This leaves more resources available for other uses and hence further increases the wealth of the community over what it would have been with competitive production of the money commodity.[21]

[21] The same point may be made in a somewhat different way. We have seen that commodity money is a part of wealth, regardless of whether it has or

Therefore, we have shown that the introduction of a monopoly-produced fiat money has increased the wealth of the community. But has this assumption affected our previous conclusion that money is an asset not offset by a corresponding debt? A little reflection on our argument of the previous section will lead to the conclusion that the method of production of money does not affect this important conclusion. For the monopolist producer of money has all the same choices open to him as any commodity producer. If the producer of money desires to increase his consumption of services, he may borrow capital goods from others and thus incur a debt (whether or not the lender requires him to pay interest) or he may produce and sell additional fiat money, which is—as we have just shown—not a debt. We conclude again, therefore, that money, whether fiat or commodity money, is not a debt of the issuer of it, but is an asset to the holders. In other words, money yields a positive flow of services to the holders of it, and does not yield an offsetting negative flow of services to either the nonholders or to the producer and seller of it.

OBJECTION: FIAT MONEY IS NOT NET WEALTH. In the literature the conclusion that fiat money is net wealth and therefore not a debt is being vigorously denied. James Tobin summarized the two main arguments that are being used in support of this position as follows:

> The community's wealth now has two components: the real goods accumulated through past real investment and fiduciary or paper "goods" manufactured by the government from thin air. Of course, the nonhuman wealth of such a nation "really" consists

---

does not have some other nonmonetary use. Suppose that it has no non-monetary use. Why should the wealth of society change if someone would, overnight, replace this commodity money with fiat money? Wealth would *not* change. Suppose that the money commodity has some other use and that someone, again, replaces this commodity money with fiat money. As far as the services of money are concerned, the community is getting no less income than before, and it is now able to rechannel the money commodity that has some other use to this use: it must be better off.

only of its tangible capital. But, as viewed by the inhabitants of the nation individually, wealth exceeds the tangible capital stock by the size of what we might term the fiduciary issue. This is an illusion, but only one of the many fallacies of composition which are basic to any economy or any society. The illusion can be maintained unimpaired so long as the society does not actually try to convert all of its paper wealth into goods.[22]

Let us consider these two arguments: First, goods are being placed in quotation marks and denied existence if they are manufactured "from thin air"; if their market value exceeds their resource cost. Market valuation of goods is being rejected on the basis of a subjective decision that these goods are "really" worthless! Are we to deny that opera singers add to national income, and that the capitalized value of this income is net wealth, since the product they produce is manufactured out of thin air? If so, a great deal of nonmonetary wealth must be removed from our accounts. Are we to deny that monopolistically produced goods, the resource cost of which is smaller than their market price, are not wealth to the extent of the difference? Then much of the tangible nonhuman wealth must be removed from our accounts; the fate of all art treasures becomes extremely doubtful. Second, the assertion is made that a good, the value of which depends on the continuing demand for it, is merely an "illusion." If so, then each and every single item of wealth is an illusion because its value, to use Tobin's words, "continues unimpaired so long as the society does not actually try to convert all of" it into other goods. The total wealth of the society is, if we accept this economic analysis, zero by definition. Clearly, neither argument could stand scrutiny if applied to anything else but money. Indeed, it is inconceivable that either argument would be used in support of a decision to remove some part of the nonmonetary ("tangible") capital from the measure of wealth. But then, why should either argument be more persuasive when we undertake economic analysis into the nature of money?

[22] James Tobin, "Money and Economic Growth," *Econometrica*, *33* (October, 1965), p. 676.

However, as the reader is surely well aware, there are numerous other arguments denying that fiat money is net wealth and asserting that it is merely a debt. Orderly presentation of our own economic analysis of commodity money, fiat money, and bank money prevents consideration of all of them at this point, especially since many cover simultaneously fiat money and bank money; the economic analysis of the latter we have not yet had a chance to present. Consequently, these opposing viewpoints will be given detailed attention upon the conclusion of our own analysis into the nature of money, in Chapters 6 through 8. At this point, all we can do is to ask the reader's forbearance and offer him assurance that the other arguments denying fiat money the character of net wealth will prove no less hollow than the two basic ones just discussed.

Effects of Changes in the Relative Price of Fiat Money

Since we have concluded that fiat money is no different from a competitively produced commodity money in its characteristics, we should expect that the analysis used in the previous section would apply without change here. And this is, indeed, the case. Consider, say, an increase in the value of our fiat money in terms of the non-money goods of the community. Such an increase makes the holders of the fiat money better off because the exchange value of their holdings of fiat money has increased or, put in income terms, the flow of services of their money holdings has increased because each unit of money now supports more transactions than before the increase in value. However, the nonholders of fiat money are no worse off, since every combination of goods available to them before the change in the price of money is available to them now. This result stems from the fact that for the nonholders of money prices have not changed, because the increase in the value of a unit of money has simply resulted in a proportional increase in the volume of services yielded by a unit of money, leaving the price of a unit of the services of money unchanged. Here we have a wealth effect stemming from the change in the value of money affecting the holders but not the nonholders of money.

Conclusion

The use of fiat money does raise problems that do not exist in the case of a competitive production of commodity money. First, a monopolistic producer of (fiat) money is able to become such only if the community is willing to give him the powers he needs to enforce his monopoly. Second, we have seen that there are significant savings of resources to be realized from a monopolistic production of money; these savings, of course, at least partly enrich the monopolist himself. It appears inevitable that the monopolist will get from the community the powers needed to enforce his monopoly only if he will place the control over the income derived from his monopolistic power in the hands of the community. Finally, there are numerous alternatives open to the monopolist for placing the money he produces into use. He may sell the money and refund the purchase price to the buyer: we shall call this a gift of money. He may sell the money and use the proceeds for his own purposes. Or he may sell the money and distribute the proceeds to the individual members of the community: we may call this payment a subsidy, or a decrease in taxes, or a transfer payment. However, since these are essentially problems of form rather than substance, analytically—though not empirically—of secondary importance, we shall leave their discussion to Chapter 8. The truly important issue discussed in this chapter is that money is in one respect identical with and in another respect completely different from all other commodities. It is different from all other commodities in that it has a technical property of yielding its owner real income that depends completely on the price ratio between other real goods and money. It is identical with all other commodities in that it is a claim of the owner on the resources of others, but it is not a debt of others to the owner. The difference between a claim based on ownership of any real resource and a

claim based on a debt of someone else is that the first merely enables
the owner to attempt to induce owners of any other good to trade
at the basis of the current market prices, whereas the second enables
the owner to insist on the repayment of a contractually stipulated
type and quantity of some other commodity.[23] The "producer" of a
debt is a debtor because he has acquired resources through no effort
of his own; they were simply transferred to him by the creditor.
The producer of a money commodity is not a debtor because he
sacrificed his effort or other resources to produce commodity money.
Were he, in a legal or economic sense, to become a debtor, the
monetary commodity would not exist at all, since he would never
produce it; he would be sacrificing his real resources to produce it
and, after production and sale, he would then be in no better position
than someone who merely induced others to transfer resources
to him.

We have also shown that fiat money is a mere substitute for commodity money. A substitute that is made possible by the exercise
of monopolistic powers by the producer of money; monopolistic
powers that—in the case of money—enhance rather than diminish
efficient use of resources. Even though no (or almost no) resources
are sacrificed in the production of fiat money, this money is nevertheless a substitute for commodity money. The reason is the special
technical property of money that makes the real output yielded by it
independent of the physical substance of it. For this reason, all the
conclusions reached with respect to commodity money must hold
with respect to fiat money. The two most important are (1) that fiat
money is a genuine part of the net wealth of the community, not
offset by any corresponding debt, and (2) that changes in the price
of the fiat money will change the wealth of society.

[23] At times, the fiat money producer gives the holders of fiat money the right
to demand a specific quantity of another commodity; e.g., gold. A slight
modification of the results obtained in this chapter is then needed. The
nature of these modifications will become obvious in the next chapter that
deals with bank money.

CHAPTER 4

Bank Money as Wealth

We are now prepared to turn our attention to the case of bank-created money. This case is, unfortunately, a complex one. As a result of this complexity, the basic similarity between the operations of the banking system and the production and sale of commodity and fiat money has had a tendency to become lost. The so called *Old View* that perceived this similarity is nowadays in general retreat, and a *New View* dominates monetary theory. James Tobin, who coined the terms we just used, expressed the currently dominant opinion most succinctly when he wrote:

> Unlike governments, bankers cannot create means of payment to finance their own purchases of goods and services. Bank-created "money" is a liability, which must be matched on the other side of the balance sheet.[1]

In this chapter we intend to show that the *Old View* still holds and that commercial banks are producers and sellers of money called demand deposits and that this money is a part of the net wealth of the community. Our analysis will contain three main parts. First,

---

[1] James Tobin, "Commerical Banks as Creators of 'Money'," in Dean Carson (ed.), *Banking and Monetary Studies* (Homewood, Ill.: Irwin, 1963), p. 415.

we discuss a general and abstract type of "private money producer," who is in the business of producing and selling private money. Initially, we impose on him no restriction other than a limit on the quantity of his output; next, we subject him to the rule that his output must be convertible into "the coin of the Realm." Second, we show that commercial banks insofar as they are producing demand deposits are such private money producers and that all the conclusions reached earlier apply to them. Specifically, we show that their output is a part of the net wealth of the community. Third, in a separate chapter, we show that certain changes in the restraints under which private money producers operate can reduce them to mere financial intermediaries.

Private Money: The General Case

For simplicity we assume that the only money in use in the economy is fiat money (in the following discussion we refer to this primary money as the "dominant money") produced by a monopolist—the government, if you like. Suppose that the government allows certain firms to enter into the production and sale of a substitute for dominant money, provided that convertibility into dominant money on the demand of a private money holder is guaranteed at a fixed exchange rate—presumably, since most conveniently, at a one-to-one rate.[2] Thus each unit of private money sold must contain an instant repurchase clause; this clause guarantees that the producer of private money will repurchase his product, on demand of the buyer or of any subsequent holder, at its original sale price.

[2] Since our problem is purely analytical, we need not inquire why the monopolistic producer of fiat money should be willing to share his monopoly. The reasons are complex. Partly they are historical: actually, the banks existed before the appearance of the fiat money producers who found it convenient to make use of them, perhaps to hide their innovation from the public eye. Also, the monopolists—as we have seen in Chapter 3—must determine the quantity of money, and these private money producers may be a very convenient tool for changing this quantity rapidly.

Assume, finally, that the private money producers are prohibited by the government from stimulating demand by bribing their customers; they are forbidden to pay interest to the holders of bank money. This last assumption is made merely for the sake of an orderly presentation and will be dropped in due course.

Benchmark: Unrestricted Private Money Producer

As a benchmark for the consideration of the private money producer, let us establish the addition to net wealth resulting from the introduction of a private money with no strings attached, i.e., all sales final. In this case, private money producers are in the same position as is the fiat money producer of the previous chapter. Hence, so long as some limit is imposed on the output of their money, the change in net wealth is simply the total sales of private money, i.e.,

$$\Delta w = \frac{M_p}{P} \qquad [4.1]$$

where (w) is the level of the community's net wealth and (M_p) is the nominal amount of private money sold. This result follows from the same analysis applicable to the fiat money producer of Chapter 3. In other words, the sale of money can only take place if the purchasers value the money at least as highly as the goods transferred to the private money producer. But since, for the private money producer all sales are final, the money sold cannot be a debt of his and therefore the money must be net wealth. To the extent that the production of private money (or dominant money for that matter) uses up resources that would have been used to increase the stock of other capital goods, the *net* change (net of reduction in other items of net wealth) in *net* wealth will be smaller. However, this simply means that the community prefers to hold its net wealth in the form of money rather than in the form of these other capital goods, and does not imply that money is not wealth.

While a positive resource cost of production of private money will affect the net change in the community's net wealth, it will not affect our decision concerning the classification of private money as net wealth. Thus, we can simplify our analysis without losing any generality if we assume that the resource cost of producing the physical units of private money is zero; that the cost of producing paper notes or accounting entries that make up the private money stock is zero.[3] Given this assumption, the increase in the producers' net wealth that results from the outright sale of private money (all sales final) is precisely equal—as in the case of the production and sale of fiat money in Chapter 3—to the change in the community's net wealth. We may, therefore, rewrite equation [4.1] as follows:

$$\Delta w = \frac{M_p}{P} - \Delta \frac{y}{r} + \Delta \frac{y}{r} = \frac{M_p}{P} \qquad [4.2]$$

where $\left(\Delta \frac{y}{r}\right)$ represents the value of the capital goods transferred by the purchasers of money to the private money producers and is of course equal to M_p.

Private Money Producer, Restricted by the Instant Repurchase Clause

We have now laid the groundwork for consideration of the economic effects of the instant repurchase clause through which privately produced money becomes convertible, on demand, into the coin of the Realm—into dominant money. This clause requires the producer of private money to repurchase his product on demand of the holder of it at a fixed price. This repurchase clause, as we shall show, (1) helps to determine the equilibrium level of output that the private

---

[3] We stress the resource cost of production of physical units of private money because, as we shall see in the discussion of the effect of the repurchase clause, it is possible for the community to impose a resource cost on the private money producer that is not connected with the production of physical units of private money.

money producer will be able to produce and sell, and (2) changes the contribution of this producer to the net wealth of society.

DETERMINATION OF EQUILIBRIUM OUTPUT OF PRIVATE MONEY. To insure that in equilibrium both private and dominant money exist, assume that these two types of money are not perfect substitutes for each other in all uses. In other words, both monies are media of exchange, but there are some exchanges that are more convenient to undertake by the use of one type rather than the other.[4] Thus, given (1) the repurchase clause requiring a one-to-one exchange ratio (or, more generally, any other fixed ratio), and (2) the prohibition of interest payments to the purchasers of private money, there will exist some proportion between dominant and private money that will make them perfect substitutes on the margin; there will exist a proportion of dominant money to private money that makes consumers indifferent between a unit of private money and a unit of dominant money. Hence, even if the private money producers did not hold any dominant money inventories as a reserve against unexpected runs of repurchases, a limit to the sale of private money would still exist. Given the two restraints specified above, this limit depends on the nominal stock of dominant money and the proportion of dominant money to private money at which the consumers are indifferent between the two types of money. In such a case the equilibrium stock of private money is

$$M_p = \frac{M_d}{\gamma} \qquad [4.3]$$

where (M_d) is the nominal stock of dominant money and (γ) is the ratio of dominant money to private money desired by consumers. If the existence of the instant repurchase clause causes the private money producers to hold some dominant money reserves, equation [4.3] overstates the equilibrium stock of private money. This overstatement results from the removal of some dominant money from the community's use whenever the private money producers sell

---

[4] We shall discuss the reasons for this later in the chapter.

their own product. In this case the equilibrium stock of private money is given by

$$M_p = \frac{M_d}{(\gamma + \rho)} \tag{4.4}$$

where (ρ) is the ratio of dominant money reserves to private money sales desired by the private money producers.[5]

THE EFFECT OF THE REPURCHASE CLAUSE ON NET WEALTH PRODUCED. Given the instant repurchase clause, the private money producer can no longer sell his money outright, but now has a restriction placed on his actions. Whereas before he had, of course, the option to repurchase his money when he so desired, now he must repurchase his money whenever the holder of it so desires. This restriction, at best, will leave the wealth of the private money producers unaffected and, at the worst, will wipe out the entire gain from the sales of private money. Hence, [4.2] above represents the upper bound to the change in the net wealth of the private money producers. Since a zero change in wealth represents the worst the private money producer can do—if he were to do worse he would not enter into the production and sale of private money—the following bounds are established for the change in wealth of the private money producers:

$$0 \le \Delta w \le \frac{M_p}{P} \tag{4.5}$$

Since the change in the wealth of the private money producers is equal to the change in the community's net wealth, we need a more exact statement if we are to succeed in determining the extent that private money represents net wealth. Careful consideration of the nature of the instant repurchase clause will enable us to measure the change in wealth more precisely. This clause forces the private money producers to be ready at all times to redeem their money with

[5] For a thorough discussion of the determinants of the equilibrium stock of a reserve money, see Milton Friedman and Anna Jacobson Schwartz, *A Monetary History of the United States 1867–1960* (Princeton, N.J.: Princeton University Press, 1964), pp. 784–789.

dominant money. If the goods purchased by them cannot be exchanged for dominant money instantly and at no cost, the private money producers will have to hold some inventories of dominant money.[6] These inventories serve as buffers against unexpected exercises of the instant repurchase clause. The bigger these inventories, the smaller the quantity of nonmonetary goods the private money producer is able to acquire for his use by selling his product because his budget constraint is

$$\frac{M_p}{P} - \Delta \frac{M_d}{P} = \Delta \frac{y}{r} \qquad [4.6]$$

where (ΔM_d) is the nominal quantity of dominant money held as inventory.

Let us now make allowance for the acquisition of some dominant money for use as a reserve against the possibility of runs of repurchases by the holders of private money. A simple noting of the wealth transfers shows that (1) the purchasers of privately produced money gained privately produced money and paid for it partly with dominant money and partly with real wealth (the first term in equation [4.7] below), whereas (2) the producers of private money lost nothing while gaining the above mentioned dominant money and real wealth (the second term in [4.7] below):

$$\Delta w = \left(\frac{M_p}{P} - \Delta \frac{M_d}{P} - \Delta \frac{y}{r}\right) + \left(\Delta \frac{M_d}{P} + \Delta \frac{y}{r}\right) - \frac{M_p}{P} \qquad [4.7]$$

where

$$\Delta \frac{M_d}{P} = \rho \frac{M_p}{P} \qquad [4.8]$$

and

$$\frac{M_p}{P} = \Delta \frac{y}{r} + \Delta \frac{M_d}{P} \qquad [4.9]$$

---

[6] The amount of reserves held may be chosen so that expected returns from the capital held is maximized subject to the repurchase clause. This would require some idea of the distribution of repurchases and knowledge of the cost of having to convert assets into dominant money on short notice.

Acceptance of equation [4.7] as the final result would lead to the conclusion that the change in wealth in this case is identical with the one that occurs in the case of a sale of fiat money (Chapter 3) or the one that results from the sale of private money not subject to the repurchase clause (equation [4.2]): this clause would have to be considered costless to the producers of private money. However, this is not the case. Looking at these inventories with the eyes of the producers,[7] we find the cost of holding them is simply the cost of being in this particular business: the producers are forced by the instant repurchase clause to forego income yielded by real assets they would have purchased in the absence of this clause. Thus the capital cost of the instant repurchase clause to the money producers is the capitalized value of the income foregone; it is equal to the value of the capital goods that could have been held if they did not have to hold dominant money reserves. Therefore, the change in net wealth is not as expressed in [4.7] but instead is

$$\Delta w = \left\{ \frac{M_p}{P} - \Delta \frac{M_d}{P} - \Delta \frac{y}{r} \right\} + \left\{ \Delta \frac{y}{r} + \left(\Delta \frac{M_d}{P} - \frac{Y_f}{Pr} \right) \right\} \qquad [4.10]$$

where (Y_f) is the money income foregone by the private money producers. We put the last two terms in this equation in parentheses

---

[7] Looking at these inventories with the eyes of the community as a whole, we find that the income the community would receive from the use of these inventories if they served as money is lost; either way, the existence of the repurchase clause introduces an additional cost of production and sale of private money. A third way of stating the *same thing* is directly related to the measurement of wealth. The producers acquire $\Delta y/r$; in the absence of the repurchase clause, they could use this wealth with the same efficiency as the original owners. With the repurchase clause, they have a choice either of using this wealth less efficiently by having it all the time in their physical possession and in instantly usable form or of holding inventories of dominant money. In the first case, the repurchase clause would make *all* of the wealth purchased by the private money producers less productive; in the second case, a part of the total is devoted to the purchases of inventories and the remainder to purchases of real wealth that can then be used at full efficiency. On the margin, these two alternative ways of accomplishing the same purpose, the satisfaction of the repurchase clause, should be equally costly; either measures the economic cost of the repurchase clause and the determination of total wealth that results from its existence.

as a reminder that these two terms precisely offset each other, since the capitalized value of income foregone as a result of holding dominant money inventories is precisely equal to the value of these inventories.[8] It might be illuminating now and it shall prove most helpful in our subsequent discussion to present the content of equation [4.10] in terms of accounting identities so familiar to all economists:

TABLE 4–1

Change in Balance Sheets: Equation [4.10]

REST OF THE ECONOMY		PRIVATE MONEY PRODUCER	
Assets	*Liabilities*	*Assets*	*Liabilities*
$-\Delta \dfrac{M_d}{P}$	(no change)	$+\Delta \dfrac{M_d}{P}$	$+\dfrac{Y_f}{rP}$
$-\Delta \dfrac{y^\dagger}{r}$		$+\Delta \dfrac{y}{r}$	
$+\dfrac{M_p}{P}$	*Net Worth*		*Net Worth*
	(no change)		$+\Delta w$

† Note that if the real assets the community pays to the private money producer are transferred to him physically, there is a negative change on the asset side of the Rest's T-account. Should the banker be satisfied with a promise to receive the real income that these real assets yield while leaving the physical possession of them undisturbed, this item would shift to the liability side of the Rest's T-account and change sign. In equation [4.10] the third term would not then read $\left(-\Delta \dfrac{y}{r}\right)$; it would read $+\left(-\Delta \dfrac{y}{r}\right)$.

Although equation [4.10] is useful because it shows *all* the changes in ncome flows and in the capitalized value of these flows that occur as a result of the production and sale of private money, many terms

[8] The reader may wonder whether we are saying that all inventories of all wealth should be removed from the wealth equation. We are not. All that we are doing is to guard against double counting. Given the repurchase clause and the necessity to hold inventories resulting from it, the community has now two alternatives: either it can gain the use of the privately produced money and lose the use of the dominant money or it can give up the use of the privately produced money and gain the use of the dominant money inventories. It cannot do both.

within this equation offset each other and hence the equation may be
more simply stated as follows:

$$\Delta w = \frac{M_p}{P} - \Delta \frac{M_d}{P} \qquad [4.11]$$

The change in the stock of money and hence, according to the
analysis presented in this and the preceding chapter, in the net
wealth of the community is precisely equal to the total sales of
private money minus the decrease in the stock of the dominant
money outstanding. Most important, we conclude that the change in
the net wealth of the community is precisely equal to the value of
sales of private money minus the resource cost of producing this
money: that private money is an asset that is *not* offset by a debt.
If commercial banking as the creator of demand deposits were
subject to no other restrictions than the one represented by the
instant repurchase clause that we imposed on the private money
producers in this section of the chapter, we could rest our argument.
However, the operations of banks are more complex, and in the next
section this complexity will be given attention. It will be discovered
that it has no effect whatever on the conclusions reached here for
the general type of "private money producer."

EFFECT OF CHANGES IN THE RELATIVE PRICE OF PRIVATE MONEY. Up
to this point all our discussions of effects of changes in the relative
price of money have been concerned with only one type of money at a
time. However, we are now considering a system containing both a
dominant (fiat) money and a general type of private money. Will this
change in the composition of the money supply affect the conclusions
reached in Chapter 3? Specifically, will the existence of the repurchase
clause cause the private money producers to be affected by changes
in the value of money in a way that offsets the wealth effect of changes
in the price of money? Consider an increase in the price of money.[9]

[9] We now assume, provisionally, that the change does not change public
demand for private money; we are assuming the quantity demanded to be
constant. In the next section of this chapter we shall amend the private
producer's mode of operation by making him buy not real but financial

Such a change will make the holders of all money, dominant or private, better off because it increases the exchange value of their holdings of money. But, the nonholders of money are no worse off because all the prices they face (including the price of the service yielded by money), and the stocks of assets they hold, remain the same. Thus, as far as the nonholders are concerned, everything remains the same. We believe we have proven this in Chapter 3; however, merely as an aid to memory let us remind ourselves that a nonholder and a potential purchaser of money is indifferent to the change in the price of money in terms of other commodities because the power of money to purchase other commodities in turn changes *pari passu.* Thus, as far as the nonholders are concerned, all opportunities that were available to them before the price change are still available; however, the holders of money now have a larger set of opportunities available. Therefore, neglecting any possible effect on the private money producers, the community's net wealth has increased. How will the increase in the value of money affect the private money producer? For simplicity let us assume that the private money producers as producers are nonholders of money except, of course, for the dominant money reserves. They can be affected only if the change in the price of money changes the quantity of inventories of dominant money that must be held against possible runs of repurchases. But, since we are assuming provisionally (cf. footnote 9) that a change in the price of all money does not change the relative usefulness of private and dominant money, the level of inventories of dominant money that must be held remains unchanged; therefore, the producers of private money will be unaffected by a change in the price of money. Therefore, we conclude that the fact that private money must be sold with a repurchase clause in no way affects the conclusion reached in Chapter 3 that changes in the price of money—now including the privately produced money—result in proportionate changes in the monetary

---

assets. Only then shall we dare to remove the constant demand assumption. However, the present discussion is still useful, since its conclusions will be shown to remain unaffected by any subsequent complications.

wealth and in less than proportionate changes in the total wealth
of the community.

Bank Money

The concept of the private money producer was used as an expository device so that we could abstract from many of the complex
modes of operation of commercial banking and demonstrate that
privately produced money is a part of the net wealth of the community.
As is true of every simplification, the concept of the private money
producer is not fully adequate. To make him viable in the face of
changes in the price of money, we must introduce refinements into
his mode of operation. We shall discover that these refinements are
precisely those that are employed by the commercial banking system.
After we have finished, it will be obvious that by describing a viable
private money producer we are, simultaneously, describing commercial banks. We shall also show that the refinements introduced
do not affect in any manner the basic conclusions reached in the
preceding section: in particular, that privately produced money is a
part of the net wealth of the community and that changes in the
price of this money change the net wealth of the community.

In what follows we shall first discuss the operating refinements
that must be introduced to make private money producers viable
and that, simultaneously, make their behavior indistinguishable
from that of commercial banks. Second, we shall discuss the reasons
that lead commercial banks to differentiate their product from a
competing product, from fiat money, and cause them to give it
the form of demand deposits. Finally, we show that some additional
restraints that the government imposes on commercial banks do
not affect the conclusions reached previously; that their sole effect
is to circumscribe more restrictively than would otherwise be the
case the size of the output of the commercial banks and to force
them to sell their product only to customers who meet government
approval.

Operating Refinements Necessary to Protect Private Money Producers from Bankruptcy

SOLVENCY REQUIREMENT. We have already seen that the instant repurchase clause requires the producers of private money to hold inventories of dominant money. However, the repurchase clause—regardless of whether it must be satisfied instantly or whether the producer is given time to convert some of his income-earning assets into dominant money to satisfy it—has another consequence that we have ignored until now. In a world in which there is not perfect certainty there is always a possibility, however remote, that *all* customers of the private money producer will exercise the repurchase clause. The only defense the private money producer or a commercial bank has against such a possibility is to remain solvent at all times. Thus the solvency requirement under which commercial banks operate is not an independent restriction, additional to the repurchase clause, but merely one implication of it. The question then arises: Does the existence of the solvency requirement affect our measure of the change in wealth resulting from the production of bank money? If a private money producer, a commercial banker, wishes to consume more than the income yielded by the wealth he purchased by selling his output of private money $\left(\Delta \frac{y}{r} \right.$ in equation [4.7] and following$\left. \right)$, he may not do so by selling these assets if such a sale would result in insolvency.[10] On the surface, a requirement that prevents the money producers from disposing of the wealth obtained from the sale of money would seem to be a burdensome one. However, as long as the money producers have access to the capital market they can, if they so desire, consume or invest the capitalized value of the income streams they purchased simply by selling their

---

[10] This last qualifying phrase has been added to make the statement accurate even in cases in which the private money producer allowed the income (y) to accumulate as an increment to his initial holdings of $\Delta(y/r)$. A sale of this accumulation—precisely as a continuous consumption of it—cannot affect the solvency of the firm producing private money.

titles to these income streams.[11] Whereas an unrestricted private
producer of money could sell the capital goods he owns and dispose
of the proceeds as he sees fit, the commercial banker subject to the
solvency requirement may simply sell his titles to the incomes yielded
by these goods and thus may also dispose of the proceeds as he may
see fit. Hence, the solvency restriction cannot affect our conclusion
that commercial banks, as private money producers, contribute
to the wealth of the community by the amount specified in equation
[4.11].[12]

BANK MONEY MUST BE SOLD FOR FINANCIAL ASSETS.   As we have
seen, the repurchase clause contains in itself the implication of the
solvency requirement; the solvency requirement, in turn, contains in
itself the need for the banks to purchase not real but financial
assets. That this is the case can be most easily shown by considering
the effect of a price change on the solvency of the private money
producer discussed in the previous section who, by virtue of our
provisional assumption, was said to buy real wealth $\left(\Delta \frac{y}{r} \right.$ in equations
[4.2] and [4.10]$\left. \right)$. Suppose that the price of money increases. Such

[11] Economically, this means that they can divest themselves, to any desired
extent, of the business of the production of private money and use the
proceeds to enter into the production of anything else or consume the
proceeds.

[12] The reader may wonder whether instead of disposing of the economic
relevance of the solvency restriction, we did not merely dispose of the
restriction by selling it to somebody else. This is not the case. The statement
that an owner must remain solvent is another way of saying that he cannot
consume his principal without selling it. But most—perhaps all—nonmonetary wealth today is of such a nature. The owners of this wealth cannot
consume the principal directly; they also *must* sell first to somebody who
wants to hold the wealth only for the income it yields, and *then* they may
consume the proceeds. A prime exception to this rule would be the Knightian
perennial "that grows at a constant (geometric) rate, except as [its] tissue
is cut away for consumption." (Frank H. Knight, "Diminishing Returns
from Investment," *Journal of Political Economy*, *LII* (March, 1944), p. 30.)
(The original word in brackets is "new." However, since Knight explicitly
permits disinvestment to occur, this must be a slip of the tongue.)

an increase will cause the value of the dominant money reserves, plus the nonmonetary wealth held, to become smaller than the value of the stock of private money outstanding. Thus, a change in the price of money will cause the private money producer to become insolvent (in the technical meaning of the word specified above). The only way of escaping this risk is to sell private money not for titles to income fixed in real terms but for titles to income fixed in money terms: to sell private money for *financial assets*. This is precisely the manner in which the actual private money producers, commercial banks, conduct their business. They sell their product, bank money, either "for cash" or "on an installment plan"; they sell it either for dominant money or for a bond executed by the purchaser and promising to the bank a stream of income fixed in money terms. Once the private money producers, commercial banks, proceed in this manner, the threat to their solvency inherent in the risk of a change in the price of money (change in the general price level) is overcome. The market value of these financial assets changes proportionately with, and therefore remains equal to, the market value of the private money produced and sold. But then equation [4.10] does not express the behavior of a private money producer who is viable in the face of price changes; it must be replaced with its modified version that reads

$$\Delta \frac{W}{P} = \left\{ \frac{M_p}{P} - \Delta \frac{M_d}{P} - \Delta \frac{Y}{rP} \right\} + \left\{ \Delta \frac{Y}{rP} + \left(\Delta \frac{M_d}{P} - \frac{Y_f}{rP} \right) \right\}$$

$$= \frac{M_p}{P} - \Delta \frac{M_d}{P} \qquad\qquad [4.12]$$

where all the variables are the same as in equation [4.10], except that capital letters now denote variables that are fixed in money terms.

It might again prove illuminating to present the revised equation [4.12] in terms of the accounting identities with which economists are so familiar:

TABLE 4–2

Changes in Balance Sheets: Equation [4.12]

REST OF THE ECONOMY		BANKERS	
Assets	*Liabilities*	*Assets*	*Liabilities*
$-\Delta \dfrac{M_d}{P}$		$+\Delta \dfrac{M_d}{P}$	$+\dfrac{Y_f}{rP}$
	$+\Delta \dfrac{Y\dagger}{rP}$	$+\Delta \dfrac{Y}{rP}$	
$+\dfrac{M_p}{P}$	*Net Worth*		*Net Worth*
	(no change)		$+\Delta \dfrac{W}{P}$

† For the position of this item, cf. the note to Table 4–1.

What are the economic consequences of this necessity to purchase financial assets? In the preceding section dealing with the private money producer, we—arbitrarily and for simplicity—limited ourselves to the simplifying assumption that he buys only streams of income fixed in real terms. But surely our conclusions would not change if, after the sale of his money for real wealth, the private money producer decided to rearrange his portfolio and exchanged some of it for financial assets. But then our conclusions would also not change if the private money producer sold his money for financial assets in the first place. Therefore, the only difference that might affect the conclusions reached earlier may be found in the fact that a commercial bank has to do what the private money producer was assumed to be free to do. Does *this* difference affect our conclusions? As long as the commercial banker has access to the capital market, he may hold exclusively financial assets in order to remain solvent and then may enter the capital market and sell the titles to the income streams yielded by these assets for sources of income streams fixed in real terms. Thus, as long as the existence of the solvency requirement has not changed the relative prices of assets, every opportunity that was available to the banker is still available to him. Therefore, this second consequence of the solvency requirement will also not affect the change in wealth that occurs when we introduce private money; the change in the community's net wealth will still be measured by the sales of private money minus the private money producers' holdings of dominant money reserves.

NOTE: SALE OF MONEY FOR FINANCIAL ASSETS REDISTRIBUTES THE PRICE RISK. We have seen that the repurchase clause forces the banks to satisfy the solvency requirement; the solvency requirement forces the banks to sell their product for financial assets; finally, the necessity to purchase financial assets results, in turn, in a redistribution of the risk inherent in the possibility of a change in the price of money. The shift from equation [4.10] to equation [4.12] has no immediate economic consequences whatever; the change in wealth that either one of these equations will show as a result of private money production will be identical. The sole difference between these two equations is to be found in the manner in which they allocate susceptibility to some future possible price change among the various sectors of the economy:[13]

1. A money producer sells his product (commodity money or fiat money) for real wealth. There is, subsequently, a decline in the price of money:
    a. the current owner of money is made worse off;
    b. the rest of the community (including the producer of money) is unaffected.
2. A private money producer sells his product for financial assets. There is, subsequently, a decline in the price of money:
    a. the current owner of privately produced money is, again, worse off;
    b. the rest of the community *as a whole* is, again, unaffected. However, the sale of money for financial assets has the

---

[13] We say deliberately "among sectors," since the necessity to engage in this hedging operation is not likely to affect the distribution of risk among persons. The price risk preferrers will simply move now into the sectors that assume the price risks; the price risk averters will move out of it.

consequences that there are now additional contracts specified in money terms:

(1) the original purchaser of private money is committed to pay to the banker a stream of income fixed in money terms; the fall in the price of money makes him better off;

·(2) the private money producer, who is receiving this income flow in money terms is, of course, worse off.

The two redistributive effects described in 2b(1) and 2b(2) will manifest themselves in offsetting changes in the net wealth (accounting term, net worth) of the nonbanking sector and the banking sector, the former gaining precisely what the latter is losing. However, the nonbanking sector also contains the current owners of the product of the banking sector, bank money, and on this wealth it suffers a loss described above by the 2a effect, identical to that described by 1a effect. Since the value of private money is bigger than the value of financial liabilities, the nonbanking sector is a net loser; its net wealth (net worth) falls. Since the net wealth of both the banking sector and the nonbanking sector falls, obviously the total wealth of the community falls. The net amount of the loss is measured, since the 2b(1) and the 2b(2) effects offset each other, by the 2a effect. Note that this result conforms fully with the conclusions reached above (in the section "Effect of Changes in Relative Prices of Money on Wealth") and demonstrates again that the Operating Refinements introduced into the behavior of the private money producer do not affect the main analysis of his effect on the net wealth of the community.[14]

---

[14] We might point out that if we forget the 2(a) effect and concentrate only on the two offsetting 2(b-1) and 2(b-2) effects, or if we—as is more frequent— forget the 2(b-2) effect and concentrate on the partly offsetting 2(a) effect and 2(b-1) effect, we are likely to conclude that we have found support for the hypothesis that money is but an asset of some and a liability of others and that the absolute amount of them cannot affect the wealth of the community. Both conclusions are the essence of the *New View* to which we referred at the beginning of this chapter. Cf., e.g., Joseph W. Conard, "The Causes and Consequences of Inflation," Commission on Money and Credit, *Inflation*,

The two refinements just discussed, the solvency requirement and the sale for financial assets requirement, leave completely unaffected our analytical conclusion that privately produced money net of reserves is, like fiat and commodity money, net wealth of the community. At the same time, the introduction of these two requirements makes the private producer fully viable in the sense that there is now no microeconomic or macroeconomic mechanism that would prevent his *continuous* economic existence.[15] Also, the introduction of the two requirements so modifies the mode of operation of the private money producer that it makes him indistinguishable from a commercial banker. Thus all the conclusions reached about commodity money production, fiat money production, and private money production also apply to the production of bank money. This money may be—and sometimes is—physically indistinguishable from fiat money; it may be bank notes. However, like many other producers, banks find it profitable to differentiate their product from the competing product.

Product Differentiation: Demand Deposits

In our discussion of the determinants of the equilibrium stock of private money, we simply assumed that the two types of money, dominant money and privately produced money, are not perfect substitutes for each other. Although both are media of exchange,

---

[15] We stress the word "continuous." Certain short-run problems that can be surmounted by purchases of financial assets of suitable maturities are discussed in the Appendix to Chapter 5, item (7-i).

Growth, and Employment (Englewood Cliffs, N.J.: Prentice-Hall, 1964), p. 135; George L. Bach and Albert K. Ando, "The Redistributional Effects of Inflation," *Review of Economics and Statistics*, *XXXIX* (February, 1957), pp. 1–13; Don Patinkin, *Money, Interest, and Prices*, 2nd ed. (New York: Harper & Row, 1965), pp. 296–297; finally, as a demonstration of strict justice, Boris P. Pesek, "A Comparison of the Distributional Effects of Inflation and Taxation," *American Economic Review*, L (March, 1960), pp. 147–153.

we assumed that some exchanges can be more conveniently undertaken by the use of one or the other. Given this, and given the requirements that both be convertible at par, the conclusion followed that there is some proportion of both upon the attainment of which the community will be indifferent (on the margin, of course) between the holding of either. We have also seen that this proportion determines the capacity of the private money producers to produce and sell private money (equation [4.4]); hence, it also determines the size of the income streams that the producers of private money will be able to exchange for their output of this money. However, none of the discussion or of the conclusions reached depends on the *form* of private money. Hence, the more attractive the private money producers make their product, the bigger will be the sales of it (the smaller will be the (γ) in equation [4.4]) and the bigger the gain of the producers. Suppose that to make their product more attractive, these private money producers introduce a number of innovations:

—Their product is insured against loss or theft *from the current owner* until he decides to use it and signifies so by signing it;

—their product is made in one single all-comprehensive denomination in that the current owner determines the denomination at the time of use simply by writing out any amount he chooses;

—their product is insured against loss or theft *from the purchaser* in that it is made property only of the buyer whose name is written on the note itself;

—their product is such that it, automatically, gives to the current owner of it evidence that he has paid his bills and thus protection against a dishonest purchaser of private money (and seller of some other wealth);

—their product depends for its existence on record-keeping by the private money producer, which may be made available to the purchaser free of charge or for a nominal charge.

All these items will make the product of private money producers distinctly superior to the dominant money, at least in some uses. Thus, such extra features tend to increase the equilibrium stock of private money by decreasing the proportion of their money holdings consumers desire to hold as dominant money; they increase the demand for the banker's product.

Clearly, none of these extra features of private money affects our measure of the change in wealth resulting from the introduction of this money, even though it may affect—indeed, is designed to affect—the absolute magnitude of the change. The change in net wealth of the community will still be the value of sales of private money minus the holdings of the dominant money reserves. But surely the reader must have noticed that when we were describing the extra features designed to increase the attractiveness of private money, we were simply describing the characteristics of demand deposits. Thus, whatever we have said in the preceding sections about private money also applies to the special type of money that becomes divorced from any physical substance and becomes a mere accounting entry—a demand deposit.

Public Control of the Banking Industry

We have shown in the fiat money section of Chapter 3 that, because of the fact that the real income yielded by money is independent of the stuff money is made of, this income is independent of the value of resources utilized to produce money. This makes production of substitutes for commodity money advantageous. We have also shown that competitive production of resource-cheap substitutes for commodity money is impossible because competitive producers, by equating marginal costs to marginal revenue, would so increase the output of the substitute as to reduce its value close to zero and convert the substitute into commodity money. By doing this, they would destroy the ability of the money substitute to serve as money because, with value so low, huge quantities would be required to facilitate an average-valued transaction. By destroying the usefulness of money substitutes the producers would, of course, simultaneously destroy themselves. A competitive money industry is suicidal. If commercial banking producing demand deposits is a competitive private money industry, it is also suicidal[16] and public control of it is essential if a decision is made to permit its existence and utilize it as a tool of producing money other than fiat money. However, this point is a complex one and will be discussed more fully in the next chapter.

Public control of the private money industry takes numerous forms: restrictions on entry into the industry; prohibition of interest payments to the customers of this industry; requirement that a part of the proceeds of the sale of private money be lent interest-free to the central bank (reserve requirements on demand deposits); requirement that a part of the funds borrowed by the private money producers be lent interest-free to the central bank (reserve requirements on time deposits); and, finally, a myriad of rules that specify (a) to whom the private money producer may sell his product on credit (from whom he may purchase financial assets), and (b) the conditions of the credit extended, especially the duration of it; these rules are usually summarized in the "short-term, *bona fide*, commercial paper" principle.

The sole issue that we are interested in here is whether privately produced money is net wealth and whether our measure of the contribution of this money to net wealth is the correct one. It is obvious that these tools of public control of the private money industry do not affect this issue any more than do the rules restricting the output and sale of, say, weapons, affect the decision that weapons are net wealth. In its end effect, public control of the private money industry restricts the output of this industry and could—in this purely analytical context—as well be replaced by a simple statement of the quantity of output of the private money industry that the producer of the dominant money will permit—a statement such as the one we applied to our otherwise unrestricted private money

---

[16] Lest the impression is gained that this terse summary conflicts with equation [4.4] that yields an *equilibrium* output of private money other than zero, let us point out that even that equation was arrived at on the basis of the stated assumption that the private money producer is prohibited from payment of interest to the purchasers of private money.

producer discussed in connection with equation [4.1]. The sole exception is the reserve requirement that, instead of producing a specific limit on output, makes this limit a function of the amount of the dominant money that the private producers are able to attract. In equation [4.4] we have seen that the size of the output of the private money producer depends on the size of the reserves that he has to hold to make himself able to satisfy the instant repurchase clause. The minimum reserve requirement simply augments the ratio ρ used in that equation. While the absolute amount of wealth the private money producer is able to produce becomes smaller, the economic analysis of private money presented in this chapter remains completely unaffected.

Conclusion

In the first section of this chapter we have shown that private money producers are indistinguishable from the producers of fiat money discussed in Chapter 3; they add in precisely the same way to the net wealth of the community. The imposition of the repurchase clause and the prohibition of interest payments do furnish an automatic economic mechanism restricting the output of these private money producers that is not imposed on the fiat money producer. Yet, as far as the changes in wealth are concerned, the imposition of the repurchase clause does not affect qualitatively the conclusions reached. As in the case of the commodity money producer (but to a smaller extent), this clause makes the net addition to net wealth supplied by the private money producers smaller because it forces an expenditure of resources in the production of money. The commodity money producer has to withdraw from other uses the resources necessary to produce the money commodity; the private producer of money has to withdraw from other uses the dominant money inventories. The key question as to whether private money net of reserves of dominant money is a part of net wealth, it is possible to answer in the affirmative.

In the next section we supplemented the result obtained by

imposing on the private money producer all the additional restraints and modes of operation resulting from these restraints that govern the behavior of private commercial banks producing demand deposits: the minimum reserve requirement, the solvency requirement, and the necessity of selling bank money for financial assets. We have shown that none of these affects the conclusion reached in the preceding section that covered private money producers. But then the conclusion is inescapable that commercial banks, insofar as they are producing a medium of exchange called demand deposits, *are* private money producers. Thus, all the conclusions that we reached are applicable not only to the abstraction, called by us "private money producers," but also to the phenomenon very much in evidence in the world around us, the producers [17] of demand deposits called commercial banks. These banks sell their product, demand deposits, to their customers for financial assets, for titles to streams of incomes that, conceptually, may be permanent but that, in reality, happen to be finite. If they do so, these sales of their product on an installment plan give rise to what is in the literature called "derivative deposits." Of course, all buyers of these demand deposits have a choice of buying them for the present capitalized value of such streams of future incomes; they have a choice of buying them for cash. If they do so, these sales give rise to what is in the literature called "primary deposits." In both cases, the repurchase clause and its logical consequence, the solvency requirement, create the purely superficial impression that we are facing a loan of resources and a debt rather than an exchange of two pieces of wealth accompanied by special contractual arrangements—arrangements, we might add, that are not typical in the case of transactions involving nonmonetary wealth but not unheard of either. A repurchase clause is, occasionally, attached to contracts involving a sale of nonmonetary wealth.

---

[17] We use persistently the terms "to produce money" and "producers of money"; we avoid studiously the terms "to create money" and "creators of money." "The producer" is a *terminus technicus* of value theory; "the creator" has become the weasel word of monetary theory. There it is used both by those who believe that banks produce money and by those who assert that banks are merely intermediaries incapable of producing net wealth.

The Case of Financial Intermediaries

Our task is still not finished. The *New View* that is currently sweeping monetary theory essentially asserts that demand deposits are only debts and not net wealth because commercial banks that produce them are indistinguishable from "other" financial intermediaries that do create debts, such as "bank deposits, savings and loan shares, insurance policies, pension rights."[1] In the light of the preceding analysis, we must now reverse the reasoning. If the above analysis shows that commercial banks by producing demand deposits produce money and net wealth, doesn't it follow that other financial institutions do the same? Are items like time deposits and shares in savings and loan associations also money and also net wealth? Life insurance policies, pension rights? Surely, this is a legitimate question and it must be given an answer. To develop it analytically will require a few more pages; however, nothing will be lost if we squash any suspense the reader might feel by anticipating the results and revealing that the answer yielded by economic analysis is a

---

[1] James Tobin and William C. Brainard, "Financial Intermediaries and the Effectiveness of Monetary Controls," *American Economic Review, LIII* (May, 1963), 385.

negative one. We shall end up by affirming the validity of the *Old View*: that *only* commodity money, fiat money, and demand deposits (and, as we show in Chapter 7, travelers checks) are money and net wealth.

Let us simply continue our discussion of privately produced money. Commercial banks producing time deposits and other financial institutions (e.g., savings and loan associations) introduce two basic modifications into their product. First, the law enables these institutions[2] to pay interest to the purchaser of their product. Second, this private "money" is precluded by law from serving as a medium of exchange and hence as money. As we develop the argument, it will become obvious that these two modifications are ultimately related. Indeed, in perfect competition among financial institutions, the payment of interest, by itself, would deprive the private "money" of the capacity to serve as a medium of exchange and hence to be money and, conversely, any rule that prevents the products of these institutions from serving as money forces these institutions to pay interest to the holders of it. In what follows, we analyze the economic consequences of the permission to pay interest and we show that private "money" yielding interest cannot be wholly money and therefore cannot be wholly net wealth. It may be partly money and partly debt (a bond) and, in full competitive equilibrium, it will be only a bond. Terminologically, we do not want to prejudge the issue and therefore we are reluctant to abandon the term "private money" that has served us well throughout Chapter 4. On the other hand, it seems absurd to use a term that the authors already know to be inapplicable and that their analysis will show to be inapplicable. To strike a middle course, we shall call the private money containing the two additional modifications just specified "private money-debt"; this term is neutral enough to leave us free to close our

[2] Note that we stress the issue of the source of these interest payments. The commodity money, fiat money, and demand deposits will also yield interest payments to the owner if he lends them to someone else, as will any other part of wealth of the community. The key difference here is that it is *the producer* of the private "money" who pays interest.

analysis with a conclusion that the product under discussion is only money, or only a debt (a bond), or a mixture of both.

Effect of Production of Money-debt on Wealth

In the preceding chapter we have seen that the producers of bank notes and demand deposits are producing net wealth. Since the resource cost of production of this bank money is assumed, for simplicity, to be zero, except for the cost of holding inventories of dominant money, and since the cost of inventories was subtracted from the total value of output of the private money producers, the increase in net wealth of these producers is pure profit. As in every competitive industry, there must be an economic mechanism that will lead the competitors to attempt to increase profits and, in doing so, reduce them to zero. In Chapter 4 we discussed in detail the purely economic factors that prevent private money producers from expanding their output beyond the equilibrium level; see our discussion of equation [4.4]. However, in that discussion we merely assumed another restraining factor and did not discuss its economic importance: we assumed that the producer of dominant money prohibits payment of interest to the holders of privately produced money. This makes it impossible for the private money producers to bribe their customers to hold more privately produced money than they would otherwise; it makes it impossible for them to purchase a decrease in the factor (γ) in equation [4.4]. Also, it makes it impossible for them to buy themselves out of the necessity of holding reserves by bribing their customers not to exercise the right given by the instant repurchase clause as frequently as before; they cannot purchase a decrease in the factor (ρ) in the same equation. Let us now drop this restriction and let us analyze the economic consequences of such an action.

If private money producers start paying interest to the holders of their product, the old equilibrium will become disturbed because the product of private money producers, money-debt, now yields two incomes: (1) it yields, as before, the imputed income that every unit of money yields, and (2) it also yields interest payments at whatever rate of interest is established by the private producers. A new equilibrium will not be reached until a unit of private money-debt of a given value yields *a sum* of these incomes that is equal to the income yielded by a unit of dominant money of the same value or, more generally, by any item of wealth of the same value.

This analytical conclusion is of extreme importance for the analysis that follows. Within the realm of value theory, it is admittedly trivial and obvious. However, within the realm of monetary theory it is often neglected and neglect of it leads to untenable analytical conclusions. Specifically, we frequently find considerations of the possibility of some assets bearing the market rate of interest (demand deposits, time deposits, bonds) and also serving as money; cf., e.g., footnote 13, or a section in Chapter 7 entitled "Money as the Limiting Case of Interest Bearing Debt." In these considerations, no attention is being paid to the restraint of value theory upon *the sum* of incomes yielded by a joint product. Even though the principle is elementary, neglect of it is so widespread that we feel it will be profitable to offer a numerical example and to analyze its meaning. Assume an economy containing refrigerators (as an example of nonmonetary wealth), commodity money (as an example of monetary wealth), debt certificates such as bonds or time deposits (as an example of no net wealth), and demand deposits which previously served as money, a medium of exchange, and which—we are told—from now on will pay the market rate of interest. Then given a market rate of interest of 5 per cent per annum,

(*a*) twenty dollars' worth of a refrigerator earns one dollar's worth of imputed income consisting of the value of refrigerating services;

(*b*) twenty dollars' worth of commodity money earns one dollar's worth of imputed income consisting of the value of the service of facilitating exchanges and of eliminating the bother of barter;

(*c*) twenty dollars' worth of debt certificates earns the owner (and costs the borrower) one dollar of "interest" income or, if nonmonetary wealth has been lent, one dollar of "rental" income;

(*d*) twenty dollars' worth of demand deposits

(*aa*) previously earned one dollar's worth of imputed income as in item *b*,

(*bb*) and will now also earn, we are told, one dollar of paid interest income as in item *c*.

Obviously, the statement of the conjunction of incomes *aa* and *bb* yielded by item *d* is inconsistent with equilibrium. *Either* the bankers will raise the price of this item to forty dollars; whether they sell it in a tie-in sale or split it up into pure demand deposit money yielding income *aa* and pure debt certificates earning income *bb* (or, identically, *c*) is of no import for our discussion. *Or* competitive forces (reflecting the assumed zero cost of pure accounting money) block the bankers from charging a higher price; then the initiation of interest payments reduces the price of the money service yielded by demand deposits (income *aa*) to zero.

> In a world of reasonable certainty, every sale would be equivalent to a lease; that is to say, if a source were to rent for one dollar per year and if the rate of interest were 5 per cent, people would be indifferent whether they paid one dollar per year as rent or twenty dollars for an outright purchase.[3]

But what is true about the level of these terms of trade is also true about the change in these terms: people will also be indifferent whether they pay one dollar per year less as rent, or receive one dollar per year more as interest payments, or pay twenty dollars less for an outright purchase. From this follows that when demand deposit money starts to pay the market rate of interest, the price of this money is reduced to zero. This may be seen best by considering a consumer who wishes to borrow twenty dollars' worth of demand

---

[3] Milton Friedman, *Price Theory* (Chicago: Aldine, 1962), p. 245.

deposits. Before the introduction of interest payments, such a loan
would cost him one dollar per annum and this expense would be
justified by the imputed income *aa*. After the introduction of interest
payments, this item will now also yield one dollar per year in interest
payments *bb* so that the net cost of borrowing it has been reduced
to zero; thus the price of it has been reduced to zero. Need one
add that, *as long as* this item continues to serve as money, a source
of purchasing power, the demand for it will be insatiable?

Any item that may be borrowed at zero net interest (or zero rent)
must have a zero price; this follows directly from the above quoted
principle of equivalence of rent and purchase. What are the economic
consequences of the fall in the price of a good to zero? In the case
of nonmoney goods (such as item *a*) we would face a conversion of a
good into a free (nonmoney) good and thus a step towards universal
plenty. A refrigerator the price of which would fall from twenty
dollars to zero (or which would start earning one dollar per annum
in interest payments) will still cool my groceries and thus be a useful
free good. In contrast, to say that money has become a free good is a
contradiction in terms. If commodity money (item *b*) or demand
deposit money (item *d-aa*) start to sell for a zero price (or start
earning one dollar per annum in interest payments) they become
completely incapable of serving as a medium of exchange by virtue
of the price-service relationship existing in the case of money. Since
a free good is incapable of serving as money, a drop in the price of
the demand deposit *d*, a money good, from twenty dollars to zero (or
a start of an income stream of one dollar per annum in interest
payments) converts this good not into a free good but into a non-
good. (If this former good is inscribed with a promise to pay interest,
this document is then called a debt certificate.) A good that may be
had for the wishing and thus sells for a zero price and an instrument
that yields the market rate of interest and thus may be borrowed at
zero cost have in common that their potential for serving as money
is nil.

It is now obvious that once an item such as demand deposits, that
is used as money, starts paying the market rate of interest, it will

earn not one equilibrium income but two of them; the holder will start receiving a return that is twice as high as the equilibrium rate of return in the rest of the economy. There will be excess demand for this item and equilibrating forces will be brought into play that will assure that, ultimately, (1) demand deposits will continue serving as money only if interest payments cease, or (2) interest payments will continue but then demand deposits will cease serving as money, or (3) some intermediate position will be found in which demand deposits will serve as an inferior type of money and will earn some interest return lower than the market return but high enough to compensate for the inferiority and to bring *the sum* of the incomes earned (*d-aa* and *d-bb*) precisely up to the equilibrium rate of return. The equilibrating mechanism that will accomplish this will be discussed in this chapter.

However, our main concern in this part of the book is the definition of the wealth equation. Let us, therefore, set aside for the moment the economic mechanism that determines the new equilibrium values of all the relevant variables and let us simply assume that a new equilibrium is reached. What will be the contribution of the privately produced money-debt to wealth?

In the case of private money in the form of demand deposits, we have seen (equation [4.11]) that the change in the net wealth of the community is equal to the value of demand deposits minus the value of dominant money inventories that must be held by the private money producers, the commercial banks. Or, in other words, it is the capitalized value of income yielded by this form of money minus the capitalized value of the income foregone as a consequence of holding the above inventories. In the case of private money-debt, equation [4.11] must be revised since the income yielded by private money-debt now contains two parts: one is the income yielded from its use as a medium of exchange and the other is simply the interest payments made by the producers of this money-debt to the owners of it. The first, as we have seen in the preceding chapter, is not offset by any negative income received by the producers of private money or anybody else; the second is, however, so offset. Taking explicit

account of this, we must rewrite equation [4.11] to make it applicable
to the case of privately produced money-debt:

$$\Delta w = \frac{(MD)}{P} - \Delta \frac{M_d}{P} - \frac{Y_i}{Pr} \qquad [5.1]$$

where

$$Y_i = r_p(MD) \qquad [5.2]$$

The symbol (MD) denotes private money-debt; Y_i the money interest
payments made by the producer of this money-debt; and r_p the rate
of interest paid by the producers of private money-debt. The equation is identical with equation [4.11] except for the addition of the
last term, the rationale for which is an obvious one. A part of the
value of private money-debt (the first term in equation [5.1]) is due
merely to the commitment of the producers to pay interest to the
owners of it. If these producers could sell their product for a lower
price, we would net out part of the first term in the equation and the
third term in it so that it would read

$$\Delta w = \left[\frac{(MD)}{P} - \frac{Y_i}{Pr} \right] - \Delta \frac{M_d}{P} \qquad [5.1a]$$

However, with the repurchase clause in existence, sales of private
money (not money-debt) for an amount indicated by the first term
of equation [5.1a] would still be subject to a requirement that they
be repurchased on demand for an amount indicated by the second
term of equation [5.1a]: sales below par (or, more generally, below
the rate fixed by the instant repurchase clause) would obviously
bankrupt the private money producers in short order. Consequently,
such sales are impossible and only interest payments (or services
yielding an equivalent imputed income) are a possible tool for
increasing the attractiveness of privately produced money-debt.

Therefore, the change in the net wealth of the community that
results from the production of private money-debt yielding interest
is, in general, equal to the sale of private money minus the value
of inventories of the dominant money held by the money-debt producers minus the value of the bond component of this money-debt.

Or, to say the same things in terms of capitalized income flows: it is the income yielded by the money-debt minus the income foregone as a result of the necessity of holding inventories minus the interest payments made by the producers of the private money-debt, all capitalized at the market rate of interest. However, these results should not surprise us, because that part of the money-debt that bears interest is equivalent to a bond and, hence, simply represents a transfer of existing resources from the purchasers of the private money-debt to the producers of the private money-debt.

Effect of Changes in the Relative Price of Money-Debt on Wealth

Consider an increase in the price of money-debt and, hence, because of the fixed exchange rate, an identical increase in the price of dominant money. Such a change makes the holders of private money-debt better off, since they may have the same real value of private money-debt and more of everything else. This same change does not affect the nonholders of private money-debt because for them, all prices and stocks of assets have remained unchanged. Thus, the community is made, on balance, better off when the relative price of money increases. But what of the private producer of money-debt? If interest is paid on money-debt, the producers of that money-debt will be made worse off by the increase in the price of money-debt because the contractually fixed interest payments will now require a greater stock of the producer's real assets.[4] Therefore, that part of the change in the real value of the money-debt due to the change in the real value of the bond component of it must not be counted as a change in the net wealth of the community as a whole. However, as long as the private money-debt has a nonzero imputed income as money, the increase in the wealth of the public will exceed the decrease in the private money-debt producer's wealth. Therefore, we reach a much more restricted conclusion concerning the effects

---

[4] The producer may avoid the problem by shifting it to somebody in the community. This can be accomplished by his holding financial assets exclusively.

of changes in the relative price of money on wealth: only for that portion of the value of private money-debt that is due to its being a medium of exchange will price changes affect the net wealth of the community.

Competitive Equilibrium of Private Money-Debt Production

We should be able to do better than merely conclude that private money-debt is partly money and partly debt. For empirical relevance, the decision as to the equilibrium relative shares of these two parts is of extreme importance. To obtain an answer to this question it is necessary to inquire (as we have done in Chapter 4 for privately produced money) into the determinants of the equilibrium values of the output of money-debt and of the interest payments on this money-debt. Let us assume, therefore, that there is a producer of dominant money who permits the private money-debt industry to be started. He requires, as in Chapter 4, that this industry attach to its product the instant repurchase clause; however, he does not require, as in Chapter 4, the private money-debt industry to abstain from the payment of interest. (For the sake of full understanding, let us stress explicitly that we are *not* now considering the mechanism by which the private money industry of Chapter 4 converts itself into a private money-debt industry upon the removal of the restriction against interest payments; we are starting from scratch and considering the economic consequences of a competitive money-debt industry unrestricted by the prohibition of interest payments.) Since no private firms would enter the production of money-debt if they were to earn losses, the rate of interest paid must not be so large as to make the capitalized interest payments greater than the proceeds from the sale of private money-debt net of dominant money reserves. In other words, the sale of private money-debt must, at worst, leave the wealth position of each single producer unchanged. Hence,

$$\Delta w = \frac{Y}{Pr} - \frac{Y_i}{Pr} \geqslant 0 \qquad\qquad [5.3]$$

where

$$Y = r[(MD) - \Delta M_d] \qquad [5.4]$$

But, since from [5.2] we know that $Y_i = r_p(MD)$, it follows from [5.3] and [5.4] that the maximum rate of interest on private money-debt consistent with a nonzero production of it is

$$r_p^{\max} = (1 - \rho)r \qquad [5.5]$$

Thus, the maximum rate of interest consistent with some private money-debt being produced and sold is a function of the reserve requirement and the market rate of interest; the minimum rate is, of course, zero.[5] We can further narrow the problem of the determination of the equilibrium rate of interest payments by assuming that the dominant money producer allows freedom of entry into the money-debt industry as long as entrants meet the restrictions imposed upon them. Under these circumstances, the equilibrium rate paid on money-debt will equal the maximum rate, because for any lower rate excess returns will be earned by the firms in the industry and entry will occur. Thus, in the case of freedom of entry, in the competitive case, the equilibrium rate of interest paid on money-debt will be the maximum rate (equation [5.5]).

However, since the extent to which private money-debt, subject to interest payments, represents a debt of its producer is measured by the capitalized value of the interest payments promised, the proportion of total sales that will be offset by debts of the private money-debt producer will be

$$\pi = \frac{\dfrac{Y_i}{r}}{(MD)} \qquad [5.6]$$

[5] If, however, the cost of production of private money-debt is positive, then the maximum rate of interest consistent with a nonzero output of private money-debt will be smaller than that given by equation [5.5]. For example, assume that production costs are a constant proportion of the value of private money-debt output, say, $k(MD)$, then equation [5.5] would read,

$$r_p^{\max} = [1 - (\rho + k)]r. \qquad [5.5a]$$

where (π) represents the proportion of the stock of private "money" that is offset by a debt of the private "money" producers. But, with freedom of entry

$$Y_i = Y = r[(MD) - \Delta M_a] \tag{5.7}$$

so that under these conditions equation [5.6] becomes

$$\pi = (1 - \rho) \tag{5.8}$$

Thus, the proportion of the equilibrium stock of competitively produced private money-debt that is net wealth is given by the reserve requirement. Therefore, permitting freedom of entry into the money industry and assuming that sufficient dominant money exists to allow the competitive equilibrium to occur, we must rewrite equation [5.1] to read

$$\Delta w = \frac{(MD)}{P} - \Delta \frac{M_d}{P} - \frac{Y_i}{Pr} = 0 \tag{5.9}$$

This result should not surprise us since, as we have shown in Chapter 3, competitive production of money leads to all money being commodity money. Thus, the value of each unit of money-debt as a medium of exchange must equal its resource content. But, since we have assumed that dominant money reserves represent the only cost of production to the private money-debt producers, this resource content is, of course, the dominant money reserves. If, however, all dominant money becomes immobilized before the competitive equilibrium is reached, then equation [5.9] will be positive because the rate of interest paid on money-debt will be less than r_p^{max} (see equation [5.5]).

Finally, should the dominant money reserves become unnecessary because the dominant money producer does not require any and because the producer of money-debt is able to arrange his portfolio so that he can instantaneously satisfy any customers of his who wish to exercise the repurchase clause, the interest rate paid on the money-debt will be equal to the market rate of interest (substitute (ρ) equals zero in equation [5.5]). Saying the same thing in a different way, the product sold will be only a bond and will not be money at all (substitute (ρ) equals zero in equation [5.8]) so that

$$\Delta w = \frac{D}{P} - \frac{Y_i}{rP} = 0 \qquad [5.10]$$

No private money is produced and no dominant money is immobilized. If we choose to, we may view the money-debt (joint product) producer of equation [5.9] as a producer of two distinct products. As far as the money part of the product is concerned, he is a producer of 100 per cent reserve money and thus a monetary intermediary; as far as the debt part of the product is concerned, he is a pure debt intermediary. The debt producer of equation [5.10] is then a pure debt intermediary, borrowing money and lending money. However, from the standpoint of the effect either type has on net wealth, they are indistinguishable; neither adds anything to net wealth (apart from the value of the intermediating service itself that is, in the context of our interest, of a third order of importance).

Banks, Intermediaries, and the Price Level

But, if equilibrium in a private money-debt industry that is precluded from paying interest on its output results in a positive addition to net wealth (equation [4.12]) and if equilibrium in a private money-debt industry that is allowed to pay interest on its output results in no change in net wealth (equations [5.9] or [5.10]), then the initial change in net wealth which occurs when the restriction on interest payments is removed from a previously existing private money-debt industry must be negative and equal in absolute value to the net contribution of the restricted private money-debt industry. What will be the effect of this on the price level? Since the answer is surprising, let us approach it slowly:

(*a*) Suppose that the economy employs only fiat money. Elimination of monopolistic restraints results in an *increase* in the total quantity of money and, as shown in Chapter 3, the combined wealth, portfolio, and real balance effects will start reducing the price of money or increasing the general price level. Ultimately, the former falls to zero and the latter rises to infinity; unrestrained production destroys fiat money.

(*b*) Suppose that the economy employs commodity money and fiat money. Elimination of monopolistic restraints results in an increase in fiat money and in direct and indirect reductions in price of fiat money in terms of commodity money: fiat money starts to sell below (commodity money) par, or starts to bear interest, or—as in the Civil War—both. Ultimately, unrestrained production destroys fiat money as in (*a*). However, since commodity money continues to exist, this represents merely a *decrease* in the total quantity of money and thus the above three effects will increase the price of money and decrease the general price level. We get results which are opposite to those reached in (*a*).

(*c*) Suppose that the economy employs dominant money and bank money. Elimination of monopolistic restraints results in an increase in bank money and in direct and indirect reductions in price of bank money in terms of dominant money. Without the repurchase clause bank money starts to sell below (dominant money) par, as during wildcat banking; without the interest clause bank money starts to bear interest, as during the Twenties. Ultimately, absence of price restraints causes competition to destroy *net* bank money (equation [5.9]) or bank money altogether (equation [5.10]). However, since dominant money continues to exist, this represents merely a *decrease* in the total quantity of money leading, as in (*b*), to an increase in the price of money and a decrease in the general price level.

This conclusion may, at first, sound absurd. The reason for this is that any mention of a removal of restrictions imposed upon banking automatically brings to mind removal of the familiar quantitative restraints (discussed at the end of Chapter 4), while the maintenance of the two key qualitative restraints (instant repurchase clause and prohibition of interest payments on demand deposits) is being assumed. Relaxation of the quantitative restraints, while the qualitative ones are being maintained, results naturally in a bigger output of bank *money* and therefore in an increase in the general price level; these increases continue until the competitive equilibrium output of private money, given by equation [4.4], is reached. However, in the paragraph above we are not considering the removal of quantitative restraints upon output of predetermined quality. We are considering the consequences of a removal of one of the two key qualitative restraints, in the wake of which a deterioration of the quality of the private money first into a money-debt and, ultimately, into a pure debt is inevitable.

But, it might be asked, if private money-debt is a medium of exchange why is it not entirely money? The answer to this question is twofold. First, we have assumed that dominant money and bank money are not perfect substitutes in all uses; that is, there are some transactions where it is preferable to use dominant money and some transactions that are better conducted with bank money. Thus, even if one type of money costs more to use than another, its use would generally not fall to zero. Secondly, if interest is paid on bank money and it continues to yield service as a medium of exchange, there will be excess demand for bank money as long as the sum of the value of the two streams of income on bank money exceeds the value of the stream of service of dominant money. Therefore, if we are to reach equilibrium, the total value of the service yielded by a unit of bank money must, at the margin, equal the total value of service yielded by dominant money. Since some given interest rate is being paid, what must occur is that the public substitutes bank money for dominant money in transactions for which dominant money is more efficient. This is reasonable because bank money now pays an additional rate of return so that the cost of using it is smaller. As long as we assume that the iso-transaction-time loci (for given amount of transactions) are convex to the origin, differences in costs of using the two types of money will not result in the disappearance of either. If equilibrium is to be established at any *given* rate of interest paid on private money with both types of money in use, the total value of returns per unit of each type of money must be equal (remember that their exchange value is fixed at one-to-one). As entry into the private fully competitive money-debt industry continues, the rate of interest paid will rise, and the value of this money-debt as a medium of exchange must fall. Since entry will continue until no excess returns are earned in the industry and since costs of production are assumed to be zero, the interest rate paid on private money-debt must equal, at the margin, the market rate of interest if equilibrium on the production side is to be achieved (equations [5.9] or [5.10]). However, if the interest rate paid on private money-debt is equal to the market rate of interest, then the value of this money-debt as a medium of exchange must have fallen to zero if we are to be in equilibrium on the demand side. As a result, private money-debt has become entirely a bond, and the money supply is once again equal to the supply of dominant money alone so that the price of this dominant money will rise; the general price level will fall.

Additional Restraints on Banks and Intermediaries

There are two additional issues that need to be discussed before we can close this purely analytical section and consider the problem of the extent to which our theory of financial intermediaries fits any specific institution we might find in the economy. The first is the problem of whether our analysis would be affected if the private money producers discussed in Chapter 4 and the private debt intermediaries discussed in this chapter were permitted to pay more than the market rate to their lenders. The second issue concerns the economic effect of restrictions that a government may impose on the debts of intermediaries.

INTEREST PAID TO LENDERS. Throughout Chapters 3 and 4 we have specified, when discussing the restriction on interest payments, that it applies to interest payments on privately produced money *in the hands of the public*. In this chapter we have seen that unless each single competitive producer of private money is prohibited from paying interest as defined above, he will find it profitable to do so. The question appears inevitable: if it is profitable for an individual firm effectively to lower the price of the product it sells, and if it is precluded from so doing, isn't the next obvious response going to be that the firm will attempt to accomplish its objective by paying more for the factor of production that is essential for its output of private money: for dominant money? In other words, isn't it essential for the validity of the above analysis and especially for the validity of the analysis of Chapter 4 to also cut off this avenue by which the competitive process of money destruction and conversion into pure debt may operate?

The private money producer, by obtaining (given a reserve ratio of, say, 20 per cent) one dollar of dominant money can produce and sell five dollars of his money. But that means that if the market rate of interest is, say, 5 per cent, he can sell his money for financial assets worth $5.00 that will earn him 25 cents per annum. If he borrows a dollar of dominant money for anything less than five times the market rate, for anything less than 25 cents, he will be ahead. Thus, it would seem that an unrestricted banker would be able to—and that competitive process would force him to—pay a rate of interest to his lenders, time depositors, that is drastically higher than the market rate. However, as has been the case so frequently before, the repurchase clause intervenes. True enough, the above situation depicts a banker who reaches equilibrium by lending at 5 per cent and borrowing at 25 per cent. However, the rest of the community certainly is not in equilibrium because one of the assets available to it now is much more profitable than all others: loans to the banker. The simplest way of gaining the advantage this situation offers is to take the banker's privately produced money, exercise the repurchase clause and obtain dominant money, lend it to the banker and borrow the privately produced money that this dominant money makes possible, exercise the repurchase clause, etc. This makes it obvious why, throughout Chapters 4 and 5, it was completely unnecessary for us to impose any restrictions on the banker as far as the rate of interest he pays to his lenders is concerned. Any banker who would attempt to pay to his lenders a rate higher than the market rate would bankrupt himself through the operation of the repurchase clause.[6] Notice, however, that while the banker is unable to offer a rate of interest higher than the market rate, he is able to incur *internal* expenses of borrowing that other borrowers cannot incur; e.g., he can run a more expensive advertising campaign than can a financial intermediary.

EFFECTS OF A DENIAL OF THE ROLE OF MEDIUM OF EXCHANGE TO MONEY-DEBT. If the producer of dominant money not only permits the producers of money-debt to pay interest on their output but also forbids the use of this product as a medium of exchange, the problem is further simplified. The only income money yields is the income resulting from the services money performs as a medium of exchange. True enough, money serves also as a store of value, but its performance in this role depends on the ability of money to serve as a medium of exchange: the latter is the *conditio sine qua non* for the former. As a result, if the product of the private producers is denied by law the capacity to serve as a medium of exchange, we know that the money-debt cannot be money at all; it must be only a debt, and this debt must pay the market rate of interest. Nobody would be willing to sacrifice his resources for an asset that does not yield any other income or is forbidden to yield any other income but the one yielded by any other debt as long as this asset does not yield the market rate of interest. In that case equation [5.1] must be revised because money-debt that is prevented from serving as a medium of exchange cannot be money at all. Hence,

$$\frac{(MD)}{P} = \frac{D}{P} = \frac{Y_i}{Pr} \qquad [5.11]$$

---

[6] Thus our analysis is in agreement with Milton Friedman's proposal according to which Congress should pass a law repealing "any price fixing on time deposits." (Milton Friedman, "A Program for Monetary Stability," in Marshall D. Ketchum and Leon T. Kendall (ed.), *Conference on Savings and Residential Financing* (Chicago: The United States Savings and Loan League, 1962), p. 26.)

and the change in net wealth appropriate for this case is

$$\Delta w = \frac{Y_i}{Pr} - \frac{Y_i}{Pr} = 0 \qquad [5.12]$$

In other words, the private money producers are simply not permitted to exist and we reach, directly, the results obtained in equation [5.10]; notice, not of equation [5.9] but of [5.10]. We face a pure intermediary, a mere transmission belt of obligations of one part of the community to another part of the community. The same result obtains, of course, even in the absence of any legal rules if the community simply does not find it advantageous to use the item that we have called money-debt as money.

Financial Intermediaries in our Economy

In the above discussion we derived rules governing an abstract type of private producer who sells a joint product: money and bonds. We have seen that the extent to which privately produced money-debt represents a net addition to wealth and not just a redistribution of existing wealth is a function of the difference between the rate of interest paid on private money and the market rate (equation [5.6]). However, this conclusion holds only in the case of a private producer of a pure type—one who does not furnish his customers with any other income except the two we discussed. The financial intermediary that we actually find in the real world is a more complex phenomenon in that it provides services other than those we have considered. Insofar as this is the case, the principles just worked out must be modified to take account of this fact. Let us first consider a typical financial intermediary: a savings and loan association or a mutual savings bank. Next, we shall consider a commercial bank.

A savings and loan association performs at least three additional services for the purchasers of its bonds. First, the product of this intermediary is a bond that is convertible into dominant money at par. As a result, it is a bond devoid of any interest rate risk, this risk being defined as the variability in the market price of an asset due to a change in the market rate of interest. Thus, the association is performing an insurance function, and because of it we would expect the rate of interest it pays to be lower than the market rate even if the bond sold in no way performs the function of a medium of exchange. Second, the association performs the service of freeing the investor of the necessity of investigating the credit worthiness of individual borrowers and spreads the risks resulting from a default on any single loan; for this reason, again, we would expect the rate of interest it pays to be lower than the market rate. Third, the association performs the service of removing indivisibilities from financial assets. It sells its bonds in (practically) perfectly divisible denominations, whereas most other financial assets are sold only in discrete denominations. Again, for this service the association should expect to be paid—the form of payment again being a rate it has to pay to its customers that is lower than the market rate. Therefore, we would expect that even competitive production of private debt by pure financial intermediaries (equation [5.11]) would not result in the interest rate paid on this private money-debt being equal to the market rate of interest. Therefore, the fact that existing rates of interest paid by financial intermediaries are less than the market rate does not imply that these financial intermediaries are producing money-debt that is at least partially money. Only if the difference between the rate of interest paid on the money-debt issued by financial intermediaries and the market rate of interest exceeds the value of the services performed by the financial intermediaries can we conclude that they are producing a money-debt that is partially money.

There is, however, another way of deciding this issue without being obliged to engage in difficult computations of costs and imputed returns. This way leads directly to a decision that whatever the difference between the rate paid and the market rate, it represents only the value of additional services rendered by the association. If we were to observe the product of the association serving as a medium of exchange, as money, we would know that at least part of the difference between the rates is due to the fact that the association is selling a joint product: partly money and partly bond. But, we do not observe the product of these savings and loan associations serving as a medium of exchange (this shall be discussed in detail in Chapter 7). Therefore, any difference between the rate paid and the market rate must be due to the value of the additional services provided; it cannot be due to the product of the association serving as money. This confirms the earlier conclusion that the product of these pure financial intermediaries is a bond and nothing else.

Next, let us look at a *commercial bank*, the books of which show that it has demand deposits and savings deposits. This enterprise is more complex than a savings and loan association because it contains, under one roof, two separate businesses. The money-producing branch (referred to hereafter as the M-Branch) sells demand deposits for financial assets (cash or promissory notes) and is a producer of net wealth as shown in Chapter 4. The intermediating branch (the D-Branch) sells, precisely in the same manner as a savings and loan association, bonds (savings deposits) and lends the proceeds of these sales to others. These bonds may be sold for cash, for private money produced by other banks that will be converted into cash, and for private money produced by the fraternal M-Branch. In the case of the first two items, the bank as a whole will maximize profits if the D-Branch lends these items only to its own M-Branch that will utilize them for additional production of private money (equation [4.11]). If the receipts of the D-Branch are the bank's own money, all that can be done with them is to lend them to others. When the D-Branch buys the money produced by the fraternal M-Branch, the net effect is a reduction in the quantity of the private money produced by this bank (*negative* change in wealth, equation [4.11]); an eventual subsequent loan by the D-Branch to others merely restores the *status quo ante*. The only return realized, if a loan can be made, is the fee for intermediating services. If it were possible, each commercial bank that wants to specialize in money production and wants no part of the intermediating business would find it profitable to maintain a special type of a D-Branch that would sell bonds (savings deposits) solely for cash or for demand deposits produced by other banks. This cannot be done, however, since the repurchase clause attached to all private money makes any such rule ineffective. Therefore, unless a commercial bank wants to forego completely the gains that can be realized from production of demand deposits on the basis of borrowed reserves of dominant money, it has to operate an unrestricted D-Branch alongside its M-Branch, even if that D-Branch does lead to some decrease in the net demand for the product of the fraternal M-Branch.[7]

[7] It might be noted in passing that Horace Secrist discovered in 1930 that "where ratios of time deposits to total deposits are high, ratios of net earnings are low." Almost thirty years later, Joseph Ashheim found that "the higher the ratio of time to total deposits, the less profitable are banks of a given size group." Deane Carson analyzed the issue further and discovered that "there is a tendency of the time-deposit ratio to exert an important influence on earning ratios independently of bank size" and that "bank groups with large time-deposit ratios tend to have (on the average) low earnings." Finally, David and Charlotte Alhadeff estimated that the absolute loss in 1956–1957 resulting from an increase in savings deposits amounted to over 140 million dollars.

In the absence of empirical evidence, assume that the ratio of externally produced money (cash and other banks' demand deposits) to internally produced money (bank's own demand deposits) is the same in the total receipts of each of the D-Branches of all commercial banks. Since the M-Branch has been shown above to be much more profitable than the D-Branch (that yields merely an intermediating fee), the higher the share of the D-Branch in the total business of the bank, the smaller the profits of this bank. Thus the first three empirical results are precisely those we would expect to find. Even when placed in conjunction with the last piece of evidence, they all fail to make us wonder, with Deane Carson and others, whether the fact that banks maintain D-Branches and that these compete for business signifies that the bankers are "unaware of their self-interest" and "illogical." According to our analysis, the banker is a profit maximizer as long as any eventual losses by the D-Branch are more than offset—in equilibrium, just offset—by gains that the D-Branch enables the M-Branch to produce. None of the above empirical evidence has any bearing whatever on that issue. (Horace Secrist, *Banking Ratios* (Stanford, Calif.: Stanford University Press, 1930), p. 154; Joseph Ashheim, "Commercial Banks and Financial Intermediaries: Some Fallacies and Policy Implications," *Journal of Political Economy*, *LXVII* (February, 1959), p. 63; Deane Carson, "Bank Earnings and Competition for Savings Deposits," *Journal of Political*

Let us now return to our key problem: What is the change in net wealth that results from the operation of a commercial bank that maintains both demand deposits and savings deposits, that maintains both the M-Branch and the D-Branch. The net change in wealth is simply the sum of the changes in net wealth produced by each branch separately. For the M-Branch, the change in net wealth is given by equation [4.11]; for the D-Branch, the change in net wealth is given by equation [5.10]. Notice, however, that the absolute size of the change will be different in the case of a commercial bank that operates only an M-Branch (considered in Chapter 4) and of a commercial bank that also operates a D-Branch because the D-Branch, simultaneously, increases the reserves available to the M-Branch and decreases the demand for the product of the M-Branch.

Conclusion

We have shown that any type of "money" that bears interest paid by the producer of these "monies" can be, at best, only partially money and is, certainly, partially merely an asset of one member of the community and a debt of another member of the community: it is also a bond. In particular, we have shown that a typical financial intermediary cannot be construed as being a producer of monetary wealth at all. It produces only a debt, a bond, as long as the rate of interest it pays on deposits differs from the market rate by no more than the value of services provided; this must be the case if the item under scrutiny does not serve as a medium of exchange and hence

Economy, *LXVII* (December, 1959), pp. 583 and 587; David A. Alhadeff and Charlotte P. Alhadeff, "A Note on Bank Earnings and Savings Deposit Rate Policy," *Journal of Finance*, *XIV* (September, 1959), p. 408; Leland J. Pritchard, Edward E. Edwards, and Lester V. Chandler, "Should Commercial Banks Accept Savings Deposits?—I, II, and III," in Marshall D. Ketchum and Leon T. Kendall (ed.), *Readings in Financial Institutions* (Boston: Houghton Mifflin Co., 1965), pp. 37–74).

does not yield to the owner any additional income that could compensate for the differential between the two rates of interest. Thus, we conclude that financial intermediaries that sell their bonds (savings deposits, shares in savings and loan associations, shares in credit unions, etc.) and lend the proceeds do not produce money; they do not produce net monetary wealth.

Theory of Banks and Financial Intermediaries

Even though the issue of whether money is net wealth and which of the items that come into consideration may be classified as money is the key concern of this book, we found it impossible to obtain a solution without opening the Pandora's box containing what is in the literature called "banking theory." At the same time, our method of approach was determined by the requirements given by our main problem. Although banking theory is spread all through Chapters 3, 4, and 5, nowhere does it appear in a systematic form. Thus the light that our analysis throws on banking theory is, at this moment, diffused. Because this theory is an important part of economics, it appears useful to focus on those conclusions that have bearing on it in an orderly and systematic manner. No more than that will be done; hence, the reader who finds banking theory of no interest may wish to skip this Appendix.

1. *Money is net wealth:* We have shown that all money that is not immobilized as reserves is net wealth because it yields positive income to the holder without yielding negative income to anyone else. We have also shown that the real income yielded by a unit

of money is determined by the price of this unit. In Chapter 3 we have shown that commodity money and fiat money qualify as "money" in the above sense; in Chapter 4 we have shown that bank money (bank notes and demand deposits) also qualifies; in Chapter 5 we have shown that money-debts also qualify to the extent to which they are money and not a debt. This conclusion clashes with the current banking theory, according to which bank money (bank notes and demand deposits) is merely an asset of the holder that is offset by a liability of the producer.[8]

2. *No dominant money exists; unrestricted banking:* In an economy in which dominant money does not exist (equivalent to our case of zero reserves of dominant money) an unrestricted banking industry will destroy itself by competitively driving the price of its product down to zero. This case implies a purposeful stride toward a barter economy. However, this conclusion clashes with the current banking theory according to which such a "banking system implies . . . an aimless drift of nominal money, nominal bonds, and the price level."[9]

3. *No dominant money exists; restricted banking:* In an economy in which dominant money does not exist, a banking industry restricted either by the two key qualitative restraints—an obligation to repurchase money for assets for which money was sold, and a prohibition of interest payments to holders of money— or by some restraint upon the quantity of output, will produce a positive output of monetary wealth; this output will have a positive price. This conclusion also clashes with current banking theory:

Evidently, if nominal money and nominal prices are indeterminate with a *laissez-faire* banking system, they are indeterminate when a competitive banking system is supplanted by a monopoly.[10]

---

[8] Since this current view is known well enough not to require documentation, we shall offer it only when the need to do so arises, in Chapter 8.

[9] John G. Gurley and Edward S. Shaw, *Money in a Theory of Finance* (Washington, D.C.: The Brookings Institution, 1960), pp. 253–254.

[10] Gurley and Shaw, *ibid.*, p. 256.

As pointed out in the preceding paragraph (item 2), the first part of the sentence is incorrect because the price of competitively produced private money is determinate; the second part of the sentence is as much a *non sequitur* for the money industry as it is a *non sequitur* for any other industry. If we have a product, *any* product, the marginal cost of production of which is assumed to be zero, then the following propositions of value theory hold:

> *a.* Competition among producers of any good, monetary or nonmonetary, results in a determinate output and a zero price; a reciprocal of this price is, by definition, indeterminate. (Note that in the case of money, the real income yielded by nominal units produced is directly proportional to price so that zero price is identical with zero real value of output.)
>
> *b.* Output restrictions (outside restraint, monopoly, etc.) result in a determinate output and price, both positive; the reciprocal of this price is also determinate.[11]

4. *Dominant money exists; unrestricted banking:* If dominant money exists but the banking system is not restricted by the two qualitative restraints, the banking industry will destroy itself as a money producer by being competitively driven to deteriorate the quality of its product: money will be converted into a money-debt and, ultimately, into pure debt.

5. *Dominant money exists; imperfectly restricted banking:* In an economy in which dominant money exists, a banking system subject to only one of the two key qualitative restraints, to the repurchase clause, will convert itself either (a) into a one hundred per cent reserve banker (producing only as much of private money as the dominant money he immobilizes) and a debt intermediary, or (b) into a pure debt intermediary.

6. *Dominant money exists; restricted banking:* In an economy in

---

[11] This is just another example (we mentioned two others in Chapter 3, footnotes 16 and 17) of the danger for economic analysis inherent in the practice of concentrating on the reciprocal of the price of money rather than on the price itself.

which dominant money exists, private money producers restricted either by the imposition of a fixed quantity of output or a fixed price will be forced to produce private money which is, on the margin, a perfect substitute for dominant money and thus is, just as dominant money, a part of net wealth. However, fixing the permissible quantity of private money would force the monopolist producer of fiat money (or the regulator, if commodity money is the dominant money) into the quicksand of allocating output quotas to individual firms of the private money industry. In contrast, *fixing the price* of private money enables the monopolist (or regulator) to leave every other decision to the competitive forces operating within the industry. In view of the fluctuations in the price of money, a rule fixing the price of private money does not have enforceable meaning unless stated in terms of the dominant money. A price fixed in these terms will be assured by the *joint* effect of

  a. a requirement that private money producers exchange both types of money on demand at a fixed exchange rate (the instant repurchase clause) and

  b. a requirement that the producers abstain from indirect price reductions which arbitrage based on *a* cannot block (the no-interest-payment clause).

Note that either requirement without the other is not sufficient since *a* without *b* permits indirect price reductions and *b* without *a* permits direct price reductions.

Thus, even if the marginal cost of producing private money is less than the market price of money, the imposition of a price fixed in terms of dominant money is sufficient to make the output of private money determinate. Since the private money output is determinate, the price of money is determinate and, hence, the price level is determinate. This conclusion, again, clashes with the current banking theory according to which "nominal money, nominal bonds, and money prices of goods and labor are . . . determinate" if ". . . the Central Bank stipulates not only the nominal reserves of commercial banks but the reserve-balance rate as well."[12] Neither stipulation nor the set of them is necessary or sufficient for the above stated determinacies to exist.

7. *Economic effects of the two qualitative restraints:* As we have seen above, the existence of the two qualitative restraints is essential if there is to be an equilibrium output and an equilibrium price of private money other than zero. Since the two qualitative restraints are so important, we shall look at them in some detail:

The prohibition of interest payments to holders of private money simply prevents the conversion of pure private money into private money-debt or private debt. All we may add is that, in view of the fact that this restraint is essential for the existence of private money, it cannot be viewed as being due merely "to historical accident and political pressures" and as "violating standard criteria of welfare economics."[13]

On the other hand, the effects of the second qualitative restraint, the instant repurchase clause, are so complex and manifold that they merit systematic enumeration:

  a. Most directly and obviously, the instant repurchase clause fixes the exchange rate between privately produced money and some other asset, typically dominant money. In the absence of it, the instant exchange rate would fluctuate (e.g., wildcat banking).

  b. This clause prevents the rate paid to the banking industry's lenders from being higher than the market rate; this applies, especially, to the holders of debt certificates of this industry called time deposits.

---

[12] Gurley and Shaw, *op. cit.*, pp. 261–262. A similar restriction made by Patinkin is discussed in Chapter 9.

[13] M. L. Burstein, *Money* (Cambridge: Shenkman Publishing Co., 1963), p. 185. Cf. also a statement by Milton Friedman that "a law repealing the provision that the banks may not pay interest on demand deposits" would be "a minor reform, but worth while." ("A Program for Monetary Stability," in Marshall D. Ketchum and Leon T. Kendall (ed.), *Conference on Savings and Residential Financing* (Chicago: The United States Savings and Loan League, 1962), p. 26.)

   c. By preventing the commercial banker from creating a D-
      Branch that would specialize in intermediating only for the
      M-Branch, the clause makes the internal cost of borrowing
      dominant money through sales of bonds (savings deposits)
      higher than are the payments to the lenders of dominant
      money; it makes the internal rate on borrowed dominant
      money higher than the market rate.
   d. The clause is extremely likely to result in the need of the
      banking industry to hold reserves of dominant money;
      notice, however, that this is not necessary for a determinate
      equilibrium output of this industry to exist.
   e. The clause forces the current owners of the banking industry
      to forego the consumption of the proceeds realized from the
      sale of private money and to consume merely the income
      these proceeds yield: it imposes a solvency requirement.
      In this manner it converts *any* wealth owned by the banks
      into one that is akin to physical capital that yields a perma-
      nent income stream of consumables, but which is not con-
      sumable itself.
   f. Through the solvency requirement, the clause prevents the
      sale of private money either for a discount (if it is sold for
      cash) or for assets that earn less than the market rate of
      interest (if it is sold for titles to income-earning assets other
      than cash).
   g. Through the solvency requirement, the clause also forces the
      private money producers to purchase not titles to income
      streams fixed in real terms but only titles to income streams
      fixed in money terms; it forces purchases of financial assets
      only.
   h. As a consequence of 7–g, the clause redistributes the price
      risks toward the private money producers and imparts to
      them a bias in favor of falls in the general price level. In a
      restricted but otherwise competitive industry, this is of no
      importance; if the industry is permitted to conspire in
      restraint of trade or to influence the output of fiat money,

this might become important. Notice, however, that this bias is counteracted (fully? partly? not at all?) by the fact that macroeconomic upheavals usually associated with price declines might bankrupt those from whom banks have purchased financial assets and, hence, might lower the level of wealth owned by the banks themselves.

  i. As a result of the solvency requirement, private money producers are forced to purchase financial assets that are not perpetuities. Regardless of whether banks are subject to qualitative or quantitative restraints, economic changes may force a decrease in the output of private money (cf. equation [4.4] in the case of qualitative restraints or cf. reduction of quantitative restraints). To decrease output, banks must sell some of their financial assets—if they sell just maturing financial assets, for a fixed price; if they sell assets that have not yet matured, for any price that a rediscounter will pay. In other words, the necessity to liquidate assets that have not yet matured may result in insolvency. Thus one of the implications of the solvency requirement is that the banks must not purchase perpetuities. The shorter the maturity of the financial assets they purchase, the smaller the risk that a necessity to reduce output will result in temporary but unavoidable insolvency.

8. *Quantitative restraints:* In item 7 above, we specified two restraints essential for the existence of the equilibrium output of private money other than zero. However, the producer of dominant money may not be willing to tolerate this equilibrium output and may wish to restrict it further. This could be done simply by an edict specifying the quantity permissible (and by allocating shares of it to various banks). Typically, however, less direct methods are preferred. Some have the effect of reducing the demand for private money (increasing the factor (γ) in equation [4.4]). Others affect the production function faced by the banking industry.

  a. Demand deposit minimum reserve requirements directly increase the factor (ρ) in equation [4.4].

   b. Disqualification of some demanders from purchases of privately produced money, bank money, for financial assets other than cash diminishes demand and increases the factor (γ). (There are myriad rules that specify who is eligible to purchase private money for noncash financial assets; who is eligible to borrow the product of the banks.)[14]

   c. Upper limit on lending to any one customer has the same effect of decreasing the demand for bank money and increasing the factor (γ).

   d. Licensing rules that prevent either new banks or branching out of existing banks decrease the attractiveness of bank money to those living in territories not adequately serviced; they increase the factor (γ).

   e. The supply of raw materials that the private money producers need (dominant money) is diminished by a rule that imposes an upper limit on the rate of interest paid by the banking industry, as long as this upper limit is below the market rate of interest.

   f. The cost of borrowing facing the industry is increased by a rule requiring the banks to lend a fraction of the borrowed funds interest-free; this is the effect of minimum reserve requirements on saving deposits.[15]

---

[14] For a detailed discussion of the depressing effect of controls on credit sales and of some exceptions to it, cf. Alpha C. Chiang, "Instalment Credit Control: A Theoretical Analysis," *Journal of Political Economy, LXVII* (August, 1959), pp. 363–376.

[15] Note that insofar as banks borrow bank money, their own product, by issuing time deposits as debt certificates they *must* be acting as mere intermediaries because the only possibility of a profit lies in lending this product to others. However, if they borrow dominant money, the bank *qua* intermediary will lend this dominant money to the bank *qua* producer of bank money because that is where the maximum profit lies. The measures (8–*e*) and (8–*f*), while aimed only at the latter part of borrowing, hit both parts and thus not only restrict banks *qua* money producers but also discriminate against banks *qua* intermediaries. Ezra Solomon makes the latter point in an excellent article that completely departs from the current banking theory, "Financial Institutions in the Saving-Investment Process II," Marshall D. Ketchum and Leon T. Kendall (ed.), *Readings in Financial Institutions* (Boston: The United States Savings and Loan League, 1965), p. 33.

g. Production of new types of private money or conversion of some existing assets into money so as to escape the above regulations may be prohibited (rule against transferability of time deposits by check, rule against production of private coins). Travelers' checks appear to be the sole major component of the private money supply that is today escaping regulation.

h. By requiring the banks to sell their product only for cash or for *short-term* financial assets, the controlling organ makes it possible for itself to change its mind in the future and to restrict more than before the industry's output without exposing itself to the (just) charge that by doing so it is impairing the solvency of the banking system.

Note that we are not saying that the sole purpose, or even one of the purposes of these rules is to restrict the industry's output. All that we are saying is that, irrespective of the purpose that the legislator had in mind when he imposed them, they do affect the industry's output as specified above.

The older approach to banking theory used to assert that banking is regulated because it produces money. James Tobin and William C. Brainard recently offered a refinement of this theory that was concisely summarized by Abba P. Lerner as "saying that banks are not regulated because they create money; they create money because they are regulated."[16] Lerner himself offered another hypothesis claiming (if we may in turn summarize his statement) that banks are regulated because they create money and create money because they are regulated. This, in the light of the foregoing, is precisely the case. Yet, there is no paradox; brief reflection will indicate that this is true about any other industry that is assumed to have zero cost of production.

As *monetary theory* turns out to be simply general value theory applied to a good that has the special technical characteristic of yielding real income the level of which is directly proportional to

---

[16] Abba P. Lerner, "Financial Institutions and Monetary Policy: Discussion," *American Economic Review, LIII* (May, 1963), p. 404.

the price per unit, so the *theory of the money industry* turns out to be simply general value theory applied to the industry that produces this good. If unrestricted competition is assumed, we than speak about the *theory of the commodity money industry*. If unrestricted competition is not assumed, in one case the only significant variable that enters this industry's production function is the fractional reserve of dominant money; we then speak about the *theory of the banking industry*, about "banking theory." In another case, no significant variable enters the industry's production function; we then speak about the *theory of fiat money*. Yet, even though the mechanics of the analysis are much more complex in these two cases, especially in the banking one, the principles used and the conclusions reached in the commodity money, fiat money, and bank money cases are precisely the same as those that general value theory yields when applied to any other industry.[17] Most importantly, we conclude that a competitive industry will, and a restrictively regulated industry will not, produce a value of outputs that is equal to the value of inputs.

Where a difference does appear is in the evaluation of this conclusion. Since a nonmoney good yields real income that is independent of the price and quantity of the good, the competitive solution causes maximization of income enjoyed by the society. Since a money good yields real income that is directly proportionate to the price per unit of this good, the competitive solution by equating price per unit to zero cost of production would not maximize income yielded by this good—it would remove it from total wealth completely. Thus, as any other industry, the banking industry is able to produce value of output in excess of value of inputs[18] only if it is

---

[17] It must be admitted, though, that the subtlety of the general value theory mechanism that yields equilibrium in this industry merely on the basis of two simple restraints (no interest payments and repurchase clause) is, for the sheer esthetic pleasure it gives, unsurpassed.

[18] A full statement should read: if the dominant money is commodity money, banks produce wealth in excess of social and private resource cost; if the dominant money is fiat money, banks produce wealth in excess of private cost and at zero social cost.

regulated and it is regulated so as to do so because, in the case of this industry, this leads to the maximization of the society's welfare. The minimum regulation that is necessary to assure that banks will produce money consists of the two qualitative restraints. Given those, the banking industry will reach a competitive equilibrium output of money given by equation [4.4]. As a result, the two qualitative restraints merely assure the possibility of existence to the privately produced money while leaving the size of output of private money, if any, to the market; thus, they do not violate the standard criteria of welfare economics. On the other hand, the innumerable quantitative restraints (some of which were stated in item 7) prevent the banking industry from reaching this competitive equilibrium. Simultaneously, they prevent the public from reaching what the public considers to be the optimum structure of the money supply—the quantitative restraints block optimization of the structure of the public's money wealth portfolio. As a result, the quantitative restraints do conflict with the standard criteria of welfare economics.[19]

---

[19] Notice that this conclusion does *not* deprive the government of its ability to regulate the size of the money supply and the general price level—merely of its ability to affect the structure of the money supply.

CHAPTER 6

An Accounting
Interpretation of Money

A powerful reason for the perennial confusion in the economic analysis of money is to be found in the accounting conventions adopted by the banking industry. These accounting conventions show private and central bank money as liabilities. If economists accept them as given, they are inescapably driven to the conclusion that bank money—and, by logical extension of the argument, fiat money—are merely debts and the producers of them merely intermediaries. Indeed, it seems that the entire money-is-a-debt argument rests on only two pillars: (1) references to the balance sheets prepared by the banking industry and taken over by the profession and (2) "that most irresistible of all weapons of scholarship, infinite repetition." [1] There exists a failure to realize that accounting—however "objective" its output may appear to be—is merely a tool reflecting, in a formal manner, analytical decisions made beforehand and assuring that all subsequent manipulations with the items that are subject to these prior analytical decisions will be

---

[1] We feel that this charming Stiglerian phrase is exceptionally apt in this context. George Stigler, "The Economist and the State," *American Economic Review, LV* (March, 1965), p. 4.

logically consistent. But this being the case, economists may accept the balance sheets prepared by the banking industry only if they are willing to abdicate their own responsibility for making analytical decisions and if they are prepared to accept unquestioningly the analytical decisions made by the bankers. What is worse, they abdicate this responsibility not to some modern banker but to one who lived centuries ago: it was he who worked out the accounting conventions by which the banking industry lives today for the perfectly good reason that the resulting balance sheets—right or wrong analytically—are still a perfectly satisfactory tool for making private business decisions.

In this chapter we do not propose to use accounting to prove or disprove either the currently dominant theory of money to be presented in Chapters 7 and 8 or the one presented in Chapters 3 through 5; accounting as a tool subject is inherently incapable of performing such a feat. What we do propose to do is to present an accounting interpretation of both approaches. In doing so, we have two basic purposes in mind:

1. To persuade the reader that the balance sheet proof that is being offered today by the supporters of the money-is-a-debt hypothesis is invalid because it is based on circular reasoning: first, the debt hypothesis is built into the T-accounts prepared for various economic sectors and then these T-accounts are pointed to and their content is verbalized as proof of the very same hypothesis.
2. To present our analysis of money as net wealth in terms of accounting for fear that, the power of accounting being what it is in modern economics, a failure to do so would reduce the persuasiveness of our argument.

In what follows we shall contrast the traditional, *industry-type balance sheets* as prepared by the banking industry and as reproduced in economics texts with *economic analysis balance sheets*. The make-up of the former does not need any description here, since they are quite familiar even to undergraduates. The latter are based on economic principles that in general and abstract terms may be described as follows:

1. *Assets.* On the assets side of the balance sheet we show the present market value of all sources of income being received by the sector in question. This income is *either* produced by the net wealth of the sector, regardless of whether owned or merely used by the sector, *or* by various rights that this sector has to receive income from other sectors.
2. *Liabilities.* We show as liabilities the present market value of obligations of the sector in question to pay income to other sectors.
3. *Net worth.* The net worth of the sector for which accounts are being prepared is simply the difference between Assets and Liabilities in possession of the sector in question. Stated differently but identically, net worth is the capitalized value of net income received by the sector in question; it measures that part of the net wealth of society that is in ownership of the sector in question.

There are two special issues that must be given consideration in terms of accounting before we proceed. First, we need to explore the consequences of a repurchase clause for our measure of assets and liabilities; second, we need to explore the consequence of an *instant* repurchase clause on these two items. The problem, in its nature, is general and concerns all sorts of economic activity. A repurchase clause is automatically attached to all debts but may also be attached to other items. For instance, every piece of wealth that is lent, rented, or leased is covered by such a clause; at times, even items sold may be so covered, as certain restrictive covenants covering the sale of land and housing attest. An *instant* repurchase clause is less frequent but still not unheard of. For instance, a debt that commits the borrower to repay it on demand is so covered. Goods purchased from a department store or a mail-order store that may be returned to the store "unless you are fully satisfied" represent another example. However, in the case of the banking industry the two problems mentioned above are especially important because the *entire* output of the banking industry is covered by an instant repurchase clause and a great part of the borrowing by this industry is also covered in this manner, if not by law then by actual practice.

Liabilities, Net Worth, and the Repurchase Clause

Let us define a repurchase clause as the right of an owner of an item to present it to somebody else and demand a payment, typically fixed and predetermined, in return. Let us now consider the following three cases:

1. Consider a financial intermediary—or any other intermediary— that borrows resources and gives to the lenders its own debt certificates; that lends resources and receives from the borrowers their debt certificates. The lender to the intermediary who owns the intermediary's debt certificate is covered by the repurchase clause in that he can turn this item in and demand that it be repurchased at a fixed price; he may receive in payment either his own debt certificate that the intermediary happens to hold or he may receive cash. The T-accounts expressing this situation will look as follows:

TABLE 6–1A

Both Industry-type and Economic Accounts

PRIVATE SECTOR		INTERMEDIARY	
Assets	*Liabilities*	*Assets*	*Liabilities*
Debt of Inter- mediary 1,000			Debt to Private Sector 1,000
	Debt to Inter- mediary 1,000	Debt of Private Sector 1,000	
	Net Worth Same as before		*Net Worth* None

2. A producer of business machines, say, of copying machines, produces one additional machine worth $1,000; this machine becomes an addition to his net worth. If he sells it, two pieces of wealth will be exchanged and the matter ends right here. Suppose that the producer chooses—as many producers do—not to sell his product but only to lease it to others. He hands the machine to his customer, receives back a debt certificate signed by the customer, and the transaction is completed. Because of the leasing arrangement, however, the borrower of the machine is covered by the repurchase clause. He can turn this item in and demand that it be repurchased; in payment he may receive either his own debt certificate or—if the manufacturer happened to sell it to a discounter—he may receive cash. The T-accounts expressing this case will read as follows:

TABLE 6–1B

Both Industry-type and Economic Accounts

PRIVATE SECTOR		MANUFACTURER	
Assets	*Liabilities*	*Assets*	*Liabilities*
	Debt to Manu-		
Machine 1,000	facturer 1,000		None
	Net Worth		*Net Worth*
		Debt of Private	
	Same as before	Sector 1,000	1,000

3. Banks come along and produce $1,000 of bank money; for simplicity, assume that they print $1,000 of bank notes. They sell this product for cash or they lend it and obtain debt certificates in return. The holders of bank money are also covered by a repurchase clause. They may turn in the bank notes and demand that they be repurchased; in payment they may receive either their own debt certificates or cash. How do we express *this* case in accounting terms? Shall we follow the precedent furnished by Table 6–1A or the precedent furnished by Table 6–1B?

Let us write out both possibilities and consider them carefully:

TABLE 6–1C
Industry-type Account

PRIVATE SECTOR			BANK	
Assets	*Liabilities*	*Assets*	*Liabilities*	
Debt of			Debt to	
Bank 1,000			Private	
			Sector 1,000	
		Debt of		
	Debt to	Private		
	Bank 1,000	Sector 1,000		
	Net Worth		*Net Worth*	
	Same as before		None	

TABLE 6–1D
Economic Account

PRIVATE SECTOR			BANK	
Assets	*Liabilities*	*Assets*	*Liabilities*	
Bank	Debt to			
Money 1,000	Bank 1,000		None	
	Net Worth		*Net Worth*	
		Debt of		
		Private		
	Same as before	Sector 1,000	1,000	

According to Table 6–1C, the bank is an intermediary and the transaction consists of an exchange of debts; according to Table 6–1D, bank notes are an item of net wealth leased to the private sector. Clearly, both treatments cannot be right, and the question of which treatment is correct must be asked and answered. Current monetary theory has chosen the first approach and states:

> Consolidation [of balance sheets] eliminates all private domestic financial assets [bank money] and their offset in private domestic primary debt.[2]

[2] John G. Gurley and Edward S. Shaw, *Money in a Theory of Finance* (Washington, D.C.: The Brookings Institution, 1960), p. 136. Cf. also an identical statement on pp. 16–17.

Money and Wealth

There is only one difficulty: as the only proof that the above analysis into the nature of money is the correct one, we are offered Table 6–1C. Indeed, it is a startling fact that in the entire literature we have found no other justification for the decision to choose Table 6–1C over Table.6–1D other than verbalizations of the content of Table 6–1C itself; Table 6–1D is not even considered. Thus, an unquestioning acceptance of the century-old decision by some bank accountant to follow the path of Table 6–1C is all that supports the fundamental decision made by economic analysis to deny to bank money—and subsequently by extension, to fiat money—the character of net wealth. As, e.g., Edward S. Shaw asserts, all modern money is a debt:

> . . . an IOU, even though there is nothing that it promises to pay, no interest to yield to the holder, and no maturity date.[3]

That, however, means that the debtlike nature of money is not a matter of economic analysis and proof but an article of faith— faith, we might add, that so much conflicts with economic analysis that the moment economists get away from the consideration of accounting identities of Table 6–1C, they immediately start talking about money in terms clearly indicating that money is net wealth and implying that Table 6–1D is the only sensible accounting way of handling it. E.g., Don Patinkin speaks about money as follows:

> Hence, for an optimum collection, the marginal utility afforded by a dollar's worth of cash balances (the marginal "convenience yield" of these balances) must be equal to this marginal subjective cost.[4]

Consider the above statement that money viewed as debt promises to the holder no outside interest income and no repayment and thus is no burden to the producer, in conjunction with the statement that money yields, *by itself*, imputed income to the holder. If the

---

[3] Edward S. Shaw, "Money Supply and Stable Economic Growth," in Neil H. Jacoby (ed.), *United States Monetary Policy* (New York: Frederick A. Praeger, 1964), p. 75.

[4] From Don Patinkin, *Money, Interest, and Prices*, 2d ed. (New York: Harper & Row, 1956, 1965), p. 91.

good discussed were not money, is there any doubt that these two statements would be completely sufficient to lead us to conclude that this good is net wealth and no debt—net wealth no different from the copying machine of Table 6–1B? But then, all we need to do to reconcile accounting and economic analysis is to abandon the hidden economic hypothesis on which the accounting interpretation of Table 6–1C is based and to accept the accounting interpretation of Table 6–1D. All we have to do is to reassert the supremacy of economic analysis over one of its tools, accounting, and make accounting serve economic analysis rather than be a master of it.

Assets and Reserves; Effects of the *Instant* Repurchase Clause

Suppose that the Copy Corporation (an imaginary manufacturer of copying machines) not only leases its copying machines and thus, automatically, endows them with a repurchase clause but that it also (a) permits its customers to transfer these machines to anyone else as they see fit, and (b) promises to any eventual holder that it will repurchase these machines for cash on the demand of the holder; that it will honor the repurchase clause instantly. Such a promise does have economic consequences that need to be expressed in accounting terms. Let us now analyze these consequences.

If the corporation produced and sold but one machine, as shown in Table 6–1B, the result of the *instant* repurchase clause would be that the company would have to sell, immediately upon leasing the machine, the debt certificates for cash so as to have means to honor the instant repurchase clause. But that means that the machine that the Copy Corporation produced would yield it no income whatever because it would be obliged to exchange an income-bearing asset for an asset that will lie idle in the company coffers: it could just as well sell its machines for wooden nickels. Obviously, this case is not interesting, since, as long as there are production costs associated with the output of the machines, the above described arrangement is not economically feasible. Suppose, however, that the corporation produces 1,000 machines and sells them for one million dollars worth of goods. These goods may consist of any real wealth of the community: nonmoney wealth or money wealth and if—as is likely—they are money wealth it may be any type of money. Let us, however, for brevity and simplicity, assume that the dominant money is *gold*. Let us further suppose that experience teaches this company that the users of copying machines will not turn in more than 20 per cent of them at any time in their exercise of rights contained in the instant repurchase clause. Thus, to prepare itself to satisfy this clause the company will have to hold on hand, at all times, $200,000 of gold; the remainder of the proceeds, $800,000, it can hold, as before, in the form of debt certificates given to it by the customers. How should we treat this case in our T-accounts?

One possibility would be to eliminate the reserve from the T-accounts completely. An example might illustrate the logic of such a treatment. Suppose that the consumers sell back to the company the rights contained in the instant repurchase clause in exchange for a promise that the reserves previously needed will be somehow incorporated into the product sold; if these reserves consist of gold, that this gold will be melted into the metals of which machines are built. Obviously, nothing substantive would change and neither the company nor the consumers would be better or worse off. Yet, the gold reserves would cease to parade in the company's coffers and confuse us into thinking that they are an asset comparable to other assets found in the company's T-account. However, regardless of how well justified by economic analysis, a complete disappearance of reserves held by the company to satisfy the instant repurchase clause might prove disturbing and hamper our communication with the business community and with the accountants. There is an alternative way of treating the reserves held to satisfy the instant repurchase clause that appears more satisfactory in this respect. We may treat these reserves as an asset that is automatically offset by a liability of equal size:

TABLE 6–1E
Economic Accounts
Instant Repurchase Clause Treated As Debt
Part 1. Account Before Production and Lease

PRIVATE SECTOR		MANUFACTURER	
Assets	*Liabilities*	*Assets*	*Liabilities*
Gold 2,000,000	None	None	None
Nonmoney wealth 10,000,000	*Net Worth* 12,000,000		*Net Worth* None

Part 2. Account After Production and Lease

PRIVATE SECTOR		MANUFACTURER	
Assets	*Liabilities*	*Assets*	*Liabilities*
Gold 1,800,000			Value of the burden of instant re-
Nonmoney wealth 10,000,000		Gold reserve 200,000	purchase clause 200,000
Copy machines 1,000,000	Debt to Copy Corp. 800,000		
	Net Worth 12,000,000	Debt of Private Sector 800,000	*Net Worth* 800,000

What is the economic interpretation of this approach? The gold held by the company as an asset is offset by what the accountants call "reserve liability," and this reserve liability expresses the economic value of the instant repurchase clause. It is the capitalized value of the income foregone as a result of the existence of this clause; for discussion of this in terms of economics, compare our discussion of equation [4.10]. The gold held as reserves is an asset because it earns for the holder an imputed income represented by the value of the knowledge that he can honor the repurchase clause; the offsetting reserve liability yields the owner a negative income consisting in the burden of the knowledge that he must honor the instant repurchase clause.

Accounting Interpretation of Bank Money

Having discussed some fundamental accounting problems, let us now turn our attention to the accounting interpretation of the theory of money presented in Chapters 3 through 5 and to the accounting interpretation of the currently dominant theory of money. As a benchmark for our discussion, let us present the T-accounts of an economy that uses only competitively produced commodity money and in which banks do not exist:

TABLE 6–2
Commodity Money Economy: A Benchmark

PRIVATE SECTOR		BANK	
Assets	*Liabilities*	*Assets*	*Liabilities*
Gold 10,000	None	None	None
Nonmoney wealth 10,000			
	Net Worth		*Net Worth*
	20,000		None

Bank Industry Is Introduced

Suppose that a private money producer in the sense outlined in Chapter 4 appears—a banker who is subject to the repurchase clause and to two major consequences of this clause, the solvency requirement and the need to sell his product, bank money, for financial assets. For the purpose of numerical example, let us assume that his business experience indicates that his ability to honor the repurchase clause instantly, as required, will be satisfied if he holds 20 per cent of this output of bank money in the form of dominant money, gold, as reserves. The remainder of his proceeds he is then able to use for purchases of income-earning (financial) assets. For the sake of orderly presentation, we shall—quite artificially—divide the discussion into three parts: (1) the creation of primary deposits, (2) the creation of derivative deposits, and (3) the creation of time deposits. Despite the big numerical size of the banker's operation, chosen so as to enable us to work with easy-to-follow figures, we are of course assuming that he is not going to affect the general price level. Price level changes, although they would not affect the substance of the accounting interpretation of the banker's activity, would necessitate confusing changes in the numbers measuring the value of individual items.

Creation of Primary Deposits

Assume that the banker persuades the public that his bank-produced money is, at least in some uses, superior to the dominant money, gold, and sells $1,000 of bank money for $1,000 of gold. Notice that he does persuade the public to exchange one income-earning asset for another income-earning asset—to sell an asset for another asset. He does not persuade the public to lend him an income-earning asset in exchange for a promise to pay income to the public; he does not persuade the public to lend him gold. After the sale is completed but before any other transaction occurs, the T-accounts of the two sectors will read as follows:

TABLE 6–3
Industry-type Account
Acquisition of Primary Deposits

PRIVATE SECTOR			BANK	
Assets		*Liabilities*	*Assets*	*Liabilities*
Gold	9,000			
Debt of Bank (Bank Money)	1,000	None	Gold 1,000	Primary deposits 1,000
Nonmoney wealth	10,000			
		Net Worth 20,000		*Net Worth* None

Assume further, purely for the sake of orderly discussion, that at this moment the banker ceases to produce money; in terms of the industry-type account, that he stops upon the creation of primary deposits. He simply uses the assets he acquired to satisfy his operating needs ($200 of gold goes into reserves) and to purchase income-earning assets (the remaining $800 of gold is spent to buy debt

certificates of the private sector). The T-accounts after these transactions are completed will read as follows:

TABLE 6–4
Industry-type Account
Purchase of Income-earning Assets

PRIVATE SECTOR				BANK	
Assets		*Liabilities*	*Assets*		*Liabilities*
Gold	9,000		Gold Reserve	200	
Gold	800	Debt to Bank 800	Debt of Private Sector	800	
Debt of Bank (Bank money)	1,000				Primary deposits 1,000
Nonmoney wealth	10,000				
		Net Worth 20,000			*Net Worth* None

If we want to prepare T-accounts that will make sense from the standpoint of economic analysis, we have to replace Tables 6–3 and 6–4
with Tables 6–5 and 6–6. The two new economically meaningful
tables will read as follows:

TABLE 6–5
Economic Account
Production and Sale of Bank Money

PRIVATE SECTOR			BANK		
Assets		*Liabilities*	*Assets*		*Liabilities*
Gold	9,000	None	Gold Reserve	200	Repurchase reserve 200
Bank money	1,000				
Nonmoney wealth	10,000	*Net Worth* 20,000	Free Gold	800	*Net Worth* 800

After the bank uses, as in Table 6–4, the free gold to purchase
income-earning assets, the accounts will read as follows:

TABLE 6–6
Economic Account
Purchase of Income-earning Assets

PRIVATE SECTOR			BANK		
Assets		*Liabilities*	*Assets*		*Liabilities*
Gold	9,000		Gold Reserve	200	Repurchase reserve 200
Gold	800	Debt to Bank 800			
Bank money	1,000				
Nonmoney wealth	10,000	*Net Worth*	Debt of Private Sector	800	*Net Worth* 800
		20,000			

Creation of Derivative Deposits

However, the assumption of Tables 6–4 or 6–6 that the banker employs the free gold to purchase income-earning assets is not sensible. By paying out gold he would be sacrificing the very raw material that he needs to produce his own product, bank money. Instead of misusing his free gold as shown in Tables 6–4 or 6–6, he will utilize it as reserves and produce another $4,000 of his product, bank money, and with it he will purchase income-earning assets:

TABLE 6–7
Industry-type Account
Creation of Derivative Deposits

PRIVATE SECTOR			BANK		
Assets		*Liabilities*	*Assets*		*Liabilities*
Gold	9,000				
Debt (bank money)	1,000		Gold Reserve	1,000	Primary deposits 1,000
			Debt of Private		Derivative
Debt (bank money)	4,000	Debt to Bank 4,000	Sector	4,000	deposits 4,000
Nonmoney wealth	10,000	*Net Worth* 20,000			*Net Worth* None

TABLE 6–8

Economic Account

Production and Sale of Additional Bank Money

Assets		Liabilities		Assets		Liabilities	
Gold	9,000						
Bank money	1,000			Gold Reserve	1,000	Repurchase reserve	1,000
Bank money	4,000	Debt to Bank	4,000				
Nonmoney wealth	10,000	*Net Worth*		Debt of Private Sector	4,000	*Net Worth*	
			20,000				4,000

Creation of Time Deposits

Since the production of bank money is profitable, the banker has every incentive to attempt to acquire as much dominant money, gold in our case, as he is able to. Suppose that the banker borrows some dominant money from the private sector and pays interest on it; as would any other borrower of wealth. Assume (1) that he is able to borrow $1,000 of gold and that this loan is called a time deposit; (2) that he insists on having an appropriate notice if the time depositor wants to withdraw his loan and hence he does not need any reserves against time deposits; and (3) that the government does not discriminate against time deposit borrowers by requiring them to have part of the loan constantly on hand. After the banker has borrowed $1,000 of dominant money and used it up in production and sale of bank money, the T-accounts will read as follows:

TABLE 6–9
Industry-type Account
Creation of Time Deposits and Additional Derivative Deposits

PRIVATE SECTOR		BANK	
Assets	*Liabilities*	*Assets*	*Liabilities*
		Gold Reserve 2,000	
Gold 8,000			
Debt of Bank (demand dep.) 1,000			Primary deposits 1,000
Debt of Bank (demand dep.) 4,000	Debt to Bank 4,000	Debt of Private Sector 4,000	Derivative deposits 4,000
Debt of Bank (time dep.) 1,000			Time deposits 1,000
Debt of Bank (demand dep.) 5,000	Debt to Bank 5,000	Debt of Private Sector 5,000	Derivative deposits 5,000
Nonmoney wealth 10,000			
	Net Worth 20,000		*Net Worth* None

TABLE 6–10
Economic Account
Sale of Bank Money Produced with Borrowed Reserves

PRIVATE SECTOR		BANK	
Assets	*Liabilities*	*Assets*	*Liabilities*
		Gold Reserve 2,000	Repurchase reserve 2,000
(1) Gold 8,000			
(2) Bank money 1,000		Debt of Private Sector 4,000	
(3) Bank money 4,000	Debt to Bank 4,000		Debt to Private Sector
(4) Debt of Bank (time dep.) 1,000			1,000
(5) Bank money 5,000	Debt to Bank 5,000	Debt of Private Sector 5,000	
(6) Nonmoney wealth 10,000	*Net Worth* 20,000		*Net Worth,* 8,000
(7)			

The net worth of the banker is now $4,000 higher than in Table 6–8 for the simple reason that he has gained $5,000 of income-earning assets but lost $1,000 of assets by acquiring $1,000 of liabilities (time deposits). Similarly, the economy as a whole has gained the use of $5,000 of bank money but lost the use of $1,000 of gold in the process. The economic interpretation of the economic accounts of Table 6–10 (and, of course, of all the preceding accounts on which this table is based) is straightforward:

1. The public holds $1,000 of demand deposits for which it paid gold outright (line 2). These demand deposits must be earning the public income as would any other item of wealth it owns: otherwise it would not have bought them and it would not hold them.

   True enough, by the repurchase clause the public reserves to itself the right to return this merchandise and ask for a refund. Should the public ever decide to do so, the net worth of the banking sector would be, of course, wiped out. This does not affect our measure of wealth and net worth. Should the demand for any commodity in the future fall to zero, the net worth of the owners of it will be wiped out; any producer of a good who sells it with a repurchase clause removes this risk from the shoulders of others and assumes it himself.

2. The public now holds $4,000 of demand deposits that some members of the public (not necessarily the current owners) borrowed from the bank industry (line 3). These deposits (as in item 1 above) must be yielding the owners of them income; otherwise, they would not hold them and the original borrowers would not have been willing to pay for their use.

3. The public holds $1,000 of debt certificates in the form of time deposits; they yield the public an income that the borrower, the banker, must pay (line 4).

4. The items in line (5) have the same character as those in line (3).

5. The banking industry by its activity has provided the public with $10,000 of assets, bank money, that earn the public income; to

do so, it had to remove from the public's use $2,000 of gold. Not surprisingly then, the net worth of this sector measures the contribution of this sector to society's wealth, $8,000 (line 7).

Output by One Bank or by the Banking System?

Even though, in the preceding discussion, we used the term "Bank," it makes no difference whether the T-accounts are assumed to apply to one bank or to the banking system as a whole. If a bank gains *permanently* the $1,000 of dominant money as assumed in Tables 6–3 and 6–9, then the T-accounts describe the expansion of production of bank money by this bank; if the gain is to the industry as a whole, then these accounts describe the increase in the output of the industry as a whole in which individual banks will participate in proportion to their share of the gain in dominant money. The operative word in this sentence is the word "permanently." When a single bank is assumed to be the *initial* gainer of the $1,000 of dominant money, this means that one single demander of bank money (Table 6–3) or one single lender to a bank (Table 6–9) happened to select Bank A. However, as the original purchasers of the bank money produced by Bank A on the basis of its gain in dominant money spend it, the subsequent holders may not share this preference for Bank A. Either they prefer dominant money; in that case Bank A —and, of course, the industry as a whole—will lose the gain in dominant money and hence we return to the original situation. Or they also prefer bank money, but do not want Bank A money but Bank B, C, . . ., X money; they use Bank A money to purchase money produced by Banks B, C, . . ., X. Since, for these other banks, it is also true that their holdings of dominant money determine output, these banks will naturally exercise the repurchase clause covering Bank A money and force it to share the gain of dominant money with them. The initial gain of reserves flows out of Bank A and is distributed and redistributed within the industry in accordance with the final equilibrium demand for the product of each single small bank. To use the simplest example possible, assume that in Table 6–6 there is not one bank but, say, five banks and assume that *the ultimate equilibrium demand* for bank money is such that they share in the output of it equally. The only difference will be that we have five bank T-accounts instead of one and each will contain entries one-fifth as high as those in Table 6–6. Instead of one bank using up $200 of gold to produce $1,000 of bank money, we have five banks, each using up $40 of gold to produce $200 of bank money. The T-account of the private sector in Table 6–6 is unaffected by this multiplication of banks, unless we want to identify the output produced by each single bank and have five $200 bank money entries instead of one $1,000 entry. The consolidation of the balance sheet of the private sector with five bank balance sheets yields the same result as, in the original Table 6–6, was yielded by the consolidation of the two balance sheets. This makes it obvious that:

1. An initial gain in dominant money reserves, regardless by which bank it is realized, is redistributed among all banks in accordance with the demand for the final product, bank money, of each bank.
2. Each single bank increases its output of bank money by some multiple of its increase in reserves.
3. The banking industry, precisely as any other industry, can be said to produce the sum of the increases in output produced by the member firms.

We felt it incumbent upon us to discuss this point here because in many banking texts we find statements such as the one made by Paul A. Samuelson:

> The banking system as a whole can do what each small bank cannot do: it *can* expand its loan and investments many times the new reserves of cash created for it. . . .[5]

---

[5] Paul A. Samuelson, *Economics* (New York: McGraw-Hill, 1955), p. 296.

Conclusion of the Bank Money Part

Because of space limitations and also because this book is devoted to analysis and not to a detailed description of the banking system, we concentrate on the barest essentials of the production and sale of bank money. This we have done at some expense, both in terms of realism and in terms of elaboration of details. In actual T-accounts, the various demand deposit items (such as shown in Table 6–10) will be aggregated; this makes the task of tracing the origins of the aggregate difficult. The banker will, of course, use his own or his stockholders' funds. If he uses bank money, this will simply re-allocate the total output of the industry; if he uses dominant money, the result will be the same as the one we described in connection with primary deposits (Tables 6–3 through 6–8). As far as borrowed funds are concerned, we explicitly ignored the fact that time deposits also happen to be covered by the *instant* repurchase clause (in practice if not by law); this forces the banker to set aside part of the dominant money gained as reserves and makes the expansion of his output of bank money smaller than shown in Table 6–10. Also, the government discriminates against debt certificates having the form of time deposits by forcing the banker to relinquish a (small) percentage of the funds he borrowed in favor of the Federal Reserve System. Also, time deposits may be purchased not only with dominant money but with bank money as well; in that case they do not furnish the raw material needed for additional production of bank money as described in Table 6–10. Finally, in computing the net worth of the banker, we have ignored the fact that, like many other producers of goods, he commits himself to furnish in the future certain free goods and services that appear necessary for the purpose of maintaining the demand for his product. For instance, he commits himself to furnish free checks to his customers (even though nowadays banks try to avoid the expense by offering for sale "personalized checks") and to furnish free accounting service. Such commitments of future income represent, of course, a current liability of the banker and should be subtracted from his net worth.

Accounting Interpretation of Fiat Money

Let us now very briefly consider the accounting treatment of fiat money produced by the government. As before, in Table 6–11 we start with the T-accounts of a nonmoney (barter) economy and in Table 6–12 we have the government produce and sell $100 of fiat money.

TABLE 6–11

Economic Account

Nonmoney Economy

PRIVATE SECTOR			GOVERNMENT	
Assets	*Liabilities*		*Assets*	*Liabilities*
Nonmoney wealth 900	None		None	None
	Net Worth			*Net Worth*
	900			None

TABLE 6–12

Economic Account

Sale of Fiat Money

PRIVATE SECTOR			GOVERNMENT	
Assets	*Liabilities*		*Assets*	*Liabilities*
Fiat money 100	None			None
Nonmoney wealth 800				
	Net Worth			*Net Worth*
	900		Nonmoney wealth 100	100

Since we want to relate our accounts to one case specifically discussed in the literature, let us next make the assumption that the government transfers the wealth it purchased back to the private sector:

TABLE 6–13

Economic Account

Transfer of Goods Purchased

PRIVATE SECTOR		GOVERNMENT	
Assets	*Liabilities*	*Assets*	*Liabilities*
Fiat money 100		None	None
Nonmoney			
wealth 900	None		
	Net Worth		*Net Worth*
	1,000		None

In the case of bank money and central bank money, economists were faced by T-accounts, prepared by the producers of these monies, based on the implicit hypothesis that these monies are debts. The governments, in contrast, do not publish their balance sheets and economists therefore had to decide what accounting treatment to give fiat money. Reasoning by analogy, they decided that if bank money is a debt, fiat money must also be a debt. They made fiat money a liability of the government (Table 6–14A); this caused the T-account of the government not to balance, and this shortcoming was repaired by adding to the net worth column of this T-account a negative worth item of equal size:

TABLE 6–14A

Debt Hypothesis Superimposed on Table 6–13

PRIVATE SECTOR		GOVERNMENT	
Assets	*Liabilities*	*Assets*	*Liabilities*
Fiat money 100	None	None	Fiat money 100
Nonmoney			
wealth 900			
	Net Worth		*Net Worth*
	1,000		− 100

An accounting treatment fully identical with the one given to the banking system would have required a different approach. A bank (cf. Table 6–1A) as an intermediary is said to have its liabilities offset by its assets, with a net worth of zero; the assets are the debt certificates held by the bank. Thus perfect equivalence would require that we replace the debt certificates that give the bank the power to call upon the resources of the other sector by a similar asset; say, "The Power to Tax." In that case, the T-accounts would read as shown in Table 6–14B.

TABLE 6–14B

Alternative Version of Table 6–14A

PRIVATE SECTOR			GOVERNMENT	
Assets		*Liabilities*	*Assets*	*Liabilities*
		Power to be	Power to	
Fiat money	100	taxed 100	tax 100	Fiat money 100
Nonmoney				
wealth	900			
		Net Worth		*Net Worth*
		900		None

Since the government's power to tax covers all the items shown on the asset side of the private sector's T-account, we can make the net worth (the net wealth) of the community any number we choose (between zero and the total value of these assets) merely by defining some of these assets as the liability of the government.

As in the case of bank money, the economic accounts of Table 6–13 can be given a straightforward economic interpretation. In Table 6–12 the public demonstrated that it considered fiat money as an income-earning asset; it demonstrated this by its readiness to sacrifice other income-earning assets to purchase fiat money that— as the current economic literature does not hide—earns for the owner no outside income and has no maturity date. Unless the income that fiat money earns in its own right is at least as high as that yielded by the goods the public sacrifices in the act of purchase, fiat money would never be sold: but this means that the public considers fiat money as income-earning asset and hence net wealth. The producer and seller of this net wealth, the government, is free to dispose of the proceeds as it sees fit; in this it is different from the banking system that, bound by the repurchase clause, is able to enjoy the income yielded by the proceeds but not to dispose of the proceeds themselves. In Table 6–13 we show the government utilizing this ability to dispose of the proceeds by transferring them back to the private sector.

In contrast, the economic meaning of Table 6–14A is impossible to fathom. The banks in the preceding section were at least claimed to be intermediaries: their alleged debt has been offset by an asset of an equal size, and their net worth has been said to be zero. In the case of government as depicted in Table 6–14A, we face a typical deadbeat: he has liabilities but no assets. That, however, is of no concern to him at all because the alleged debt he faces costs him nothing to hold and has no maturity date. An imaginary debtor is facing the burden of an imaginary debt. The public is also unconcerned with the poor credit rating of this debtor, manifested by his negative net worth, since it was well satisfied to shift from a barter economy of Table 6–11 to the monetary economy of Tables 6–12 and 6–13. It must be a matter of indifference to the public that we decide to enter the two offsetting entries in Table 6–14A. Thus, except for affecting the size of wealth as measured by economists, these two entries leave *every* economic unit unaffected and unconcerned. The economic meaning of all this is so inscrutable that the reader might wonder if Table 6–14A is not the familiar strawman set up only to be knocked down; let us conclude this section by pointing out that the results obtained in Table 6–14A are identical with those reached in a book that surely expresses the current theory of fiat money;[6] the same type of table can be found in almost any other book dealing with monetary theory.[7]

[6] Gurley and Shaw, *op. cit.*, p. 16. (In our approach, accounts for the "Business Sector" and "Consumer Sector" are consolidated into "Private Sector.") See also tables on pp. 135, 137, and 146.

[7] Cf. e.g., Don Patinkin, *op. cit.*, 1st ed., p. 203 and 2d ed., pp. 296 and 304; or Kenneth E. Boulding, *Economic Analysis, Macroeconomics*, 4th Edition, (New York: Harper & Row, 1966), p. 115; or Board of Governors of the Federal Reserve System, *Flow of Funds Accounts, 1945–62* (Washington, D.C.: Board of Governors of the Federal Reserve System, 1963), p. 7.

Conclusion

We want to conclude by stressing the fact that we certainly do not believe that the industry-type balance sheets or the economic balance sheets presented here either prove or disprove any hypothesis. Specifically, they cannot determine whether the money-is-a-debt hypothesis or the money-is-net-wealth hypothesis is the correct one. Regardless of how objective the T-accounts prepared by the use of accounting methods may appear, we trust that we have shown that they do not and cannot prove anything that was not decided beforehand. If we feel that the money-is-a-debt hypothesis is the correct one, we prepare—knowingly or unknowingly—the T-accounts for various sectors by following the method of the industry-type accounts. This guarantees that a subsequent consolidation of the sectoral T-accounts into the balance sheet of the economy as a whole will dispose of money without a trace; we might then mislead ourselves into the conclusion that consolidation of balance sheets "proves" that money is a veil and has no net existence. If we feel that there are analytical grounds for asserting that money is net wealth, we follow the same rules of accounting and obtain what we call the economic balance sheets; although no subsequent consolidation can then dispose of money as an item of net wealth, we surely do not mislead ourselves and do not want to mislead the reader into believing that this "proves" that money is net wealth.

However, accounting does have the advantage of enabling the user to marshal the items that he considers relevant for a decision in a manner that makes it easy to trace these items and to relate them to other, associated items. In our brief discussions of the economic meaning of the two alternative methods of accounting, based on two alternative hypotheses as to the nature of money, we attempted to make use of this advantage to demonstrate the shortcomings of the money-is-a-debt hypothesis and the superiority of the money-is-net-worth and therefore money-is-net-wealth hypothesis.

CHAPTER 7

Liquid Assets:
Money and Debts

Money Supply in Current Thinking

Much of the current literature attempts to persuade the reader that either money is impossible to separate properly from debt or that if it were separable, it would not be the relevant set of assets from an analytical standpoint. R. S. Sayers, in his review of modern British monetary theory and policy, expresses this view as follows:

> I suspect that, because money in the abstract sense is an unambiguous concept, people have subconsciously believed that there must also be a simple answer to the question of what is money in the concrete sense. They have been looking for a sharp line of distinction where only Marshallian shading has reality. This pursuit of a will o' the wisp . . .[1]

[1] R. S. Sayers, "Monetary Thought and Monetary Policy in England," *Economic Journal, LXXX* (December, 1960), p. 711. Similarly, on this side of the Atlantic, Kenneth E. Boulding wrote recently as follows: "For purposes of exposition it is often convenient to draw a sharp line at some point in the scale of liquidity and say, 'everything more liquid than this is money, and everything less liquid than this is not money.' It is important to realize, however, that wherever this line is drawn will be a more or less arbitrary point. Consequently, arguments as to whether a certain thing is or is not money are usually a waste of breath."—*Economic Analysis, Macroeconomics*, 4th ed. (New York: Harper & Row, 1966), pp. 71–72.

As evidence that this view is quite prevalent in the profession, we point to works dealing with monetary policy, such as the *Radcliffe Report* and the *Report of the Commission on Money and Credit*. In both these significant works, the view expressed above by R. S. Sayers has found a receptive audience.

The difficulty of separating money from debts has led to two opposite trends. On the one extreme, lack of a workable distinction that would enable us to separate the huge and complex mass of financial assets into money and debts has caused monetary theorists to admit progressively fewer and fewer assets to the money club.[2] However, with the facts of life indicating that financial assets have important consequences for equilibrium of the economy as a whole, economists have felt compelled to search for a substitute concept that could be assigned this burden. The substitute for the "money-nonmoney" dichotomy is, with increasing frequency, becoming the "liquid-nonliquid" dichotomy. Thus, much of modern monetary theory concerns itself with a broad class of assets called liquid assets rather than with the progressively narrowing class of assets called money. For instance, R. S. Sayers outlines the modern position as follows:

> [It is] this wide concept of liquid assets that we must put in the place conventionally occupied by "the supply of money," as the monetary quantity influencing total effective demand for goods and services. And we must interpret it widely enough to include credit that can be brought into existence concurrently with a decision to exercise demand.[3]

In this statement we find that the concept of the supply of money has deteriorated to such an extent that it is prefaced by the slightly derisive term "conventional"; it is put in quotation marks presumably to indicate its emptiness. But, what are these "liquid assets" that are to replace money, and indeed have done so in such studies as the

---

[2] These issues shall be discussed in detail in Chapter 8, Money in Current Analysis: A Comparison.

[3] R. S. Sayers, *op. cit.*, p. 712.

Radcliffe Report and the Brookings *Econometric Model?*[4] Since "liquidity" is a continuum, there does not seem to be any limit to the coverage: all assets are "liquid," provided we allow an appropriate time for liquidation. But that is not all. The same writer also suggests that liquid assets should include only the positive side of the picture, that credit should not be "netted out." If a bond is introduced into the economy, we should consider it a liquid asset, but we should not consider the fact that it is a debt of its issuer.[5] But then, we allow "liquid assets" to be any arbitrary multiple of the net wealth of the community.

Concepts such as "liquid assets," initially devised simply as a tool enabling the empirical researcher to surmount the analytical difficulty of separating money from debts, have the unfortunate tendency of implanting themselves in the purely theoretical structure of economics and from there causing confusion on all levels of analysis. In particular, on the policy-making level, the consequences of all this appear to us to be quite serious. If monetary wealth cannot be defined—or does not exist—neither can the producers of money be defined:

> The supply of credit . . . is no monopoly of the banks; the power of the banks to create credit (and it is credit, not money, that is relevant here) thus provides no justification for control of the banks while other credit agencies are left uncontrolled.[6]

Control of banks becomes "discriminatory." The logical policy conclusion is that we either cease this discrimination altogether or we extend controls to practically everybody. On the other side of the Atlantic, Gurley and Shaw actually did draw this latter conclusion when, as one solution, they consider the extension of "financial

---

[4] Committee on the Working of Monetary System, *Report* (London: Her Majesty's Stationery Office, 1959), pp. 170–171; J. S. Duesenberry *et al.*, *The Brookings Quarterly Econometric Model of the United States* (Chicago: Rand McNally, 1965), p. 210.

[5] R. S. Sayers, *op. cit.*, p. 713.

[6] R. S. Sayers, *ibid.*, p. 714.

controls to the nominal debt issues of nonmonetary intermediaries and *spending units* [emphasis ours]."[7]

As we have just shown, the economics profession finds it so difficult to separate money from debts that many are inclined to give up the search altogether and lump them both in an agglomeration that frequently receives the name of liquid assets. The reason for this is that there are numerous and confusing similarities between money and debt certificates:

First, both money and debt certificates are shown by empirical research to affect the general price level, thus giving rise to an argument that there is no reason to consider them separately.

Second, both money and debt certificates are parts of the wealth portfolio of the owner of them; both are his store of value. This gives rise to the argument that we should not be concerned only with money, but with every store of value that affects the behavior of its owner.

Third, both money and debt certificates give their owner the right to demand from someone else a specified quantity of money; both contain a repurchase clause. But then, an argument has been made that they cannot be distinguished even if it were found desirable to do so: they are both—strictly analytically—debts of the non-owners and thus not net wealth of society as a whole.

Fourth and last, in the limit there is no difference between money and debt certificates; this fact leads to the argument that money as "noninterest-bearing debt" is but the limiting case of the broad category of interest-bearing debts.

Even though we believe that Chapters 3 through 5 provide, sometimes explicitly and sometimes implicitly, an answer to all these arguments, the fact remains that all four are so prevalent in the modern literature, have such intricate underpinnings, and are given so much weight that it seems imperative to give each of them systematic and direct consideration. In this way we intend to assure the reader that none of them affects the analysis presented here; in particular,

[7] John G. Gurley and Edward S. Shaw, *Money in a Theory of Finance* (Washington, D.C.: The Brookings Institution, 1960), p. 299.

that none of them affects our conclusion that commodity money, fiat money, demand deposits, and that modern innovation, travelers' checks, are all money and net wealth of the community. Discussion of these arguments is not easy because they are analytically so disconnected as to defy simultaneous treatment; they must be disposed of one by one.

Money and Debt Both Affect Prices

Observations suggest that both money and credit (debt) affect the price of money. Or, if we prefer to express the same thing in a more roundabout way, that both affect the aggregate demand for goods and services and through it the general price level—the reciprocal of the price of money. If this is the case—and since macroeconomic analysis is not our concern here, let us merely stipulate that this is the case—doesn't this fact provide a persuasive argument in support of the claim that money and credit (debt) are one and the same thing? As R. S. Sayers explained (above), not only money but also trade credit (looking at it from the other side, consumer debt) generate total demand. He goes on to discuss money and the velocity of money and concludes that these concepts have no meaning:

> The artificiality of the concept lies, in short, in its reliance on a distinct and identifiable category of money; and one danger of using it lies in its encouraging us to overlook the relevance, to the pressure of total demand, of sources of credit outside this defined category.[8]

Since money, called credit money, and "other" credit both affect aggregate demand, we are told not to attempt to make any distinction between them. Because "banks as creators of credit and other firms as users or intermediaries" both affect the total demand, we are told that any distinction between them is "if not completely false at

[8] R. S. Sayers, *op. cit.*, pp. 713 and 715.

least misleading."[9] Of course, if we conclude in advance that money is a debt, it is then easy to make a case in favor of not making a distinction between money and credit. Let us, however, without prejudging the issue, inquire as to whether the criterion used is a meaningful one: whether the fact that two things, money and credit, affect prices is enough to justify an assertion that for this reason we should not make a distinction between them.[10]

Suppose that instead of considering the producers of money and of money-credit, we consider the producers of cars and of car-credit:

1. If the producers of cars increase their output, they are increasing *the supply* of cars and this, we would expect, would affect the price of cars.

2. Given the demand for car transportation, this demand can be satisfied by a wide range of stocks of cars. The more efficient are the methods of utilizing any given stock, the smaller is going to be the demand for the stock. Car rental agencies are one of the tools employed by the community to make the use of any given stock of cars as efficient as possible. Therefore, if the car rental agencies increase their output, they are affecting *the demand* for the stock of cars and this, we would expect, would also affect the price of cars.

It is interesting to note that Don Patinkin, when he considers the case of the alleged commercial bank "intermediaries" and of other kinds of financial intermediaries, reaches precisely the same consion. Although in Part II (but not Part I) of his book he is standing four-square on the current orthodoxy that both banks and "other" financial intermediaries create only debts, he somewhat incongruously but—as we have just seen—correctly concludes that

---

[9] R. S. Sayers, *op. cit.*, p. 713.

[10] Ezra Solomon, in an excellent article that lies outside the scope of the current orthodoxy, wittily pointed out that a question as to why distinguish money from financial assets leads directly to a question as to "why distinguish money from mud pies?"—"Financial Institutions in the Saving-Investment Process-II," Marshall D. Ketchum and Leon T. Kendall (ed.), *Readings in Financial Institutions* (Boston: Houghton Mifflin Co., 1965), p. 28.

. . . the banking system affects the economy by changing the supply of money; whereas nonbanking intermediaries do so by changing . . . the demand for money, and hence the velocity of circulation.[11]

We have seen in the above example that both the producers of cars and the producers of car credit affect the price of cars. Using the reasoning with which we started the discussion in this section, we are forced to conclude that the concepts of the demand for cars and of the supply of cars are "artificial" and that there is no difference between Ford Motor Company and Hertz. It seems to us extremely dubious that *this* conclusion would be accepted kindly by the profession. We see no reason why this reasoning should be any more persuasive when applied to the producers of money and producers of money-credit—to banks and financial intermediaries. It surely is not persuasive enough to justify a decision to abandon the concept of the money supply and to adopt, instead, the mixture of money and evidences of loans of money represented by the concept of "liquid assets."[12]

[11] From Don Patinkin, *Money, Interest, and Prices*, 2nd ed. (New York: Harper & Row, 1956, 1965), p. 302.

[12] Lest we be misunderstood, let us point out that there *are* contexts in which a composite variable containing, simultaneously, money and debt certificates may be useful enough to mislead us into a conclusion that it does have an analytically meaningful content. Since empirical relevance is at issue here, two empirical examples may best help us to make our point: 1. For the purpose of calculating an aggregate supply function for a given sector, physical possession of wealth and thus ability to use wealth (monetary and nonmonetary) may be most relevant, not the ownership of this wealth. 2. On the other hand, for the purpose of calculating an aggregate demand function for a given sector, ownership of wealth (monetary or nonmonetary) appears most relevant, not physical possession. (a) The hard way of obtaining this variable is to reassign to this sector the wealth it owns but has lent to other sectors and to eliminate from the wealth of this sector items that are merely in the physical possession of this sector. (b) Alternatively but identically, wealth owned and possessed by the sector, nonmonetary plus monetary, plus evidences of debt (debt certificates) of other sectors to this sector may become the independent variable. However, if we select the short cut represented by method (b), we should not mislead ourselves into concluding that good empirical results prove that the concept of liquid assets, the sum of monetary wealth and debt certificates, is a meaningful one either empirically or theoretically.

Money and Debt Both Are Stores of Value

The second reason for the difficulty of making a distinction between money and debts is that they both serve as stores of value. Milton Friedman and Anna Jacobson Schwartz expressed this point most succinctly when they wrote:

> The use of the narrower total is often defended on the grounds that only the items it contains are a medium of exchange ... The implicit criterion for choosing the total to which to apply the term "money" is by no means clearly appropriate. Money is a term that has been used to refer not solely to a medium of exchange but also and, in our view more basically, to a temporary abode of purchasing power enabling the act of purchase to be separated from the act of sale.[13]

Our main answer to this argument is that the analysis of money developed in the preceding chapters applies to money as a medium of exchange that also happens to act as a store of value; it does not apply to all stores of value. In particular, only a medium of exchange has the technical property of yielding real income that is completely independent of the resource content of this good and that changes not only with the physical quantity but also with the price of this good. As a result, the wealth of society may be changed through no expenditure of resources; also, the wealth of society may be changed merely through a change in the price of this good. It is these two consequences of the special technical property of money that force separation of money from other wealth. Neither of these two key arguments can be shown to hold—indeed, do not hold—for other stores of value, regardless of whether they are net wealth (e.g., physical capital) or whether they are merely debts. But then, it is not an arbitrary decision whether we stress, to discover what is money, the role resources play as a medium of exchange or as a store of value. Economic analysis forces a decision, and forces that it be made in

[13] Milton Friedman and Anna Jacobson Schwartz, *A Monetary History of the United States 1867–1960* (Princeton, N.J.: Princeton University Press, 1963), pp. 649–650.

favor of the medium of exchange role. An associated difficulty with the argument just quoted is that once we abandon the medium of exchange role and concentrate on the store of value role, we render ourselves completely impotent to make an analytically defensible distinction between money and other things; indeed, the definition of money becomes a completely arbitrary one, since innumerable other things beside money serve as stores of value. (1) Nonmonetary wealth (e.g., physical capital) acts as a store of value; it is able to do so only because it yields, in its basic use, income; (2) debt acts as a store of value because it, simultaneously, acts as a negative store of value for someone else; (3) monetary wealth acts as a store of value because it yields, in its basic use as a medium of exchange, income. Take away the ability of capital to yield whatever physical income it yields, render a debtor impotent to discharge his obligations, deprive money of its ability to yield income as a medium of exchange, and capital, bonds, and money—all become worthless as stores of value. The capacity of anything to serve as a store of value is, obviously, a derived one. *All media of exchange* (*monies*) *are stores of value but not all stores of value are media of exchange* (*monies*). This point has been stressed in the last century by Carl Menger;[14] early in this century, Ludwig von Mises[15] restated it with great vigor.

[14] "But the notion that attributes to *money* as such the function of also trans- ferring 'values' from the present into the future must be designated as erron- eous. . . . it is . . . clear that other commodities are still better suited for it. . . . It appears to me to be just as certain that the functions of being 'a measure of value' and a 'store of value' must not be attributed *to money as such*, since these functions are of a merely accidental nature and are not an essen- tial part of the concept of money."—Carl Menger, *Principles of Economics* (Glencoe: The Free Press, 1950), pp. 279–280.

[15] "After Menger's review of the question, further discussion of the connection between the secondary functions of money and its basic function should be unnecessary. Nevertheless, certain tendencies in recent [i.e., circa 1911] literature on money make it appear advisable to examine briefly these secondary functions and to show once more that all of them can be deduced from the function of money as common medium of exchange."—Ludwig von Mises, *The Theory of Money and Credit* (New Haven, Conn.: Yale University Press, 1953), p. 34.

This, we hope, makes it clear that although money does serve as a store of value, the *conditio sine qua non* for the performance of this task is that money performs its main task of being a medium of exchange. This also, we hope, makes it clear that any attempt to distinguish between money and other things (nonmonetary non-human wealth or debt certificates) on the basis of the criterion of store of value *must fail* since all three perform this function. The only reason why the vacuity of the store of value criterion has escaped notice is that it has been applied only in an effort to distinguish between debt certificates and money. Since *here* the issue is in doubt, the failure of the criterion to yield distinction could be and, as we have seen above, was interpreted as proof that, analytically, there is none and that consequently any distinction supported by good empirical performance may be tolerated. It must be stressed, however, that had the same criterion about whether something is or is not a store of value been applied in an attempt to distinguish between physical capital and debt certificates, it also would have failed. However, a conclusion that this failure proves that physical capital is a debt (or, alternatively, that debt is physical capital) surely would not have been accepted. Rather, the inevitable conclusion would have been reached that an attempt to distinguish between money and other things on the basis of the store of value character-istic of money is hopeless because this characteristic is common to nonmonetary wealth, monetary wealth, and to debt certificates which are not net wealth.

Money and Debt Both Contain a Repurchase Clause

The next similarity between money and debt certificates is to be found in the fact that both contain a clause that gives the owner of either the right to demand and obtain from someone else a specified quantity of wealth, typically a specified quantity of money; both contain a repurchase clause. The fact, however, that both these two assets contain a repurchase clause does not indicate that both are either money or debt certificates. Let us return to our example of automobiles and impose on them a repurchase clause in several alternative ways:

1. An owner of a car lends it to a borrower and receives a debt certificate that entitles him to receive a car on demand.
2. A government passes a law establishing a "dominant automobile." All producers of cars are now obliged to include in every sales contract a clause that entitles their customers to turn in the car they purchased and to receive on demand a "dominant automobile" of equal value. The government may or may not require the producer of the "dominant automobile" to exchange one of his cars for another of his cars of equal value.

In the first case, the right to obtain an automobile on demand is clearly a consequence of a loan; the debt certificate is an asset of the owner and a debt of the borrower. No new wealth is being created when a car is lent, and the debt certificate is not a part of net wealth. In the second case, the right of the purchaser of a car to obtain a different ("dominant") car has a completely different economic meaning. The existence of this right surely cannot affect our knowledge that whenever the automobile manufacturers produce and sell one of their cars, they are adding to net wealth. All that an *instant* repurchase clause does in this case is to increase the cost of automobile production by requiring the producers to hold an inventory of the dominant automobiles. Similarly the producers of the dominant car will face increased costs because they will have to hold larger inventories of their own product than they would otherwise hold. The capitalized value of the increased cost due to the necessity of holding dominant car inventories measures the economic cost of the instant repurchase clause attached to automobiles. If the demand for the instant repurchase clause is small, car owners will exercise it seldom, the producers will be able to hold small inventories of dominant cars, and the instant repurchase clause component of the value of the joint product (cars *plus* instant repurchase clause or, in other words, cars *plus* debt) will be small; and, of course, vice versa.

If we, however, erroneously conclude that a repurchase clause signifies, in all cases, that a debt exists *equal to the value* of the item covered by the clause, we are then forced to conclude that the cars produced and sold by car producers are not a part of the net wealth of the community. To paraphrase a statement that has been made about fiat money, "cars as the asset of the private sector are netted out as debts of the automobile industry, so they disappear. Consolidation of the balance sheets rips away the car veil." Or, to paraphrase another statement about bank money, "car producers cannot produce cars to finance their own purchases of goods and services. 'Cars' are a liability, which must be matched on the other side of the balance sheet." Finally, if we care to, we might apply the same reasoning to the dominant automobiles. Since they also are cars, they must be—to paraphrase again a statement about commodity money—"the same thing though based on custom rather than law"; they are also an asset of the owner and a liability of the dominant car producer or of society as a whole and, therefore, they are also not net wealth. Is it conceivable that these statements would persuade anyone that a car is not net wealth?

Yet, the existence of this clause is currently used as an argument either supporting or, perhaps, proving the proposition that money is not net wealth. To shift from paraphrasing to quoting, Gurley and Shaw describe fiat money as follows:

> Money as the financial asset of private sectors is netted out against money as the debt of government, so it disappears. Consolidation [of balance sheets] rips away the money veil.[16]

Similarly, James Tobin writes about bank money as follows:

> Unlike governments, bankers cannot create means of payment to finance their own purchases of goods and services. Bank-created "money" is a liability, which must be matched on the other side of the balance sheet.[17]

[16] Gurley and Shaw, *op. cit.*, pp. 16–17.
[17] James Tobin, "Commercial Banks as Creators of 'Money'," in Deane Carson (ed.), *Banking and Monetary Studies* (Homewood, Ill.: Irwin, 1963), p. 415.

Finally, Harry G. Johnson points out in his review of modern monetary theory that if this logic is able to dispose of commodity money substitutes by showing them to be mere debts, why should it not apply also "to commodity moneys, which are the same thing though based on custom rather than law"?[18]

Actually, the reasoning goes the other way. Since this logic fails to apply to a commodity such as cars, why shouldn't it also fail to apply to a commodity such as money, and to substitutes for it—fiat money and bank money? The first reason for the failure is that legal facts such as the repurchase clause may or may not have economic content; even if they do, the economic meaning of the same clause is different in different cases. The second reason for the failure of the reasoning of the *New View* that money is a debt is to be found in a misapplication of accounting. It is used to furnish proof that money is but a veil to be ripped away even though an arithmetic operation such as consolidation can rip away nothing that was not, on the basis of an earlier decision, placed as a debt in the sectoral accounts to be consolidated. Accounting, being merely a tool, "proves" whatever our analytical decisions make it prove. The confusion becomes further compounded by the fact that bank money is sometimes sold for cash (dominant money) and sometimes on credit— on an installment plan. In the former case, sales are said by monetary and banking theory to give rise to "primary deposits"; in the latter case, to "derivative deposits." Also, in the latter case, it is customary to speak about "The Monetization of Debt by Commercial Banks."[19] The above example based on automobiles continues to be useful by demonstrating that these modes of speech confuse rather than enlighten by separating, quite needlessly, both terminologically and analytically, value theory from monetary and banking theory. If

[18] Harry G. Johnson, "Monetary Theory and Policy," *American Economic Review, LII* (June, 1962), p. 343.
[19] E.g., "Topic 2" of the Conference on Saving and Residential Financing was "The Monetization of Debt by Commercial Banks." Cf. Marshall D. Ketchum and Leon T. Kendall (ed.), *Conference on Saving and Residential Financing* (Chicago: The United States Savings and Loan League, 1962), p. 102.

automobiles were covered by a repurchase clause, would we say that
cash sales of the automobile producers give rise to primary deposits
and that sales on an installment plan give rise to derivative deposits?
Would we say that sales of cars on an installment plan result in
"Car-ization of Debt by Automobile Producers?" Neither the
repurchase clause nor the fact that money is sold partly for cash and
partly on credit provide any justification for treating money any
differently than we treat any other part of society's wealth.

Money as the Limiting Case of Interest-bearing Debt

As we have seen above, fiat money—although it is also sold subject
to a repurchase clause—is more difficult to classify as a liability of the
producer because the repurchase clause is in terms of fiat money
itself; under these conditions the repurchase clause gives to the
purchaser of fiat money the economically empty right to present
this instrument for payment and receive back a mint-fresh copy
of the very same instrument. As a result, the money-is-a-debt proponents have tried to surmount this difficulty by using the argument
that fiat money is simply government debt that does not pay interest.
Often the mathematical concept of the limit is used to explain away
the difference between something and nothing, between interest payments going to an owner of a debt certificate and no interest payments
going to the owner of fiat money. For instance, Don Patinkin
calls fiat money the noninterest bearing debt of the government;[20]
Harry G. Johnson, in his review of modern monetary theory, then
explains the peculiar presence of an alleged noninterest-bearing
debt in the midst of interest-bearing debts by pointing out that the
former is merely "the limiting case"[21] of the latter. A search of
the literature has failed to reveal what rate of interest is being
assumed to approach zero in the limit. However, there seem to be
two possible interpretations of the statement that money is the

[20] Don Patinkin, *op. cit.*, 1st ed., pp. 202–203.
[21] Harry G. Johnson, *op. cit.*, p. 343.

limiting case of interest-bearing debt. Perhaps it may be interpreted to mean that as the market rate of interest approaches zero the distinction between money and debts disappears; therefore, money is the limiting case of interest-bearing debt. Or, perhaps, debts are observed to pay various nominal rates of interest,[22] presumably because of the different risk characteristics of the issuers; in this case, money is being viewed as the limiting case in which the nominal interest rate paid on a debt becomes zero. Note that in these two cases, two different concepts of interest rates are being used. In the first case we are discussing the market rate of interest, and in the second we are discussing the income payments accruing to an asset expressed as a percentage of market value of this asset. This latter nominal rate of interest may or may not be equal to the market rate of interest. Let us consider each of these cases in turn.

Market Rate of Interest in the Limit

As has been shown in Chapter 3, money is net wealth because it yields income to its owner and yields no negative income to anybody else. In contrast, debt certificates are not net wealth because even though they yield positive income to their owner, they yield precisely the same negative income to the debtor. This income is called interest payments, and depends, of course, on the equilibrium market rate of interest. From this, however, it follows that as the equilibrium rate of interest approaches zero, the distinction between money that is wealth and debt certificates that are not wealth becomes smaller. In the limit, when the interest rate is zero, the distinction disappears completely and we have no way of distinguishing between money and debt certificates. That, however, fails to cause us any dismay because, if the equilibrium rate of interest is zero and the marginal product of capital is nonzero, then the values of goods must be zero.

---

[22] The nominal rate of interest is herein defined as the money income of the asset divided by its market value. Thus, in a joint product asset, e.g., the money-debt of Chapter 5, which is one-half debt and one-half asset, the nominal rate of interest will be one-half as high as the market rate of interest.

Thus all nonmoney goods become free goods; all money goods become no goods (notice, not free goods but *no goods* by virtue of the technical property of money by which money yields a flow of services that changes proportionately with the price of money); all debts cease to be positive assets for some and negative assets for others. Paradise is a reality and all that is left for economists to do is to debate the puzzle of whether wealth becomes infinite or zero. However, that doomsday of our discipline seems far off. As Frank H. Knight put it,

> Even if invention and all forms of social progress ceased, and saving went on at an indefinitely high rate, the interest rate would never fall to zero; for there is no limit to the possibility of using capital to increase the supply of innumerable commodities which could never become free goods.[23]

Nominal Rate of Interest in the Limit

There may be another meaning in which the terms "interest rate" and "the limit" to this rate are being used. Whatever *the* market rate of interest, the nominal rate paid on any specific asset may range from zero to this market rate depending on the uncertainty associated with the various assets and, more fundamentally, on the extent of other income streams accruing to these various assets. Let us consider each point in turn.

UNCERTAINTY "IN THE LIMIT." Faced by the problem of explaining the coexistence of interest-free debts (money) and interest-bearing debts (bonds), J. R. Hicks gives the following answer:

> The theory of liquidity preference is conventionally approached by asking how is it possible that an individual (or entity) may simultaneously hold bonds (that do bear interest) and money (that does not). The theory of rational conduct under uncertainty does unquestionably provide an answer to this problem.[24]

[23] Frank H. Knight, *The Ethics of Competition* (New York: Augustus M. Kelly, 1951), p. 264.
[24] John R. Hicks, *Capital and Growth* (New York: Oxford University Press, 1965), p. 284.

Nevertheless, this answer to the problem does appear highly questionable. If the *full* explanation of the rate differential is to be found in uncertainty, it follows that the smaller the uncertainty the smaller the differential until, in the limit, certainty is reached and the differential must disappear. But this can only be true if two conditions, implicit in the above answer to the problem, hold:

1. Analytically, it must be true that the *sole function* of money is to provide protection against uncertainty and the *sole reason* why bonds yield income is that it is an uncertain income.
2. Empirically, it must be true that the degree of uncertainty and thus the uncertainty premium (or certainty premium) are changing, *pari passu*, with all the observed changes in the rate of interest.

Leaving aside the empirical issue, it seems sufficient to point out that Hicks himself does not believe that protection against uncertainty is the sole role of money because a few pages earlier he introduced money in the economy with the explanation that it is needed to conduct exchanges. But surely exchanges of goods due to division of labor would not disappear as uncertainty disappears and this, by itself, denies the implicit assumption (1) and therefore denies the correctness of the above answer to the problem of the rate differential. Since money is needed to conduct exchanges, to serve as a medium of exchange, it has a role to play quite independently of the existence of uncertainty or certainty; for performing this role it will earn income that bonds, because they are not performing this role, cannot earn. From this it follows that uncertainty may explain part of the observed rate differential, but not all of it.

LIQUIDITY "IN THE LIMIT." Because the rate of interest paid on money is permanently zero, whereas the rate paid on bonds is positive and changing, we understood the above argument to claim that the rate of interest yielded by *bonds* is a premium for uncertainty that would disappear, with uncertainty, "in the limit." Don Patinkin understands this argument in the same way and also objects to it.

However, he merely reverses the reasoning. Uncertainty leads to illiquidity, and the zero rate of interest yielded by *money* is the penalty for liquidity that would disappear with uncertainty and the resulting illiquidity in the limit:

> . . . the end result of making bonds completely liquid is to eliminate not the rate of interest but the use of money. In this *limiting case* [emphasis ours] the medium of exchange would consist only of bonds, whose rate of interest would continue to reflect the traditional forces of thrift and capital productivity.[25]

But that means we jump from the frying pan into the fire. By Patinkin's own analysis, money as such produces income; either as a consumer's good it produces final income or as a producer's good it produces intermediate income.[26] If bonds came to be used, as he states, as money,[27] they would yield to their owner this income that money as money yields; but they would also be bonds and they would, as he states, also earn for the owner the equilibrium rate of interest. Thus, if the positive rate of bonds is due to uncertainty then bonds "in the limit" will earn zero equilibrium income, but if the positive rate on bonds is due to illiquidity then bonds "in the limit" will earn two equilibrium incomes.

VARIOUS SERVICES YIELDED BY ASSETS "IN THE LIMIT." Let us therefore put aside uncertainty (or liquidity) that may explain part of the difference in rates paid on money and bonds but that cannot explain all of it and that cannot therefore explain the peaceful coexistence of money and interest-bearing bonds. Let us, instead, consider the nominal rate of interest accruing to risk-free assets.

[25] Don Patinkin, *op. cit.*, 2d ed., p. 109. (For a similar statement, see Paul A. Samuelson, *Foundations of Economic Analysis* (New York: Atheneum, 1965), p. 123.)

[26] Don Patinkin, *ibid.*, pp. 160–161.

[27] A similar claim has been expressed by James Tobin. However, since his argument makes money disappear by making the demand for it disappear, we discuss Tobin's point in a chapter dealing with the demand for money (Chapter 14).

These rates may range from zero to the market (equilibrium) rate, depending on the extent of other income streams accruing to the asset under scrutiny. If we are dealing with an asset that has some flow of services as a medium of exchange, then the discussion of *money-debt* in Chapter 5 is relevant here. The ratio of the nominal rate paid to the market rate measures the extent to which the asset in question is a debt. The difference between the nominal rate paid and the market rate represents, of course, the unpaid rate that is received by the owner, in kind, by virtue of the asset being money. Obviously then, unity minus the ratio of nominal to market rate measures the extent to which the asset in question is money.

In this special sense, the statement that money is the limiting case of interest-bearing debt has an element of truth in it. If the nominal rate on money-debt is zero, then the money-debt is entirely money; if the nominal rate on money-debt is equal to the market interest rate, then the money-debt is entirely a debt certificate. This, however, makes it clear that there is no discontinuity here that permits money to be a part of wealth and a vehicle for the wealth effect if the nominal interest rate on money-debt becomes zero in the limit. If the money-debt were serving as a medium of exchange, it would have always been a vehicle for the wealth effect. All that happens when the nominal rate becomes zero is that the entire asset becomes money, and, hence, the entire value of it becomes a vehicle for the wealth effect. Hence, the fact that a zero nominal rate of interest on money-debt makes it entirely money in no way implies that money is a debt. In fact, quite the opposite is the case. The same is true about the refrigerator money in Chapter 3. If the income that refrigerator money, the *money-good*, yields in the limit is entirely the income that any refrigerator yields, then the money-good is entirely a refrigerator and not money. If the income the refrigerator money yields in the other limit is entirely money income and no refrigerating income whatever, the money-good is entirely money.

Finally, there is a third possibility: *good-debts* are extremely widespread in the economy even though they are ignored both by economic analysis and by empirical studies of wealth. At the present time and in the United States, most cars, appliances, office equipment, and much of industrial equipment is sold with a warranty, explicit or implied, that commits the producer and seller of these goods to provide the purchaser for a specified period of time with free repair service, free parts, free training of the operators of the equipment, and so on. Such a warranty promises the buyer that he will receive a stream of (imputed) income in future years. The market value of such a warranty—in some cases it is even purchasable separately—represents the value of a bond that is being sold by the producer to the buyer. Thus the market price of these good-debts sold expresses partly the value of the good sold and partly the value of the bond sold. As in the case of money-debt and money-good, so in the case of the good-debts the statement that nonmoney capital goods are but limiting cases of interest-bearing debts has also an element of truth in it. In one limiting case, there is no warranty and the seller is committed to zero interest payments in the future. Then the nominal rate in this limit is zero and the good-debt is entirely a good. In the other limiting case, there is no good and the seller is committed to pay to the purchaser a stream of income that any borrower would pay. Then the nominal rate is the market rate and the good-debt is entirely a debt.

It thus appears that the arguments that fiat money is noninterest-bearing debt, that in the limit there is no difference between interest-bearing debts and noninterest-bearing debts, and that therefore money and debt certificates are one and the same thing do not seem to have any meaning. They fail completely to explain the peaceful coexistence of interest-bearing debt and the so-called noninterest-bearing debt in cases in which the market rate of interest is not zero, they reduce to an empty truism in the case in which the equilibrium rate of interest happens to be zero; they are irrelevant for a decision of whether money is a part of wealth if they happen to operate not with *the* equilibrium rate of interest but with one of the huge number of nominal rates of interest, all of which can exist—and, in the case of good-debts, actually do exist—at any one time.

Distinction Between Money and Debt

Throughout our discussion we have stressed one important point: money *is* and *must be* a medium of exchange. The only characteristic of money that distinguishes it from any other capital asset is the fact that the flow of services from a unit of money changes proportionately with the price of money. This unique and important characteristic of money is due to the character of the flow of services of money, its use as a medium of exchange. Thus, when we attempt to classify any specific asset in the wealth portfolio of any wealth owner, there are two issues that must be decided. The first of these is the condition that is necessary for the asset to be at least partially money: its use as a medium of exchange. If the asset under consideration does not serve as a medium of exchange, then that is the end of our scrutiny. If, on the other hand, we find that the asset under consideration does serve as a medium of exchange, then further inquiry becomes necessary. We must then discover whether the asset in question is a medium of exchange and nothing else, or is it perhaps some mixture of medium of exchange and debt certificate. In other words, does the instrument in question perform only one service and yield one income, that yielded by money, or does it perform two services and yield two incomes—one income, that is to be attributed to money, and another one, that is to be attributed to a loan of resources made by the owner of this instrument? Let us proceed with this line of inquiry by first considering various assets that are often included in the definition of "liquid assets" and separate those that are at least partially money from the others. After we have selected those assets eligible for the money club, we shall subject them to further scrutiny to determine the extent to which they are money.

Monetary Assets

It is clear that the problem of whether something serves or does not serve as a medium of exchange is an issue that no economic theory is able to answer on some *a priori* basis; it is a purely empirical problem. As always, when we descend from the well-ordered world of theory into the confused and complex world of reality, we are likely to discover that analytical concepts become fuzzy along the edges. Yet, we believe that the following discussion will show that the concept of a "medium of exchange" is more fortunate than most major concepts of economic theory: the fuzziness along the edges is —when compared with such concepts as "consumption good"— negligible.

Fiat money cannot possibly be mistaken for anything but a pure medium of exchange. The only income it yields to the owner is the income that any other commodity money would yield; the value of the power to facilitate transactions. It yields no negative income to any alleged debtor.[28] *Demand deposits* are also serving as a medium of exchange. In some uses, they are an imperfect substitute for fiat money (paying by personal check in a foreign city); in other uses, they are superior to fiat money (settling large transactions, paying to a designated person only, insured against loss or theft). As a medium of exhange, in some uses more and in some uses less perfect than fiat money, demand deposits must also be yielding to the owner almost the same income that fiat money yields: they must be a part of net wealth. Whether they should be entered into the wealth equation by their full value (net, of course, of the dominant money reserves) or by some fraction of it—to account for some imperfection —we shall discuss in the next section. *Travelers checks* are also serving as a medium of exchange. In contrast with the other monies, they are purchased at a premium. However, the premium is so small that it seems likely that a valuation of the imputed income furnished by the producer would establish that they are sold at a discount and that they are, therefore, a somewhat imperfect substitute for fiat money.

[28] One of the authors wishes to give belated credit to the numerous students in his money and banking introductory course who found it impossible to accept the argument that a five-dollar bill that entitles them to five one-dollar bills is a debt that the government owes them.

On the other hand, *time deposits* and *shares in savings and loan associations* are, already, on the other side of the dividing line. They clearly do not serve at the present time, and in the United States (to drive home again the point that we are facing an empirical issue),·as media of exchange. Indeed, they seem to be even inferior to many parts of nonmonetary wealth as far as barter is concerned. On the other side of the dividing line are also items that are wealth and considered to be "close substitutes" for money, such as corporate stock and such evidences of debt as corporate bonds and government bonds. Indeed, U.S. savings bonds, which are frequently considered to be the closest substitute for money, are by law precluded from serving as a medium of exchange and are merely debt in its purest form. All other items that are parts of nonmonetary wealth may be, at times, subject to barter between two persons; even a three-cornered barter may very rarely occur. We submit that only if we throw away all the empirical knowledge we have are we able even to contemplate the possibility of, say, cigarettes, serving at the present time and in the United States as a medium of exchange.

A question may be asked whether the rejection of the items just discussed is not too dogmatic. Commercial banks and savings and loan associations frequently pay the monthly bills of their depositors; is there any substantive difference between a demand deposit and a share in these associations? Time deposits can frequently be shifted into a demand deposit on the basis of a phone call; isn't any distinction between them artificial? In answer it must be said that these similarities hide a basic difference. Money, a medium of exchange, must be used to facilitate exchanges; it must enable the buyer to buy a good, any good, of his choice and to pay for it with money. It is obvious that the items just discussed do not perform this role, since they must first be presented for payment to the borrower, the bank that created the time deposit or the association that created the share, and *only the proceeds* of this sale, money, may be used to pay the bills of the owner of the debt certificate in the form of time deposit or saving share. As in the case of all other wealth, money is what money does. If time deposit books were conveniently usable not just for collection from the borrower but for payments (or if, as was the case in the past, they were transferable by check), they would be money; if they paid interest at the same time, they would be money-debt in the sense discussed earlier. But they are not, and what remains is that these items, even though not money, are highly liquid. Liquidity, however, is irrelevant for a decision whether an item is a medium of exchange. Common stock may also be sold almost instantly for money, so can many standard commodities, and so can even the most "illiquid" asset if the owner happens to be in a company of expert dealers in this item. The reason why confusion such as the one contained in the question with which we started this paragraph arises is that sometimes we forget (cf., e.g., footnote 25) that *every money is a liquid asset, but that not all liquid assets are money.*

An asset is perfectly liquid if it is instantly salable to a specific firm or firms for a specific item, typically money. A good is perfect money if it is instantly salable to anybody for anything. Economic practices of any community *could* make a decision of this empirical issue hard or impossible since there is no analytical reason why any or all things could not be money. It is fortunate but probably not incidental (in present economies, gravitating towards high specialization of all resources) that the role of money also turns out to be a highly specialized function. True enough, we do not have "perfect" money: a hundred dollar bill turns out to be unacceptable in a small drug store, a check in a foreign city may be hard to cash, but on the whole it is amazing how perfect our actual money is. Similarly, there are many nonmonies that come close to perfect liquidity. Yet, we submit that at the present time and in the United States there is a deep, wide, and unmistakable chasm between the most perfectly liquid nonmonies and the most imperfect of monies.

Apportioning the Value of Money-debt Between Money and Debt

However, this is no place to rest since our task is but half finished. Our next problem is whether the items that are eligible for the monetary wealth category, because they serve as a medium of exchange, belong there by their full value or whether they belong there only by a fraction of their value; in other words, whether they are only money or whether they are money and also something else: monetary wealth *and* nonmonetary wealth, monetary wealth *and* debt certificates. As we have shown in the preceding chapter, the extent to which an asset that serves as a medium of exchange is debt can be measured by the value of the flow of nonmedium of exchange services per unit of money value of the asset relative to the market rate of interest. In the particular case of money-debt discussed in the previous chapter, the value of the nonmedium of exchange flow of services per unit of money value was simply the rate of interest paid on money-debt. However, it is not necessary that everything that serves as a medium of exchange be partially a debt and partially money. It may be partially a capital asset (e.g., the refrigerator money of Chapter 3) and partially money. The reason for neglecting the so-called nonliquid assets from consideration as possible media of exchange is that the more time required to convert the capital asset into one of the assets that is entirely money, the less likely that the asset in question will be generally acceptable in transactions. It is on this ground that we have not considered the nonfinancial assets as candidates for the medium of exchange role. While, in fact, some nonfinancial assets may serve as nonlegal media of exchange and have a portion of their value attributable to this fact, we feel that at least in the United States they are of a second order of importance.

What can we say about fiat money, demand deposits, and travelers' checks; the three items that do serve as media of exchange? Since the production and sale of these monies do not exactly correspond to the pure theoretical constructs presented in Chapters 3 through 5, several questions must be answered before that analysis can be applied:[29]

---

[29] In certain periods of our history demand deposits have paid interest and time deposits have been transferable by check; cf. Friedman and Schwartz, *op. cit.*, p. 4. In addition, even currency has at times paid interest; cf. W. C.

1. Are the three items that do serve as media of exchange pure money, or are they a joint product?

   The answer to this question is important for our measurement of the size of the net monetary wealth in the United States.

2. As far as the money component of the three items is concerned, is this money component in its entirety a pure substitute for commodity money or does it contain an element of pure commodity money?

   The answer to this question is important for a decision as to the extent that money producers are able to take advantage of the conceptual possibility of producing money at zero resource cost.

3. As far as the pure commodity money component of the three items is concerned, is this component due to an expenditure of real resources at the time of production or was part of this expenditure of resources deferred until some future time?

   The answer to this question is important for our measurement of the size of *non*monetary wealth in the United States.

Since the issues raised here are purely empirical ones, the answers to these questions cannot affect the analysis presented in Chapters 3 through 5. However, answers are not easy to give since the questions asked above are so new that little, if any, of the empirical evidence required is available. Thus, all we will be able to do is outline the analytical underpinnings of the questions and in a few cases give some indication of the magnitudes involved; considerable more research needs to be done before most of the empirical issues to be raised here can be resolved.

MONEY, MONEY-GOODS, AND MONEY-DEBTS.   As we have shown in Chapter 3, all items of wealth must yield the same equilibrium rate

---

Mitchell, *A History of the Greenbacks* (Chicago: The University of Chicago Press, 1903), pp. 174–175. It is for this reason that every so often we add to our definition of money supply and thus of monetary net wealth the qualifying phrase, "at the present time and in the United States."

of return. Thus, if an item of wealth yields income as a medium of exchange and also as a good or a debt, then the sum of these two incomes must be equal to the income yielded by any other item of wealth of equal market value. Also, if the flow of services of this item as a good or as a debt increases, then the value of this item as a medium of exchange must fall until the sum of the two incomes again results in a rate of return equal to the rate of return on other items of wealth. Hence, the fraction of an item of wealth that is money depends on whether that item also serves as a source of income, either as a good or as a debt (a bond), and this fraction may be different at different points in time.

In the light of the above, what is the status of the three items that do serve as money in the United States at the present time? *Currency*, whether coin or paper bills, yields no nonmoney income to the owner and thus is entirely money. Note that this does not imply that there are no servicing costs to maintaining the stock of currency outstanding but that these costs are not debts; they are production costs of currency for without them currency could not serve as money. (A more complete discussion of this point will be presented below.) *Demand deposits*, while serving as a medium of exchange, may also yield additional income in the form of accounting services furnished to the owner. In contrast, the internal costs of servicing demand deposits, i.e., the costs of check clearance and related activities, do not represent income to the user of demand deposits in addition to the income yielded by demand deposits in their role as a medium of exchange. Rather, these services simply make possible or enhance the medium-of-exchange flow of income of demand deposits and thus are simply production costs of demand deposits. To the extent that demand deposits yield accounting services to the owner they are not money. However, the supply cost of these services is probably small since they are produced as a by-product of the service costs of demand deposits: the marginal cost of producing monthly bank statements does not seem to be much higher than the cost of paper, some accounting machine time, and mailing costs. The demand price—introspection suggests—is a low one as well. But then, the market value of these accounting services is likely to be low relative to the flow of income from demand deposits as a medium of exchange. In other words, demand deposits as we find them today in the United States are primarily money and the good component of them (the accounting services) is probably of negligible size. In the case of *travelers' checks* the major nonmoney income is the insurance against loss due to negligence or theft. Since empirical evidence of the costs of this insurance is unavailable—in fact, the quantity of travelers' checks outstanding and the reserves held against these outstanding travelers' checks are also unknown—we will not even hazard a guess concerning the good component of this money-good.

In conclusion we may state that out of the three types of wealth that serve as media of exchange in the United States, one type, currency, is at the present time entirely money (whether the costs of production are borne entirely at the time of production and sale or deferred to some later date). Two other types are money-goods; in this case the good component consists of a flow of services, either accounting or insurance services, that (a) are provided to the owner of the money-good, and (b) represent a commitment of resources on the seller's part and consequently reduce the wealth of the seller.

MONEY COMPONENT: COMMODITY MONEY OR PURE MONEY SUBSTITUTE? As we have shown in Chapter 3, competitively produced pure commodity money will have a resource content of value that is equal to the market value of this wealth. In view of the special technical property of money (yielding real income the size of which is completely divorced from the quantity of the substance serving as money and that is, therefore, completely divorced from the substance itself) it is possible to produce the same quantity of monetary wealth monopolistically and achieve substantial saving of resources. In the extreme case of a pure substitute for competitively produced commodity money the saving of resources reaches 100 per cent. All the present analyses of fiat money and bank money, as well as our own analysis as presented in Chapters 3 and 4, make the simplifying assumption that in our economy the theoretically possible maximum resource economies can be and are fully utilized by actual money producers. In other words, it is customary to make the simplifying assumption that the so-called fiduciary issues are produced either at zero expenditure of resources or that this expenditure is so negligible as to warrant neglect.

This is, admittedly, a simplifying assumption which we all know not to be entirely true. *Fiat money* consists of three types: coin, Treasury and Federal Reserve System notes, and Federal Reserve System deposits. In the case of coin there is a significant mixture of pure commodity money and of pure money substitute. While cost data are completely inadequate, it appears that—very roughly— the resource cost and thus the commodity money component of coin represents one-half of the market value of coin: by resource cost we mean, of course, the cost of copper, silver, and nickel metals and the cost of coining. Treasury and Federal Reserve System paper money, in contrast, are merely printed pieces of paper produced at resource cost that is negligible in relation to the market value of these wealth items. Only the most fastidious researcher will insist that these two monies are a mixture of commodity money and money substitutes. Federal Reserve deposits are pure accounting entries. Since the resource cost of producing them is not fully borne at the time of production and since much of it occurs day after day, we shall reserve discussion of this item until later. *Bank money* contains resource costs partly incurred at the time of sale and partly deferred. Leaving the deferred cost aside for the moment, let us mention the one incurred at the time of sale. As shown in Chapter 4, they very economic nature of bank money requires the major part of bank money that is not sold for dominant money be sold for titles to income streams produced by the purchaser rather than merely exchanged for the sources of these income streams. Whenever a good (monetary or nonmonetary) is sold for titles to income streams, it becomes essential to investigate the ability of the purchaser to honor his commitments. Thus, one of the resource costs of production of bank money is to be found in the utilization of resources to investigate the credit-worthiness of the purchaser of bank money on an installment plan. Again, data on this are either completely missing or we could not discover them. As a result, we feel unable to make even a rough guess as to what an extent bank money is commodity money and to what extent it is a pure money substitute. All we can say with a fair degree of certainty is that empirical evidence indicates that demand deposits contain, to some significant degree, a pure money substitute component. Were they pure commodity money, with resource cost equal to their market value, demand deposit production should be no more profitable than any other type of economic endeavor. As Footnote 7 in Chapter 5 indicates, this is not the case. In the case of *travelers' checks*, the only resource cost of producing the money component of this money-good at the time of production is the printing of the checks and the fee paid to the distributors. The printing cost appears, as in the case of Federal Reserve notes, negligible; about the retail costs we have no information.

COMMODITY MONEY COMPONENT: IMMEDIATE OR DEFERRED RESOURCE COSTS. The problem of incurred and deferred resource cost faces us both in the case of nonmonetary wealth and in the case of monetary wealth. It will be instructive to consider first nonmonetary wealth. Assume that we select any wealth item that requires a specific expenditure of resources and declare this item to be a "standard" one. Assume further that a competing producer chooses to spend a smaller quantity of resources and produces a technically inferior product yielding the same output but depreciating faster. In the case of nonmonetary wealth, the producer has two choices: he can either sell this inferior product for a lower price or he can sell it for the same price for which the standard good sells and promise the purchaser free labor and parts that will fully make up for the deficiency of his product. If he selects the second avenue, the result is that any measurement of wealth that does not take account of the obligation of the producer to spend resources in the future overstates national wealth: the owner of the inferior product owns resources that are, for the moment, in physical possession of the producer of this inferior item. It may be noted parenthetically that nonmonetary wealth today is replete with all sorts of explicit or implicit warranties promising future performance. These warranties have economic value, represent resources held—legally, "owned" by the producers—which are economically committed and are not, therefore, income earning assets for the producer and, therefore, are not net wealth. As far as we know, most producers of nonmoney wealth do not show the market value of these warranties as a liability and as a result the existing measurements of national wealth overstate, perhaps seriously, the size of the nonmonetary wealth in the United States.

In the case of pure substitutes for commodity money, "pure fiduciary issues," this problem of resource cost deferral cannot arise since these monies are produced, by definition, at zero resource cost. However, in the case of commodity money the deferral problem is as relevant as it is in the case of nonmonetary wealth. As we have seen, all monies in use in the United States today have a commodity money component; i.e., none is produced at zero resource cost. As far as this commodity money component of total monetary wealth is concerned, the producers frequently find it advantageous to produce a product at a small present expenditure of resources and make up this resource deficiency by promising additional expenditure of resources in the future. (As we have shown in our discussion of equation [5.1A], the repurchase clause forecloses the possibility enjoyed by producers of nonmonetary wealth of producing an inferior product and simply charging a lower price.) Coin money and note money producers promise to exchange the deteriorating commodity component of money free of charge. The commodity money substitutes depend on the enforcement of the monopolistic privilege (fight against counterfeiters) and this also requires a continuous expenditure of resources. The demand deposit component of net monetary wealth by its very nature requires account keeping, printing of checks, etc.: resource costs all of which are, however, incurred not at the time of production but are a continuous burden.

This has two consequences. First, the capitalized present value of these future resource-expenditure commitments is a part of the resource cost of producing net monetary wealth presently in existence. This capitalized value must be added to the resource costs incurred at the time of production when we make the decision (as discussed in item (2) above) of the extent that current net monetary wealth is composed of commodity money. Second, the total wealth owned by the producers of money wealth (just as the wealth of the producers of nonmoney wealth) is overstated by the value of resources held—legally, "owned" by the producers—which are economically committed and are not, therefore, income earning assets for the producer and, therefore, are not net wealth. As we know, producers of money wealth do not show the market value of these warranties as a liability and as a result the existing measurements of national wealth overstate, perhaps seriously, the size of the *nonmonetary wealth* (notice that we say "nonmonetary") in the United States.

Why do we insist on the subtraction of these as yet unspent but committed resources from nonmonetary wealth? First, just as in the case of nonmonetary wealth produced by the method of deferring expeditures of resources, it is not the net wealth of the owner of the product that is smaller; it is the wealth of the producer of this item who skimped on resources today and must make up the deficiency tomorrow. Second, in the case of nonmoney goods discussed earlier, a researcher interested only in total wealth and not the structure of its ownership will not incur an error regardless from whose accounts he subtracts the deferred resource costs. In the case of money this is not true because the product is monetary wealth and the resources still to be sacrificed nonmonetary. Since monetary wealth—especially in the case of price changes—has a different technical property than nonmonetary wealth, it becomes crucial that the subtraction be made from the correct part of wealth; i.e., the nonmonetary part. Specifically, subsequent price changes will change the monetary wealth of the owners of money while leaving the nonowners and therefore the owners of nonmonetary wealth unaffected.

This is also true about the owner of the negative nonmonetary wealth consisting of the obligation to sacrifice nonmonetary resources to maintain the monetary wealth, produced by the use of the method of cost-deferral, in working order. The real resource cost of, e.g., exchanging worn-out banknotes or making accounting entires remains unchanged regardless of whether the purchasing power of a unit of money (say, a dollar) increases from three packs of cigarettes to six packs of cigarettes.

The point just discussed focuses attention on a problem that has received no attention by those who analyze money and little or no attention by those who measure nonmonetary wealth. We have pointed out that a producer of any wealth—monetary or nonmonetary—frequently has the choice of either spending the full resource cost of the product prior to the sale of it or of deferring some part of this resource cost until a later date. If the latter is the case, a part of the resources shown as owned by such a producer is fully committed to a specific use, cannot earn any income for the producer, and must be therefore subtracted from our measure of his net wealth.

It is necessary to stress with great emphasis that the third point, even though it declares that one part of monetary wealth has as its counterpart a debt of the producer, has no relationship whatever to the current money-is-a-debt argument. The simplest way of demonstrating this is to point out that the current theory of money declares pure money substitutes, "fiduciary issues" produced at zero resource cost now and in the future, to be a debt and therefore not a part of net wealth. Our analysis, *in contrast*, shows that such pure "fiduciary issues" can never give rise to a debt; the last point discussed shows, however, that pure commodity money—just as any other nonmoney commodity—may be produced by the use of the resource-cost-deferral method and, if it is so produced, gives rise to a commitment of nonmonetary resources by the producer. It is then his real nonmonetary debt, and must be therefore subtracted from his nonmonetary wealth; nonmonetary wealth, since the resources that must be used to maintain the commodity component of money must be nonmonetary. It is the nonmonetary resources that were being withheld initially by the use of the resource-cost-deferral method and it must be the same resources that need to be furnished later on as required.

However, to return to the empirical issue on hand. In the case of *fiat money*, the deferred cost represents the cost of exchanging worn coin and notes and the cost of enforcement of the monetary monopoly. In the case of *demand deposits*, the cost of printing of checks and of accounting; in the case of *travelers' checks*, the cost of accounting.

CONCLUDING REMARKS.   In view of the novelty of the questions that we discussed in this part of the chapter, it might be useful to close the discussion by offering the reader a schematic representation of the empirical problems that must be solved whenever we attempt to analyze the economic content of an item that is discovered in any specific economy to serve as money; in the United States, currency, demand deposits, and travelers' checks:

**Schema of the Allocation of Economic Contents to Any Item
Observed to Serve as a Medium of Exchange**

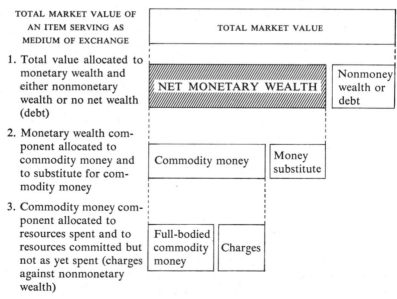

TOTAL MARKET VALUE OF AN ITEM SERVING AS MEDIUM OF EXCHANGE	TOTAL MARKET VALUE	
1. Total value allocated to monetary wealth and either nonmonetary wealth or no net wealth (debt)	NET MONETARY WEALTH	Nonmoney wealth or debt
2. Monetary wealth component allocated to commodity money and to substitute for commodity money	Commodity money	Money substitute
3. Commodity money component allocated to resources spent and to resources committed but not as yet spent (charges against nonmonetary wealth)	Full-bodied commodity money	Charges

The *schema* suggests the kind of information needed to quantify the extent to which an item is net monetary wealth and a gross addition to nonmonetary wealth. A gross addition, since any resource commitments due to (a) the cost-deferral production of the pure commodity money (and (b) the same in the production of the nonmonetary wealth component) result in double-counting of this nonmonetary wealth and must be allowed for.

As far as the net monetary wealth component of the three items under consideration is concerned, we concluded that currency is 100 per cent money and nothing else; demand deposits have a fraction of their value, probably a very small one, which is nonmonetary wealth (free accounting service); travelers' checks also do have such a fraction about the size of which we would not hazard a guess. We concluded that all three items of monetary wealth do have a commodity money component in that their production requires expenditure of resources; in the absence of any cost figures, quantification of this component is impossible at the present. Finally, we have seen that the commodity money component of all three items is due partly to the expenditure of resources at the time of sale and partly to a subsequent expenditure of resources; the very same absence of cost data makes impossible a quantification of the extent to which nonmonetary wealth owned by the producer is overstated.

Money Supply in Real Terms

As we have done on numerous other occasions throughout our discussion, we must emphasize again that all that we are considering here is the initial consequence of a change in the quantity of money on wealth. It is extremely likely that this change in wealth will cause a change in the behavior of the consumer and that, as a result, the general equilibrium of the economy will become disturbed. One of the variables that is likely to be affected is the general price level which is, of course, just the reciprocal of the price of money. This, in turn, will again change wealth because changes in the price of money, given the quantity of money, affect the level of monetary wealth in the same way as changes in the quantity of money, given the price of it. Analysis of these changes is, of course, a problem for macroeconomic analysis and is reserved for Part V of this book. At this point, all that needs to be done is to emphasize that the *ultimate* effect of the change in the money supply on wealth depends on the change in the level of prices that this change in money supply will cause. This, however, only amplifies and strengthens the validity of the principles for defining the money supply that we have discussed in this chapter. To count, after the introduction of demand deposits into the economy, only fiat money as the money supply—a procedure followed, e.g., by the *Radcliffe Report*—is to grossly underestimate the money supply. The reason is that the introduction of this substitute for dominant money increases the total money supply and, most probably, affects the price of money. To take, then, the currently existing price of money, co-determined as it is by the existing total money supply, and to value only the dominant money in terms of this price understates monetary wealth. The only consistent procedure would be—if only a fraction of the money supply were to be used—to make an estimate of what the price of money would be if only that fraction of money were in existence and then to value the nominal quantity of this fraction in terms of this estimated price. A procedure that is "iffy" at best and, should the rigid quantity theory happen to hold, pointless at worst.

Conclusion

In this chapter we have outlined the reasons that we feel have caused modern monetary theory to contemplate the abandonment of the concept of money and to replace it, with increased frequency, with the sum of monetary wealth and debt certificates called "liquid assets." There are two broad categories of arguments that are being used to support such reasoning. The first states that a separation of money from debt certificates, even if it were possible, is not desirable because empirical evidence suggests that both have the same economic consequences. The second argument states that, even if it were desirable to undertake such a separation, the concept of liquid assets would still have to be used because, empirically, such a separation is impossible.

The argument that both money and debt certificates (credit) affect the equilibrium level of prices seems to be true but is irrelevant. It can be easily shown that the former does so by affecting the demand factors. Similarly irrelevant is the argument that the use of the concept of liquid assets seems to yield, empirically, good results.[30] In the light of the above analysis, this is not surprising. If we analyze the economic behavior of any specific sector of the economy, it is extremely likely that some concept of liquid assets will seem to be a good explanatory variable because it is a measure of the monetary wealth of that sector plus that part of the nonmonetary wealth that is in the ownership but not in the physical possession of that sector. In other words, liquid assets are simply a measure of a certain fraction of a total wealth of a sector: a fraction bigger than the monetary wealth and smaller than the total wealth. As long as this fraction remains stable over time, liquid assets may be found to be a good proxy for either. The argument that money and debt certificates cannot be distinguished also fails to survive scrutiny. True enough, there are several very misleading similarities between both. They both have negligible or no intrinsic value, both are parts of the wealth portfolio of the owner, both contain a repurchase clause, and both are indistinguishable "in the limit." The last three are completely irrelevant, since they apply not only to money and debt certificates but to nonmonetary wealth (say, to purely physical capital) with equal force. If they prove that it is impossible to distinguish between money and debt certificates, they also prove that it is impossible to distinguish between purely physical capital and debt certificates—a conclusion that is obviously unacceptable.

The remaining similarity—the absence of intrinsic value in the

---

[30] Cf. Friedman and Schwartz, *op. cit.*, p. 650, where good empirical results are said to justify a concept of "money" containing both money and debts, time deposits.

case of both money and debt certificates—is more serious. Here the only answer can be that economic analysis is able to prove that money is one part of wealth that can yield positive income to its owner and no negative income to its producer or to the nonowner, and that this income is completely divorced from the physical substance of money. In contrast, debt certificates yield income to the owner only because they yield negative income of equal size to the debtor.

Finally, we have shown that when economic analysis is used in an effort to separate money from debt certificates in the huge mass of financial assets—all of which have no intrinsic value—the empirical difficulties encountered in this effort are negligible. The role of money in a modern society such as the United States appears to be so specialized (and government regulations contribute significantly to this) that even though there is conceptually no reason why many commodities and many debt certificates could not serve as money, we discover that in reality extremely few do. When financial assets are scrutinized, some reveal themselves immediately as money and nothing else (except for the warranty component), some as debt certificates and nothing else. The intermediate grey area in between, that is to be expected whenever we apply analytical concepts to the real world, proves to be next to nonexistent. This is in sharp contrast with the fact that almost all consumption goods are capable of being investment goods and—more than that—do at some time of their existence serve as such. If ease or difficulty in empirical application of analytical concepts should decide whether it has a place in analysis, the "money-nonmoney" dichotomy would have a much safer place than the well-established "consumption-investment" dichotomy. Thus we would conclude that there is no justification for the view that the analytically and empirically clear-cut concept of monetary wealth and of money supply should be replaced by the agglomeration called "liquid assets."

CHAPTER 8

Money in Current Analysis: A Comparison

In the preceding chapters we proceeded without systematic references to the currently dominant theory. It is now necessary to discuss thoroughly this dominant theory to enable the reader to compare it with the analysis presented here. For two reasons, such a comparison is a task of some expositional complexity. First, we find in the current literature a persistent use of "coined" phrases to describe what the various writers believe to be fundamentally different types of money: simply "money," commodity ("hard") money, fiat money, outside money, inside money, money plus deposits, central bank money, commercial bank money, money introduced by financial intermediaries—even such indefinite evidences of calls upon credit called credit cards. Frequently, different economic analyses are given to these different labels despite the fact that many of these monies are, as we intend to show, economically indistinguishable. Conversely, one and the same "coined" phrase frequently describes two or more dissimilar methods of introducing money into circulation. These methods must have different analytical consequences; yet, the fact that one label serves to cover all such cases causes the current literature to give them but

one economic analysis. Second, many proponents of the dominant
theory argue that money in general or some part of money covered
by a specific coined phrase is an asset of the owner that is offset
by a debt of others. Changes in money are then said to be incapable
of changing the net wealth of society as a whole, but only the asset
and debt positions of the various members of the community. If
this money does affect economic behavior, it is—this argument claims
—not because of changes in net wealth but merely because of asymmetrical responses of the various decision makers to changes in
assets and debts. The "wealth effect" of a change in the real quantity
of this money is reduced to a "distribution effect." Thus, according
to current analysis, several types of monies may have identical
consequences for final equilibrium, but this identity is said to be
merely the result of the fact that in the case of one type of money
there is no debt, whereas, in the case of another type of money there
is a debt, but it is ignored. A discussion of all these issues simultaneously would court confusion. To avoid this danger we will
divide our discussion into two parts.

First we will discuss only that aspect of the various monies resulting in specific economic consequences. As long as the concept of
money employed by a writer is such that, according to that writer,
changes in a given type of money have economic consequences, this
concept and these consequences are discussed. The basis for discussion and for comparison is what we call *the economically relevant
wealth equation.* From an accounting standpoint, this is a gross
wealth equation because it includes all items said, by the writers
discussed, to affect economic behavior, regardless of whether consolidation of the balance sheets of the various decision makers
would leave an item in or net it out. From an economic standpoint,
all the items that affect economic behavior are left in the equation
despite the fact that some pairs of items (positive and negative) would
disappear if all decision makers were assumed to respond equally
to all assets *and* to all debts. If we voice disagreement in this section
with the writers discussed, it is not because of any differences in the
analysis of the basic nature of money. It is because in some cases we

find inconsistency between the definition of the specific type of money employed by the writer discussed and his subsequent analysis of consequences of changes in this money: most frequently, such definitions imply changes in two or more income streams as money is placed in circulation, whereas the subsequent analysis pays attention to fewer changes in the income streams.

Second, after we have discussed each type of money and the method of introducing it into the economy employed by the various writers, we shall discuss the effect of a change in the quantity of this money on the levels of economically relevant wealth and net wealth in the community: we discuss *the net wealth equation.* In terms of accounting, we ask whether this money would disappear if there were rigorous consolidation of all balance sheets. In terms of economics, we ask whether this money would have economic consequences for the final equilibrium if the assumption that different decision makers respond to changes in assets and debts differently were replaced with the assumption that all decision makers respond in a symmetrical way. In these sections we establish whether the writer discussed considers "his" money to be (or not to be) a part of the net wealth of the community. Any expression of our disagreement found in this section dealing with the net wealth equation is, of course, more fundamental and cannot be resolved by a mere restoration of some forgotten income stream; it turns on the basic analytical issue of whether money in general—and a specific type of money under discussion in particular—is, or is not, net wealth. Any disagreement will be merely stated, not defended, since detailed defense of our own position has already been offered in the preceding chapters. There we showed that all money, regardless of whether it happens to be commodity money, fiat money, or bank money, is a part of the net wealth of the community. In the light of this analysis, the economically relevant wealth equation is identical with the net wealth equation. Changes in money have economic consequences shown in the economically relevant wealth equation not because some decision makers are ignoring their debts, but because there are no debts to ignore.

Before we start, it seems desirable to explain our reasons for singling out some writers for discussion and for asserting that it is they who represent the "currently dominant theory." By dominant, as we have already said, we do not mean a majority opinion: we have no way of discovering the majority opinion and we doubt that such a discovery would be relevant in any case. Rather, we mean the opinion of those who have dealt, systematically and in print, with the topic under discussion: the nature and economic consequences of money. Even with this restriction, a selection is still inevitable because even among those writers there is a frequent repetition of the same argument—but also some diversity of opinions. Who are, then, the writers whose opinions really carry weight; who represent the current orthodoxy? One guideline for our decision was provided by the selection of writers that we find in such a prestigious review of current monetary theory as the one written by Harry G. Johnson as a leading article in the *American Economic Review*.[1] In the section dealing with our topic, Johnson chose to discuss the views of Patinkin, Tobin, Gurley and Shaw, Pigou, Metzler, and Haberler: we took this list to be representative of the currently dominant theory. Another guideline was provided by semiofficial studies such as the *Radcliffe Report* and the *Report of the Commission on Money and Credit*. These undertakings, products of committees and subcommittees, typically contain only analytical approaches that can boast of a very broad consensus; it cannot be by chance that here, also, the influence of the analysis based on the money-is-a-debt argument is unmistakable. Simultaneously, there is—as always—a group of economists who seem to be out of the mainstream, partly or fully. Milton Friedman and Martin Bailey ignore the money-is-a-debt argument completely and state flatly that money is a part of what we call economically relevant wealth *and* of net wealth.[2] Gottfried Haberler is—at least partly—on the

---

[1] Harry G. Johnson, "Monetary Theory and Policy," *American Economic Review, LII* (June, 1962), pp. 304–305.

[2] Milton Friedman, *Price Theory* (Chicago: Aldine Publishing Co., 1962), p. 245. Martin Bailey, "Saving and the Rate of Interest," in Earl J.

other side of the fence. Arnold Collery questions the dominant argument with respect to commodity money;[3] J. M. Culbertson, similarly, attacks the notion that banks do not create money and claims that bank money is a special asset.[4]

In our comparison, we state the views of the writers as we understand them: if, as is at times the case, a writer seems to be on both sides of the fence, we try to decide what opinion is the main guide of his work and what opinion may be merely a careless slip into what he himself might consider to be a bad habit. If possible, we take the most recent writing to be his most considered opinion. We do not present criticisms by others of the opinions discussed in the following comparison, mainly because there are, by and large, none. Our topic seems to be an example of perfect coexistence. The current dominant theory, that we believe sharply contradicts professional opinions that prevailed between, say, 1860 to 1950, became dominant with little controversy. In 1955 the term "financial intermediaries" was coined and applied to commercial banks. Practically without discussion, the term and the monetary analysis it implies became parts of the established doctrine. A few years later, it appeared in the title of a book by R. W. Goldsmith;[5] the term and the analysis behind it entered the semiofficial reports mentioned earlier; the term itself received the final accolade of becoming a heading in the *Index of Economic Journals* prepared by the American Economic Association. In this volume, it was even applied—posthumously, so to speak—

---

[3] See note 41.

[4] J. M. Culbertson, "Intermediaries and Monetary Theory," *American Economic Review*, *XLVIII* (March, 1958), pp. 119–131.

[5] R. W. Goldsmith, *Financial Intermediaries in the American Economy Since 1900* (New York: Princeton University Press, 1958).

Hamilton, Albert Rees, and Harry G. Johnson (eds.), *Landmarks in Political Economy* (Chicago: The University of Chicago Press, 1962), pp. 592–593. It must be admitted, however, that Milton Friedman in another of his works does succumb to the current orthodoxy and speaks about money as noninterest-bearing debt. Cf. Milton Friedman and Anna Jacobson Schwartz, *A Monetary History of the United States 1867–1960*, (Princeton, N.J.: Princeton University Press, 1963), pp. 649–650.

to articles that deal with commercial banking as a producer[6] of money, not as a middleman or "intermediary."

This makes it clear that the comparison that follows is highly selective in that it covers but a few writers whose analysis we consider to be of key importance and in that we only cover a few dissenting voices. Our sole purpose is to give the reader a very brief review of what some distinguished and influential members of the profession think about money and its role in the wealth equation, not to write a history of this part of doctrine. Consequently, omission should not be interpreted as an expression of disrespect; inclusion, we trust, will give no offense.

Commodity Money

Discussions of commodity money have dwindled to a trickle in recent years. This lack of interest is understandable, since this type of money has almost disappeared from all but international monetary relations; it is also unfortunate because many arguments based on the money-is-a-debt approach become immediately suspect when translated into commodity money terms.

I. *The Effect on Net Wealth.*   Most of the writers who do consider commodity money have no trouble assigning to it the attribute of genuinely belonging to the net wealth of the community. For example, Gottfried Haberler asserts that for institutional reasons even ". . . what is nominally credit money may be safely treated *as 'real' money like gold"* [emphasis ours].[7] Similarly, J. R. Hicks

---

[6] To the term "producer" we give the meaning of someone who genuinely increases the net money supply and net wealth of the community. We do not give it the emasculated meaning of someone who creates one asset by extinguishing another; a mere intermediary "borrow[ing] loanable funds . . . issuing indirect securities in exchange . . . transmit[ting] the borrowed funds to spending units . . ., receiving in exchange direct securities. . . ." (J. G. Gurley and E. S. Shaw, "Financial Aspects of Economic Development," *American Economic Review,* XLV (September, 1955), pp. 519–520.

[7] Gottfried Haberler, *Prosperity and Depression* (Geneva: League of Nations, 1941), p. 500.

points out that wealth will change and hence the wealth effect will occur in the case of "hard" money of whatever kind, especially metallic money.[8] Thus these authors and many others feel that commodity money is, indeed, a part of net wealth, and hence we may express the effect of a change in commodity money as follows:

$$dw = d\frac{M_c}{P} \qquad [8.1]$$

where (w) denotes *net* wealth and (M_c) commodity money. Lately, this separation of commodity money from what is called "credit money" seems to have disappeared. Thus, we find Harry G. Johnson in his review of monetary theory asking what appears to be merely a rhetorical question whether commodity money is not the same as fiat money, both debts of society.[9] This question must be answered in the negative. Consider, for example, an increase in the quantity of commodity money accomplished by a new gold discovery. Such an increase is then considered by the gold purchasers to be an increase in their assets. But, if the gold miners consider the gold sold as their liability, then the change in the net wealth of the community must be zero:

$$dw = d\frac{M_c}{P} - d\frac{D}{P} = 0 \qquad [8.2]$$

where (D) is the value of the debts of the society. The gold miners surely do not view the situation in this manner; does the society as a whole? The new gold gives the producer or the purchaser claims on the wealth of other members of the society—but so does any new wealth item produced, say, a machine. It, too, can be sold at the market price. Clearly, this is not a useful way of viewing the situation, since it implies that the total wealth of society is, by definition, zero. It also might be pointed out that the *net* change in net wealth resulting from gold production (or any other production)

[8] J. R. Hicks, *Value and Capital* (London: Oxford University Press, 1948), p. 334.
[9] Harry G. Johnson, *op. cit.*, p. 343.

is negative because resources that are used up only result in the zero change in wealth alleged in equation [8.2]. We submit that all this shows clearly that the proposition that commodity money is offset by a debt of equal size cannot stand scrutiny.

II. *The Effect on Economically Relevant Wealth.* The writers who consider commodity money to be a part of the net wealth of the community, of course, also think that it is a part of economically relevant wealth. Those who deny this money the character of net wealth by claiming that it is a debt are silent on this topic; however, since they do consider even fiat money to be a part of economically relevant wealth, they must be, *a fortiori*, giving this characteristic to commodity money. Hence, in all cases with which we are familiar,

$$dw^* = d\frac{M_c}{P} \qquad\qquad [8.3]$$

where the symbol (w^*) expresses the gross wealth concept the authors have discussed and which they feel affects the behavior of the decision-making units—*economically relevant wealth.*

Fiat Money

In the case of commodity money, no attention is being paid to the method chosen by the producer of this money to dispose of his product. In contrast, in the fiat money case the current literature places great emphasis on the method selected by the fiat money producer to dispose of his product. The reader is given to understand that it makes a basic analytical difference whether fiat money is sold, say, for goods and services or, say, for titles to streams of income (e.g., fiat money called "outside money" and fiat money called "inside money"). It appears intuitively obvious that such distinctions are no more warranted than would be a decision to call gold that a gold miner sells for goods and services "outside gold" and gold that he sells for titles to such goods "inside gold" and to conclude that these "two" golds have two different characteristics. And indeed, the analysis that we shall present will prove that the method of introduction of fiat money into the economy, while it does have some secondary distribution effects with which the literature does not concern itself, is of no consequence for a decision of whether fiat money is a part of the net wealth of the community. To furnish such proof we must structure our discussion on the basis of the various methods of introduction of fiat money stressed by the current literature. In what follows, we shall separately consider the case of a gift of fiat money, the case of a sale of fiat money for goods and services, and the sale of fiat money for securities, both domestic and foreign.

Production and Gift of Fiat Money

In its outright form, this may be considered to be a rare case empirically; but if its importance is judged by the amount of discussion it receives in the literature, it must be considered the most prevalent of all methods of money introduction. For example, Lloyd A. Metzler, in his paper which contributed so much to the exploration of the nature of the wealth effect, assumes that the quantity of money changes ". . . by a currency reform in which one unit of new money is exchanged for two units of old."[10] Robert A. Mundell, who followed Metzler and introduced some improvements in his analysis, also treats the simple case of money introduction as a gift.[11] In other works the simple case of a gift of money is not explicit in the analysis, but is assumed implicitly. This point becomes obvious only when we read the passages considering the effects of the monetary change, for it then becomes apparent that no consideration is given to the possibility that the government may have acquired and the public lost some resources through the

[10] Lloyd A. Metzler, "Wealth, Saving, and the Rate of Interest," *Journal of Political Economy*, *LIX* (April, 1951), p. 97.
[11] Robert A. Mundell, "The Public Debt, Corporate Taxes, and the Rate of Interest," *Journal of Political Economy*, *LXVIII* (December, 1960), p. 623.

introduction of money.[12] For example, whenever Don Patinkin in his
First Edition discusses a change in the quantity of money other
than a purchase of securities (open-market operations), he always
specifies his problem along the following lines: "Assume now that
this initial equilibrium is disturbed by a doubling of the amount of
money. This causes . . ."[13] Since he never specifies any other change
that accompanies a change in money, a gift of money must be the case
he has in mind. In his Second Edition he continues this practice.[14]
However, in one section he suggests that his discussion might not be
a full analysis of the gift of money case but an incomplete analysis
of some more complex sale of money cases. He writes that an analysis
of a simple case of an increase in the quantity of money is a "com-
parative-static analysis," whereas "the dynamic impact of an
increase in the quantity of money depends on the way in which it
is introduced into the economy"[15] and, in the next eight pages,
proceeds to consider "the dynamic" problem of the method used to
introduce money into circulation. It might not be inappropriate to
add that here he does not seem to do full justice to comparative
statics that can, surely, handle a gift of money (or cheese) as efficiently
as a sale of money (or cheese). Another example of an analysis based
on a gift of money is one of the variants of the Gurley and Shaw
"outside-money case"; a variant that we shall denote as Outside
Money Case I.[16] In this case, money is given away through the
device of transfer payments.[17] This, of course, is a case of money
distinct from the Metzler case. Metzler gives money to the existing

[12] This point is well recognized in inflation theory; e.g., Martin Bailey, "The
Welfare Cost of Inflationary Finance," *Journal of Political Economy*, *LXIV*
(April, 1956), pp. 93–110.

[13] Don Patinkin, *Money, Interest, and Prices*, 1st ed. (New York: Harper &
Row, 1956), pp. 192 ff.

[14] Don Patinkin, *Money, Interest, and Prices*, 2d ed. (New York: Harper &
Row, 1956, 1965), pp. 44, 74, 259, 266, 275, 276, 281, and 329.

[15] Don Patinkin, *ibid.*, pp. 236–237.

[16] Gurley and Shaw treat all their Outside money cases as being identical but,
as we shall show, all are economically dissimilar.

[17] John G. Gurley and Edward S. Shaw, *Money in a Theory of Finance* (Washington, D.C.: The Brookings Institution, 1960), p. 15.

holders of money in proportion to their money assets; in the Outside Money Case I, the transfers presumably go to consumers whose incomes are below some level, or who are unemployed, or whom the state finds deserving for some other reason. James Tobin has gently chided the profession for concentrating so many of its guns on the money give-away case:

> Sometimes we are asked to imagine that everyone wakes up to find his cash stock has doubled overnight ... This mental experiment is harmless and instructive, provided its results are not considered indicative of changes in the money supply engineered by normal central bank procedures. The overnight miracle increases equally money stocks and net worth; the gremlins who bring the money are not reported to take away bonds or IOU's.[18]

However, in defense of the profession, this case does adequately describe currency reforms and also gives us a starting point for the discussion of the other types of money introduction.

I. *The Effect on Net Wealth.* From among the writers whom we have discussed in this section, only Lloyd A. Metzler does not refer to the fiat-money-is-a-debt argument at all: it may be that he overlooked it, it may be that he assumed it as given and left it to the reader to make his own qualifications, it may be that he disagreed with the argument.[19] Should the last assumption be the true one, his net wealth equation would read

$$dw = d\frac{M}{P} \qquad [8.4]$$

Most of the current writers in monetary theory do, however, deny

[18] James Tobin, "Money, Capital, and Other Stores of Value," *American Economic Review, LI* (May, 1961), p. 29.

[19] It should be noted that in the literature Lloyd A. Metzler is depicted as holding the view that the money he discusses is a debt; indirectly by R. A. Mundell (see note 11) and explicitly by Arnold Collery and Harry G. Johnson (see note 41). In Metzler's article we found no justification whatever for this imputation.

to fiat money the character of net wealth. Thus, for instance, Don Patinkin writes in both his First Edition and Second Edition:

> We note finally that, in a certain sense, the real-balance effect is itself a distribution effect. For our fiat paper money is the debt of the government. . . .[20]

Precisely the same argument is used by Gurley and Shaw when they discuss their Outside Money cases:

> Given the nominal amount of this outside money, its real value varied inversely with the price level, and each such change in its real value represented a *wealth transfer* [emphasis ours] between the private sectors and government.[21]

James Tobin also states that "The means of payment of a country— at least in part governmental in origin—are generally demand 'debts' of the central government."[22] If we, despite all our misgivings, take the money-is-a-debt argument as given, the conclusion with respect to the gift of money case then is that it cannot cause a change in the net wealth of the community. The change in net wealth is

$$dw = d\frac{M}{P} - d\frac{D}{P} = 0 \qquad [8.5]$$

where (D) is the value of the debt of the fiat money issuer.[23]

II. *The Effect on Economically Relevant Wealth.* The representatives of the *New View* realize that fiat money, even though it is asserted not to be net wealth, does have economic consequences. To account for these they introduce fiat money into the economically

---

[20] Patinkin, 1st ed., *op. cit.*, pp. 202–203, and 2d ed., *op. cit.*, p. 288.

[21] Gurley and Shaw, *op. cit.*, p. 73.

[22] James Tobin, *op. cit.*, p. 29.

[23] Even though the quotations are quite clear, to avoid any chance of confusion, we might stress that the results shown in the equation above are not due to any eventual changes in the level of prices that the change in the quantity of money may cause. Net wealth is *not* said to remain unchanged because some subsequent, equilibrating change in prices cuts down the real value of money. Net wealth is said not to change because, irrespective of the level of prices, the assets of fiat money by the owner are claimed to be at all times precisely offset by the debts of the issuer of fiat money.

relevant wealth equation by making special assumptions about the
economic behavior of various decision makers in the economy.
For instance, Don Patinkin justifies his analysis that assigns economic
consequences to changes in fiat money by stating:

> Thus the preceding analysis has been based on the tacit—though
> realistic—assumption that the government, alone of all economic
> units, is unconcerned with the real value of its outstanding (non-
> interest bearing) debt, and plans its demand for commodities
> accordingly.[24]

Gurley and Shaw face the same problem because they use the same
justification as Patinkin for introducing their outside money into
the relevant wealth equation. They discuss the assumptions that
underlie their conclusions with respect to the effects of changes in
the real quantity of fiat money and state that the resulting "wealth
transfer affected the private demands for money, goods, and labor
but it was assumed not to affect government demand."[25] In all the
gift-of-money cases cited above, the change in the level of economically relevant wealth, before the price level has adjusted to the new
quantity of money, is simply the real value of the money gift,
namely:

$$dw^* = d\frac{M}{P} \qquad\qquad [8.6]$$

and is equal to the change in wealth which accompanied an increase
in commodity money. This conclusion is, as in the case of commodity
money, independent of the money-is-a-debt argument, since the
supporters of this argument usually assume that the issuer of money
ignores the level of his debts in making his decisions.[26] Hence,
even if the debts of the issuer of money increased by an amount

---

[24] Patinkin, 1st ed., *op. cit.*, p. 203, and 2d ed., *op. cit.*, p. 288.

[25] Gurley and Shaw, *op. cit.*, p. 73.

[26] Actually, [8.8] could have been more generally written as $dW = dM - kdD$;
where D is the outstanding debt of the issuer and k is a constant varying
between 0 and 1, depending on the extent to which the issuer of money
behaves like the remainder of the community. k will be unity if the issuer
considers his debts exactly like any other decision-making unit, and zero
if he ignores them.

equal to the increase in the wealth holdings of the nonissuers, only the change in nonissuers' wealth affects economic behavior.

Production and Sale of Fiat Money for Goods

This is the usual method used by the government to introduce fiat money into the economy: the government uses the newly created money for direct purchases of goods and services. All such purchases may equally well—and more instructively—be called sales[27] of money for wealth. An example of an explicit discussion of money introduced in this manner is the Gurley-Shaw Outside Money II. The authors state that one method of introducing outside money is the purchase ". . . of goods and services . . ." by the issuer; in our terms, the sale of money for the services of human and nonhuman capital or for the capital itself.[28] However, the statement that money is being sold for goods and services tells us but half of what we need to know to analyze this case. We are told that the public gained money assets, but we do not know what happens to the goods and services purchased by the producer of money. Several major possibilities appear:

1. The producer of fiat money is a part of the private sector.

2. The producer of fiat money is the government. Then this government is faced with the necessity of deciding what to do with the goods and services it has acquired. It may increase its own use of resources, it may decrease taxes, or it may distribute the goods purchased as subsidies in kind. Gurley and Shaw seem to consider this last case when they write:

[27] Perhaps the reason for much of the confusion concerning the sale of money emanates from the fact that few, if any, governments sell money directly but most resort to such subterfuges as selling bonds (debt) to their central banks (buying money from their central banks). Also, there seems to be an aversion to term anything a sale unless the thing used for the purchase is money. Hence money, simply by convention, cannot be sold. But isn't any "barter" really a "sale" of one item for another, our conventional modes of speech notwithstanding?

[28] Gurley and Shaw, *op. cit.*, p. 73.

So far as its [the government's] spending displaces private spending, there is no effect on private incomes but private money balances gain.[29]

3. Another possibility, if the government is the producer of fiat money, is that it will decide to "sterilize the goods it purchased"; throw the goods into the sea or bury the goods in a Fort Knox. Gurley and Shaw, in their Outside Money Case III, are assuming case (3), since in one of their several descriptions of what they call *the* outside money case they write: ". . . outside money [is] based on the monetary system's holding of gold . . ."[30]

I. *The Effect on Economically Relevant Wealth.* There are three cases that merit consideration when fiat money is sold for goods:

1. A private producer of fiat money gains goods and services; the buyers gain money assets. Thus the net effect of this transaction on the economically relevant wealth is merely

$$dw^* = d\frac{M}{P} \tag{8.7}$$

2. The producer of fiat money is the government and the proceeds are distributed in some fashion. Then the change in economically relevant wealth will be

$$dw^* = d\frac{M}{P} - d\frac{y}{r} + \left[-d\frac{t}{r}, d\frac{u}{r}, d\frac{y_g}{r}\right] \tag{8.8}$$

where dt, du, and dy_g stand for the permanent income equivalents of the changes in taxes, subsidies, and government output of goods and services, respectively (they are separated by commas in [8.8] to indicate that any one or all may change as long as the total change does not exceed dy). Any one of the three, of course, benefits the public: the first two directly, the last inevitably because whatever the government produces, it produces—by

---

[29] Gurley and Shaw, *ibid.*, p. 29.
[30] Gurley and Shaw, *ibid.*, p. 135.

definition—for the public. Assuming that the public is indifferent as to the form in which it receives its income,

$$-t + u + y_g = y \qquad [8.9]$$

the negative second term in equation [8.8] will be precisely offset by the positive third term[31] so that the net change in the economically relevant wealth is, again,

$$dw^* = d\frac{M}{P} \qquad [8.10]$$

Should the public value the income yielded by private goods more (less) highly than it values any one of the three alternative income transfers,

$$-t + u + y_g < y \qquad [8.11]$$

then all we can say about the change in the economically relevant wealth is

$$0 < dw^* \lessgtr d\frac{M}{P} \qquad [8.12]$$

Taking the simpler case of [8.10], there might be one thing that puzzles the reader. Money is sold for goods; that is, these goods have a positive price. Yet, after the transaction is completed, the private sector has, by the equation just quoted, no less non-monetary wealth (and income) than before. Shouldn't the private sector then be willing to sell the goods it owns for *any* price: negative, zero, positive, infinite? The explanation is simple. No specific seller of wealth for money has any assurance that it will be *he* who will get the tax decrease, the subsidy, or the additional government output that the wealth he is selling will make possible. For all he knows, someone else may be the beneficiary of the

---

[31] Don Patinkin, in discussing the same issue in his Second Edition, concludes that an exogenous supply of bonds (third term in [8.8]) simultaneously represents an offsetting exogenous demand (second term in [8.8]) and concludes that "The government is a veil" which either ignores the first term of equation [8.8] or asserts that the public ignores the Outside money and thus conflicts with the whole of Patinkin's analysis of this Outside money.

government largess. This, of course, also shows that even though the economically relevant wealth equations expressing the gift of money (equation [8.6]) and the sale of money for goods (equation [8.10]) are identical, their sameness tends to hide the fact that in the case of a sale of money there is an accompanying redistribution of nonmonetary wealth within the private sector. If we consider such distribution significant, it would be better to hold on to equation [8.8] rather than to use equation [8.10].

3. The government decides to sterilize the goods it purchased by throwing the goods into the sea or burying the goods in a Fort Knox. Then the change in the economically relevant wealth will allegedly be

$$dw^* = d\frac{M}{P} - dR = 0 \qquad [8.13]$$

where dR is the value of the goods given up for the money. Since the goods are sterilized or disposed of, we need not consider the additional problem of the disposition of the proceeds of the sale. The burial at sea is a clear case. Whether the Fort Knox case is represented better by equation [8.8] or [8.13] depends on our evaluation of the underlying situation. In a closed economy, [8.13] appears more appropriate; should any time in the future the discovery be made that these "reserves" are unnecessary, we might—from the standpoint of current economic relevance— ignore them until then. In an open economy, these assets may very well represent (publicly owned) stores of value held against some future national emergency; equation [8.8] then depicts the same case better.

II. *The Effect on Net Wealth.* Should we accept the money-is-a-debt argument, we would have to revise the economically relevant wealth equations [8.7], [8.8], and [8.13] by adding to them the debt term to obtain an expression for the net wealth equation:

$$dw = d\frac{M}{P} - d\frac{y}{r} + \left[-d\frac{t}{r}, d\frac{u}{r}, d\frac{y_g}{r}\right] - d\frac{D}{P} = 0 \qquad [8.14]$$

where the bracketed term is interpreted as in [8.8], or

$$dw = d\frac{M}{P} - dR - d\frac{D}{P} = -dR \qquad [8.15]$$

If we reject the money-is-a-debt argument, as, we believe, must be done, the difference between the net and economically relevant wealth equations disappears. The relevant equations [8.7], [8.8], and [8.13] are, simultaneously, the net wealth equations.

Production and Sale of Fiat Money for Securities

We have now reached the most common type of money sale; the familiar open-market operations fall in this category. Here the producer of money sells his product not for real wealth or current services of equal value but for titles to a stream of income, securities. Economically it cannot make any difference (but may cause some gains in efficiency) whether the purchaser obtains physical possession of a piece of wealth or whether he leaves physical possession undisturbed and accepts instead written proof that he is the owner—accepts a "security." However, since in the literature a distinction is being made between a sale of money for goods and services and for securities, we now briefly cover the security case and discuss separately the sale of money for government securities, private securities, and foreign securities. In the discussion, we assume that the securities are perpetuities; this does not affect the argument and makes the arithmetic simpler. If realism is desired, it is easy to transform any specific security yielding an income stream of finite length into a perpetuity yielding the permanent income equivalent of this stream.

GOVERNMENT SECURITIES. Consider the sale of money by the producer of fiat money for government-produced financial assets. In the United States, this type of money sale is the most important one, for it is the primary means by which the government affects the quantity of money outstanding. Gurley and Shaw cover this possibility with the Outside Money Case IV. In the same passage in which they consider the possibility of Outside Money III backed by gold, they also speak about "outside money [is] based ... on government securities ..."[32] They impose the restriction that the producer of money be a separate monetary monopoly, but this restriction does not affect the analysis except that it clouds the money-is-a-debt issue. Patinkin also considers the sale of money for debt of the government. He bases his analysis on the following changes that result from such a sale: "... the *increase* in the amount of money is necessarily accompanied by a corresponding *decrease* in the government bonds outstanding."[33]

I. *The Effect on Economically Relevant Wealth.* These changes, according to Patinkin, result in the following changes in the level of the economically relevant wealth:

$$dw^* = d\frac{M}{P} - d\frac{g}{r} = 0 \qquad [8.16]$$

where (g) stands for government interest payments, so that any effect from the transaction is said to come from a portfolio effect. However, as in the previous case, the income stream from the proceeds of the money sale has become lost; we must remember that the government now needs to pay less interest on its outstanding debt, since it has been reduced. Therefore, it requires less taxes to finance these lower interest payments and, if we take this into account, then the term representing the decrease in the public's asset holdings in equation [8.16] disappears.[34] Thus, the correct change in the level of economically relevant wealth is

$$dw^* = d\frac{M}{P} - d\frac{g}{r} + \left(-d\frac{t}{r}\right) = d\frac{M}{P} \qquad [8.17]$$

[32] Gurley and Shaw, *op. cit.*, p. 135.
[33] Patinkin, 1st ed., *op. cit.*, p. 208.
[34] That is, this term will disappear as long as the rates at which human and nonhuman income streams are capitalized are identical.

In his Second Edition, Don Patinkin realized the omission of taxes and states a more limited proposition:

> [If] individuals do not discount their future tax liability at all . . . an open-market purchase in this case does not *initially* . . . generate a wealth effect . . . for it merely replaces bonds by an equivalent amount of money. . . .[35]

If they do discount the tax load fully, he points out that this leads to the results indicated above by equation [8.17]: his system reduces to one in which bonds may be ignored.[36] Note that [8.17] above is identical to the change in the level of economically relevant wealth which has occurred in the gift of money case and in the sale of money for goods and services case.

II. *The Effect on Net Wealth.*   If we accept the money-is-a-debt argument for this case, we again must conclude that the effect of such a sale on the level of net wealth is zero, since the increase in the monetary assets of the public will be exactly offset by an equal increase in the debts of the government. Thus, the change in net wealth will be equal to

$$dw = d\frac{M}{P} - d\frac{D}{P} + d\frac{t}{r} - d\frac{g}{r} = 0 \qquad [8.18]$$

where $\left(d\frac{t}{r}\right)$ is the capitalized value of the tax reduction which is necessarily equal to the value of government security purchases if the rates of interest used to capitalize human and nonhuman income are the same. On the other hand, if we reject the money-is-a-debt approach, the debts of the government are unaffected by the sale of money and the change in the level of net wealth is again equal to the change in the level of economically relevant wealth, namely:

$$dw = d\frac{M}{P} \qquad [8.19]$$

---

[35] Don Patinkin, *Money, Interest, and Prices*, 2d ed. (New York: Harper & Row, 1956, 1965), p. 294.

[36] ". . . system [3]–[6] above reduces to the already familiar one of Chapter X: 1." (*Ibid.*, p. 294.)

PRIVATE SECURITIES. Suppose that the fiat money producer instead of selling his output for his own securities sells it for somebody else's securities. Lloyd A. Metzler in his article already quoted has the government purchase titles to private wealth. He calls such purchases open-market operations, despite the fact that this term is normally used to cover only the purchases of government securities. Analytically, however, there can be no objection to this because the change involved is insignificant: it makes no difference whether the government sells its product, fiat money, not to reduce its obligations to pay income but to increase its rights to receive income. On the other hand, Gurley and Shaw feel that the difference is fundamental and to stress it they give the government fiat money used for this purchase the name Inside Money. They describe this money as follows:

> Money is still [as in the case of outside money] government debt, but it is issued in payment for government purchases of private securities. It is a claim of consumers and firms against the world outside the private sectors, but it is counterbalanced by private debt to the world outside, that is, to government in this model. It is based on internal debt, so we refer to it as "inside" money.[37]

There is a difference between the Metzler case and the Inside Money case in that the former is based on securities expressed in real terms and the latter, in nominal terms. That, however, is of no import in a discussion in which only the initial effects of money creation are given attention, and it requires only slight change in analysis when equilibrium of the system is discussed.

I. *The Effect on Economically Relevant Wealth.* The sale of money for privately issued securities results in an increase in the monetary assets of the public and a reduction in their privately issued financial assets by an equal amount. If the analysis were carried no further, then the change in the level of economically relevant wealth would be

$$dw^* = d\frac{M}{P} - d\frac{y}{r} = 0 \qquad [8.20]$$

[37] Gurley and Shaw, *op. cit.*, p. 73.

where $\left(d\dfrac{y}{r}\right)$ is the capitalized value of the permanent income stream yielded by the privately issued securities and is precisely equal to the value of the money sold. Gurley and Shaw do not carry it any further, as this quotation indicates:

> Suppose that an initial equilibrium position is disturbed by an open-market operation in which the Banking Bureau buys bonds from consumer portfolios to increase the nominal stock of money. The immediate result is that, at the initial bond rate and price level . . . consumers' portfolios are over-supplied with real money and under-supplied with real bonds.[38]

Don Patinkin in his Second Edition adopted the Inside Money case completely; however, he has the private banking system rather than the government creating inside money. Like Gurley and Shaw, he states that a change in the quantity of inside money in the hands of the public will be precisely offset by an opposite change in the quantity of bonds held: ". . . a (say) decrease in the quantity of money influences the system [13]–[15] not through the wealth effect, but through the opposite and matching changes directly generated in the excess supplies of bonds and money."[39]

However, if in the Gurley and Shaw case we account for the increased income of the government by decreasing taxes or increasing subsidies by the same amount (or if we, in the Patinkin case, account for the increased income the owners of banks realize from the securities they purchased for the Inside Money they created) the change in the economically relevant wealth actually is

$$dw^* = d\,\frac{M}{P} - d\,\frac{y}{r} + \left[-\,d\,\frac{t}{r},\, d\,\frac{u}{r},\, d\,\frac{y_g}{r},\, d\,\frac{y_b}{r}\right] \qquad [8.21]$$

where the bracketed term is interpreted as in [8.8] and all the symbols are the same as before and dy_b expresses, in the Patinkin case, the

[38] Gurley and Shaw, *ibid.*, p. 77.
[39] Patinkin, *op. cit.*, 2d ed., p. 298. For another example, cf. George Horwich, *Money, Capital, and Prices* (Homewood, Ill.: Richard D. Irwin, Inc., 1964), p. 88.

extra income realized by the bank proprietors. Thus a full statement of the consequences of the open-market operations with "inside money" should read:

The immediate result is that, at the initial bond rate and price level, the consumers' portfolios are

(a) oversupplied with real money,

(b) undersupplied with real bonds, *and*

(c) in the Gurley and Shaw case, oversupplied with capitalized value of tax reductions or, in Patinkin's case, oversupplied with additional capitalized yield of bank securities.

It is worth emphasizing that, completely irrespective of the issue of whether money is or is not a debt, once full account is taken of *all* income changes resulting from a change in money, all differences among government-created Inside Money (Gurley-Shaw), bank-created Inside Money (Patinkin), *and* government-created Outside Money (Gurley-Shaw and Patinkin) disappear.[40] The three apparently distinct cases are just one single case of the public gaining the use of money and the money producer (public or private) gaining the use of whatever the public gave up in payment. The distinction, so much emphasized by Gurley and Shaw and by the literature dealing with their analysis would have never arisen if the authors had considered the effects of the sale of money on government revenues and expenditures.

II. *The Effect on Net Wealth.* Since the effect of this case on the level of economically relevant wealth is identical to the analysis of the sale of money for government-issued securities, and since the only difference between economically relevant wealth and net wealth lies

---

[40] The Inside Money Case does assume a purchase of securities fixed in nominal terms; but so does the Outside Money Case IV. In addition, this refinement has no substantive distinction. Others have also considered the additional problems that are caused by securities fixed in nominal terms (cf. Don Patinkin, 1st ed., *op. cit.*, p. 205). Besides, this refinement is irrelevant for our present discussion, since here—as Gurley and Shaw themselves put it— we are considering but the initial consequences of a sale of money: "the immediate result, . . . at the initial bond rate and price level. . . ." (Gurley and Shaw, *op. cit.*, p. 77).

in the offsetting debt of the government which arises in the money-is-a-debt approach, this case is identical to the sale of money for government-issued securities. Thus, the change in the level of net wealth for the money-is-a-debt approach is

$$dw = d\frac{M}{P} - d\frac{D}{P} + \left(-d\frac{t}{r}\right) - d\frac{y}{r} = 0 \qquad [8.22]$$

and the change in the level of net wealth for the money-is-a-net-asset approach is

$$dw = d\frac{M}{P} + \left(-d\frac{t}{r}\right) - d\frac{y}{r} = d\frac{M}{P} \qquad [8.23]$$

Gottfried Haberler, in his discussion of the very same problem, pointed out that, if prices subsequently change proportionately with the change in nominal money and wipe out the first term in equation [8.21], the public's loss of wealth will be measured by the second term and the government's gain, by the third term: a perfectly correct statement. Arnold Collery misunderstood Haberler's argument and criticized him for saying that money is a debt and that an increase in the price level will cause the public to lose (first term in equation [8.22]) and the government to gain a decrease in its debt (second term in the same equation). Syed Ahmad sprang to the defense of the argument that Haberler did not make. By now, this nonexistent statement by Haberler is so well established as a fact that it is being used (e.g., by Harry G. Johnson in his survey of monetary theory) to depict Haberler as a supporter of the dominant view. This canard should be laid to rest.[41]

FOREIGN SECURITIES.   This case is rarely discussed in the literature; Gurley and Shaw, however, do cover it in the Outside Money Case V. Besides transfer payments, purchases of goods and services, securities, and gold, outside money may also be ". . . based on the monetary

---

[41] Gottfried Haberler, "The Pigou Effect Once More," *LX* (June, 1952), p. 245; Arnold Collery, "A Note on the Saving-Wealth Relation," *LXVIII* (October, 1960), p. 509; Syed Ahmad, "The Saving-Wealth Relation," *LXX* (June, 1962), p. 287: all above, *The Journal of Political Economy*. Harry G. Johnson, "Monetary Theory and Policy," *American Economic Review, LII* (June, 1962), p. 341.

system's holdings of . . . foreign securities. . . ."[42] The economic consequences of this method of disposing of fiat money depend on the purpose followed by the foreign seller. He may be purchasing fiat money of another country to use either as reserve backing for his own currency, or as an internationally acceptable medium of exchange, or he may be merely intending to purchase in the country producing the fiat money in question some other goods.

The first two cases of purchases of fiat money for use outside the issuing country are simple ones. Indeed, they are so simple that it will prove extremely instructive to give them somewhat more detailed attention. As long as the fiat money remains outside the issuing country, this country has gained income-yielding foreign securities and lost nothing: its income and wealth must be bigger than they were before. The temptation then becomes especially strong to assert that this is simply due to an interest-free loan by another country, the evidence of which, the debt certificate, is the fiat money. Yet, precisely here the money-is-a-debt argument is even more untenable than in the case of domestic sales of fiat money. A loan of a given resource necessarily means that the lender loses a resource and a borrower gains it. An international purchase of fiat money is—even more clearly than a domestic purchase—neither a charitable gesture nor something forced upon the purchaser by the legislative power of the local government.[43] It is an ordinary business

---

[42] Gurley and Shaw, *op. cit.*, p. 135.

[43] Joseph A. Schumpeter, *History of Economic Analysis* (New York: Oxford University Press, 1954), p. 1090, describes this strange theory of the value of money as follows: "In Germany what may be described as tempest in a teapot was raised by Knopp's *State Theory of Money*. This book presented a theory of money that turns upon the adage: Money is the Creature of Law." We mention it here because recently this theory appears to have experienced some revival. Albert G. Hart, Nicholas Kaldor, and Jan Tinbergen in their article, "International Commodity Problems" (U.N. Conference on Trade and Development, E/CONF.46/P/7, February 17, 1964), p. 8, state that "within any one nation with a "managed paper currency" . . . the acceptability of the obligations of the central bank is backed up by the power of the government to define the rules as to what constitutes "legal tender" and to put substance into those rules by deciding in what form to accept payment of taxes."

transaction in the course of which the foreign buyer gives up his assets to gain the use of something that is equally valuable to him— the use of fiat money. This money *must* be yielding him an income, on the margin, as high as the securities sacrificed to purchase this asset, this net wealth. The foreign buyer of fiat money surely did not lose, and his own voluntary act of purchase is the best evidence of it; the domestic producer of fiat money demonstrably gained. Can there be any doubt that this increase in fiat money represents a net increase in world's wealth—an increase received by the fiat money-producing country? The only thing that tends to confuse this conclusion is the fact that this increase is reversible. The country that purchased the money may reverse the transaction, sell the fiat money back, and thus give an appearance that "a loan is being called." Is, however, today's wealth to be judged by possible but unforeseen changes in demand that may happen tomorrow? All that the right of the holding country to reverse the transaction signifies is that all owners of monetary wealth—as do all owners of other wealth in existence today— have the power and the ability to destroy this wealth tomorrow by not desiring it any more. If all economic units, to take an extreme case, decided to quit using money, money would of course cease to be wealth; if all economic units ceased watching TV, all the wealth consisting of TV-stations and TV-sets would cease to be wealth. The former case proves that money is a debt and not net wealth no more and no better than the latter case proves that TV-sets and stations are a debt and not net wealth.

   I. *The Effect on Economically Relevant Wealth.* If the foreign purchaser of fiat money desires to hold it as reserves or to provide himself with a means of exchange in international trade, the fiat money-producing country simply gains the income y_a yielded by foreign securities:

$$dw^* = d\frac{y_a}{r} \qquad [8.24]$$

From the standpoint of the foreign country that buys the fiat money,

$$\dot{w}^* = d\frac{M}{P} - d\frac{y_a}{r} = 0 \qquad [8.25]$$

The change in the world's wealth is, of course, the sum of equations [8.24] and [8.25]; in other words, $d\dfrac{M}{P}$.

If the foreign purchaser acquires fiat money merely to spend it in the issuing country, the nonmonetary wealth taken out is then exactly offset by wealth represented by foreign securities so that, in the issuing country, the net change in wealth is

$$dw^* = d\frac{M}{P} + d\frac{y_a}{r} - d\frac{y}{r} = d\frac{M}{P} \qquad [8.26]$$

II. *The Effect on Net Wealth.* If we accept the money-is-a-debt argument, the money-producing country gains foreign securities and a debt

$$dw = d\frac{y_a}{r} - d\frac{D}{P} = 0 \qquad [8.27]$$

the foreign country gains money and loses securities, so that its change of wealth is also zero:

$$dw = d\frac{M}{P} - d\frac{y_a}{r} \qquad [8.28]$$

If we reject the debt argument, as we think we must, either the two equations [8.24] and [8.25] or the equation [8.26] express both the net and the gross change in net wealth. Whether the former or the latter is applicable depends, of course, on whether the foreign country holds the money or spends it in the money-producing country.

Bank Money

Economists agree that a true financial intermediary does not add to the net money supply, since it simply acts as a broker for lenders and borrowers. In this way it is no different from a stockbroker, who cannot be said to add anything to the quantity of a given stock outstanding, but is simply engaged in the act of bringing buyers and sellers together. He may, however, by his very existence and by the brokerage services he offers stimulate people to issue more stock than they would issue otherwise; in this, indirect, manner he may be said to "create" stock. Leaving this indirect effect aside, all that financial intermediaries do is to redistribute, temporarily, the existing monetary wealth. They themselves add nothing to wealth, except for the capitalized value of the income that the society pays for their services.

Recently, there seems to be a move afoot to put commercial banks into the class of true financial intermediaries and thus remove demand deposits from the net money supply and net wealth. For example, Gurley and Shaw assert that theirs is a gross money concept defined as follows:

> We count as money any debts of the monetary system that are means of payment generally accepted on markets for labor services, current output, and primary securities. Thus we regard the nominal stock of money in the United States as the sum of currency held by spending units and demand deposits subject to check after adjustment for checks drawn but not yet charged against deposit accounts.[44]

They then go on to contrast this gross money doctrine with a net money doctrine asserting that "consolidation eliminates all private domestic financial assets and their offset in private domestic primary debt."[45] Thus, they imply that bank money is a debt and hence not a part of the net wealth of the community and therefore not a part of the net money supply.

Don Patinkin in his First Edition accepts the argument that bank money is not a part of net wealth and goes even further than Gurley and Shaw in that he "largely" removes bank money from the economically relevant wealth equation:

> In particular, we can disregard its [i.e., the price level's] effects in increasing the real value of individuals' demand deposits, for this

---

[44] Gurley and Shaw, *op. cit.*, p. 134.
[45] Gurley and Shaw, *ibid.*, p. 136.

is largely offset by the corresponding increase in the real value of individuals' debts to banks.[46]

On the preceding page, he makes demand deposits a liability of the banking sector while an asset of the households; his reason for ("largely") eliminating bank money from the economically relevant wealth equation is, presumably, his feeling that bank money is obviously a debt and that his assumption that the fiat money producer ignores his debts is inapplicable to private firms. In his Second Edition, he adopts completely the Gurley and Shaw Inside Money analysis except that he disposes of the impotent government, the only task of which is to create Inside Money and engage in open-market operations. He has the banking system create the Inside Money:

> Let us now take account of the fact that in reality most money in a modern economy is of the inside type: that is, based on the debt of endogenous economic units. This in turn is a consequence of the fact that money in such an economy is largely the creation of a private banking system . . . inside money is offset by a corresponding debt to the banking system.[47]

As in Gurley and Shaw, so in the Second Edition of Patinkin "the wealth effect in the form of the real-balance effect is consistently absent from *all* markets."[48] All that is left is a disturbance in the individual's wealth portfolio: "the level of prices is still determinate by virtue of its impact on the *excess* demands for bonds and money."[49] J. R. Hicks goes even further than Patkinkin:

> It is money, not a bond, in the sense that it bears no interest; nevertheless, it merely registers a debt from one of the "individuals" (who may be a bank) in the economy to another. In this

[46] Patinkin, *op. cit.*, 1st ed., p. 204. The specification of the effects of the price change is incomplete and consequently the claim that the effects are self-cancelling is erroneous. However, we discussed this in detail in Chapter 4 of the present book, pp. 95–97ff., and thus it must suffice here to make a reference to those pages.

[47] Patinkin, *op. cit.*, 2d ed., pp. 295–296.

[48] Patinkin, *ibid.*, p. 297.

[49] Patinkin, *ibid.*, p. 298.

case the positive and negative holdings of money must have been initially equal, just as the positive and negative holdings of bonds must certainly have been equal.[50]

Clearly, this excludes banks completely as producers of net money. Therefore, if we accept this argument and still want to have the level of bank money affect economic behavior, we must not use a concept of net wealth but rather some gross wealth concept.

I. *The Effect on Economically Relevant Wealth.* How will an increase in the nominal amount of demand deposits affect the level of economically relevant wealth? If we follow the Gurley and Shaw analysis and use the "gross money concept," we get

$$dw^* = d\frac{M_b}{P} \qquad [8.29]$$

where (M_b) is the level of demand deposits outstanding. If we use Patinkin's First Edition analysis, we get a change which is approximately equal to zero, since he argues that the asset value of the demand deposits is "largely" offset by the value of individuals' debts to the banks:

$$dw^* = d\frac{M_b}{P} - d\frac{D}{P} \simeq 0 \qquad [8.30]$$

Finally, if we follow Hicks' or Patinkin's Second Edition analysis, then the change is identically equal to zero:

$$dw^* = d\frac{M_b}{P} - d\frac{D}{P} = 0 \qquad [8.31]$$

(but the portfolio balance is disturbed and thus some effects follow in any case). Lastly, if we use the analysis presented in Chapter 4 of this book, we see that only a part of the increase in the quantity of demand deposits is an addition to the level of economically relevant wealth, since some of the dominant money must be sterilized

[50] J. R. Hicks, *Value and Capital, op. cit.*, p. 334. He reiterates this position and applies it to fiat money as well in *Capital and Growth* (New York: Oxford University Press, 1965), p. 282.

for use as reserves. Thus, the change in the level of economically
relevant wealth becomes

$$dw^* = d\frac{M_b}{P} - \rho d\frac{M_b}{P} \qquad [8.32]$$

where (ρ) is the reserve ratio so that ($\rho d\, M_b$) is the change in dominant
money required to make the increase in the production and sale of
demand deposits possible.

II. *The Effect on Net Wealth.* Greater uniformity[51] of opinion
exists in the case of the net wealth equations because the analyses

---

[51] Joseph Aschheim, "Commercial Banks and Financial Intermediaries:
Fallacies and Policy Implications," *Journal of Political Economy, LXVII*
(February, 1959), p. 61, may be an exception; however, he is extremely
difficult to classify. He states that demand deposits are money and time
deposits are not "because demand deposits circulate as a widely accepted
means of payment," and time deposits do not. From this he draws the
policy implication that what we call the M-Branches of commercial banks
should be controlled and what we call the D-Branches should be freed
from regulation. Both these views perfectly coincide with the analysis
presented in Chapters 3 through 5 of the present book. However, when
Aschheim's assertion that demand deposits are money meets the Gurley-
Shaw-Tobin assertion that all monies are debts, any chance of a productive
debate disappears since Gurley, Shaw, and Tobin accept the Aschheim
thesis, whereas Aschheim accepts (or at least never objects to) the Gurley-
Shaw-Tobin thesis. Thus James Tobin was able to terminate the debate
by stating: "The means-of-payment characteristic of demand deposits
is indeed a feature differentiating bank liabilities from those of other intermediaries. Insurance against death is equally a feature differentiating life
insurance policies from the obligations of other intermediaries, including
banks. It is not obvious that one kind of differentiation should be singled out
for special analytical treatment."—"Commercial Banks as Creators of
'Money'," in Dean Carson (ed.), *Banking and Monetary Studies* (Homewood,
Ill.: Richard D. Irwin, Inc., 1963), p. 412.

Without analytical proof that the means-of-payment characteristic
differentiates money from debts by making money a part of net wealth,
the issue raised by Aschheim reduces to one of taxonomy; without such
proof there is, indeed, no reason for singling out any one of the above items
for special analytical or policy treatment. Since Aschheim failed to supply
it and merely asserted his view, his basically correct thesis could not gain
acceptance.

(For a statement almost identical with the one by Tobin, cf. Gurley and
Shaw, *op. cit.*, p. 199.)

used by Gurley and Shaw, Patinkin, and Hicks all result in no change in the level of net wealth as a result of a change in the quantity of bank money. They all agree that this type of money is precisely offset by debts of the public to the banks and that the net wealth equation is the same as equation [8.31]. Only if the money-is-a-debt argument is rejected—and in Chapter 4 we did reject it—do we get a change in the net wealth of the community and, as we have shown, this change is precisely equal to the economically relevant wealth change of equation [8.32]. Once again, when we realize that money is an asset that is not offset by a corresponding debt of equal magnitude, we find that the net wealth equation and the economically relevant wealth equation are one and the same, and both contain demand deposits. Thus, in this analysis—in contrast to the Patinkin and Hicks thesis—these deposits do affect the equilibrium values of the endogenous variables, especially the level of prices and they do so—in contrast to the Gurley and Shaw thesis—without any special assumptions about the behavior of some decision-making units. Using a term that did not exist when the Currency-Banking Controversy was resolved: changes in the level of bank money do, according to the above analysis, lead to a wealth effect.

Conclusion

The issues discussed in the sections dealing with the economically relevant wealth equation are—with the exception of the case of bank money—not of basic empirical importance. All that our discussion has revealed is that in some cases some authors defined a specific type of money in such a way that a change in this money had to involve a change in two or more income streams and that, in their subsequent analysis, they failed to take some of these changes in income streams into account. Necessary amendments, even though bound to change quite seriously the specific analytical results obtained, do not involve any basic issues. But this means that all the writers discussed above (except Patinkin and Hicks as far as the bank money is concerned) agree on one fundamental thing: that the quantity of money and changes in this quantity affect economic behavior and hence the equilibrium level of the endogenous variables.

Basic disagreement does appear in the case of the net wealth equation. The content of this equation, the presence or absence of some type of money, reveals what the author discussed thinks is the reason for the causal relationship shown in the economically relevant wealth equation. In the case of one type of money, commodity money, there is at present disagreement even among the adherents of the dominant theory. In the case of all other types of money, there is general disagreement between the analysis we present in this book and the dominant theory. According to our analysis, *all* money (commodity money, fiat money, central bank money or commercial bank money) in circulation[52] is a part of the net wealth of the community and affects economic behavior because of this. In the opinion of the currently dominant theory all the non-commodity monies have economic consequences merely because some decision makers ignore their debts.

Thus, in summary we may say that (1) there is general agreement—bank money excepted—that a causal relationship exists between money and the equilibrium level of the endogenous variables, and (2) there is a disagreement as to the reasons for this causal relationship. If money is *excluded* from net wealth, this reason must be some asymmetry in the responses of some decision makers—asymmetry not explicable by economic analysis. If money is *included* in the net wealth equation, this reason becomes the perfectly rational and analytically predictable behavior of all decision-making units. However, as long as there is an agreement about the causal relationship, is there any point in attempting to settle the issue of the reason for this relationship? Is an effort to settle the "why" merely a

---

[52] We limit ourselves to these major items, although realizing full well that insofar as the producer of, say, travelers' checks acts as a bank or the banking system—operates with fractional reserves—he also adds to the total money supply and thus to wealth.

manifestation of empirically irrelevant intellectual curiosity—a mere penchant for academic theorizing? We believe that it would be a gross error to argue this way. In any analysis, the theoretically and empirically relevant parts cannot be neatly separated; a confusion in the former is bound to be reflected in a confusion in the latter.

CHAPTER 9

Money As Net Wealth:
A Summary

Thirty years ago, J. R. Hicks complained about the confusion and contradictions we find in monetary theory and suggested a new approach to the profession:

> I should prefer to seek illumination from another point of view— from a branch of economics which is more elementary but, I think, in consequence better developed—the theory of value. . . . It was marginal utility that really made sense in the theory of value; and to come to a branch of economics which does without marginal utility altogether! No wonder there are such difficulties and such differences![1]

It appears that thirty years later monetary theory is worse, rather than better, off. The malady from which it suffers is contained in a nutshell in the following statement by Edward S. Shaw:

> Modern money is a debt . . . of the monetary system—the commercial banks, the Federal Reserve Banks, and the Treasury

[1] J. R. Hicks, "A Suggestion for Simplifying the Theory of Money," in Friedrich A. Lutz and Lloyd W. Mints (eds.), *Readings in Monetary Theory* (Homewood, Ill.: Irwin, 1951), pp. 13–14.

accounts. It is issued to the other sectors ... in payment by the
monetary system for purchase principally of nonmonetary
securities and monetary metals. It is an IOU even though there is
nothing that it promises to pay, no interest to yield to the holder,
and no maturity date.[2]

If proof is needed that Hicks' injunction was not followed, the
above quotation is the quintessence of it. Modern money, based on
purchases of assets for the strange IOU's described above, is, we
submit, completely inexplicable by the theory of value. There is no
conceivable explanation why a consumer should sacrifice his resources in favor of the monetary system—the commercial banks,
the Federal Reserve Banks, and the Treasury accounts—for debt
certificates that promise to pay nothing, yield no interest, and will
never be repaid. The main reason for this state of affairs appears to
be the fact that during these thirty years, one type of money after
another has been excluded from net wealth and has become classified
as a mere asset of some and a liability of others. By now, demand
deposits, fiat money, even—in some cases—commodity money are
denied the character of wealth and are asserted to be merely debts.

As the definition of money changed, so did the definition of the
producers of money. The revolutionary idea of 1820 that banks
produce money came to be universally accepted at the close of the
Currency-Banking Controversy in 1860:

> Bank notes were, of course, universally accepted as a circulating
> medium ... Deposits by this time were almost as universally
> classified as circulating medium as were notes ... Among those
> whose statements justify any inference on the subject the pre-
> ponderance of opinion apparently was that the banks do perma-
> nently increase the aggregate volume of the circulating medium,
> and not merely during periods of boom.[3]

The question of whether bank notes and demand deposits were not

[2] Edward S. Shaw, "Money Supply and Stable Economic Growth," in Neil
H. Jacoby (ed.), *United States Monetary Policy* (New York: Frederick A.
Praeger, 1964), p. 75.
[3] Lloyd W. Mints, *A History of Banking Theory* (Chicago: The University
of Chicago Press, 1945), pp. 178–179.

only circulating medium but also net wealth, no one, as far as we know, discussed, since the influence of wealth on the economy was not under consideration. However, Alfred Marshall is quoted by Mints as saying that checks are a substitute for coin;[4] since coin— produced by an expenditure of resource—was surely considered a part of wealth, it would be surprising if a substitute for it would have been denied this characteristic.

The agreement, true enough, was not unanimous. Even at that time, we are told by Lloyd W. Mints,

> ... the perennial confusion on the subject of whether deposit banks are merely middlemen continued to a discouraging extent. ... most of these men failed to see the distinction between primary and derivative deposits and ... considered banks to be merely intermediaries between borrowers and lenders.[5]

However, what was in 1860 an individual aberration, by 1960 seems to have become the new orthodoxy—orthodoxy strong enough to find shelter in semiofficial documents that typically aspire to express nothing but the general consensus of the profession: the *Radcliffe Report* in Britain and the *Report* of the Commission on Money and Credit in the United States. In both of them, banks are once again mere middlemen distinguished from a car rental agency merely by the adjective in the term "financial intermediaries." Monetary wealth dissolves in the mass of debts existing in society; inevitably, money producers also disappear in the mass of producers of debt and dealers in debt. By now, it is impossible to find any substantive distinction among a Treasury department, a central bank, a commercial bank, an investment house, a firm producing credit cards, even individual spending units. They *all* are said to be engaged in the production of nominal debt issues.

Bank money is a debt because it is offset on the bank's balance sheet; fiat money is but a limiting case of government interest-bearing debt; commodity money is the same thing even though

---

[4] Lloyd W. Mints, *ibid.*, p. 179.
[5] Lloyd W. Mints, *ibid.*, pp. 179–180.

only by custom, since not by law; bank money is acceptable because
it is convertible into fiat money; fiat money is acceptable because it is
convertible into commodity money; if fiat money is not convertible,
it is acceptable because of government compulsion; fiat money makes
the consumers better off, but does not make the debtor worse off,
since the government can ignore its debts; commercial banks are
private enterprises, but behave like a government and also ignore their
debts; producers of credit cards compete with the government and
the banks, since money and credit cards both give the consumer the
power to demand goods—the list could go on and on, each argument
answering one question and raising many others. The very multi-
plicity and dishomogeneity of all these arguments supporting the
money-is-a-debt hypothesis provides sufficient grounds for sus-
picion. A theory is not necessarily correct because it is simple and
elegant; however, a theory that must be supported from all sides by
such an ungainly maze of scaffolding is extremely likely to be wrong.

More fundamentally, however, the money-is-a-debt argument
places monetary theory in a most difficult position. Difficult *empirically*, because, despite the alleged net nonexistence of money, evidence
keeps indicating that money and changes in it do have major
economic consequences. Difficult *analytically*, since a good that does
not exist—in net terms—cannot have a price; since the reciprocal
of the price of money is the general price level, this price level is also
indeterminate. As Don Patinkin put it succinctly in his Second
Edition:

> ... what we have here is the indeterminacy of Wicksell's "pure
> credit" economy in which all transactions are carried out by
> checks, while banks hold no reserves. The economic interpretation
> of this indeterminacy is straight-forward: in order for the absolute
> price level to be determined by market-equilibrating forces,
> changes in it must impinge on *real* behavior in *some* market—i.e.,
> must create excess demands in some market.[6]

The only way to overcome, simultaneously, both the empirical and

[6] From Don Patinkin, *Money, Interest, and Prices*, 2d ed. (New York:
Harper & Row, 1956, 1965), p. 303.

analytical difficulty seems to be the construction of ever-changing assertions of some asymmetry in the behavior of some economic decision-making units. In the literature, they appear under various names. At times, the asymmetry is asserted, but no special technical name is given to it; at other times, the consequences of it are given the name "the distribution effect"; most recently, they were said to be due to "the fallacy of composition." Regardless of the name, these assertions of asymmetry used to be made with an air of apology. By now, necessity has been converted into virtue and the asymmetry is being elevated to a principle that permeates any economy and our analysis of it:

> But, as viewed by the inhabitants of the nation individually, wealth exceeds the tangible capital stock by the size of what we might term the fiduciary issue. *This is an illusion, but only one of the many fallacies of composition which are basic to any economy or any society* [emphasis ours].[7]

What are these fallacies of composition on which economic analysis is allegedly based?

With respect to fiat money, nowadays fashionably called Outside Money, the customary assumption has been well stated by Don Patinkin:

> Thus the preceding analysis has been based on the tacit—though realistic—assumption that the government, alone of all economic units, is unconcerned with the real value of its outstanding (non-interest-bearing) debt, and plans its demand for commodities accordingly.[8]

If so, then we have the public that responds to changes in the real value of money assets and the government that does not respond to changes in the real value of its debts. First, the empirical fact that changes in the quantity of money do have economic consequences

---

[7] James Tobin, "Money and Economic Growth," *Econometrica, 33* (October, 1965), p. 676.

[8] Patinkin, *op. cit.,* 1st ed., p. 203, and 2d ed., p. 288.

despite the net nonexistence of money thus becomes explained by the differential response of debtors and creditors. Second, by the same token, the general price level becomes determinate, since it now ceases to be a matter of indifference whether the economy—as a unit—has a money-debt worth one dollar or 100 billion dollars. There are, however two difficulties with this approach. First, as Harry G. Johnson pointed out, this makes monetary theory (and the determination of the general price level, we may add) "dependent on adventitious institutional or historical details."[9] Without the government acting in this special manner, or without government, there is no solution. Second, even if Don Patinkin should be correctly describing the behavior of the government, he is clearly in error when he states that the government *alone* acts this way; in economic *relations* there is no such thing as acting alone. No one can ignore his debts unless someone else lets him. Thus the alleged irrationality of the government has its inevitable—and extremely disturbing— counterpart: the irrationality of the consumers themselves. If, in fact, fiat money is a noninterest-bearing bond, what economic mechanism induces the consumers to lend their resources interest-free and thus makes them countenance the government behavior assumed by Patinkin? It is surprising that this assertion of such strange behavior on the part of the private sector has escaped not only criticism but even notice. It might be found barely tolerable to impute to the government actions inexplicable by economic theory because the analysis of the economic behavior of the government is one of the underdeveloped fields in economics. However, the counterpart of this imputation does seem intolerable: presumably rational consumers acquiesce, at a heavy cost to themselves, to this government behavior.

Gurley and Shaw attempted to surmount these difficulties by inventing the concept of Inside Money, accepted by Don Patinkin in his Second Edition. As we have shown in Chapter 8, if *all* income flows are taken into account, there is no difference between Outside and Inside Money. Waving this issue aside, however, the innovation —despite the claims of the authors—does not obviate the need to assert asymmetrical behavior; it merely changes the actors who are assigned the role. As Gurley and Shaw express it, the invention of Inside Money results in the determinacy of the general price level (and, we might add, in the possibility of empirical economic consequences of a change in money) for the following reason:

> Change in the price level from an equilibrium position has no net effect, it is true, on aggregate private wealth, but it does have effects on the composition of this wealth that will tend to drive the price level back to its starting point. Price inflation and deflation have no net effect on aggregate wealth; the distribution effects between private debtors and creditors we are pledged to put aside; but there is still a portfolio mix or diversification effect that makes the price level determinate.[10]

In a numerical example that follows this statement, Gurley and Shaw point out that if prices double, the private sector experiences a change in the ratio of real money to real bonds; thus at the new price level, there will be "excess real demand for money [and] excess real supply of bonds and goods, so that the system is destined to grope its way back to the initial level of prices . . ."[11] This result is due, however, only to the fact that the private sector (households) and the business sector are kept separate, and only the response of the first is considered. Should the business sector have the same behavior as the private sector, or should the consumers realize that they own the business sector and that a change in their portfolio is precisely offset by an opposite change in the portfolio of businesses they own, the Gurley and Shaw solution disintegrates. Instead of improving matters, it makes them worse: it is easier to conceive that the households do not realize they own the government

[10] John G. Gurley and Edward S. Shaw, *Money in a Theory of Finance* (Washington, D.C.: The Brookings Institution, 1960), pp. 74–75.
[11] Gurley and Shaw, *ibid.*, p. 75.

than to conceive that they do not realize they own the business sector.

Don Patinkin in his Second Edition offers a third possible way of escaping from the problem of price indeterminacy:

> In brief, a necessary condition for the determinacy of the absolute price level in the foregoing system (or, equivalently, a necessary condition for money to play a meaningful role in this system) is that the central bank concern itself with some money value—and in this sense be willing to suffer from money illusion. But this is a somewhat overdramatic statement of the obvious and already emphasized fact that in order for money prices to have economic significance, someone's real behavior must be dependent upon one or more of them.[12]

Instead of the government sector or the business sector reacting to changes in the real value of money differently from the reaction of others, it is now the central bank that performs this task of a *deus ex machina*.

The last sentence in the above quotation puts in a nutshell the difficulty that all the above three approaches face: how does one argue simultaneously that money has no net existence and that, nevertheless, economic behavior depends on it? Unless one makes explicitly some special assertions about the behavior of at least some economic units not derivable from general economic analysis of rational economic behavior and unless by doing so one makes corresponding implicit assertions about the behavior of all the remaining units, this difficulty appears insurmountable. And yet, all these difficulties—empirical and analytical—disappear without a trace if we abandon the notion, untenable in the light of the analysis presented in this part of the book, that modern money is a debt of the government (fiat money), of the banking system (demand deposits), and of private money producers (travelers' checks)—a notion that, if our reading of the history of doctrine is correct, would have been

[12] Don Patinkin, *op. cit.*, 2d ed., p. 309.

rejected by 1860: in that year we would have been told that fiat money and bank money (net of reserves) are substitutes for and thus additions to commodity money.[13] Since commodity money was produced like any other commodity, it was considered a part of net wealth; surely these other monies—had the question been raised—would also have been classified as net wealth. The quantity theorists might even have thrown in, for good measure, a word of caution by pointing out that changes in the supply of money will not necessarily change the level of wealth since, given the demand for money, ultimate price changes may destroy any initial additions to the level of monetary wealth.

Why is it that a century later we see the general acceptance of the denial (a) that money is net wealth, (b) that it has—as such—empirically verifiable economic consequences, and (c) that the price of money (or its reciprocal, the general price level) is determinate? We see two main reasons for this situation. First, analytically the money resource has been persistently treated as something to which general value theory is not applicable, instead of being treated as just another resource, with a specific technical property, that is subject to value theory analysis as is any other resource. This exclusion of money from the scope of value theory forced, and simultaneously permitted, the invention of all sorts of special assumptions designed to enable monetary theory to be both a part of general theory and at the same time something distinct from it. Second, it does not seem accidental that the retrogression from the status quo of, say, 1860 reached the most serious proportions in the middle of this century: it was during these last two decades that one item after another has been denied admission to the money club and that the center of gravity of monetary analysis kept shifting more and more rapidly to actual and even potential debts. During these decades, economic analysis started to rely extremely heavily on the national

[13] However, we would not have agreed entirely with his view, since, at the time, some time deposits were subject to check and some demand deposits paid interest. Thus, some part of the time deposits was very likely money, and some part of the demand deposits was very likely debt.

income accounting identity and on the input-output identity. The case of money, with its special ability to yield real income completely unrelated to inputs therefore presented a serious problem. The T-accounts of the national income statements must balance. Since modern money wealth is produced, virtually, at no cost, it must have been extremely difficult to conclude that zero inputs can result in positive outputs.[14] Similarly, mere changes in the price level are, in the case of nonmonetary wealth, incapable of changing real (deflated) income. Without the recognition of the fact that the money resource has the unique technical property of changing its yield proportionately with the change in the price of it, it was impossible to recognize that income yielded by money changes if prices change. It was much more likely that the conclusion would be made that changes in the price of money (in the general price level) cannot change real wealth and real income—a statement that fits perfectly with the notion that money is a debt. The difficulty of handling money in the national income accounts and wealth accounts has been compounded by the fact that the banking system follows the convention of not showing in its T-accounts the money it produces as its net worth. In this way, both macroeconomic accounting (national income and wealth accounts) and microeconomic accounting (income and asset statements of the banks), which should be mere tools of analysis, became its masters.

---

[14] Notice, however, that as far as the difference between resources used up and value of wealth is concerned, money is not an isolated case: rare stamp collections, rare coin collections, first editions, trivial letters and mere autographs by celebrities, all represent cases in which the value of output is much greater than the value of inputs. In general, natural and artificial monopolies, all result in production of wealth items, the value of which exceeds—at times much exceeds—the resource inputs. Much of the discussion arguing that money is not net wealth rejects (only in the case of money) the valuation attached to this item by the market and substitutes for it resource-cost valuation; for the most explicit argument of this nature, cf. Chapter 3, footnote 21. Why in the case of money, and only money, scarcity is denied the ability to codetermine value and why, as a result, market valuation is being rejected in favor of a resource-cost valuation is left unexplained in all these arguments.

Summary of Part II

In an attempt to apply the currently dominant monetary theory in our exploration of the effects of wealth on economic behavior, we soon realized why Harry G. Johnson, when speaking about this monetary theory, somewhat plaintively stated that "the question naturally arises whether this is the best that can be done."[15] In an attempt to do better we found it necessary to start afresh. We attempted to follow Hicks' injunction stated at the opening of this chapter and discovered, to our pleasure, that the general theory of value is no more difficult to apply to the analysis of money than it is —to use A. C. Pigou's simile—to apply to the analysis of lead or tobacco.[16] After completing our analysis, we concluded that the answer we would have obtained a century ago still holds—that commodity money, fiat money, central bank money, demand deposits, and that modern addition, travelers' checks, are all money when in circulation; that is, when not immobilized in the hands of the producers of money as reserves. In addition, the sources of these monies (the producers of the money commodity, the government, and the banks) are all producing money, not merely transferring wealth from one person in the community to another. Hence, money in real terms, measured in terms of its purchasing power, is a part of the net wealth of the community—a part that we have called net monetary wealth to emphasize that we do not mean some concept of gross wealth as it is currently being employed. But, since monetary wealth is a part of the total wealth of the community, it is bound to codetermine the behavior of the decision-making units of the community and thus to affect the equilibrium of the economy. Let us now restate, in summary form, the major conclusions of our analysis.

MONEY AS NET WEALTH. We found that money yields income to the owner without yielding a negative income to the producer of

[15] Harry G. Johnson, *op. cit.*, p. 343.
[16] A. C. Pigou, "The Value of Money," in Friedrich A. Lutz and Lloyd W. Mints (eds.), *op. cit.*, pp. 163–164.

it or to anybody else. Consequently, money must be a part of the net wealth of the community; it is *not* a debt.

DISTINGUISHING CHARACTERISTIC OF MONEY. Yet, there must be some reason why for centuries "economic theory" was applied to nonmonetary wealth and "monetary theory" to monetary wealth. And indeed, there is one, and a very fundamental one. A unit of nonmonetary capital goods, to which general value theory is traditionally applied, yields physical, real, income that is independent of the price of the capital good in question. In contrast, a unit of monetary capital goods yields real income that is directly proportional to its price. This characteristic of money, familiar to monetary theorists for some time,[17] is due to the nature of the service yielded by money—the facilitation of exchange—so that every change in the price of money is precisely matched by a proportional change in the flow of services from a unit of money. That is, a change in the price of a unit of money changes the value of the transactions that this unit of money is, technically, able to facilitate. This property of money would in the case of "physical capital" be termed a *technical property*; for example, an apple tree would have this property if it were to yield *X* per cent more apples whenever the price of apple trees increased by *X* per cent. As a result, those conclusions of value theory reached for resources yielding constant real (physical) output, regardless of the price of the resource, will be different from the conclusions reached by value theory for a resource with a different technical property; e.g., the one just stated. Unless this is kept firmly in mind, the impression is gained that value theory is inapplicable to money and that value theory and monetary theory are two distinct theories. Actually, as we have seen in Part II of the present book, there is but one economic theory equally applicable to nonmonetary and to monetary wealth.

[17] Cf., e.g., Milton Friedman, *Price Theory* (Chicago: Aldine Publishing Co., 1962), p. 245: ". . . the stock of money . . . differs from [other wealth] because the production services rendered by money do not depend closely on the number of physical units there are, but primarily on the mere existence of a stock."

RELATIONSHIP TO THE QUANTITY THEORY OF MONEY. This simple, inherent, and purely technical property of money has been so much associated with the quantity theory of money (which makes use of this property to reach a more complex proposition) that it seems desirable to show explicitly that the former is completely independent of the latter. However, it seems preferable to demonstrate this by discussing some capital good completely different from money—so different that the purely automatic reflexes economists acquire in the case of money are prevented from taking over. Let us assume that it is the apple trees that have the technical property specified above and let us go a step further and state, in addition, a *quantity theory of apple trees:*

> The demand of the public for apples is such that an increase in the quantity of apple trees, *ceteris paribus*, will cause the price of apple trees to fall (and thus will cause the output of apples by each apple tree to fall) until in a new equilibrium the new output of apples by the new quantity of apple trees is the same as was the old output of apples by the old quantity of apple trees. If we choose to measure the quantity of apple trees not in terms of their numbers but in terms of the quantity of apples they produce, then this "real" quantity of apple trees will be the same in the old and in the new equilibrium.

It is easy to see that the validity of the quantity theory of apple trees stated above depends on the validity of that part we placed in parentheses: on the statement of the purely technical property of our (hypothetical) apple trees. It is also easy to see that any eventual denial of the above-stated hypothesis as to the specific nature of the demand for apples has no bearing whatever on the validity of the statement about the technical property of apple trees.

All the reader needs to do to shift back to money, the technical property of the money resource, and the quantity theory of money is to substitute in the above statements the terms "the nominal quantity of money" (for apple trees), "the real income yielded by nominal money" (for apples), and "given the output of goods and services of the economy" (for *ceteris paribus*). All the above arguments

remain unaffected by this substitution: in particular, the one stating
that the correctness or incorrectness of the empirical propositions
contained in the quantity theory of money has no bearing whatever
on the analytical statement that the real income yielded by money
changes—at all times and regardless of whether the system is or is not
in equilibrium—proportionately with the price of money. Irving
Fisher seems to have seen that the quantity theory of money ultimately rested on this purely technical property of money when he
wrote the following passage in his celebrated *Purchasing Power of
Money*:

> The quantity theory of money thus rests, ultimately, upon the
> fundamental peculiarity which money alone of all goods possesses
> —the fact that it has no power to satisfy human wants except a
> power *to purchase* things which do have such power.[18]

Thus, Irving Fisher's statement implies that the quantity theory holds
if the services of money change proportionately with the price of a
unit of money; it does not imply that the services of money change
proportionately with the price of a unit of money *if* the quantity
theory holds.

ANALYTICAL IMPLICATIONS SYSTEMATICALLY STATED.   After establishing the crucial technical property of money and its complete
independence from the validity of the quantity theory, let us now
state in a systematic fashion the analytical implications resulting
from the application of the theory of value to a resource with the
technical property stated above:

1. Any commodity that yields a positive income to the owner and no
   negative income to the nonowner is a part of the net wealth of
   the community. Because of the existence of the primary income
   that such a commodity yields, the commodity may be held either

[18] Irving Fisher, *The Purchasing Power of Money* (New York: Augustus
M. Kelley, 1963), p. 32.

to fulfill its primary role or to serve as a store of value, or both.[19]

2. Money is a commodity that yields a positive income to the owner and no negative income to the nonowner. Thus money is a part of the net wealth of the community. As such, it may also serve as a store of value.

3. Assume that the price level is constant. An increase in the quantity of any resource, whether this resource is monetary or nonmonetary in nature, must cause an increase in the income of the community and thus in the community's net wealth.

4. Suppose that we reverse the direction of the argument by holding the quantities of resources constant and changing the prices. In the case of nonmonetary resources, the owners are made better off by a price increase, and the nonowners are made worse off. But, if the resources in question are monetary ones, then the owners are made better off, and the nonowners are not affected at all, since the productivity of the monetary asset itself changed as a result of the technical property that money has (and apple trees do not have). Thus, a change in the price of a unit of money, with the quantity constant, causes the real monetary wealth of the community to change proportionately and causes the total wealth of the community to change in the same direction.

5. Whereas changes in the demand for any nonmonetary commodity will, given the supply of that commodity, change the price of that commodity, the flow of services emanating from the commodity will remain unchanged. But, a monetary commodity has a technical property that causes the real income flowing from this commodity to change proportionately with the price of this commodity. For this reason, in the case of money, and money only,

---

[19] Note that the reverse of this proposition does not hold and we are not stating that it does: while every item of net wealth may be capable of serving as a store of value, not *every* store of value is net wealth. For instance, a debt certificate is also a store of value for the holder of it, but it is not net wealth, for it has its inevitable counterpart; namely a negative store of value for the debtor.

we have the following unique situation: if the quantity of the money resource (the nominal quantity of money) is constant, demand for the service of money will create its own supply at no expenditure of resources but merely through the change in the price of money.

6. Since the demand for the services of money creates its own supply at no expenditure of resources, it follows that the total real income yielded by money is independent of the nominal quantity of money in existence.[20] In other words, as long as money exists, the money work to be done—to facilitate transactions and to serve, between transactions, as a store of value—may be performed by any nominal quantity of money. But if the physical quantity of a given substance does not matter, the substance itself does not matter. Any other substance or no substance at all will do equally well. This opens the gates for all sorts of cheap substitutes for that part of net wealth represented by commodity money; this opens the gates for pieces of paper bearing the legend (*X*) *number of units of money* (fiat money) and for mere accounting entries (demand deposits).

The existence of these resource-cheap substitutes (i.e., substitutes the market price of which exceeds the marginal cost of production) depends on the prevention of competition among their producers. In the case of fiat money, this is accomplished by an outright monopoly that fixes the quantity produced. In the case of bank money, this is accomplished by fixing the price charged by otherwise competitive bank money producers (i.e., by the imposition of the instant repurchase clause and of the no-interest-payments clause).

[20] As we have already shown, those conclusions of value theory applicable to those resources that have one technical property (e.g., of yielding constant output, constant real income, regardless of the price of the resource) are inapplicable to those resources that happen to have another technical property (e.g., of yielding output, real income, that changes proportionately with the price of this resource). In the present context, those conclusions of value theory that state that competitive conditions will maximize output hold for the former but not the latter. Specifically, they do not apply to money.

7. Since there is nothing in the theory of value that prohibits any physical resource from yielding more than one distinct flow of services, money may also yield more than one distinct flow of services. Of course, in order that the resource under scrutiny be money, *one* of the flows of services emanating from it must be due to the use of this resource as a medium of exchange. The capitalized value of *this* flow of service must be included in monetary wealth and thus in the net wealth of the community. However, the second flow of services may or may not be an item of net wealth.

   If, on the one hand, the second flow of services is not offset by a negative flow somewhere else in the economy (e.g., our refrigerator money of Chapter 3), then the entire value of the resource will be net wealth, partly monetary and partly nonmonetary. If, on the other hand, the second flow of services is due to a negative flow of services to somebody else in the economy (e.g., our money-debt of Chapter 5), then that part of the value of the resource due to its use as money will be monetary wealth, and hence net wealth, and that part of the value due to the second flow of services will not be a part of net wealth.

8. If the money resource is a joint product—i.e., yields at least one income flow in addition to the flow of services as a medium of exchange—then the usual theory of joint products can be applied. Since, in equilibrium, all resources must yield equal flows of services per unit of value, then the sum of the flows of incomes per unit of money must equal the flow of income from any other resource of the same value. Therefore, we can separate the money component of the above joint product by measuring the change in net wealth that occurs when the money resource is introduced into an economy in which it did not exist. If this change in wealth is equal to the total value of the money substance produced and sold minus any resource cost of producing money, then this money is entirely a component of net wealth, and the income flows to the owners of it are not offset by negative income flows to any nonowner (e.g., our refrigerator money of Chapter 3).

If, on the other hand, the change in net wealth is less than the total value of the money substance produced and sold minus the resource cost of producing the money, then at least some part of the flow of income from the money resource must be offset by a debt (e.g., our money-debt of Chapter 5).[21]

9. The joint product analysis of value theory is applicable only if the resource under scrutiny is permitted to serve and does serve in two or more capacities. An effective law that would forbid the refrigerator money of Chapter 3 to serve as refrigerators (or as money) would make the application of the joint product analysis of the value theory superfluous, since we would know in advance that the resource under scrutiny is permitted to yield but one income: the money income (or the refrigerating income). The same is true should an effective law forbid the use of an instrument as money (or as a debt certificate). Even in the absence of any law, the community may simply choose not to make use of the potentially joint product and to use some item only for one, specialized function: only as a refrigerator, only as money, only as a debt certificate. Although value theory recognizes the possibility of joint products, it does not require that they exist. If they are forbidden by an effective law, or if the habits of the community are such that they simply do not happen to exist, then an attempt to apply the theory of joint products is, of course, superfluous.

Thus, in determining those assets that serve as money and represent monetary wealth we can discard any resource that does not serve as a medium of exchange. In addition, by the use of the

---

[21] Conceptually, even a combination of both is possible: a refrigerator covered by a warranty and used also as a medium of exchange would emanate three distinct incomes: (1) refrigerating income, (2) medium of exchange income, and (3) income paid to the owner by the producer who issued the warranty. The capitalized value of these three incomes would represent (1) non-monetary net wealth of the community, (2) monetary net wealth of the community, and (3) debt certificate (a bond) and, thus not net wealth. We would face a refrigerator-money-debt.

above method we can determine the extent to which any resource that does serve as a medium of exchange represents money and, hence, is monetary wealth. By the use of this analysis we have determined that at the present time and in the United States the money supply consists entirely of fiat money (currency outside banks), demand deposits, and travelers' checks. It might be added that the commodity and fiat money measure must exclude reserves held (voluntarily and because of legal requirements) by the producers of fiat money, demand deposits, and travelers' checks; the value of warranties attached to monetary wealth should also be excluded. Lastly, we concluded that other assets that are often included in the money supply are not money at all, are wholly debts, and should not be included in monetary wealth.

Conclusion

We believe that this summary clearly indicates that the acceptance of the Hicksian precept of the usefulness of the theory of value for monetary theory is worthwhile—actually, so much so that it indicates that the dichotomy between value theory and monetary theory is not based on the difference in theory but solely on the technical properties of the items analyzed. Our discussion shows that there is but one theory, economic theory. When applied to analyze a part of wealth that happens to have the technical property of yielding real output that is independent of the price of this wealth, it is traditionally called "value theory." When applied to analyze a part of wealth that happens to have the technical property of yielding real output that is a function of the price of this wealth, it is traditionally called "monetary theory."

Application of economic theory shows that money is a part of net wealth of the community and that it, alone of all the resources in the community, yields a stream of real income that changes proportionately with its price. In addition, we have shown that once the theory of value is applied, there is no analytical difficulty in distinguishing between money and other forms of assets, whether these assets are capital or financial; i.e., whether the assets under question are genuine parts of net wealth or are simply debt certificates. Finally, the world around us seems to contribute to the basic simplicity of the analysis by preferring to use as money specialized resources that serve as money and nothing else. The use of joint products as money is, at least at the present time and in the United States, quite rare and possibly nonexistent. Thus, the conclusions reached in Part II of this book are simple analytically and are simple to apply.

PART III

NONMONETARY
WEALTH

At the outset of our inquiry we have seen that there is, at present, uncertainty as to whether some specific types of money or even any money at all may be included as a net component of the wealth equation. In Part II of this book we believe to have resolved this problem and have shown that commodity money, fiat money, demand deposits, and travelers' checks are a net part of the wealth of the community insofar as they are in circulation and not immobilized as reserves of the money producers. The time has now come to turn our attention to the other items entering the wealth equation—to nonmonetary wealth. In contrast with money, the issues facing us here are not fundamental. There is no question that the nonmonetary part of wealth is wealth; the question is merely whether nonmonetary wealth should appear in the wealth equation as one homogeneous unit or whether there is theoretical justification for listing various parts of the wealth of the community separately. Stated in this terse fashion, this problem may appear trivial. What difference can it make whether we show in any equation the sum of the components or whether we show the individual components? Yet this problem does have some serious analytical and policy-making implications. If only the sum is shown, we are denying that changes in the structure of the components may affect wealth; especially, we are denying that changes in government taxes and in government debt may affect total wealth. If the individual components are shown, the reverse is true; the structure of income streams and changes in government taxes and debts is said to be capable of affecting wealth.

Another way of stating the same problem is to say that a decision must be made whether the capitalization rates by which incomes are converted into parts of wealth are or are not identical. Should we conclude that they are—or that in a general theory they should be assumed to be—there would be no need to continue with Part III; we would have our definition of wealth, and we could proceed with the analysis of the effect this wealth has on economic behavior. Actually, in the next chapter we shall conclude that there are analytical and empirical grounds for a difference between capitalization rates; this will make it necessary to discuss in a subsequent chapter the various sources of incomes, and the incomes to which these capitalization rates are attached.

CHAPTER 10

Rates of
Capitalization of
Nonmonetary Incomes

Macroeconomic Implications of Unequal Capitalization Rates

In our discussion of money in current analysis (Chapter 8) we assumed, to avoid introduction of extraneous issues, that the rates of interest at which various income flows are capitalized are identical. For nonmonetary wealth w_{nm} we were using the equation

$$w_{nm} = \left(\frac{y_h}{r_h} - \frac{t_h}{r_{t_h}}\right) + \left(\frac{y_n}{r_n} - \frac{t_n}{r_{t_n}}\right) + \frac{g}{r_g} \qquad [10.1]$$

in which taxes on human and nonhuman income (t) finance government interest payments (g) and all the (r's) in the denominators are the same. This assumption, however, leads to a conflict with the "real world" as seen by many economists. As we shall document shortly, it is considered objectionable to be forced to conclude that changes in government debt have no consequences for the wealth of society and lead merely to "transfer payments" and, if there are consequences nevertheless, that they are merely due either to

257

changes in the distribution of income among individuals ("distribution effects") or to changes in the structure of a given wealth portfolio of individuals ("portfolio effects"). In most analyses, these two effects are usually assigned a second order of importance and are frequently assumed away.

To surmount this difficulty many economists make, implicitly or explicitly, special assumptions about the relationship of the various capitalization rates in equation [10.1]. Lloyd A. Metzler[1] in a pioneering article made the implicit assumption that taxes necessary to finance government debt are not capitalized at all, so that an open-market purchase of government bonds results in an offsetting increase in monetary wealth and a decrease in nonmonetary wealth; the only effect left is the portfolio effect. This is equivalent to saying that

$$r_t = \infty \qquad [10.2]$$

Robert A. Mundell[2] drew attention to these implicit assumptions and revised them in a manner he considered more appropriate. Specifically, he stated that for the holders of nonhuman wealth it makes no difference to their valuation of their wealth position if they acquire additional income yielded by government debt or by private securities and lose, simultaneously, an equal amount of income as a consequence of new taxes on nonhuman income ("corporate taxes"). This is equivalent to saying that

$$r_n = r_{t_n} = r_g \qquad [10.3]$$

On the other hand, if taxes are imposed on human wealth ("personal income taxes"), wealth is said by Mundell to increase, which can only mean that he is assuming that

$$r_n < r_{t_n} \qquad [10.4]$$

---

[1] Lloyd A. Metzler, "Wealth, Saving, and the Rate of Interest," *Journal of Political Economy*, *LIX* (April, 1951), pp. 93–116.

[2] Robert A. Mundell, "The Public Debt, Corporate Taxes, and the Rate of Interest," *Journal of Political Economy*, *LXVIII* (December, 1960), pp. 622–626.

Thus, in the case of a change in debt associated with taxes on human wealth Mundell obtains, due to the unequal capitalization rates, a wealth effect. Similarly, Don Patinkin in his Second Edition bases part of his analysis on a lower capitalization rate for taxes than for income. His wealth equation[3] does not contain human wealth so that, transcribed into our notational framework, it reads

$$w = \frac{y_n}{r} + \frac{M}{P} + \frac{g}{r} \qquad [10.5]$$

Strangely enough, taxes necessary to finance government interest payments do not appear in this equation either explicitly or implicitly; the latter is obvious from the fact that he declares the first term in the above equation to be "constant." To carry on with the discussion, let us amend his wealth equation for the missing taxes so that it will read

$$w = \left(\frac{y_n}{r_n} - \frac{t_n}{r_{t_n}}\right) + \frac{M}{P} + \frac{g}{r_g} \qquad [10.6]$$

In principle, Patinkin permits the rate of interest applicable to taxes to range anywhere between equality with other rates and infinity:

$$\infty > r_{t_n} > r_g \qquad [10.7]$$

Specifically, his statement is that "k is a constant (greater than zero and less than one) reflecting the degree to which individuals do not discount the future tax liabilities connected with government bonds."[4] In practice, he briefly explores the possibility that the

---

[3] Don Patinkin, *Money, Interest, and Prices*, 2d ed. (New York: Harper & Row, 1956, 1965), p. 295.

[4] Don Patinkin, *ibid.*, p. 289. Since the factor k is a constant that is defined merely in arithmetic and not in economic terms, it is uncertain as to what it measures. Equation [10.7] is just one possible interpretation of it, but even then the economic meaning is in doubt. It could depict "imperfect discounting of perfect income streams" or "perfect discounting of imperfect income streams." If the latter, it could mean that the streams have the same quality as other income streams but are considered less certain. (While I formerly bought milk for myself, now the government taxes me and buys milk for

tax discount rate is equal to the other rates and dismisses it by pointing out that this would make bonds drop out of the model and could be true only if the government "so perfectly represents the corporate will" as to be merely a "veil."[5] In the remainder of his analysis he makes "the crucial—though reasonable—assumption that there is an imperfect discounting of the tax liability associated with bonds"[6] and obtains on this basis a new effect, "the net-real-financial-asset effect."[7] In another empirical defense of this analytical assumption Patinkin points out that without this assumption there would be no difference between deficit financing $\left(d\dfrac{M}{P}, \right.$ the differential of equation [10.5]$\bigg)$ and open-market operation $\left(\text{only } d\dfrac{M}{P} \text{ would be left, since then } d\dfrac{g}{r_g} = -d\dfrac{t_n}{r_{t_n}}\right).$[8] However desirable on intuitive grounds it may be to have a model that is able to make such distinctions and that does not confine government bonds to net nonexistence, there are obvious dangers in incorporating empirical assertions into general economic analysis simply to get

[5] Don Patinkin, *ibid.*, p. 294.
[6] Don Patinkin, *loc. cit.*
[7] Don Patinkin, *ibid.*, p. 290.
[8] Don Patinkin, *ibid.*, p. 294.

---

me. I consider the tax to be permanent, but the subsidy impermanent.) Alternatively, it could mean that even though the factor costs of the goods taxed away and given back are the same, their contribution to the consumer's satisfaction is different. (The government taxes away my milk, which I like, and gives me back butter of equal factor cost, which I don't like.) Patinkin's statement made a few pages later that k would be unity if the government perfectly expressed the popular will suggests that this is what he has in mind: perfect discounting of imperfect income streams. But imperfection that would result in k other than unity could also be due to a myopia that would cause the consumers to plug into the capitalization formula an incorrect time variable in some cases. Obviously, all these various interpretations of k (and of the "imperfect discounting" it is said to express) have widely different economic implications and would each affect our measure of wealth differently. In what follows, we shall attempt to avoid the use of the term "imperfect discounting," since—in contrast with such terms as perfect competition—it does not have, at present, a standard meaning.

analytical results which we, *a priori*, feel to be empirically right. The tradition against admitting such assertions into analysis is strong, and Harry G. Johnson in his review of modern monetary theory upholds it vigorously. He rejects all "effects" based on the assertion of imperfect capitalization of taxes by pointing out that in a world of reasonable certainty, all capitalization rates would be identical.[9] In this chapter we intend to show that it is possible to preserve the net presence of government debt in the wealth equation, without paying the heavy price of introducing empirical assertions into general economic analysis. All that needs to be done is to shift the focus of attention from the capitalization rates applicable to taxes on wealth (human and nonhuman) to the capitalization rates applicable to the wealth itself (human and nonhuman). Specifically, we intend to show that equality of *these* rates, even in a world of "reasonable" certainty, requires satisfaction of a set of conditions unobtainable in the past, present, and in the foreseeable future. Indeed, were it not for our strong aversion to prophecy, we would be tempted to say "unobtainable ever."

Before we open the discussion of this issue, let us point out briefly that once a decision is made that the capitalization rates on human and nonhuman incomes are unequal, capitalization of the burden of taxes imposed on these two incomes by the use of rates that are identical with the rates applicable to the incomes themselves will accomplish precisely the same thing aimed at by Metzler, Mundell, and Patinkin and at the same time free us from the necessity of making empirical assertions that may hold at one time and not at another time, that may hold in one society but not in another society. To show this, let us at the moment merely assume that the rates applicable to human and nonhuman income are different because these incomes, for some reason or other, are inherently different. Then the level of nonmonetary wealth becomes endogenous to the macroeconomic system and will be changed by endogenous changes in the distribution of income even if the total income remains

[9] Harry G. Johnson, "Monetary Theory and Policy," *American Economic Review*, LII (June, 1962), p. 343.

constant. Therefore, such a "distribution effect" can no longer be ignored. Secondly, the structure of income and thus the level of nonmonetary wealth may be affected by government action. For example, if the government levies taxes on both human and non-human income, then the distribution of these taxes, for any given distribution of government expenditures, will affect the level of nonmonetary wealth. In addition, if we allow for the existence of government interest payments financed out of taxes, then changes in the level of government debt may change wealth. This, we believe, shows sufficiently that the issue of the customarily asserted equality of the capitalization rates on various types of income is an important one for the correct specification of the macroeconomic system. If, as was asserted above by Harry G. Johnson, these rates must be assumed to be equal, then the nonmonetary component of wealth must be expressed as the total permanent equivalent of any given stream of total income capitalized by the market rate of interest. If, on the other hand, there should turn out to be reasons for an assertion that these rates are different, then we must separately account for the various income streams in the wealth equation, with each income stream capitalized by the rate of interest applicable to it.

Conditions for Equality of Capitalization Rates

Let us now explore in some detail the problem of capitalization rates applicable to various streams of income—specifically, the problem of the rates of capitalization to be applied to human income on the one hand and to nonhuman income on the other hand. In the treatment of nonhuman capital it is generally recognized that equilibrium in an economy without uncertainty, even a growing one, will result in the equalization of the returns on all types of non-human capital.[10] Thus, when human resources began to be viewed

[10] See, for example, Frank H. Knight, *On the History and Method of Economics* (Chicago: The University of Chicago Press, 1956), p. 193.

as capital equivalent to nonhuman capital, it seemed reasonable to extend this analytical conclusion concerning the equality of rates of return to cover both types of capital. On the other hand, economists have, almost from the dawn of the science, asserted that human resources were somehow different from nonhuman resources. Many reasons were given for this difference; the most frequently quoted were written by Alfred Marshall. In a famous section of his *Principles*, Marshall presents five peculiarities of the labor factor: (1) the worker sells his work, but retains property in himself; (2) the seller of labor must deliver it himself; (3) labor is perishable; (4) the sellers of labor are often at a disadvantage in bargaining; (5) a great length of time is required to provide additional supplies of specialized ability.[11] Of these five peculiarities of labor, economists have subsequently discarded all but one as not being a distinguishing factor of labor, or as not being relevant in a competitive situation, or both. The one remaining factor that distinguishes labor from all other types of capital is the physical nonseparability of human capital from the owner of this capital.

This fact of nonseparability represents a combination of Marshall's first two principles and implies, in the absence of slavery, no market for human capital. Thus, if the owner of human capital desires to consume his capital, he is disadvantaged relative to the owner of nonhuman capital as long as a market for the latter exists. Once human capital is purchased, it is technically impossible to consume it, since it becomes an inseparable part of the owner; as a result, the resale value of human capital becomes zero the moment it is purchased. As a result, it is less capable than nonhuman wealth to act as a store of value to the owner. Indeed, in one respect, the inferiority just discussed is an absolute one: human wealth ceases to yield any income when the owner of it dies and thus is, in contrast with nonhuman wealth, incapable of serving as a store of value to be used to enrich the owner's heirs. However, this special aspect of the general issue will be discussed only in Chapter 16.

[11] Alfred Marshall, *Principles of Economics* (New York: The Macmillan Co., 1953), pp. 560–569.

In what follows, we shall explore the general issue by pursuing two lines of inquiry. First, we shall consider very briefly the case in which this nonseparability is assumed away and specify conditions necessary for the equality of the capitalization rates in this case. Next, we shall drop the separability assumption and inquire what substitute assumptions must be made to permit the equality of capitalization rates to continue.

Human Wealth Separable

Let us make all the usual static long-run equilibrium assumptions and let us also assume a world in which it is possible to transfer skills and knowledge from one owner to another with the same ease with which the ownership of a piece of physical capital can be transferred—a world in which the knowledge of, say, matrix algebra may be transferred from one owner to another one as easily as some machine tool. Note that the fact that the owner of human capital may teach someone else does not imply separability. This teaching is simply a flow of services from the human capital and not the capital itself. What we mean by separability is that the owner of the knowledge of matrix algebra sells this knowledge so that the buyer has it and the former owner no longer does. In this world, human and nonhuman capital would yield identical rates of return as long as the following conditions hold: (1) the utility functions of the members of society do not contain as an argument *the type* of capital from which their income streams emanate and (2) all types of capital have the same degree of riskiness or consumers are indifferent to risk. In this case every opportunity that is open to a consumer holding nonhuman capital is also open to the holders of human capital. Thus, if the discounted present value of future income streams yielded by any wealth (human or nonhuman) is to be maximized (which is the condition for maximization of utility in this case), all forms of capital held by the consumer must yield the same rate of return.

Assumptions Compensating for Nonseparability

However, our assumption of separability of human capital from its owner is obviously highly unrealistic; indeed, we know that it does not exist and that it has never existed in the past. Let us, therefore, search for other assumptions or conditions that may be capable of serving as a perfect substitute for it. In one respect, the lack of separability of human capital from its owner is a problem because a market for human capital does not exist. It might be argued, however, that this is simply something that the community has imposed on itself, since in communities where *slavery* is not illegal, a market in human capital does exist. If slavery or the absence of it is all there is to this problem, then this man-made imperfection could be taken into account in a solution of any specific problem but would be, like rent controls, unworthy of incorporation in any general analysis. Let us therefore see if the absence of antislavery legislation would overcome the lack of separability of human capital from its owner. Milton Friedman writes on this point as follows:

> The fact that human capital sources cannot in our society be bought and sold means . . . that human capital does not provide as good a reserve against emergencies as non-human capital . . . In the second place, this fact reduces the scope of market forces in investment in human capital. . . . Finally, the fact that human capital sources cannot be bought and sold is the basic reason for Marshall's second peculiarity: it is only for this reason that the seller of labor must deliver it himself. . . . The owner of land, for example, has no reason to be concerned whether the land is used in a way that is "pleasant" or "unpleasant" or the owner of a horse whether the horse is used in work that it "enjoys" or does not "enjoy," provided both types of work involve the same effect of the land's or the horse's subsequent productivity. The owner of labor power, on the other hand, does have reason to be concerned.
>
> These peculiarities would disappear only in a slave society and there only for the slaves.[12]

[12] Milton Friedman, *Price Theory* (Chicago: Aldine Publishing Co., 1962), pp. 201–202. (Note that in the original, the last sentence appears first.)

Essentially, Friedman's condition of a slave society is the logical equivalent of making human capital separable from its owner since, as far as the slaves are concerned, they are—like any nonhuman capital—subject to sale; analytically, they are converted into non-human wealth. However, we must emphasize Friedman's qualification that this is true *only* with respect to the slaves; in the case of slaveowners, we face the same problem as before. Since a slave society, by definition, must contain both slaves and slaveowners, by instituting slavery we have not found a perfect substitute for the separability requirement. All we have done is to lessen the numerical magnitude of the problem; while in the absence of slavery all human wealth is burdened by the lack of separability, in the case of a slave society only a part of human wealth bears this burden. Thus, the assumption of the existence of a slave society cannot solve the problem of nonseparability and thus nonmarketability of human wealth; it is not an adequate substitute for separability.

As we have just seen, the nonseparability of human wealth becomes a problem only for those owners of human capital who want to divest themselves of some of their human capital before it has depreciated entirely; and the nonmarketability is a problem only because the market value of human capital becomes zero as soon as the investment in this capital is made. For any consumer who has a zero probability that he will desire to divest himself of his human capital prior to the time this capital is fully depreciated, the nonseparability and thus the nonmarketability of human wealth is irrelevant. This probability can be zero only if the owners are certain that no event will occur in the future that will make them alter their consumption plans or the structure of their wealth portfolio. Thus, *perfect knowledge* of the future (which, of course, means perfect certainty as well) is required if we want to find a perfect substitute for separability. However, perfect knowledge, by itself, is not enough. Consider an individual who desires an income stream for a period of n years. Assume that the production functions governing the output of either type of wealth are identical and that they both yield capital that will produce a given income stream at the lowest cost only if this capital has durability of $(n + x)$ years. Then, even with perfect knowledge and identical production functions, nonhuman capital will still be preferable over human capital since in the n-th year the unused portion of the former can, and the unused portion of the latter cannot, be sold.

There is therefore a second requirement, in addition to perfect knowledge, that is required if we are to specify a set of assumptions that will perfectly compensate for the lack of separability of human capital. Assume that the production functions governing the output of human and nonhuman capital are such that they permit, on the margin, the two capitals of equal production costs to yield the same permanent income equivalents if the former has a durability of, say, h years and the latter a durability of, say, n years. Assume further that the production function governing the output of human capital is such that the cost of producing human capital of any durability other than h years is merely a linear function of time passing through the origin. Thus, this function has the special characteristic that any addition to or subtraction from the durability of h years adds or subtracts from the cost of producing a given unit of human capital no more than the discounted present value of income gained or lost as a result of this change in durability.[13] Then, with perfect knowledge, the consumer will be able to choose, at no cost, the durability of human capital that he requires and, hence, will be indifferent between human and nonhuman capital. Or, to state the same thing differently, the issue of durability is made to disappear by assuming that the cost of producing human capital of *any* durability is always precisely equal to the discounted stream of income yielded by this capital. Thus, these two assumptions become

---

[13] What is required here is that the cost of producing human capital that produces a unit of income for h years as a function of h be the following:

$$c_h = \frac{1 - (1 + r_h)^{-h}}{r_h}$$

where c_h is the cost of production of, and r_h is the rate of return on, human capital. Of course, for the case of perfect knowledge and our above cost function, r_h will equal the rate of return on nonhuman capital.

the logical equivalent of the separability of human capital from its owner, because whenever the owner of human capital who has perfect knowledge desires to divest himself of his human capital, that capital will have just depreciated to zero and will have disappeared.

In conclusion we may say that two incomes of equal size would have the same value to the owner of the human and nonhuman sources of these incomes if these sources were equally easily separable from him: if knowledge of, say, matrix algebra could be as easily sold to others to use as is, say, a machine tool. This, as we all know, is not the case. The lack of separability of human wealth from its owner would be fully compensated for by the existence of two other conditions: (a) perfect knowledge, and (b) a special type of production function governing the output of human capital.[14] However, (a) the lack of perfect knowledge is only too painfully obvious to anyone who either writes or reads economic tracts; (b) the lack of this special type of production function is no less obvious to anyone who would want to acquire the knowledge of, say, matrix algebra for an afternoon's use and who would want his acquisition costs to be proportionately lower than are the costs facing, say, a lifelong user of this knowledge. Thus it needs no elaborate discussion to prove that the pair of conditions that are, conceptually, capable of substituting for separability of human capital cannot be satisfied. But then, two incomes of equal size cannot have the same value to the consumer. The one yielded by human wealth must be inferior to one yielded by nonhuman wealth, and therefore the capitalization rate applicable to human income must be higher than the rate applicable to nonhuman income. A macroeconomic model must allow these rates to be different and must allow changes in the distribution of total income between human and nonhuman income to affect the level of nonmonetary wealth. Specifically, it must contain the statement

---

[14] One cannot, of course, prove a negative: that there does not exist a set of conditions that compensate for nonseparability less onerous than the one we came up with. The burden of proof that there is such a set and that it is satisfied in any specific economy, consequently, must rest upon an eventual critic of the thesis just presented here.

that the capitalization rates on human income, because of the lack of separability or of the conditions compensating for it, is higher or— in the limiting case—equal to the capitalization rate on nonhuman income. If a solution in terms of the equality of these capitalization rates is desired nevertheless, it may be stated simply as a special case.[15]

Capitalization Rates in Reality

There is another, partly analytical and partly empirical, reason providing additional and weighty support to the assertion of inequality of capitalization rates just made. Most of the economic literature dealing with the equalization of rates of return on all types of investment implicitly assumes that the flows of capital under consideration are, purely analytically, definable and are, empirically, measurable. Unfortunately, this is not the case. There is no conceptual difficulty in measuring the gross income, operating cost, and thus the net income of a machine. Indeed, all the empirical measurements of nonhuman income and wealth express, with greater or smaller empirical precision, only the net income yielded by nonhuman sources of income. In contrast, economic theory has, up to now, proved to be completely sterile when asked to make a distinction between gross income, operating costs, and net income yielded by the human resource. A catalogue of the attempts to make such a distinction is a catalogue of exercises in subjective value judgments.

Some of these attempts make no effort to be taken in any other but humorous vein; George Stigler's quantification of the cost of food subsistence, yielding an answer of some forty dollars per year, is of such nature.[16] His purpose is not to obtain an answer but to

---

[15] Notice that in a special sense the difference between the capitalization rates is consistent with the conclusion of economic analysis that in equilibrium there will be equalization of all rates. In equilibrium, the difference between the rates will be precisely so high as to compensate for the inferiority of human capital, so that "the pure rate" on income yielded by *homogeneous* capital will be the same. In the same sense, the price of a unit of "transportation" of defined quality will be the same regardless of whether it is furnished by a Volkswagen or a Rolls-Royce.

[16] George Stigler, "The Cost of Subsistence," *Journal of Farm Economics*, *XXVII* (May, 1945), pp. 303–314.

demonstrate either the difficulty or, possibly even the inherent absurdity of the question. Burton A. Weisbrod, with greater seriousness, defined the operating costs of the human resource as the value of total consumption so that the net income yielded by the human resource becomes the savings of its owner. He states that ". . . if we are interested in the value of the person to others then his productivity net of consumption is most relevant." [17] That this criterion is analytically completely unacceptable for the purpose of quantifying human wealth should be made quite obvious by the application of it to nonhuman wealth: the value of a machine to others and thus its share in wealth would be simply the gross output of the machine minus the consumption of the owner of this machine, with consumption defined to contain both the supplies of the raw materials used up by the machine and the supplies of caviar used up by the owner. In another study, R. M. H. Hashimi [18] approached the problem by assuming that food expenditures measure the operating costs. While an unclothed male worker might find few employment opportunities, food expenditures themselves cannot possibly measure operating costs. Should the productivity of human resources remain unchanged but should the owners of this resource choose to consume more food or more expensive types of food and less housing or clothing, our measure of operating costs would rise and our measure of net income yielded by the human resource would fall. Gary S. Becker [19] uses a different approach, in which the cost of producing gross human income is taken to be the investment necessary to produce this income. Essentially, this is the opportunity

---

[17] Burton A. Weisbrod, "The Valuation of Human Capital," *Journal of Political Economy, LXIX* (October, 1961), p. 426.

[18] R. M. H. Hashimi, *Studies in Functional Income Distribution* (East Lansing, Mich.: Michigan State University Press, 1960), p. 6.

[19] Gary S. Becker, *Human Capital* (New York: National Bureau of Economic Research, 1964). Note, however, that *this* approach does have clear merits. Although a discovery that gross human income exceeds the opportunity cost of producing this income is difficult to interpret, since it is consistent with either equilibrium or lack of it, a discovery that opportunity costs exceed gross human income must mean that there is overinvestment in human capital, irrespective of the level of operating costs.

cost approach that yields the clear implication that the difference between the gross income and costs as defined measures the above-the-equilibrium income—an implication that is supported by the calculation of "the internal rate of interest" that differs from the market rate of interest. This approach, however, can be valid only if the implicit assumption is made that the operating costs of producing the gross income are zero; thus even this approach leaves the problem raised above unsolved.

A review of the attempts made in the course of the last hundred years to define the operating cost of the human resource suggests strongly the basic futility of all of them.[20] The reason for the formidable difficulties encountered is simple enough. Even a slaveowner would find it extremely difficult to establish what are the operating costs of human capital. While he might find it fairly simple to establish an optimum relationship between the operating costs and output of a "prime field hand," the problem becomes well nigh insoluble the more complex the activity. In a modern economy, the maximization of the difference between the total output of a unit of human resource ("from each according to his ability") and the total operating costs of this resource ("to each according to his need") reveals itself as an impossible task. This is, very probably, the reason why the institution of slavery is moribund: by presenting insoluble managerial problems it is economically inefficient.

Let us now return to the problem of the capitalization rates. Even should we grant the hypothesis that in equilibrium the capitalization rates on human (r_h) and nonhuman (r_n) income are equal,

$$r_h = r_n \qquad [10.8]$$

this conclusion would be without any importance and could be safely ignored by economic analysis as long as economic theory is unable to make a distinction among (a) gross human income, (b) operating costs of the human resource o_h, and (c) net human

[20] Helen H. Lamale, "Changes in the Concepts of Income Adequacy over the Last Century," *American Economic Review*, *XLVIII* (May, 1958), pp. 291–304.

income y_h. Until then, all that will be available for both analytical and empirical work will be a wealth equation

$$w_R = \left(\frac{o_h}{r_h} + \frac{y_h}{r_h}\right) + \frac{y_n}{r_n} \qquad [10.9]$$

with only *the sum* of the first two terms being known: conceptually and empirically. But that means that for net human income we have available only a proxy, gross human income. Since we know that this proxy (y'_h) is bigger than net human income, we must apply to it a proxy capitalization rate (r'_h) that also must be bigger than the true capitalization rate and bigger than the capitalization rate applicable to nonhuman income even if the special case of equation [10.8] should hold:

$$w_R = \frac{y'_h}{r'_h} + \frac{y_n}{r_n} \qquad [10.10]$$

and

$$r'_h > r_n \qquad [10.11]$$

Note that this result is perfectly consistent either with the hypothesis expressed in equation [10.8] or with the hypothesis—presented in this chapter—that denies the validity of equation [10.8]. Consequently, a discovery that in any specific society inequality [10.11] happens to hold neither supports the conclusion that disequilibrium level of investment in human capital exists nor confirms the analysis of the preceding section of this chapter.

There is still another, minor, correctible, and purely empirical reason for making use of the inequality [10.11] if we happen to employ in empirical work gross human income as yielded by national income accounting. Data on wage and salary incomes (i.e., incomes yielded by human sources of income) are not, in contrast to data on the capitalized value of income yielded by nonhuman sources of income, corrected for the impermanency of these incomes. A rough correction for this difference in definitions is possible; we say rough because some assumption about the mutual relationship between gross income and operating costs over time must be made. If we assume that there is a constant ratio of the above two items over time, we may write

$$\frac{y'_h}{r'_h} = \sum_{n=a}^{\infty} \left[y''_h P_a^n \frac{1}{(1 + r'_h)^{n-a}} \right] \qquad [10.12]$$

where y''_h is the measured income of a human resource in any one specific year, and where P_a^n is the probability of the human resource of age a being alive at age n. Such an adjustment converting the measured income into its permanent income equivalent has been recently undertaken by Burton A. Weisbrod.[21]

Conclusion

This chapter shows that there are not one but several weighty reasons for making the rate of capitalization applicable to a unit of income produced by a human source bigger than the rate of capitalization applicable to the same unit of income produced by a nonhuman source. First, we are unable to measure net human income and therefore we must use the concept of gross human income alongside the concept of net nonhuman income. Second, even if we waive this problem or set it aside in expectation that it will be solved sometime in the future, we have shown that the inferiority of sources of net human income would remain even if the market in these sources were perfect and slavery existed and even if knowledge were perfect. Looking at the issue as a demand problem, one can see that perfect knowledge would disqualify the purchase of *some* sources of human income while not disqualifying the purchase of *any* source of nonhuman income simply because an owner of human wealth may not and an owner of a nonhuman wealth may disinvest and use the proceeds in any way he sees fit. Looking at it from the supply side, even with perfect knowledge but with a lack of separability, one cannot use all the cheapest methods of producing human sources of income, whereas one may and will use the cheapest methods of

[21] Burton A. Weisbrod, *op. cit.*, p. 427.

producing nonhuman sources of income. The reason for this is that the supplier of sources of human income, endowed with a durability that proves to be the cheapest one technically and economically, would find either no demanders for his product or only few demanders whose production plans happen to be equal in length or longer than the durability of the good itself.

Thus, a general macroeconomic formulation must allow the capitalization rates applicable to human income to be higher than the capitalization rates applicable to nonhuman income. The assumption that these two rates are equal should be treated as a special case, applicable only in cases in which it is desired to assume that human income is separable from its owner (or that perfect knowledge plus the special type of the production function specified above exist) and that the analytical and empirical difficulty of defining and measuring net human income has been surmounted.

CHAPTER 11

Components of
Nonmonetary Wealth

In the preceding chapter we have seen that there are purely theoretical grounds for separating total nonmonetary wealth into its major components, human and nonhuman wealth. In that discussion we made no distinction between privately owned nonhuman wealth and government-owned nonhuman wealth other than a simple noting of the source of the income flows. In other words, we used the same rate of interest to capitalize government nonhuman income flows and privately owned nonhuman income flows. However, in our discussion of money in current analysis in Chapter 8, we did note this distinction and also noted that these capitalization rates might be different. In this chapter we intend to explore this distinction and the modifications of the wealth equation that the presence of the government might make necessary. Fortunately, the fact that the issues involved are not of any fundamental analytical importance makes this chapter a mercifully short one.

Nonhuman Wealth and Disposable Nonhuman Wealth

The proposition that nonhuman nonmonetary wealth, much of which is represented by purely physical capital, belongs in the wealth

equation needs no defense. In his *General Theory*, John Maynard
Keynes recognized explicitly that this wealth affects the behavior
of the consumer (specifically, his consumption and saving decisions)
both in the short[1] and in the long run. Concerning the short-run
effects of changes in the rate of interest on nonmonetary nonhuman
wealth he wrote as follows:

> Perhaps the most important influence, operating through changes
> in the rate of interest, on the readiness to spend out of a given
> income, depends on the effect of these changes on the appreciation
> or depreciation in the price of securities and other assets. For if a
> man is enjoying a windfall increment in the value of his capital,
> it is natural that his motives towards current spending should be
> strengthened, even though in terms of income his capital is worth
> no more than before; and [*vice versa*].[2]

In spite of this apparently strong feeling that the level of nonhuman
wealth would, in the short run, affect the level of consumption
Keynes did not incorporate the capitalized value of nonhuman
income streams into his analytical structure. This failure to incorporate the effect of the level of nonhuman wealth on the level of
consumption was repeated by the followers of Keynes and, in part
at least, by his critics, Gottfried Haberler and A. C. Pigou. Both
Haberler and Pigou concentrated entirely on the monetary part of
wealth in answering the Keynesian attack on the classical case of
full-employment equilibrium. As a result, the nonmonetary part
of nonhuman wealth disappeared from discussion until Lloyd A.
Metzler, in 1951, reintroduced it by including it in the wealth equation
of his formal macroeconomic model.[3] Metzler pointed out that, in
the short run, changes in the rate of interest will change the capitalized value of a given flow of nonhuman income and that this
change will then affect saving. He proceeded to show that changes

---

[1] For a more extended discussion of this issue, cf. Chapter 1.
[2] John Maynard Keynes, *The General Theory of Employment Interest and
Money* (New York: Harcourt, Brace and Co., 1936), p. 94.
[3] Lloyd A. Metzler, "Wealth, Saving, and the Rate of Interest," *Journal of
Political Economy*, LIX (April, 1951), pp. 93–116.

in the stock of money would change the equilibrium rate of interest if accompanied by opposite changes in private holdings of non-human nonmonetary assets—i.e., if the change in the stock of money is accomplished by an open market operation—since the change in the value of the nonhuman nonmonetary wealth held by the private sector would affect the level of saving.

However, in his discussion Metzler failed to allow the change in government receipts and their subsequent disbursement to affect the level of nonmonetary nonhuman wealth. In particular, he assumed that any change in the income of the Central Bank would be offset by changes in taxes so that security purchases or sales by the central bank ". . . will redistribute income between former asset owners and taxpayers but will not influence the total of disposable income."[4] But, since this redistribution was assumed not to affect the level of nonhuman nonmonetary wealth, Metzler must have implicitly assumed either that any change in taxes on nonhuman income was not capitalized into changes in the level of nonhuman wealth or that any change in the level of taxes is accomplished by changing taxes on human income. Thus, Metzler capitalized only the gross level of nonhuman nonmonetary wealth. This approach is clearly inadequate if the taxes on nonhuman income streams are changed since, unless such changes are considered by the holders of nonhuman assets to be of one period duration, these taxes would be capitalized into wealth. In fact, it was just this oversight that allowed Metzler to arrive at his conclusion that acceptance of the wealth-saving relation resulted in the rate of interest becoming a monetary phenomenon.[5]

[4] Lloyd A. Metzler, *ibid.*, p. 109, ftn.
[5] Metzler's conclusion follows from the fact that, using his definition of wealth, an open market purchase of securities will reduce the level of non-human wealth and thus lead to an increase in the saving function. But since he assumes that the investment function does not shift, by virtue of the fact that income in the community has remained constant, the shift in the saving function results in a decrease in the equilibrium rate of interest. Thus, monetary changes can affect the rate of interest and it has become a monetary phenomenon.

A few years later, Robert A. Mundell introduced the level of real taxes on nonhuman income streams as a negative nonhuman income stream capitalized at the same rate of interest as the nonhuman income streams themselves.[6] Thus, he assumes that the taxes are viewed as permanent by the holders of nonhuman assets, resulting in the following nonmonetary nonhuman wealth equation:

$$w_{nm} = \frac{(y_n - t_n)}{r_n} \qquad [11.1]$$

where w_{nm} is the level of nonmonetary nonhuman wealth, y_n the nonhuman income stream, t_n the taxes on the nonhuman income stream, and r_n is the rate of interest used to capitalize nonhuman income—i.e., r_n is the rate of return on nonhuman capital investment. Using this definition of wealth, Mundell proceeded to show that Metzler's conclusion that acceptance of the wealth-saving relation resulted in the rate of interest becoming a monetary phenomenon was false in one major case.[7] That is, if the government changes the taxes on nonhuman income by the full amount of the income from the assets purchased or sold in the open market operations, then the net income from nonhuman sources will not have changed and hence, nonhuman wealth will not change. But, if nonhuman wealth does not change then Metzler's mechanism for the change in the equilibrium rate of interest does not work; namely the saving function does not shift because of the open market operation so that if, as Metzler assumed, the investment function remains the same the rate of interest will be unaffected.

[6] Robert A. Mundell, "The Public Debt, Corporate Taxes, and the Rate of Interest," *Journal of Political Economy*, *LXVIII* (December, 1960), pp. 622–626.

[7] Mundell's model is not directly comparable to Metzler's, since he assumed that the level of taxes on nonhuman income also affected the investment function so that the case we are considering would lead to the saving function remaining constant but would shift the investment function. In particular, for an open market purchase of securities and a subsequent reduction in the level of taxes on nonhuman income, the saving function would remain unchanged but the investment function would shift upward and lead to an increase in the rate of interest.

In view of this discussion we believe that it is the level of net nonhuman income streams that is the relevant flow of income to be capitalized in arriving at the level of nonmonetary nonhuman wealth. Or, alternatively, it is the level of disposable nonhuman income that determines the behavior of consumers, given the rate of interest, and not the gross income received. However, we must add the proviso that in order for the same capitalization rate to be used on the income and the taxes on that income, it is necessary that the consumers anticipate that the level of taxes is permanent.

Human Wealth and Disposable Human Wealth

In general economic theory, and especially in capital theory, human resources are recognized as an important part of the community's total wealth.[8] Yet, in macroeconomic models human wealth is rarely introduced into the wealth equation. In fact, most of these models implicitly assume that the interest rate used to capitalize human income streams is unity; or, to state the same thing in an alternative way, that the time horizon for human income is one year.[9] Of course, this assumption by itself is not sufficient to justify the exclusion of human income from the wealth equation; the current level of human income should be included. But this need not be done if current human income is separately accounted for in the consumption function and in the demand for money function. However, recent developments in the theory of the consumption function make it very clear that there is a need to give formal consideration to more than the current human income. In fact, the two major new theories of the consumption function, the life cycle theory and the permanent income hypothesis, incorporate the past, present, and

---

[8] Cf., e.g., Frank H. Knight, *The Ethics of Competition* (New York: Augustus M. Kelley, 1951), p. 173, or Martin Bailey, "Saving and the Rate of Interest," in E. J. Hamilton, A. Rees, and H. G. Johnson (ed.), *Landmarks in Political Economy* (Chicago: The University of Chicago Press, 1962), p. 587.

[9] E.g., in the articles specified in notes 3 and 6 above.

expected future income of the consumer into the analysis and obtain results that appear significant both analytically and empirically.[10] Consequently, in Chapters 13 through 15 we develop an analysis that generalizes the permanent income and life-cycle approaches. For all these reasons, the time seems ripe for an incorporation of human wealth, or more precisely, of the capitalized value of human income flows, into the general macroeconomic framework. In incorporating the capitalized value of the flow of human income in the wealth equation, we shall follow the lead of the previous section and assert that it is the net flow of human income, given the rate of interest, that determines the behavior of consumers. Thus, the level of human wealth may be represented as

$$w_h = \frac{(y_h - t_h)}{r_h} \qquad [11.2]$$

where w_h is the level of human wealth, y_h is the flow of income from human sources, t_h the level of taxes on human income, and r_h is the rate of capitalization for human income—i.e., r_h is the rate of return on investment in human capital. We are again faced with the problem of assuming that the capitalization rate on the flow of human income is identical to the capitalization rate for the taxes on that human income. However, in this case this assumption may be less important, since estimates of the time horizon applicable to human income indicate that this horizon is quite short[11] and hence any myopia of the consumers with respect to taxes would not significantly affect the results obtained by assuming it away.

---

[10] Milton Friedman, *A Theory of Consumption Function* (Princeton: Princeton University Press, 1957), and Franco Modigliani and Richard Brumberg, "Utility Analysis and the Consumption Function," in Kenneth K. Kurihara (ed.), *Post Keynesian Economics* (New Brunswick, N.J.: Rutgers University Press, 1954), pp. 388–436.

[11] Milton Friedman, "Windfalls, the 'Horizon,' and Related Concepts in the Permanent Income Hypothesis," in *Measurement in Economics* (Stanford: Stanford University Press, 1963), p. 7, estimates that "the horizon is on the average something like three years [and] implies a subjective discount rate of 0.333."

Government Debt

There is a third type of wealth owned by the private sector: that represented by government debt. In the past, this debt was frequently considered to be a part of wealth. However, in his review of monetary theory and policy, Harry G. Johnson objected to this practice by pointing out that government debt is not net wealth of the private sector:

> The existence of government debt implies the levying of taxes to pay the interest on it, and in a world of reasonable certainty these taxes would be capitalized into liabilities equal in magnitude to the government debt; . . .[12]

In his Second Edition, Don Patinkin seems to have accepted this point since he writes:

> Hence if the private sector discounts its further tax liabilities in the same way that it discounts future interest receipts, the existence of government bonds will not generate any net wealth effect.[13]

While these statements express a fact that seems to be, at times, neglected in discussions of the burden of the public debt, they are not entirely accurate for three reasons:

1. The government itself may own sources of income that are being used to pay interest on government debt. Government bonds would then be nothing else but evidences of ownership of this wealth in the physical possession of the government.
2. The government may draw upon its power to produce money to finance the interest payments. However, this is actually a special case of point 3 discussed below, since this action is the equivalent of a tax on money balances (regardless of whether the price level rises or stays the same).

[12] Harry G. Johnson, "Monetary Theory and Policy," *American Economic Review, LII* (June, 1962), p. 343.
[13] From Don Patinkin, *Money, Interest, and Prices*, 2d ed. (New York: Harper & Row, 1956, 1965), p. 289.

3. Or, as Harry G. Johnson visualizes, the government may be paying the interest income out of taxes. However, as we have shown in Chapter 10, it does not follow that the taxes will be capitalized in liabilities *equal* in magnitude to the value of the government debt.

These three reasons for our refusal to accept the above quoted statement all rest on different footing. If the government bonds are of the first type, they are merely evidences of the fact that certain physical wealth is in the possession of the government but is owned by the private sector. In case 2, the problem is ambiguous. If the quantity of money is being increased in times of full employment, the holders of monetary wealth are bearing the burden of this government debt, since every increase in the money supply will lower the price of money, and this measures the amount of the tax imposed on the owners of monetary wealth. If the aggregate supply function does not happen to be perfectly inelastic, the increase in the money supply will increase the level of income; the problem of deciding who loses and who benefits in this case appears to us to depend very much on purely subjective value judgments. Only in the third case is the situation unambiguous in that interest payments received by some are precisely matched by taxes paid by others.

This, however, as we have shown in the preceding chapter, does not signify that the level of wealth is going to remain unchanged if government bonds are created. For the owners, they represent nonhuman wealth; if taxes are necessary to pay interest on this debt and are imposed on nonhuman nonmonetary wealth, there is a presumption that—as Johnson asserts—the positive wealth represented by bonds will be precisely offset by the capitalized value of taxes imposed on nonhuman wealth. However, if these taxes are imposed on human wealth, the difference in the discount rates applicable to either assures that government debt will represent a positive component of wealth, though not by its full amount, since

$$dw = d\frac{g}{r_n} - d\frac{t_h}{r_h} > 0 \qquad\qquad [11.3]$$

Given the fact, however, that *all* taxes irrespective of the purpose they serve have been already excluded from the wealth equations in the first two sections of this chapter, it is necessary to make government debt (the first term of the above equation) an independent part of the wealth equation.[14]

Government Wealth

Finally, the government may own nonhuman wealth, and in some cases this wealth may be significant. It may be accounted for explicitly by including a flow of income emanating from this government wealth capitalized at an appropriate rate of interest or it may be assumed that the income from this wealth is used to reduce the taxes that otherwise would be necessary to provide the government services demanded by the community (as we have done in Chapter 8). However, this does not solve the problem, since the value of the flow of services from government wealth may exceed the interest payments on government bonds. However, for want of a better theory of private responses to government actions we shall have to stand on the decision outlined above. Thus, we shall assume that the flow of services from the government-held wealth is invariant with respect to any endogenous variable in the macroeconomic system, that it is exogenous to the system; we may then impose the constraint that the sum of the taxes equals the interest payments on the government debt. Implicitly we are assuming that government services desired by the community are equal or exceed the total flow of income from the government's wealth and that the demand for government services remains constant (we can, of course, change this desired level and investigate the effect of such a change).

[14] Obviously, this discussion has a bearing on the burden of the debt controversy. Space limitations forbid us to range, however, that far afield. Interested readers may find the end of the controversy, with references to earlier works, in Franco Modigliani, "How to Make a Burden of the Public Debt: A Reply to Mishan," *Journal of Political Economy*, *LXXII* (October, 1964), pp. 483–485.

Conclusion

In this chapter we have discussed the various components of the nonmonetary wealth of the community. Essentially we have arrived at a definition of wealth that can be used in analysis of the effect that changes in wealth may have on the economic behavior of the various sectors of the community. Determining the direction and relative magnitude of these wealth effects will be the problem of Part IV of this book.

CHAPTER 12

Wealth in Economic Theory: Conclusion

At the outset of this book we discussed the various criticisms of the effect of changes in wealth on aggregate economic activity. These criticisms may be placed in two main categories: (1) There are those who admit that the level of wealth may well affect the behavior of decision-making units in the economy, but insist that changes in the level of prices and interest rates cannot change the level of wealth. Hence, the wealth effect cannot occur in the short run. (2) Others admit that changes in the price level or the rate of interest can affect the level of wealth in the short run, but insist that such changes in wealth do not affect the behavior of decision-making units and hence cannot affect the level of economic activity. The first group of criticisms has been the topic of discussion in Parts II and III of this book and the second group will be discussed in Parts IV and V.

The Definitional Argument and its Resolution

The primary target of the critics of the wealth effect has been the monetary component of wealth. For the purposes of their discussion the critics have generally separated money into two parts. First, the "hard" money, i.e., commodity money, was almost generally agreed to be a genuine part of the net wealth of the community and hence subject to change in real value through changes in the price level. However, even here it has been suggested by a few economists that changes in the price level cannot change the real level of wealth through changing the real value of commodity money because such changes merely make the holders of money better or worse off and the remainder of the community worse or better off by an offsetting amount.[1] Second, so called "credit" money (fiat money, demand deposits, and other forms of noncommodity money) was declared to be offset by debts of the issuers of these forms of money. Hence, any change in the price of money could not change the net wealth of the community, since any change in the wealth of the holders of credit money would be offset by an opposite and equal change in the wealth of the issuers of credit money.

But, if changes in the price level cannot change the level of the community's net wealth, neither can the issuance of credit money. The money-is-a-debt proponents are then left in the rather uncomfortable position of saying that for theoretical reasons the real level of "credit" money outstanding could not affect economic behavior and recognizing, at the same time, that the level of this money does appear to affect behavior. As we have seen above, this dilemma has been circumvented by assuming that while the holders of credit money are affected by changes in the real value of their assets, the issuers (debtors) of this money are unaffected. The primary issuer that is assumed to ignore his debts is the government, since an assumption that private firms (banks) should be unaffected by the real value of their debts is rather hard to take.[2] Thus, the money supply, except for the small part of it (zero in many communities) that is commodity money, cannot be affected by changes in the value

---

[1] Syed Ahmad, "The Saving-Wealth Relation," *Journal of Political Economy*, LXX (June, 1962), pp. 287–293.
[2] Don Patinkin, *Money, Interest, and Prices*, 1st ed. (New York: Harper & Row, 1956), p. 204.

of money unless we are willing to assume that certain decision makers ignore, at least to some extent, the real value of their debts.

Finally, it has been pointed out that although the government itself may not be affected by the value of its debts, the existence of interest-bearing debts implies interest payments on them. Thus, changes in the price level may affect the real value of the taxes necessary to service this debt, and this change would make the tax-payers (who do react to the real value of their debts) better or worse off. Therefore, it is asserted, in a world of reasonable certainty (and thus in a world containing only one capitalization rate applicable to all incomes) the assumption that the government fails to react to its real debts is incapable of explaining the effect of government debt on economic behavior.[3]

At that juncture it seemed that the wealth effect had been reduced to a mere analytical toy. The granting of an abstract analytical relevance to the wealth-saving relationship could help, as Paul A. Samuelson put it in 1963, ". . . to save face and honor for the believers in the harmony of equilibrium" while a denial that wealth can change, or would make any empirical difference if it did, could clear the air and enable us to "tackle matters of substance and not ideology."[4]

In Parts II and III, we have subjected the arguments presented above to careful analysis and we have concluded that none of them is theoretically valid. First of all, money—regardless of whether it is commodity money, fiat money, or bank money—was shown to be a part of the net wealth of the community. Second, changes in the price of money (or, if we prefer, in the reciprocal of this price, in the general price level) were shown to change the net wealth of the community because they change the real income yielded by a unit of

[3] Harry G. Johnson, "Monetary Theory and Policy," *American Economic Review,* LII (June, 1962), p. 343.
[4] Paul A. Samuelson, "A Brief Survey of Post-Keynesian Development," in Robert Lekachman (ed.), *Keynes' General Theory* (New York: St. Martin's Press, 1964), p. 333.

this special type of wealth. Third, we have shown that unless reasonable certainty is interpreted in a rather unreasonable manner (to include not only perfect knowledge but also a special condition on the cost of producing human capital of different durabilities), it alone cannot lead to identical capitalization rates on human and nonhuman income flows. In particular, we have shown that under all conditions, except in the case where perfect knowledge is combined with certain specific cost conditions on the production of human capital, the capitalization rate on human income streams will be higher than the capitalization rate on nonhuman income streams. Thus, any theory that purports to be general must allow for these rates of capitalization to be different and, at best, include equal rates as a limiting case. In addition, the persistently neglected fact that human income is analytically definable and empirically measurable at the present time only in gross terms (i.e., gross of the cost of maintaining that capital) makes the capitalization rate on human income still higher relative to the capitalization rate on nonhuman income. In fact, this actual capitalization rate on human income has been estimated to be at the present time as large as one third.[5] As a result, changes in the structure of the community's nonmonetary incomes will have economic consequences—not because of any arbitrary assumption of asymmetry of response of the various decision-making units to these incomes, but because the structure of income affects the total net wealth of the community.

Thus, in our opinion, the first serious challenge to the wealth effect must be considered a failure. The wealth effect cannot be dispatched out of economic theory by denying it the basis on which it stands: by defining wealth so as to make it impossible for a wealth effect to occur. Of course, there are other hurdles to cross: (1) Does economic theory support the conclusion that changes in wealth affect, predictably, the behavior of consumers (the wealth-saving relation), of the holders of money (the wealth-demand for

[5] Milton Friedman, "Windfalls, the 'Horizon,' and Related Concepts in the Permanent Income Hypothesis," in *Measurement in Economics* (Stanford, Calif.: Stanford University Press, 1963), p. 7.

money relation), and of the suppliers of labor (the wealth-labor supply relation)? (2) After this is established, these partial relationships need to be incorporated into a general economic model. (3) Finally, should all these efforts be successful, the task of empirical investigation of the importance of these effects can begin. Before we proceed, let us now replace the definition of wealth that we presented in Chapter 2 for discussion purposes with a definition of wealth based on the conclusions reached in Parts II and III.

The Definition of Wealth

The appropriate definition of wealth depends on the use to which the definition is to be put. For purposes of general analysis the definition should contain only those parts of wealth, the separate existence of which can be defended on *a priori* grounds, or possibly on empirical facts of apparent persistency—"brute facts," to use a term used by Paul A. Samuelson to describe this situation.[6] For the purposes of empirical analysis, certain empirical difficulties may force a complication of our definition of wealth. But, since our purposes in this book are purely analytical, we shall define wealth for the purposes of general analysis as

$$w = \frac{M}{P} + \frac{(y_n - t_n)}{r_n} + \frac{(y_h - t_h)}{r_h} + \frac{g}{r_g} \qquad [12.1]$$

where

$$g = t_n + t_h \qquad [12.2]$$

and

$$r_h > r_n = r_y \qquad [12.3]$$

List of Symbols
  M = nominal quantity of money
  P = price level
  y_h = real human income
  y_n = real nonhuman income
  g = nonhuman real income yielded by government securities

[6] Paul A. Samuelson, "An Exact Consumption-Loan Model of Interest," *Journal of Political Economy, LXVI* (December, 1958), p. 468.

t_h = real taxes on human income

t_n = real taxes on nonhuman income

r_h = capitalization rate applicable to real human income

r_n = capitalization rate applicable to real nonhuman income

r_g = capitalization rate applicable to real government interest payments

Note that after raising the issue of the flow of income from the nonhuman wealth held by the government, we have proceeded to ignore this source of income streams. We do this on the assumption that these flows are constant and simply reduce the taxes necessary to supply the volume of government services demanded, which is also a constant. Therefore, the only effect of leaving this part of wealth out of the wealth equation would be, possibly, to make the effect of changes in the rate of interest on wealth of somewhat different magnitude than otherwise. This difference depends on the rate of interest used to capitalize the flow of services from government-held wealth relative to the rates of interest used to capitalize the tax saving due to the holding of the wealth and on how the structure of these rates changes when the market rate of interest changes. Since little is known of this area we shall neglect it entirely.

Possible Modification in the Wealth Equation

If empirical faithfulness is required, this basic equation may be recast in a number of ways. Let us suggest a few major ones.

Money may be divided into its components, and account explicitly taken of the fact that the production of money requires immobilization of some other monetary wealth as reserves. As empirical research advances along the lines outlined here, both monetary wealth and nonmonetary wealth, which are at present available only in terms gross of the debt element represented by various warranties, should become measurable in net terms.

Government taxes, expressed above in real terms, may be redefined to express the fact that frequently government receipts and expenditures are fixed in money terms. The important consequence of such a redefinition may be found in the fact that the price level, which, in the above equation, affects wealth merely through the money supply then affects wealth also through changes in the real value of government expenditures and revenues: it changes the after-tax structure of the incomes entering the wealth equation.

On a lower level of generality, the existence of different levels of uncertainty that might be attached to income streams yielded by sources of income under the control of the owner (human income and private nonhuman income) and to income streams taken away from (taxes) or given to (subsidies) the private sector on the basis of government decision may prevent us from applying the same capitalization rate r_n to the second term in equation [12.1] and the same capitalization rate r_h to the third term in that equation. To state the same thing differently, this may force us to assume that there is some capitalization rate r_t different from—presumably higher than—the two rates we are using. It may be noted in passing that it is on this basis that Don Patinkin, in his Second Edition, obtains what he calls "the financial-asset effect." It is, as he states, based on "the crucial—though reasonable—assumption that there is an imperfect discounting of the tax liability. . . ."[7] The reasonableness of this assumption is, apparently, being buttressed by the following statement that points out that without it, bonds would disappear from the economic model. We do not feel it necessary to include this refinement because in our model bonds cannot disappear as long as there are—as we expect there always will be—taxes on human income.

Factors Changing Wealth

On the basis of the definition of wealth specified above, it is then possible to derive a list of factors that, if they change, will change the total net wealth of the community.

[7] From Don Patinkin, *Money, Interest, and Prices*, 2d ed. (New York: Harper & Row, 1956, 1965), p. 294.

Changes in Endogenous Factors

For a general economic theory and for a discussion of the automatic functioning of a macroeconomic model changes in the two
endogenous variables, the level of price and the rate of interest, are
of prime importance.

PRICE-INDUCED WEALTH CHANGES. Since the level of prices
determines the real value of any given nominal supply of money,
wealth is a function of the price level. In particular, increases in
the price level will reduce the real value of any given nominal stock
of money so that

$$\frac{\partial w}{\partial P} < 0 \qquad\qquad [12.4]$$

INTEREST-INDUCED WEALTH CHANGES. The level of wealth is a
function of the rates of interest used to capitalize human and nonhuman income such that increases in these rates lead to decreases in
the level of wealth. Hence,

$$\frac{\partial w}{\partial r_h} < 0 \qquad\qquad [12.5]$$

and

$$\frac{\partial w}{\partial r_h} < 0 \qquad\qquad [12.6]$$

STRUCTURE OF INCOME WEALTH CHANGES. If we assume that the
rates of interest used to capitalize human and nonhuman income
streams are not equal, then the level of wealth will be a function of
the distribution of income flows, given the total level of income.
In particular, if we assume that $r_h > r_n$, then a redistribution of
income in favor of human income will reduce wealth[8] so that

$$\frac{\partial w}{\partial \left(\dfrac{y_h}{y_n}\right)} < 0 \qquad\qquad [12.7]$$

[8] We are listing this possibility because Lawrence R. Klein obtained some
evidence that this relationship exists even though, at present, it is impossible
to say whether it is due to endogenous or policy-determined changes.
(Cf. Chapter 2, footnote 11, of the present book.)

Such changes in the distribution of income may arise through the normal market mechanisms. However, if the government tends to fix some revenues and expenditures in money terms—e.g., the interest payments on the debt and the taxes necessary to meet these interest payments—then changes in the price level will affect the structure of income as long as the taxes on human income are positive. In particular, an increase in the price level will reduce the real flow of nonhuman income in the form of interest payments on the government debt and will reduce the real taxes necessary to service this debt. But, if a portion of the taxes are levied on human income, the decrease in nonhuman income will be only partially offset by the reduction in taxes on nonhuman income, the remainder of the reduction coming on the flow of human income. Thus, the increase in the price level will result in a redistribution of income to human from nonhuman sources, and since such a redistribution will reduce wealth, the net effect will be

$$\left[\frac{\partial w}{\partial\left(\frac{y_h}{y_n}\right)}\right]\left[\frac{\partial\left(\frac{y_h}{y_n}\right)}{\partial P}\right] < 0 \qquad [12.8]$$

Policy-induced Changes in Wealth

CHANGES IN THE MONEY SUPPLY. Since the money supply is a component of net wealth, changes in it will affect net wealth. In particular, increases in the supply of money are the counterpart of decreases in the price level. Thus,

$$\frac{\partial w}{\partial M} > 0 \qquad [12.9]$$

CHANGES IN THE DISTRIBUTION OF TAXES. If we assume that the interest rate used to capitalize human income flows is greater than the interest rate used to capitalize nonhuman income flows, then changes in the taxes on these income flows will affect the level of wealth. In particular, an increase in taxes on human income accompanied by a reduction in taxes on nonhuman income (so that the total tax burden remains the same) will increase wealth. Thus,

$$\frac{\partial w}{\partial\left(\dfrac{t_h}{t_n}\right)} > 0 \qquad\qquad [12.10]$$

CHANGES IN THE LEVEL OF THE PUBLIC DEBT.   Since government interest payments are a special type of nonhuman income, an increase in these payments, as long as any portion of it is accompanied by taxes on human income, will also change wealth so that

$$\frac{\partial w}{\partial g} > 0 \qquad\qquad [12.11]$$

Obviously, these policy-determined changes are bound to disturb the equilibrium in the system and bring in their wake changes in the endogenous factors. For instance, at full employment it is quite possible that any change in wealth resulting from a policy-determined change in the quantity of money will be fully offset by an endogenous change in the level of prices. However, here we show merely the partial derivatives; the elaboration of the signs we may expect the total derivatives to have must come from consideration of the complete macroeconomic model.

Before we turn our attention to a macroeconomic model, it is necessary to explore in detail the consequences that changes in wealth may have on the various aspects of the behavior of decision-making units. Some of them are initimately related to each other: if wealth affects total consumption out of any given income, it is likely to affect the consumption of leisure in particular. When we concentrate on the demand side, we speak about the relationship between wealth and the demand for consumption goods. When we concentrate on the supply side, we speak about the relationship between wealth and the demand for leisure or, what is the same thing, the supply of labor. Finally, the consumers are also likely not only to want to hold wealth but also to hold different wealth items in proportions that they consider most satisfying. One way of taking explicit account of the consumer's desire to hold a "balanced portfolio" is to introduce nonmonetary wealth as an argument in the function expressing the public's demand for money. In Part IV, we shall consider in turn each one of these wealth-behavior relationships: the wealth-saving relationship, the wealth-supply of labor relationship, and the wealth-demand for money relationship.

PART IV

WEALTH AND
CONSUMER BEHAVIOR

After establishing a definition of wealth that is, we hope, analytically sound, it now becomes necessary to inquire into the relationship between wealth and consumer behavior. Stated as naïvely as that, there is little problem. Wealth, tautologically, determines how well off the consumer is— changes in wealth, how much better off or worse off he is today than he was yesterday. However, these homilies do not get us very far, since we do need to know how he is going to react to his change in status: Is he going to consume more and save less, is he going to work more or start to lead a more leisurely life? The responses are likely to be as many as there are consumers; the very young may respond differently from, say, the very old. Thus our first task is to present a model of consumer behavior sufficiently general as to be able to predict the responses of any rational consumer; this we shall do in Chapter 13. In the next chapter, Chapter 14, we shall formally introduce money that the consumer uses for transaction purposes and derive the determinants of the demand for this part of wealth. In Chapter 15 we use the basic model of consumer's behavior as modified by the introduction of money to derive the consumer's responses to changes in capital and wealth—to changes in his physical endowment and to changes in the market-determined variables that determine the market value of this physical endowment. However, we are not only interested in what a single consumer will do but also in what the society as a whole will do if its wealth changes: the aggregation problem comes to the fore and is discussed in Chapter 16.

CHAPTER 13

Basic Model

Wealth-behavior Relationships; A Brief Survey

Since the task of economic analysis is to discover the ways in which individuals acquire wealth in a manner least disagreeable to them and dispose of wealth in a manner most agreeable to them, it is not surprising that this analysis concludes that wealth affects economic behavior. And what is true about individuals must be true about society as a whole; namely changes in wealth may be expected to change the behavior of all consumers and thus cause changes in the major macroeconomic functions into which we reduce complex microeconomic relations. When John Maynard Keynes was paving the way to the macroeconomic model that is in general use today, he was aware of most wealth-behavior relationships and spoke about them in quite sophisticated terms; the only major wealth-behavior relationship that Keynes seems to have missed[1] is the one that relates wealth to the demand for one particular good, leisure, or to its complement, the supply of labor. As we have shown in Chapter 1, he recognized that monetary wealth and changes in it

---

[1] We say "*seems* to have missed" and even that with some trepidation, since, as we have just shown, so many other claims that he missed wealth-behavior relationships do not withstand scrutiny.

will affect the consumption and saving decisions of consumers; he recognized the endogenous price-induced wealth effect. Similarly, he recognized that changes in nonmonetary wealth will affect saving and consuming decisions; he recognized the endogenous interest-induced wealth effect. Finally, when he discussed the demand for existing wealth, he realized that the demand for one type of wealth will depend on the quantity of all the remaining types of wealth; the balanced-portfolio argument comes to the fore. Most importantly, it comes to the fore when we discuss the demand for money and its dependence on the other (nonmonetary) wealth held by the consumer:

> ... in *what form* [emphasis Keynes'] he will hold the command over future consumption which he has reserved, whether out of his current income or from previous savings. Does he want to hold it in the form of immediate, liquid command (i.e., in money or its equivalent)? Or is he prepared to part with immediate command . . . , leaving it to future market conditions to determine on what terms he can, if necessary, convert deferred command over specific goods into immediate command over goods in general?[2]

The balanced portfolio argument disappeared from the discussion of the effects of changes in wealth on economic behavior until it was rediscovered in 1949 by Lloyd A. Metzler. Subsequently, it received extensive analytical attention by many writers (Gurley, Shaw, Tobin, and others); empirically, it appears frequently neglected even today. In many investigations, the researchers limit themselves to an investigation of the effect of changes in wealth on consumption even though, on the basis of the balanced portfolio argument, we should expect repercussions also in the consumers' purchases of investment goods. In other studies, the balanced portfolio argument is ignored even as far as its effect on consumption expenditures (that include durables) is concerned. For instance, in the much quoted

---

[2] John Maynard Keynes, *The General Theory of Income Employment and Money* (New York: Harcourt, Brace & World, 1936), p. 166. Reprinted by permission of Harcourt, Brace & World, Inc. Also by permission of Macmillan & Co. Ltd. and the Trustees of the Estate of Lord Keynes.

article by Thomas Mayer, a change in monetary wealth of 28 billion dollars is reduced to a change in income yielded by this wealth. After the marginal consumption-income ratio is applied to this change in imputed income yielded by money, the conclusion is drawn that the *income effect* of a change in wealth on consumption will amount to only 1.2 billion dollars.[3] This approach is inadequate on two counts. First, even if each item in the wealth portfolio of the consumers increased proportionately, the above method would underestimate the change in consumption if present consumption is not inferior to future consumption, since, then, some part of the (balanced) increase in the portfolio would be consumed, in addition to the increase resulting from the income effect, in the first year. Second, the analysis does not start with an assumption of a balanced increase in the portfolio but with an assumption of an increase in only one component of this portfolio—in monetary wealth. Conversion of this gain in one component of the portfolio into other components, so as to establish portfolio equilibrium, must be expected to affect aggregate demand for goods and services other than current consumption: demand for durables and demand for investment goods (residential housing and other). Since money represents only a fraction of the total wealth portfolio, we would expect the balanced portfolio effect upon aggregate demand to exceed substantially the income effect.

Although there can be no doubt that Keynes stated almost all presently known wealth-behavior relationships when discussing the factors affecting the key variables entering his macroeconomic model, it is uncertain what use he made of these relationships in his analysis of the determination of equilibrium in this model. One reason for this uncertainty is that Keynes, even though a skilled mathematician, forsook the use of this tool. He expressed the opinion that "too large a proportion of recent 'mathematical' economics

---

[3] Thomas Mayer, "The Empirical Significance of the Real Balance Effect," *Quarterly Journal of Economics*, *LXXIII* (May, 1959), Table I and p. 282. For results yielding sizeably larger effects, cf. bibliography in footnote 10, Chapter 2, of the present book.

are mere concoctions . . . which allow the author to lose sight of the complexities and interdependencies of the real world. . . ."[4] The absence of a mathematical model supporting Keynes' discussion of the determination of equilibrium in his model and of the forces that change this equilibrium results in great difficulties when we attempt to decide whether some specific conclusion is supposed to be generally true or whether it holds only if certain underlying assumptions are assumed to exist. Although it would be extremely interesting to undertake a systematic inquiry of whether and to what extent Keynes made use, in his *General Theory*, of the wealth-behavior relations stated there, space and topic limitations both make it impossible. All we shall do here is to trace, at least in broad outlines, the subsequent history of the analysis of the various wealth-behavior relationships.

The first decade[5] following the publication of *The General Theory* is marked by Keynes' misfortune. To paraphrase his own statement about Ricardo, Keynes conquered his colleagues as completely as the Holy Inquisition conquered Spain.[6] As a result, instead of the normal case in which the innovator is forced to refine his analysis to the satisfaction of his critical and questioning colleagues, Keynes' supporters undertook to recast the innovator's analysis into as rigorous terms as possible. They prepared mathematical and geometric interpretations of his work which, while yielding all the significant advantages for exposition that only a concisely presented model has, deprived the theory of all "the complexities and inter-dependencies" that Keynes considered so important and that are so conducive to further productive economic thought. As a result, the effect of wealth on the economic behavior of consumers was lost in the course of transition from the book's verbal presentation to the mathematical and geometric interpretation of it; "the Keynesian cross" is the ultimate reduction of a theory *ad absurdum*. In addition, the few critics that Keynes was fortunate enough to acquire did not

---

[4] Keynes, *op. cit.*, p. 298.

[5] As in any historical survey, a "decade" means ten years, give or take a few.

[6] Keynes, *op. cit.*, p. 32.

do much better. While Gottfried Haberler still spoke broadly about "the wealth-saving relation,"[7] those who came after him focused their attention only on the money-saving relationship, and the discussion came to be dominated by the real-balance effect.[8] Even this one component of the complex wealth-behavior relationships was reduced, in the course of the discussion, to net nonexistence when a decision was made that real balances are really an asset of some and a debt of others and thus, not net wealth to society as a whole. The real-balance effect came to be viewed as just another distribution effect that Keynes happened to overlook or ignore.[9] Thus, in the analytical approaches by friend and foe alike, the rich set of relationships between various types of wealth and various types of consumer responses to changes in them became emasculated into a single relationship of doubtful analytical legitimacy.

In the second decade following the publication of *The General Theory*, this process of emasculation was reversed. Studies appeared that analyzed with rigor what was left of all the wealth-behavior relationships (the real-balance effect) and that discovered other wealth-behavior relationships and incorporated them into what is now known as "the Keynesian model." Don Patinkin in his *Money, Interest, and Prices* devoted the entire Part I to a painstaking analysis of the role of money in consumer behavior; Lloyd A. Metzler[10] rediscovered the interest-induced wealth effect and the balanced-portfolio effect and built them into a model of a fully competitive economy that is, once again, a full employment economy and only that. Almost inevitably, the realization followed that anything that makes consumers better off, any increase in consumers' wealth,

[7] Gottfried Haberler, "Sixteen Years Later" in Robert Lekachman (ed.), *Keynes' General Theory* (New York: St. Martin's Press, 1964), p. 292.

[8] A. C. Pigou, "Economic Progress in a Stable Environment," Friedrich A. Lutz and Lloyd W. Mints (ed.), *Readings in Monetary Theory* (New York: The Blackiston Co., 1951), pp. 249–250.

[9] Don Patinkin, *Money, Interest, and Prices*, 1st ed. (New York: Harper & Row, 1956), pp. 202–203.

[10] Lloyd A. Metzler, "Wealth, Saving, and the Rate of Interest," *Journal of Political Economy*, LIX (April, 1951), pp. 93–116.

causes these consumers to demand more of all goods. Not only to demand more market-produced goods and services, but also more of the nonmarket good that we call leisure. But this is just another way of saying that an increase in wealth reduces the supply of what is left of the consumer's time—that it reduces his supply of labor. Louis Hough[11] forged this particular link in the chain of the various wealth-behavior relationships.

In the third decade following the publication of *The General Theory*, two new attacks were launched against wealth-behavior relationships, the fate of which starts to remind one of "The Perils of Pauline." They both replaced the customary one- or two-period analysis with a multiperiod analysis. The first questions the view that nonmonetary wealth is able to affect consumers' behavior in a predictable manner, since a change in the rate of interest has not one but two consequences: it results in the interest-induced wealth effect and, simultaneously, it changes the terms of trade governing the exchange of present for future goods. Since these two affect the consumer's welfare in opposite directions, the net effect of both is said to be uncertain. The second analysis asserts that a change in any item of wealth (monetary or nonmonetary) cannot lead to any *lasting* change in the behavior of consumers. Since, in contrast to the other criticisms of the wealth-behavior relationships, we have not had occasion to discuss these two new ones in the preceding sections of the book, let us now outline each in some detail.

The interest-induced wealth effect, according to which changes in the rate of interest change wealth in the opposite direction and thus change savings in the same direction, was scrutinized recently by R. C. O. Matthews. His analysis, to use his own words, cast doubt "on the contention sometimes advanced that a fall in [the rate of interest] necessarily tends to stimulate expenditure by means of a wealth effect . . ."[12] He pointed out that a fall in the rate of interest

---

[11] Louis Hough, "An Asset Influence in the Labor Market," *Journal of Political Economy*, *LXIII* (June, 1955), pp. 202–215.

[12] R. C. O. Matthews, "Expenditure Plans and the Uncertainty Motive for Holding Money," *Journal of Political Economy*, *LXXI* (June, 1963), p. 205.

has two effects that affect the consumers in opposite ways: (a) a fall in the rate of interest makes the value of sources of income the size of which is fixed more valuable than before, and (b) the same fall signifies that any newly purchased sources of income streams will be less productive than the already existing ones. Thus the *net* effect may cause any one consumer to feel better off or worse off, depending on the length of his horizon.[13]

The second line of attack is to be found in an article on monetary theory by G. C. Archibald and R. G. Lipsey.[14] They open up the issue called the "invariance principle"; they claim that changes in the real quantity of money can only have a temporary effect on consumption while leaving the long-run equilibrium values unaltered.

---

[13] Syed Ahmad claims that we do not know who is better or worse off unless we know the measure in terms of which the real value of assets is assessed by the public. He poses the problem of whether ". . . people consider the real value of their assets in terms of its command over real income and not over real assets." ("The Saving-Wealth Relation and the Real Value of Assets," *Journal of Political Economy, LXX* (June 1962), pp. 289.) This is a red herring: (a) If we measure the consumer's welfare in terms of the market value of his wealth, a fall in the rate of interest will cause the value of the existing wealth to rise, whereas any future given expenditures of resources will yield the same market value of wealth as before. Thus, in these terms, current owners of current wealth are said to be better off, whereas future producers of future wealth are unaffected. (b) If we measure the consumer's welfare in terms of income that he can enjoy, a fall in the rate of interest is identical with saying that any future given expenditure of resources will yield a lower income stream while any existing wealth continues to yield the old income streams. Thus, in these terms, the current owners of current sources of income are unaffected while the future producers of future sources of income are worse off. As long as we are consistent, there is no possibility that, to quote Ahmad again, ". . . conflicting results may follow from various plausible measures. . . ." Since all we are interested in is a comparison between these two groups of consumers, it obviously makes no difference in what terms we measure consumer's welfare as long as we stick to a decision once made. The only danger is that we shall consider the welfare of the current wealth owners in (a) terms, above, and the welfare of future income producers in (b) terms and conclude that they offset each other.

[14] G. C. Archibald and R. G. Lipsey, "Monetary and Value Theory: A Critique of Lange and Patinkin," *Review of Economic Studies, XXVI* (October, 1958), pp. 1–22.

In another article, R. W. Clower and M. L. Burstein[15] follow the same line of inquiry in a model that has money and bonds and reach the same conclusion. N. Liviatan, in his reconsideration of both the above studies expressed the opinion, however, that these two cases are based on a special assumption that the long-run consumption is invariate and that they yield, not very surprisingly, the conclusion that this consumption will not change when, and if, wealth changes. To quote him directly,

> The basic thing in the "invariance principle" which contradicts our economic intuition is that it implies that no matter how rich a consumer may become as a result of a windfall, he must always eventually drift back to his original standard of living. . . . We shall first show that while A[rchibald] and L[ipsey]'s model is formally correct, their conclusion as to the invariance principle depends in a crucial way on their assumption that money is the only asset. . . . In Clower and Burstein's model the stability of the long-run equilibrium does not follow from the model itself (as is the case with A and L) but is arbitrarily assumed to exist. Clearly, if one starts with an *assumption* that a stable long-run equilibrium exists the conclusion that the windfall effect is temporary is almost trivial.[16]

Regardless of what the outcome of these debates is ultimately going to be—and we, in what follows, intend to contribute to it—the very existence of these arguments makes it obvious that a multi-period analysis of consumer behavior is essential if we are to derive analytical conclusions about the responses of the consumer to wealth (and to changes in the endogenous variables that determine wealth). It is also obvious that the line of attack indicated must be based on a multiperiod analysis of the microeconomic underpinnings of various macroeconomic relations if we are to assure ourselves that seemingly

---

[15] R. W. Clower and M. L. Burstein, "On the Invariance of Demand for Cash and Other Assets," *Review of Economic Studies*, *XXVIII* (October, 1960), pp. 32–36.

[16] N. Liviatan, "On the Long-Run Theory of Consumption and Real Balances," *Oxford Economic Papers*, *17* (July, 1965), p. 206.

obvious macroeconomic relations do not rest on clay feet. Multi-period analysis itself is not new; in the past decade, economists have devoted a great deal of attention to it. Their attention has been concentrated, however, on topics that are not of key interest to us in this book. Franco Modigliani, associated with R. Brumberg[17] in one case and A. Ando[18] in the other case, explored the income-consumption relationship by the use of a "life-cycle" approach; similarly, Milton Friedman[19] approached the income-consumption relationship by the use of the permanent-transitory income distinction based on a multiperiod analysis. Menahem E. Yaari[20] extended the scope of the inquiry to cover more variables than only income and consumption; however, his analysis is not entirely satisfactory, since it makes the utility function of the consumer independent of time and thus prevents the aging process from affecting consumers' decisions.

We believe that this survey of the fate of the wealth-behavior relationships indicates that there is merit in attempting to present a formal analysis of the problem, building upon the previous work done and making, if possible, some modest contribution to this work. Needless to say, this field is still very much virgin territory. As consumers, we know how difficult it is to make decisions today on the basis of our estimate of what the future will bring; economic analysis of this decision-making process and empirical verification of this analysis is unlikely to be any easier.

[17] F. Modigliani and R. Brumberg, "Utility Analysis and the Consumption Function: An Interpretation of Cross-Section Data," in K. K. Kurihara (ed.), *Post-Keynesian Economics* (New Brunswick, N.J.: Rutgers University Press, 1954), pp. 388–436.

[18] A. Ando and F. Modigliani, "The 'Life Cycle' Hypothesis of Saving," *American Economic Review*, LIII (March, 1963), pp. 55–84.

[19] M. Friedman, *A Theory of the Consumption Function* (Princeton, N. J.: Princeton University Press, 1957).

[20] Menahem E. Yaari, "On the Consumer's Lifetime Allocation Process," *International Economic Review*, 5 (September, 1964), pp. 304–317; and "Uncertain Lifetime, Life Insurance, and the Theory of the Consumer," *Review of Economic Studies*, 32 (April, 1965), pp. 137–150.

The Basic Model

As we have indicated above, we intend to approach the problem of the effect of wealth on consumer behavior from an individual consumer maximizing approach. To do so, we disaggregate the community into individual spending units; for the sake of convenience, we do not disaggregate the items these individual spending units purchase any more than is necessary. In other words, we are not going to be interested in the problem of how the consumer allocates his intended expenditures among the numerous individual commodities available to him, but rather how he decides on the aggregate level of these expenditures. Thus, for our purposes we shall be interested in the consumer's choice of the level of real consumption of goods and services, and leisure. Since our approach is to be an intertemporal one, we shall be interested in the levels of these arguments of the utility function for more than a single period. In addition, we do not want to restrict the consumers to a zero terminal asset position because we desire to treat the terminal asset position as an object of consumer choice. Essentially, we assume that a consumer may get utility from seeing that certain individuals (usually spouses and children) or institutions (usually nonprofit) are provided for after the consumer's death. Thus, we introduce the time path of the level of real bequest expenditures as an additional function to be chosen by the consumer. The terminal value of this function is, of course, equal to the consumer's terminal asset position and is his final bequest to his heirs. Our approach in the following discussion will be an infinite dimensional one; that is, we make use of the calculus of variations, but the mathematical exposition is kept to a minimum and explanation is given at each step.

Let us begin by considering a consumer whose present utility is a functional[21] of the time path of his real consumption of goods and

---

[21] A functional is a function that attaches a real number to a function. In this case the functions to which real numbers (utility) are attached are the time path of consumption of goods and services, bequests, and leisure, i.e., $c(t)$, $b(t)$, and $l(t)$.

services, $c(t)$; the time path of his consumption of leisure, $l(t)$; and the time path of real bequest expenditures, $b(t)$. Thus, $c(t)$, $b(t)$, and $l(t)$ are rates of consumption of goods (and services), bequests, and leisure, respectively, so that total consumption of goods (and services), bequests, and leisure for the interval $I_1 = t_1 - t_0$ may be written as

$$C_{I_1} = \int_{t_0}^{t_1} c(t)\, dt \qquad\qquad [13.1]$$

$$L_{I_1} = \int_{t_0}^{t_1} l(t)\, dt \qquad\qquad [13.2]$$

$$\beta_{I_1} = \int_{t_0}^{t_1} b(t)\, dt \qquad\qquad [13.3]$$

where C_{I_1} is the total consumption of goods and services during the period I_1; L_{I_1} is the total consumption of leisure during the period I_1; and β_{I_1} is the total amount of bequests made during the interval I_1. We write the utility functional as follows:

$$U[c(t), l(t), b(t), \tau, T] = \int_{\tau}^{T} \mu[c(t), l(t), b(t), \tau, T, t]\, dt \quad [13.4]$$

where τ is the present time and T is the end of the consumer's horizon. By horizon we shall mean the termination of the consumer's life, which for the present we shall consider is known with zero variance. Let us consider this functional with some care. It gives the level of utility associated with various functions $c(t)$, $l(t)$ and $b(t)$. Thus, the integrand of [13.4] is not a utility function. However this function does show the level of utility derived at the present time (τ) from various levels of consumption, bequests, and leisure enjoyed in all the various years (t) up to the terminal year T. The function μ can be viewed as a utility function ("instantaneous" to use Strotz's terminology) if and only if it is possible to factor (t) out of it so that μ can be written as

$$\mu = \alpha(t, T, \tau)\mu^*(c(t), b(t), l(t)) \qquad\qquad [13.5]$$

Here, the function α may be interpreted as a discount function and

μ^* as the function that indicates the level of utility associated with various levels of $c(t)$, $l(t)$, and $b(t)$.[22] Thus, for this case, [13.4] may be interpreted as the discounted present value of future utilities. An interesting implication of equation [13.5] is that the marginal rate of substitution between any two arguments is independent of time and depends only on the values of the arguments themselves. This can be shown simply by noting that the relative partials of U are as follows:

$$\frac{\partial U}{\partial c(t)} = \alpha(t, T, \tau)\mu^*_{c(t)}$$

$$\frac{\partial U}{\partial b(t)} = \alpha(t, T, \tau)\mu^*_{b(t)} \qquad [13.6]$$

$$\frac{\partial U}{\partial l(t)} = \alpha(t, T, \tau)\mu^*_{l(t)}$$

where $\mu^*_{c(t)}$, $\mu^*_{b(t)}$, $\mu^*_{l(t)}$ are the partial derivatives of μ^*. Since the partials of μ^* are independent of time and for any given t, $\alpha(t, T, \tau)$ is simply a common constant coefficient of all partials, the marginal rates of substitution are independent of time. Thus, a phenomenon such as increased preference for leisure as consumers age is not consistent with this formulation. Since we shall be interested in such changes in the consumer's preferences and since the mathematical techniques required are no more sophisticated than when a constancy in these preferences is assumed, we shall not assume separability of μ.

The next step in the analysis is to specify the means that the consumer has available to maximize his utility. In general, it will depend on his initial wealth position and on the subsequent output of income that he (as human wealth) and his assets will produce. To make it possible for him to consume more or less of his income at any particular time there must be in our economy some assets (if positive, wealth of any type; if negative, debt certificates) that the consumer may hold. Since details at this point make no difference, assume that

[22] R. H. Strotz, " Myopia and Inconsistency in Dynamic Utility Maximization," *Review of Economic Studies, XXIII* (October, 1956), pp. 165–180.

he holds all his assets in real bonds (positive or negative) that are risk-free and earn at time (t) the market rate of interest $r(t)$, where $r(t)$ is the time path of the rate of interest.

Since we have assumed that the end of the consumer's horizon occurs at time T, the budget constraint under which he operates is defined up to that time. As long as we allow borrowing and lending at the same rate of interest, it is sufficient to express the constraint in terms of values at time τ, or T. As it turns out, the arithmetic is simpler if we capitalize values rather than discount, so we have chosen the termination of our consumer's life as our point of valuation. Thus, for a fixed time path of income, we may express the budget constraint as

$$\int_{\tau}^{T} e^{\int_{t}^{T} r(u)\,du} y(t)\,dt + e^{\int_{\tau}^{T} r(u)\,du} A(\tau)$$
$$= \int_{\tau}^{T} e^{\int_{t}^{T} r(u)\,du}[c(t) + b(t)]\,dt \qquad [13.7]$$

where $y(t)$ is the time path of income, $A(\tau)$ is the real value of assets at time τ, $r(u)$ is the time path of the rate of interest, and $c(t)$ and $b(t)$ arc as previously noted. The term containing the Napierian constant e results from the fact that we are continuously compounding at rate of interest $r(t)$. The equation states that his initial assets and subsequently produced income must be equal (in their capitalized future value) to the capitalized future value of purchases of consumption (of goods and services) and bequests.[23] Leisure, of course, does

---

[23] Income is, of course, the flow of goods and services produced by the assets net of the capital consumption allowance. Saving (and investment) is that part of this income devoted to purchases of additional sources of income; consumption is that part devoted to current enjoyment. We feel it necessary to specify this, since Kenneth E. Boulding recently offered a radically different definition of consumption claiming that it is the one "also used by classical economists." According to it, consumption seems to be identical with the capital consumption allowance; it is ". . . the 'using up' or the destruction of stock of goods . . . if we had unbreakable china . . . and machines that never wore out, consumption would be much diminished. . . . It is the size of the house we live in, the elegance of the clothes we wear that give us satisfaction, not the incidental and regrettable fact that in the course

not appear explicitly in the equation that makes his means equal to the use of his means, since he does not buy leisure in the same manner as he buys consumption goods. He "buys" it by working less than he would otherwise. If we allow the consumer to select the time path of income (i.e., if we allow him to select his optimal path of leisure), then $y(t)$ must be expressed as a function of the time path of work, say, $w(t)$.

Before we do so, however, and before we use this basic model to work out the principles the consumer will follow to maximize his present utility, we want to introduce money explicitly into our model. As we have pointed out above, the returns from the use of money lie in its facilitating exchanges. Thus, holding money balances has a return to the consumer in that it reduces the transaction time involved in any given level of expenditures. Since the task of introducing money into the model we have developed is somewhat complicated and since the implications of this development are many, we have reserved the next chapter for this problem. However, this detour means that we shall not resume the current argument until Chapter 15.

---

of yielding these satisfactions, they happen to be afflicted by decay and consumption." If we understand this startling idea, the famous Knightian perennial (cf. Chapter 4, ftn. 12) would yield satisfaction (not, as Knight says, consumption) if cut off and investment if not cut off; consumption of it would be zero, since the decay of it is zero. Or, a statue or a painting that never decays (has a zero capital consumption allowance) would yield no "consumption" to the owner; just satisfaction. While we find it hard to accept the alleged classical parentage of these definitions, this is not the place to debate that issue. Thus, we limit ourselves to the statement that Boulding's definitions are not the ones we are using. (Cf. Kenneth E. Boulding, *Economic Analysis, Macroeconomics* (New York: Harper & Row, 1966), pp. 125–126.)

CHAPTER 14

Demand for Money

In a risk-free economy in which the consumers have zero elasticity of expectations, i.e., expect that future prices will equal current prices—and this is the economy with which we are dealing now—money is not desired as an asset that furnishes protection against fluctuations in the rate of interest, nor is it desired as an asset that furnishes protection against expected increases in the price of capital goods other than money. In this economy, money is desired solely because it reduces the time the consumer must spend while undertaking transactions. By its use, the consumer is able to increase his consumption of leisure time, or is able to increase his income through an increase in work time, or both.[1] Thus, there will be a return to (or benefit from) holding a part of wealth in the form of money. This being the case, it is necessary that we subtract from the budget constraint specified in the preceding chapter the capitalized value of the interest forgone as a result of the decision of the consumer to hold money and, thus, not to hold some income-earning asset. Simultaneously, we must add to our real income the return from the use of these real money balances. Let us begin by assuming that the time spent in undertaking transactions is a function of the real

---

[1] Gary Becker, "A Theory of the Allocation of Time," *Economic Journal* *LXXV* (September, 1965), pp. 493–517.

value of consumption expenditures, bequest expenditures, and real money balances (m) held so that

$$B(t) = g(c(t), b(t), m(t)) \qquad [14.1]$$

where $B(t)$ is the time path of bartering and

$$g_{c(t)} > 0, g_{b(t)} > 0, g_{m(t)} < 0 \qquad [14.2]$$

In addition, during any period of time, say $(t_1 - t_0)$, the cumulative time spent on leisure, work and bartering is assumed to equal the total elapsed time. Thus,

$$B(t) + l(t) + w(t) = 1 \qquad [14.3]$$

so that

$$\int_{t_0}^{t_1} (B(t) + l(t) + w(t)) \, dt = (t_1 - t_0) \qquad [14.4]$$

where $w(t)$ is the time path of work.

Let us now assume that the time path of income is a function of the time path of work and time itself so that

$$y(t) = f(w(t), t) \qquad [14.5]$$

where $f_{w(t)} > 0$ and for simplicity $f_{w(t), w(t)} = 0$. By applying identity [14.3] to [14.5] we can rewrite [14.5] as a function of leisure and barter so that

$$y(t) = h(l(t), B(t), t) \qquad [14.6]$$

where $h_l = h_B = -f_w < 0$. Substituting [14.1] into [14.6] we get

$$\begin{aligned} y(t) &= h[l(t), g(c(t), b(t), m(t)), t] \\ &= H(l(t), c(t), b(t), m(t), t) \end{aligned} \qquad [14.7]$$

where $H_l < 0$, $H_c < 0$, $H_b < 0$, $H_m > 0$; $H_{cm} > 0$, $H_{bm} > 0$; and for simplicity $H_{ll} = H_{cc} = H_{bb} = H_{lb} = H_{lc} = H_{bc} = H_{lm} = 0$. Thus, the consumer's income at time (t) depends on the amount of leisure consumed and the amount of money held. However, for any given functions $c(t)$, $b(t)$, and $l(t)$, the consumer will hold money so as to maximize the capitalized value of his earned income stream

$y(t)$ plus the capitalized value of his initial assets $A(\tau)$. Hence, the consumer wishes to choose the time path of money held $m(t)$ so as to make the following functional a maximum:

$$C = \int_\tau^T e^{\int_t^T r(u)\,du} H(l(t), c(t), b(t), m(t), t)\,dt$$

$$+ e^{\int_\tau^T r(u)\,du} A(\tau) - \int_\tau^T e^{\int_t^T r(u)\,du}(r(t)m(t))\,dt \qquad [14.8]$$

The Optimal Time Path of Money Holdings

Let us begin by assuming that the function H is continuous and at least twice differentiable. Then in order for [14.8] to be a maximum for a given $\hat{m}(t)$ it is necessary and sufficient that the increment of [14.8] be less than or equal to zero for all increments $h_m(t) = m(t) - \hat{m}(t)$.[2] In particular, it is necessary that the first variation of [14.8] vanish for $m(t) = \hat{m}(t)$.[3] Thus, it is necessary that the following integral vanish:

$$\delta C = \int_\tau^T e^{\int_t^T r(u)\,du}[H_m(l(t), c(t), b(t), m(t), t)$$

$$- r(t)]h_m(t)\,dt = 0 \qquad [14.9]$$

where H_m is the partial derivative of H with respect to m. For $r(t)$ continuous in $[\tau, T]$, [14.9] equal to zero for arbitrary $h_m(t)$ implies that the coefficient of $h_m(t)$ in [14.9] must equal zero for all t in $[\tau, T]$. Thus, our necessary condition becomes

$$e^{\int_t^T r(u)\,du}[H_m(l(t), c(t), b(t), m(t), t) - r(t)] = 0 \qquad [14.10]$$

[2] I. M. Gelfand and S. V. Fomin, *Calculus of Variations* (Englewood Cliffs, N.J.: Prentice-Hall, 1963), pp. 12–13.
[3] The first variation is the principal linear part of the increment ΔU, i.e., the linear functional which differs from ΔU by an infinitesimal of order higher than one relative to the max $|h_m(t)|$. See Gelfand and Fomin, *op. cit.*, pp. 11–12.

for all t in $[\tau, T]$. Since $e^{\int_t^T r(u)\,du}$ is never zero, then for [14.10] to be zero requires the following:

$$H_m(l(t), c(t), b(t), m(t), t) = r(t) \qquad \text{for all } t \text{ in } [\tau, T] \qquad [14.11]$$

Now H_m is simply the marginal revenue of holding money at time t; that is, H_m is the change in value of real income per (real) dollar change in money balances held, and $r(t)$ is the marginal cost of holding money at time t. Hence, [14.11] is the traditional result that a consumer should hold money until the marginal revenue is equal to the marginal cost. From [14.11] we can solve for $m(t)$ in terms of $c(t)$, $b(t)$, $r(t)$ and t giving us

$$m(t) = G(c(t), b(t), r(t), t) \qquad [14.12]$$

Note that $l(t)$ does not appear in [14.12] because H_{ml} is assumed zero.

Sufficiency conditions for our solution $\hat{m}(t)$ to maximize [14.8] require that the second variation be strongly negative. Thus,

$$\delta^2 C = \frac{1}{2} \int_\tau^T e^{\int_t^T r(u)\,du} H_{mm} h_m^2(t)\,dt \le k\|h\|^2 \qquad [14.13]$$

where $\|h\|$ is the $\max_t |m(t) - \hat{m}(t)| = \max_t |h_m(t)|$, and $k < 0$ is a constant. It is necessary for [14.13] to be satisfied that $H_{mm} < 0$ for all t in $[\tau, T]$. Sufficiency conditions would require in addition that the remaining terms in the Taylor expansion of C be small relative to [14.13] for all $h_m(t)$.[4] However, what will follow does not depend on these additional conditions, so that they will not be derived here.

The Comparative Statics of the Demand for Money

We are now in a position to see the effect of variations in $c(t)$, $b(t)$, and $l(t)$ on the equilibrium $m(t)$, i.e., determine the signs of the partial derivatives of [14.12]. For this we must take the variation

---

[4] Gelfand and Fomin, *ibid.*, pp. 99–100.

of our necessary condition, i.e., the variation of [14.9], which is

$$\int_\tau^T e^{\int_t^T r(u)\,du}[H_{mc}h_c(t) + H_{mb}h_b(t) + H_{ml}h_l(t)$$
$$- h_r(t)]h_m(t)\,dt = 0 \qquad [14.14]$$

where $h_c(t) = [c(t) - \hat{c}(t)]$, $h_b(t) = [b(t) - \hat{b}(t)]$, $h_l(t) = [l(t) - \hat{l}(t)]$, $h_r(t) = [r(t) - \hat{r}(t)]$ and $\hat{c}(t)$, $\hat{b}(t)$, $\hat{l}(t)$, and $\hat{r}(t)$ are the original values of the functions $c(t)$, $b(t)$, $l(t)$, and $r(t)$. As before, if [14.14] is to be zero for arbitrary $h_m(t)$, then the coefficient of $h_m(t)$ must be zero for all t. Thus

$$H_{ml}h_l(t) + H_{mc}h_c(t) + H_{mb}h_b(t) + H_{mm}h_m(t) - h_r(t) = 0 \quad [14.15]$$

for all t in $[\tau, T]$, so that by applying the signs assumed in [14.7] for H_{mc}, H_{mb}, and H_{ml} and the necessary condition derived from [14.13], we get[5]

$$\frac{h_m(t)}{h_c(t)} > 0; \qquad \frac{h_m(t)}{h_b(t)} > 0; \qquad \frac{h_m(t)}{h_l(t)} = 0; \qquad \frac{h_m(t)}{h_r(t)} < 0 \quad [14.16]$$

for all t in $[\tau, T]$.[6] Since for given t the fractions in [14.15] are ratios

[5] R. C. O. Matthews pointed out that an increase in the rate of interest makes the consumer *qua* holder of fixed-yield assets worse off and *qua* prospective purchaser of new assets better off, with the net effect uncertain. Thus he concluded that the effect of interest rate changes on demand for consumption goods is uncertain. By analogy, he extended this conclusion to the demand for money. This extension does not hold on two counts: (a) A rise in the rate disturbs the balanced portfolio of the consumer. Regardless of whether he is better off or worse off (or indifferent), he faces a fall in his nonmonetary wealth and no change in his monetary wealth. Restoration of portfolio equilibrium requires a fall in the demand for money wealth and a rise in the demand for nonmoney wealth, regardless of what happens to his demand for newly produced wealth. For obvious reasons, changes in the demand for existing stocks must dominate changes in demand for additions to these stocks. (b) In addition, we show in Chapter 16 that Matthews' analysis, although valid for each consumer, is invalid for society as a whole. To apply its conclusions to society as a whole involves us in a fallacy of composition. (R. C. O. Matthews, "Expenditure Plans and the Uncertainty Motive for Holding Money," *Journal of Political Economy*, *LXXI* (June, 1963), p. 205.)

[6] Here the variations $h_m(t)$ may be considered as differentials for fixed t in $[\tau, T]$.

of differentials they are the partial derivatives of [14.12]. Hence, we may write

$$\frac{\partial G}{\partial c} > 0; \qquad \frac{\partial G}{\partial b} > 0; \qquad \frac{\partial G}{\partial r} < 0; \qquad \frac{\partial G}{\partial l} = 0 \qquad [14.17]$$

for all t in $[\tau, T]$.

Analysis of the Result Obtained

This specification of the determinants of the demand for money raises three questions that it appears desirable to discuss in detail before we proceed with our main enterprise, the derivation of the optimum behavior of a consumer who wants to maximize an intertemporal utility function. First, the above result (equation [14.12] above) indicates that the demand for money is a function of the real value of present and future consumption, and bequest expenditures, made by the consumer, and not the number of transactions undertaken. Since the real value of the consumer's consumption, and bequests, may be taken to be determined by this income function and his assets, the above result might lead to an impression that somewhere in our analysis there is a hidden, implicit preference for the hypothesis contained in the "Cambridge Quantity Equation" over the "Fisher Quantity Equation." [7] Second, the reader might find it puzzling that in contrast with the demand for other capital goods, the demand for money should not be dependent on the price of money. Third, the fact that the above specification of the determinants of money contains both income and the rate of interest may lead to the impression that the results obtained above are identical with those contained in the well-known demand for money function found in Keynes' *General Theory*. Let us discuss each one of these three issues in turn.

[7] These terms are taken over from John Maynard Keynes, *A Treatise on Money* (London: The Macmillan Co., 1958), Vol. 1, pp. 229 and 233.

Cambridge Versus Fisher

In the literature we find two formulations of the demand for money, both bearing the name "quantity theory of money." In the Fisher formulation, demand for money depends on the number and size of transactions made by the use of money that are undertaken in the economy. In the Cambridge formulation, the demand for money depends on the community's income. If we assume that the economic organization of society is such that the number of transactions per unit of income generated is constant, then it becomes a matter of taste whether we prefer to use one or the other statement. However, it seems preferable to view the number of transactions per unit of income as being a result of optimizing behavior on the part of the consumers. Thus using income as a scale variable in the determination of the demand for money subsumes the level of transactions, but the reverse is not true.

Let us discuss the above in terms of the preceding analysis of the demand for money. We concluded that the amount of money held at a point in time was a function of the level of real consumption expenditures, real bequest expenditures, and the rate of interest. But where is the number and value of transactions? Here they are subsumed in the real consumption and bequest expenditures. That is, consumption and bequest expenditures imply transactions. However, given the level of real consumption and bequest expenditures over an interval, there is a set of various numbers and sizes of transactions consistent with these chosen levels of real consumption and bequest expenditures. Of this set the consumer chooses the element—i.e., the one number and size of transactions—that will maximize the capitalized value of his income function plus initial asset position. Thus, the consumer is able to choose within the limits of the organization of the community the number and size of transactions and the quantity of money held so as to make himself as well off as possible. Since this choice will be affected by the income function and by his initial assets through their effect on his optimal choice of real consumption, bequests, and leisure, it does not follow that the units of money held per dollar of transactions will remain constant at different levels of income and wealth. Thus, using income and wealth in the demand for money on the aggregate level does not imply that transactions are not important, but simply summarizes the effect on the number and size of transactions of changes in the level of income and wealth, given the institutional and technological constraints under which the economy operates. Using the transactions approach, on the other hand, emphasizes the effect of changes in the institutional and technological constraints of the community for given income. Thus both approaches are useful and neither excludes the other.

Price of Money Not Determining the Demand for Money

It might seem surprising that the preceding specifications of the determinants of the demand for money do not contain the price of money. There are two reasons for this. We are assuming a risk-free economy with zero elasticity of expectations. Hence, future prices of all goods, including money, are assumed to equal current prices for the duration of the consumers' horizon and beyond. As a result, the consumers are not holding speculative inventories of any good, monetary or nonmonetary, and neither present nor expected future prices determine the level of these inventories. However, in this riskless economy demand for nonmonetary goods would be co-determined by the prices of these goods: had we specified the demand for cars or apple trees or cranes, surely the prices of these goods would have appeared in the equations specifying the demand for these goods. Why then, doesn't the price of money (or its reciprocal, the general price level) appear as a determinant of the demand for the money good? We have shown in Chapter 3 that money has the unique characteristic of yielding real income that is proportionate to its price. This makes the real price of money services—i.e., the price of the services of money in terms of consumption goods— given the initial holdings of real money balances, independent of the existing price level. The only effect that the existing price level has is to determine the nominal stock of money that will be held by any consumer. It might be noted that if a nonmoney capital good existed that had this same unique property, of the flow of services yielded being proportionate to its price, then the demand for the services of this capital good would also be independent of the current level of its price, since the real price of the service—that is, the price of the service of this capital good in terms of other goods—would be independent of the price of the capital good. Again, the only effect that the price of this capital good would have is to determine the nominal units of the capital good that the consumer would have to hold to receive the flow of services that he desired. Thus, once the decision to hold a given stock of real money has been made, the stock of nominal money associated with this given real stock is given by the relationship

$$M = P\hat{m} \qquad\qquad [14.18]$$

where $\hat{m}$ is the desired level of real money balances.

The result contained in equation [14.18] has been construed by most of the theories of the demand for money to imply that the price elasticity of demand for nominal money is unitary.[8] However, such an assertion neglects the fact that [14.18] is valid only for given levels of initial holdings of real money balances. Since the real value of initial holdings of nominal money balances is affected by the level of prices, wealth is affected by changes in prices, and hence the desired level of real present and future consumption and the desired real money holdings will be changed. In particular, assume that the price level increases. Such a change in prices will reduce the value of the stock of nominal money, reduce wealth, and thus lead to a reduction in desired real consumption and desired holdings of real money balances. This reduction in the desired level of real money holdings will reduce the increase in the demand for nominal balances implied by equation [14.18] and result in an implied price

[8] Cf. Allan H. Meltzer, "The Demand for Money; the Evidence From the Time Series," *Journal of Political Economy, LXXI* (June, 1963), p. 227.

elasticity of demand for nominal money holdings of less than one.[9]
It is, of course, possible to specify economic conditions that prevent
changes we have just outlined and that, as a result, assure that the
identity [14.18] becomes converted into a function expressing the
level of nominal money consistent with equilibrium for various
price levels. If we, for instance, make the assumption that the

[9] This point is easily proven by considering our demand for money equation
for the current time τ;

$$\hat{m}(\tau) = G[c(t), b(t), r(t), \tau] \tag{1}$$

and assuming that, as we shall show in Chapter 15, current real consumption
is a function of the capitalized value of present and future income, the
capitalized value of current wealth holdings, and the rate of interest so that;

$$c(\tau) = J\left(\int_{\tau}^{T} e^{r(T-t)}y(t)\, dt,\ e^{r(T-\tau)}\left[\frac{M}{P} + a(\tau)\right]\right) \tag{2}$$

where we assume that $r(t) = r$ for all t in $[\tau, T]$ and that $a(\tau)$ is the level of
real bond holdings at time τ.
Now consider the differential of [14.18] in the text:

$$dM = P\, d\hat{m} + \hat{m}\, dP \tag{3}$$

From [1] and [2] above we get that

$$d\hat{m} = -G_c \cdot J_w \cdot e^{r(T-\tau)}\left(\frac{M}{P}\right) dP \tag{4}$$

so that by substitution of [4] into [3] we get

$$dM = \left[\hat{m} - G_c \cdot J_w \cdot e^{r(T-\tau)}\left(\frac{M}{P}\right)\right] dP \tag{5}$$

Noting that $\hat{m} = \dfrac{M}{P}$ and solving [5] for $\dfrac{dM}{dP}$ we get

$$\frac{dM}{dP} = [1 - G_c \cdot J_w \cdot e^{r(T-\tau)}]\frac{M}{P} \tag{6}$$

so that the price elasticity of demand for nominal money balances is

$$\left(\frac{dM}{dP}\right)\left(\frac{P}{M}\right) = [1 - G_c \cdot J_w \cdot e^{r(T-\tau)}] \tag{7}$$

which is less than unity, since G_c, J_w, and $e^{r(T-\tau)}$ are all positive.
    Karl Brunner tells us that this conclusion about the price elasticity of
demand for nominal money being less than unity is consistent with results
yielded by his and Allan H. Meltzer's as yet unpublished investigation of
the determinants of the demand for money.

supply of all goods and services is fixed, so that expenditures on goods yielding present and future consumption cannot change, and if we assume that the rate of interest is fixed (which may be an automatic consequence of the first assumption), then the factors determining the demand for real money are prevented from changing. As a result, the real quantity of money demanded $\dot{m}$ is prevented from changing. Identity [14.18] then becomes a function expressing the demand for nominal money; the implied elasticity of nominal money holdings with respect to the general price level (and, conversely the implied elasticity of the general price level with respect to nominal money holdings) becomes unity. The reader has surely noticed by now that the assumptions about the nature of the economy and the analytical conclusions derived by their use are those of the rigid version of the quantity theory of money.

Comparison with Keynes' Demand for Money Function

From our analysis of consumer behavior we concluded that the demand for money will depend on income and on the rate of interest. However, money demanded for speculative purposes was excluded from our analysis. Were we to put it in, the determinant of the speculative demand for this good—just as the determinant of a speculative demand for any other good—would surely be some expectational function (x) containing expectations about future interest rate and price changes:

$$m - m_1 + m_2 = l_1(y, r) + l_2(x) \qquad [14.19]$$

On the other hand, the Keynesian demand for money function,[10] while also containing income and the rate of interest as determinants, reads as follows:

$$M = M_1 + M_2 = L_1(Y) + L_2(r) \qquad [14.20]$$

---

[10] John Maynard Keynes, *The General Theory of Employment Interest and Money* (New York: Harcourt, Bruce & World, 1936), p. 199. Reprinted by permission of Harcourt, Brace & World, Inc. Also by permission of Macmillan & Co. Ltd. and the Trustees of the Estate of Lord Keynes.

The fact that one equation is stated in real terms and the other in money terms is of no interest to us at present. Other differences, however, are worth discussing because the manner in which Keynes wrote his demand function for money gave rise to what we consider to be a serious confusion in monetary theory. This confusion results from accepting the Keynes function as stated above and from several subtle, almost imperceptible, shifts in interpretation, terminology, and emphasis. First, the fact that Keynes split up the two determinants of the demand for transaction money and the demand for speculative money fostered the notion, so frequent in the literature, that we may distinguish between these two demands by referring to the determinants: that demand for money determined by income is transaction demand and that demand for money determined by the interest rate is speculative demand. Second, the term "speculative" has come to be replaced with terms very misleading in their implications: "the asset demand," "demand for money to hold," etc. Third, Keynes wrote the demand for money equation as *the sum* of the two demands. Although this is harmless when we talk about "transaction money" and "speculative money," it becomes most confusing once we start to speak about "money demanded for transactions" and "money demanded to hold." The additive feature of Keynes' equation then leads directly to the notion that money demanded for transactions may not be held at all and that there may be demand for money to hold with money not used for transactions at all. Once this view is established, it becomes easy to conclude that when we attempt to provide an operationally meaningful *definition* of money to which the above equations pertain, we may concentrate on assets that are being held—regardless of whether or not they happen to facilitate transactions. Ultimately, we end up with the declared inability of economists (discussed in Chapter 7) to distinguish between money and debts. Before we grasp this nettle, it might be useful to go back to *The General Theory* to see to what extent Keynes is reponsible for all this.

In Chapter 1 of the present book, we have seen that as far as the consumption function is concerned, Keynes carefully spelled out all the factors affecting it and then dashed off an equation completely unrelated to his discussion. Similarly, the demand for money equation reproduced above has little relation to his verbal analysis of the determinants of the demand for money. First, he disposes of the additive feature of his equation by stating that these two demands "are *largely* [emphasis ours] independent of one another" and even that statement he declares to be merely "a safe first approximation." Second, about the transaction demand he states that it will depend on income *and*, among other factors, on "the effective cost of holding idle cash"; i.e., on the rate of interest. However, strangely enough for a book containing "interest" in the title and a discussion of the effects of changes in the rate on the page following, he adds correctly but irrelevantly and misleadingly that, "if we have a short period of time in view and can safely assume *no material change* [emphasis ours] in any of these factors," we can ignore them. Third, about the speculative demand Keynes states the following:

> ... *uncertainty* [emphasis his] as to the future course of the rate of interest is the sole intelligible explanation of [speculative demand]. ... It follows that a given [amount of speculative money] will not have a definite quantitative relation to a given rate of interest of r:—what matters is not the *absolute* [emphasis his] level of r but the degree of its divergence from what is considered a fairly *safe* [emphasis his] level of r, having regard to those calculations of probability which are being relied on.[11]

While he goes on to make the speculative demand depend simply on the level of the rate of interest, this is explicitly merely a simplifying assumption. Obviously, by now nothing is left of equation [14.20]; in his verbal analysis, Keynes comes up with a demand for money function that is identical with the one expressed in equation [14.19] (except for the difference that one is stated in nominal and the other in real terms).

Let us now return to our main issue; to the notion that money may be demanded for transaction purposes but not held or that

[11] Keynes, *ibid.*, p. 201.

money may be demanded for asset purposes but not for transaction purposes. Keynes himself starts this trend in thinking when he uses interchangeably the concept of the speculative demand and the concept of the propensity to hoard. By the time that Franco Modigliani wrote his well-known mathematical version of the Keynesian model, the transition from the speculative demand to the demand for money to hold was completed. Modigliani distinguishes between "the transaction demand for money" and "the demand for money as an asset"; later, he analyzes "the classical case when the equilibrium rate of interest is sufficiently high to make the *demand for money to hold* [emphasis ours] zero or negligible."[12] Here we meet the notion that money may be held or not held at will and that there may be money used for transactions while none is "held." As time goes by, such statements become more and more explicit until we reach analyses such as the one presented by James Tobin. Under certain conditions, he states:

> Even though money is required as a medium of exchange, transactors will suffer no cost or inconvenience by holding more lucrative assets at all times except the negligible microseconds before and after transactions.[13]

As a result, as Tobin puts it, "no one will hold [money]." On the opposite side of the spectrum, we find analyses of the demand for money only for asset purposes and not at all for transaction purposes. For instance, Paul A. Samuelson considers "the social contrivance of money" as a store of value in a society "with ideal clearing arrangements [where] money as a medium of exchange might have little function."[14] In what follows we intend to show

[12] Franco Modigliani, "Liquidity Preference and the Theory of Interest and Money," Friedrich A. Lutz and Lloyd W. Mints (ed.), *Readings in Monetary Theory* (New York: The Blackiston Co., 1951), p. 223.

[13] James Tobin, "Money, Capital, and Other Stores of Value," *American Economic Review, LI* (May, 1961), p. 26.

[14] Paul A. Samuelson, "An Exact Consumption-Loan Model of Interest With or Without the Social Contrivance of Money," *Journal of Political Economy, LXVI* (December, 1958), p. 481.

that neither one of these two polar positions can survive careful analysis:

1. We cannot have transaction money unless money is held in between transactions. This can be shown by proceeding from two, opposite, directions. First, we may assume that money does not exist and inquire into the conditions for its existence. Second, we may assume that money does exist and inquire into the conditions which, if they prevail, will cause money to cease to exist:

   a. If the consumer can get rid of the good he does not want and acquire the good he wants instantaneously, money is not needed and will not exist since barter is the only efficient means of undertaking exchanges. However, if a chain of barter transactions is required to accomplish the consumer's purpose, the existence of money becomes possible —but even then it is not certain. It becomes possible because the use of money reduces the chain of transactions necessary to only two: the initial and the final one. This shows that transactions undertaken by the use of money cannot be, purely conceptually, instantaneous since, if they could be, money would not exist.[15]

   b. Now let us approach the problem from the other side: let us assume that money exists and let us assume that consumers make a decision not to hold it and merely to use it for transactions. If no one holds money, where will the transactors acquire money needed for transactions? Money becomes the proverbial hot potato: as the time during

---

[15] Note that if it were *always* possible to sell an unwanted good for money and, within microseconds, sell money for ultimately wanted goods, why should money exist? Merely to add one extra futile step to the transacting activity? The mere fact that money exists is conclusive evidence that barter is not, in general, economically feasible. Of course, once money exists, habits and customs may make it used even in cases in which barter would do. But such cases do not prove that money exists so as to complicate barter any more than an observation of a man carrying a bicycle proves that bicycles exist so as to burden pedestrians.

which money is held in between transactions approaches zero, the price of money approaches zero (the general price level approaches infinity). Given the relationship between the price of money and the real value of money, money ceases to exist.

Thus we have just shown that (a) money will not exist unless held in between transactions and (b) if not held in between transactions, money will cease to exist. Consequently we can say that an unavoidable property of money is that it is held. In the case of money, these periods of inactivity are unavoidable conceptually; in the case of many nonmoney capital goods, they are unavoidable technically. In all cases, the consumer will exert an effort to minimize these periods of inactivity of all capital goods. The intensity of this effort to minimize these idle periods (or, what is saying the same thing, to minimize the average money holding in a given period) will depend on the ability of the consumer to afford these inactive periods (i.e., on his income) and on the cost of these periods (i.e., on the rate of interest). The holding of money—or of any other capital goods that cannot be operated continuously—becomes less attractive the higher the rate.[16] If this rate is so high as to reduce the amount of money

---

[16] In contrast, loans of resources become more attractive the higher the rate. But then, since an increase in the rate of interest makes (a) holding of wealth of a given productivity (currency and demand deposits) less attractive and (b) lending of wealth (e.g., purchases of time deposits) more attractive, we would expect on *a priori* grounds that a negative relationship between interest rate and item (a) will be weakened (indeed, may be reversed and become positive) if we shift to a composite consisting of items (a) plus (b).

It is thus easy to understand that Allan H. Meltzer's investigation of this issue led to the conclusion that ". . . the effect of a rise in the rate of interest on the percentage change in the quantity of money demanded is much greater when time deposits are excluded from M than when they are included in it."—Allan H. Meltzer, "Demand for Money: Evidence From the Time Series," *Journal of Political Economy, LXXI* (June, 1963), p. 239.

Similarly, Milton Friedman and Anna Jacobson Schwartz stated that ". . . the velocity of currency plus demand deposits adjusted, at least in the postwar period, may be more sensitive to interest-rate changes than velocity of money is." (Note that in both cases the definition of "money" includes

held down to zero, it cannot be true as stated by Franco Modigliani
that

$$L_r = 0 \quad \text{and} \quad M = L(y) \qquad \text{[14.21] and [14.22]}$$

it must be true that

$$M = 0 \qquad\qquad \text{[14.23]}$$

A rate that makes the demand for money to hold equal to zero
makes it, simultaneously, worthless for the performance of the task
that money performs, that of facilitating exchanges. Thus, money
disappears from the economy completely. Precisely the same is true
about any other capital good that cannot be, for whatever reason,
operated twenty-four hours per day. If the level of the rate of interest
makes it impossible to bear the cost of the period of inactivity, these
capital goods will simply not exist.

2. The converse proposition cannot hold either: there cannot exist
   a demand for money to hold if there is not a demand for money
   for the purpose of undertaking transactions. The ability of any
   good to serve as a store of value is a derived one; derived from the
   economic value of the good in its prime task. In a society with
   perfect clearing arrangements, money is not needed and thus will
   not exist; as a result, it will not perform the store of value role
   either. Why does it exist nevertheless in Samuelson's model discussed earlier? He believes that he has specified a model in which
   wealth does not exist, in which provision of retirement income
   is impossible, and in which social coercion is necessary to

---

time deposits.) The same authors prepared a biliography of many other
studies yielding the same results. Milton Friedman and Anna Jacobson
Schwartz, *A Monetary History of the United States 1867–1960* (Princeton,
N.J.: Princeton University Press, 1963), p. 652. For definition of "money,"
cf. *ibid.*, p. 640. For the above mentioned bibliography, cf. *ibid.*, p. 646,
note 6. For cases in which the relation between the rate of interest and the
composite of items (a) plus (b) reversed itself and became positive, cf. *ibid.*,
p. 842, Index Item "Interest rates, changes in the velocity of money and
inverse relation of."

maximize welfare.[17] The collectivity in his model prints pieces of
paper and "makes a grand consensus on the use of these greenbacks as a money of exchange."[18] Unfortunately, it is left completely unexplained why consumers agree to use these pieces of

[17] The article analyzes and solves the problem of determining the rate of
interest and of providing for retirement income in a society in which nonhuman wealth is assumed not to exist. However, reading of this article
indicates that Samuelson neglects the existence of human wealth.

1. Should human wealth also be assumed away (implicitly), the whole
problem becomes insoluble since one cannot draw blood out of a turnip.
2. Actually, human wealth is implicitly assumed to remain in the model.
But then, since wealth exists, the problem which the article purports to
solve does not exist: Human income is either produced by human capital
during working years or is assured to humans as rent (say, manna from
heaven) during those years. In either case, the capitalized value of this
income *is wealth*, human wealth. If slavery is permitted, this wealth may
be purchased outright; if it is forbidden, demanders may purchase titles
to the income produced by human wealth, bonds or debt certificates.
In either case, there *will* exist a market rate of interest and there is *no*
reason whatever why it should be "the biological rate," identical with the
rate of growth of population. Regardless of population growth, it may
be positive, zero, or negative, depending on the orthodox forces of supply
and demand in the (human) capital market. The seller of human wealth
or titles to it may utilize the proceeds as consumption loans or as *investment loans* (education, training, production of children who will
become new income receivers, etc.). The purchaser of human wealth or
titles to it *is* able to provide for his retirement through the market and *no*
social collusion or conspiracy is required to reach the Pareto optimality of
perfect competition. The only social collusion necessary is a law en-
forcing private contracts—surely *no* violation of the principles of *laissez
faire.*

In other words, the analysis contained in this article is false from beginning
to end. (Cf. Paul A. Samuelson, "An Exact Consumption-Loan Model of
Interest With or Without the Social Contrivance of Money," *Journal of
Political Economy, LXVI* (December, 1958), pp. 467–482. Cf. also Abba P.
Lerner and Paul A. Samuelson, "Consumption-Loan Interest and Money,"
and "Reply," and "Rejoinder," *op. cit., LXVII* (October, 1959), pp. 512–
525; and W. H. Meckling and Paul A. Samuelson, "An Exact Consumption-
Loan Model of Interest: A Comment," "Reply," and "Rejoinder," *op. cit.,
LXVIII* (February, 1960), pp. 72–84.)

[18] Paul A. Samuelson, "An Exact Consumption-Loan Model of Interest
With or Without the Social Contrivance of Money," *Journal of Political
Economy, LXVI* (December, 1958), p. 481.

paper as money—for which in this economy with ideal clearing arrangements there is no use—and why they fail to agree to use these pieces of paper as debt certificates—which in this economy of perishables are needed. Lacking explanation, all we can do here is to deny that these pieces of paper are money as defined and analyzed in Chapters 3 and 4 and to assert that these pieces of paper are debt certificates as defined and analyzed in Chapter 5.

Conclusion

In this chapter we used the Basic Model of the preceding chapter to derive the determinants of the demand for money in a risk-free economy in which the consumers have zero elasticity of expectations. We concluded that it will depend on the consumer's income and the rate of interest. These results gave us an occasion to discuss some of the major theories of the demand for money; we have shown that these theories are not competitive but mutually consistent, each concentrating on one important element determining the demand for money. We demonstrated that the Cambridge approach to the demand for money concentrates on the ability of the community to afford having the job that money performs (facilitating trans-actions) performed; that the Fisher approach concentrates on the underlying technological determinants of the demand for money. Since each approach is complementary to the other, we concluded that there is no necessity of making a choice between them. This simultaneously suggests that some of the recent attempts to make such a choice on the basis of empirical investigations do not rest on adequate analytical foundations.[19] We also pointed out that if we discuss the demand for money measured in real terms, in efficiency

---

[19] E.g., Allan H. Meltzer wrote recently: "This conclusion is supported by numerous additional estimates, some of which are presented in the following section; it suggests that it is more fruitful to view the demand for money as influenced by cost and yield consideration rather than primarily as a means of effecting a volume of 'transactions' and subject to an income constraint." —Meltzer, *op. cit.*, p. 234.

units, price will not be a determinant of demand, since money has the technical property of changing its output equiproportionately with a change in its price. Finally, we have compared the demand for money obtained in this chapter with the demand for money in current use and we concluded that the economic meaning of the demand for money function has been subtly changing. What originally has been conceived as demand for money for the purpose to which money serves, transactions, and additional demand for speculative purposes came to be transformed into demand for transaction money ("active balances") which is not held at all and into demand for asset money ("idle balances") which need not be used for transactions at all; indeed, which may be worthless for transactions. We have seen that, analytically, this distinction cannot stand scrutiny. Money cannot exist for transactions if it is not held in between transactions, since barter is then the only economic manner of undertaking exchanges. Conversely, money cannot become a store of value if it has no economic task to perform.

CHAPTER 15

Wealth and
Consumer Behavior

In Chapter 13, we outlined the past history of wealth-behavior relations, and concluded that a multiperiod analysis of these relations is essential. We then proceeded to outline a basic model to be used in this endeavor. In Chapter 14, we focused our attention on an important part of wealth, money. Money is important because, as was shown in Chapters 3 through 5, changes in the price of it have the ability to change the wealth of its owners while leaving the wealth of nonowners and prospective purchasers unaffected. In Chapter 14, we specified the reason that consumers will demand a stock of money to be held for transaction purposes. Of course, any speculative demand may be added if it is desired to increase the complexity of the model by adding uncertainty to it. Then, we derived determinants of the demand for money. For an individual, we have seen that his demand depends on the rate of interest, his consumption expenditures (containing both present and future consumption), and on his expenditures on bequests. For society as a whole, this must necessarily mean that this demand depends on the rate of interest and income. Finally, we related these results to the theories of demand for money represented by the various versions of the quantity theory of money and to the Keynesian theory and some of the interpretations of it. Thus, we are now in a position to return to the task we set out for ourselves in Chapter 13; the maximization of intertemporal utility.

The Intertemporal Maximization of Utility

The Final Form of the Constraint

The optimizing behavior of the consumer regarding the optimal stock of money was summarized in equation [14.12]. In addition, we derived the signs of the partial derivatives of that equation by using the comparative static approach. Thus we are now able to return to our main problem as specified at the end of Chapter 13. First of all, it is necessary to construct the final form of our budget constraint—a constraint that allows for optimizing behavior in regard to the holding of money balances. In doing this, let us recall that we wrote the equation of the optimal path of money balances as

$$m(t) = G[c(t), b(t), r(t), t] \qquad [15.1]$$

where $G_c > 0$; $G_b > 0$; $G_r < 0$, and for simplicity assume that $G_{cc} = 0$; $G_{bb} = 0$; and $G_{cb} = 0$. By substituting [15.1] into the final form of our income function (equation [14.7]) and by substituting the result into the budget constraint, we get the final form for the constraint:

$$C = \int_{\tau}^{T} e^{r[T-t]} H[l, c, b, G, t] \, dt + e^{r[T-t]} A(\tau)$$
$$+ \int_{\tau}^{T} e^{r[T-t]} [c(t) + b(t) + rG] \, dt \quad [15.2]$$

where it is additionally assumed that $r(t) = r$ for all t in $[\tau, T]$. Thus, our constraint already includes the result of one maximization problem. This is, of course, not unusual in economic problems, e.g., the maximization of profits given cost functions which are minima of total costs for each output.

The Problem and Its Solution

Our problem now is that of finding functions $c(t)$, $b(t)$ and $l(t)$ that will make the utility functional [13.4] a maximum, subject to the constraint [15.2]. This is a traditional iso-perimetric problem in the variational calculus and can be handled by the use of Lagrangian methods.[1] Consider the functional

$$U^* = \int_\tau^T \{\mu(c, l, b, \tau, T, t) + \lambda e^{r[T-t]}[H(l, c, b, G, t)$$
$$- (c + b + rG)]\} \, dt \quad [15.3]$$

the maximization of which is equivalent to maximizing equation [13.4] subject to [15.2].[2] Now, as before, it is necessary that the first variation of [15.3] vanish. Thus,

$$\delta U^* = \int_\tau^T \{[\mu_c + \lambda e^{r[T-t]}(H_c - 1)]h_c + [\mu_b + \lambda e^{r[T-t]}(H_b - 1)]h_b$$
$$+ [\mu_l + \lambda e^{r[T-t]}H_l]h_l\} \, dt = 0 \quad [15.4]$$

Since [15.4] can be written as the sum of the integrals of the three terms, our necessary conditions are

$$\int_\tau^T \{\mu_c + \lambda e^{r[T-t]}(H_c - 1)\}h_c \, dt = 0$$

$$\int_\tau^T \{\mu_b + \lambda e^{r[T-t]}(H_b - 1)\}h_b \, dt = 0 \quad [15.5]$$

$$\int_\tau^T \{\mu_l + \lambda e^{r[T-t]}H_l\}h_l \, dt = 0$$

---

[1] I. M. Gelfand and S. V. Fomin, *Calculus of Variations* (Englewood Cliffs, N.J.: Prentice-Hall, 1963), p. 46. Also L. E. Elsgolc, *Calculus of Variations* (Reading, Pa.: Addison-Wesley, 1962), pp. 127–146.
[2] We are adopting the convention of dropping the notation indicating that c, l, b, G are functions of t as a notational simplification. Let it be understood that they remain functions of t. Similarly, the increments in these functions will simply be understood to be functions of t.

Assuming that μ, H and G are all continuous and twice differentiable, we can apply the result of the previous section so that if the above integrals are to be zero for arbitrary h_c, h_b, h_l, then the coefficients of h_c, h_b, h_l must be zero for all t in $[\tau, T]$. Thus, [15.5] can be written as

$$\mu_c = -\lambda e^{r[T-t]}(H_c - 1)$$

$$\mu_b = -\lambda e^{r[T-t]}(H_b - 1) \qquad\qquad [15.6]$$

$$\mu_l = -\lambda e^{r[T-t]}H_l$$

for all t in $[\tau, T]$. Equations [15.6], together with the budget constraint [15.2], may now be solved for the optimal $c(t)$, $b(t)$, $l(t)$, and λ. Then, by substitution into [15.1], we get the optimal $m(t)$. In terms of marginal rates of substitution our necessary conditions are

$$\frac{\mu_c}{\mu_b} = \frac{(H_c - 1)}{(H_b - 1)}$$

$$\frac{\mu_c}{\mu_l} = \frac{(H_c - 1)}{H_l} \qquad\qquad [15.7]$$

$$\frac{\mu_b}{\mu_l} = \frac{(H_b - 1)}{H_l}$$

for all t in $[\tau, T]$. Equations [15.7] represent the traditional result of consumer demand theory in that the marginal rates of substitution between any two of our arguments at any time t must equal the ratio of their prices. In addition, the following intertemporal relationships must hold:

$$\frac{\mu_c(t)}{\mu_c(t+j)} = e^{rj}\,\frac{\{H_c(t) - 1\}}{\{H_c(t+j) - 1\}}$$

$$\frac{\mu_b(t)}{\mu_b(t+j)} = e^{rj}\,\frac{\{H_b(t) - 1\}}{\{H_b(t+j) - 1\}} \qquad\qquad [15.8]$$

$$\frac{\mu_l(t)}{\mu_l(t+j)} = e^{rj}\,\frac{H_l(t)}{H_l(t+j)}$$

Thus, the marginal rate of substitution between consumption, bequests, and leisure at time (t) and consumption, bequests, and leisure at time $(t + j)$ must equal their prices at time (t) relative to their prices at time $(t + j)$.[3]

The reader will remember that in Chapter 13 we made it possible for the consumer to change his utility functional as he ages: indeed, this is what we would normally expect to happen. However, we might note parenthetically the necessary conditions that will make the consumer's expenditure plan for $c(t)$, $l(t)$, and $b(t)$ invariant with respect to the initial period τ; i.e., under what conditions will planned expenditures on $c(t)$, $l(t)$, and $b(t)$ remain unchanged as the decision period moves forward in time, as the consumer ages.[4] These necessary conditions are that the function $[\mu]$ be invariant with respect to time τ so that all marginal rates of substitution will remain the same as the consumer moves forward in time.

Let us now return to the normal case in which utilities are permitted to change over time. In that case it is both necessary and sufficient for equation [13.4] to be maximum, subject to the constraint [15.2], if the second variation of the utility functional [13.4] is strongly negative at the functions $\hat{c}(t)$, $\hat{b}(t)$, and $\hat{l}(t)$ that satisfy (a) equations [15.6] and (b) the budget constraint [15.2], for all h_c, h_b, and h_l that are consistent with this constraint. That is, the admissible set of variations in $c(t)$, $b(t)$, and $l(t)$ are those that make the first variation of [15.2] equal to zero. Thus,

$$\delta C = \int_\tau^T e^{r[T-t]}\{(H_c - 1)h_c + (H_b - 1)h_b + H_l h_l\}\, dt = 0 \quad [15.9]$$

must be satisfied for all (h_c, h_b, h_l). Therefore, it is necessary and sufficient for equation [13.1] to be a maximum at $\{\hat{c}(t),\ \hat{b}(t),\ \hat{l}(t)\}$

---

[3] If the function H is independent of time, then the relative prices will simply be e^{rj}; that is, the value of a dollar invested at time t at rate of interest r for j years.

[4] See R. H. Strotz, "Myopia and Inconsistency in Dynamic Utility Maximization," *Review of Economic Studies*, *XXIII* (October, 1956), pp. 165–180, for a thorough discussion of this point.

for the following integral to be strongly negative subject to [15.9]:

$$\delta^2 U = \frac{1}{2} \int_\tau^T \{\mu_{cc}h_c^2 + \mu_{bb}h_b^2 + \mu_{ll}h_l^2 + 2\mu_{cl}h_c h_l$$
$$+ 2\mu_{cb}h_c h_b + 2\mu_{bl}h_b h_l\} \, dt \quad [15.10]$$

If [15.10] is to be strongly negative, it must satisfy the following inequality:

$$\delta^2 U \le k\|h\|^2 \qquad [15.11]$$

where

$$\|h\| = \left\{ \max_t \ [|h_c(t)|] + \max_t \ [|h_b(t)|] + \max_t \ [|h_l(t)|] \right\}$$

and $k < 0$ is a constant, for all (h_c, h_b, h_l) that satisfy [15.9]. Now if [15.10] is to be strongly negative then the integrand of [15.10] must be negative for all (h_c, h_b, h_l), not all zero, that satisfy [15.9] and for all t in $[\tau, T]$. Thus,

$$Q = \mu_{cc}h_c^2 + \mu_{bb}h_b^2 + \mu_{ll}h_l^2 + 2\mu_{cl}h_c h_l + 2\mu_{cb}h_c h_b$$
$$+ 2\mu_{lb}h_l h_b < 0 \quad [15.12]$$

for all t in $[\tau, T]$ and all (h_c, h_b, h_l), not all zero, satisfying [15.9]. But, if Q must be negative definite on the set of all (h_c, h_b, h_l) satisfying [15.9], it must be negative definite on a proper subset of all (h_c, h_b, h_l) satisfying [15.9]. Thus, Q must be negative definite for all (h_c, h_b, h_l), which make the integrand of [15.9] equal to zero for all t in $[\tau, T]$. Therefore, it is necessary but not sufficient for [15.11] to hold subject to [15.9] that Q be negative definite subject to the following linear constraint:

$$e^{r[T-t]}(H_c - 1)h_c + e^{r[T-t]}(H_b - 1)h_b + e^{r[T-t]}H_l h_l = 0 \quad [15.13]$$

for all t in $[\tau, T]$. This implies that the principal minors of the matrix of the quadratic form [15.12] bordered by the coefficients of the linear constraint [15.13] are alternatively negative and positive (the even order determinants being negative, and the odd order determinants positive). In particular, the following determinant must be negative for all t in $[\tau, T]$:

$$
Q^{*\cdot} =
\begin{bmatrix}
\mu_{cc} & \mu_{cb} & \mu_{cl} & e^{r[T-t]}(H_c - 1) \\
\mu_{bc} & \mu_{bb} & \mu_{bl} & e^{r[T-t]}(H_b - 1) \\
\mu_{lc} & \mu_{lb} & \mu_{ll} & e^{r[T-t]}H_l \\
e^{r[T-t]}(H_c - 1) & e^{r[T-t]}(H_b - 1) & e^{r[T-t]}H_l & 0
\end{bmatrix}
$$

$$[15.14]$$

The Comparative Statics of the Model

The Asset Effect

Let us consider the system of equations we solved for the optimal $c(t)$, $b(t)$, $l(t)$; that is, consider equations [15.5] and the constraint [15.2]. However, for this problem let us write the capitalized value of the initial asset position as an integral so that the entire constraint will be an integral with the same limits of integration. Thus, consider the following system of equations:

$$
\int_{\tau}^{T} \{\mu_c + \lambda e^{r[T-t]}(H_c - 1)\} h_c \, dt = 0
$$

$$
\int_{\tau}^{T} \{\mu_b + \lambda e^{r[T-t]}(H_b - 1)\} h_b \, dt = 0
$$

$$
\int_{\tau}^{T} \{\mu_l + \lambda e^{r[T-t]}H_l\} h_l \, dt = 0 \qquad [15.15]
$$

$$
\int_{\tau}^{T} e^{r[T-t]} \left\{ H(l, c, b, G, t) + \frac{r(T-t)+1}{T-\tau} A(\tau) \right.
$$

$$
\left. - (c + b + rG) \right\} dt = 0
$$

In order to see the effect of a change in initial assets on the optimal level of consumption, bequests, and leisure we must take the first variation of system [15.15]:

$$\int_\tau^T \{\mu_{cc}h_c + \mu_{cb}h_b + \mu_{cl}h_l + e^{r[T-t]}(H_c - 1)h_\lambda\}h_c \, dt = 0$$

$$\int_\tau^T \{\mu_{bc}h_c + \mu_{bb}h_b + \mu_{bl}h_l + e^{r[T-t]}(H_b - 1)h_\lambda\}h_b \, dt = 0$$

$$\int_\tau^T \{\mu_{lc}h_c + \mu_{lb}h_b + \mu_{ll}h_l + e^{r[T-t]}H_l h_\lambda\}h_l \, dt = 0 \quad [15.16]$$

$$\int_\tau^T e^{r[T-t]}\left\{(H_c - 1)h_c + (H_b - 1)h_b + H_l h_l \right.$$
$$\left. + \frac{r(T - t) + 1}{T - \tau} \, dA(\tau)\right\} dt = 0$$

Again applying the result that an integral, whose integrand may be factored into two functions, one of which is arbitrary but not identically zero, will be zero if and only if the other function is identically zero, we get the following system of equations:

$$\mu_{cc}h_c + \mu_{cb}h_b + \mu_{cl}h_l + e^{r[T-t]}(H_c - 1)h_\lambda = 0$$

$$\mu_{bc}h_c + \mu_{bb}h_b + \mu_{bl}h_l + e^{r[T-t]}(H_b - 1)h_\lambda = 0$$

$$\mu_{lc}h_c + \mu_{lb}h_b + \mu_{ll}h_l + e^{r[T-t]}H_l h_\lambda = 0 \quad [15.17]$$

$$\int_\tau^T e^{r[T-t]}\left\{(H_c - 1)h_c + (H_b - 1)h_b + H_l h_l \right.$$
$$\left. + \frac{r(T - t) + 1}{T - \tau} \, dA(\tau)\right\} dt = 0$$

where the first three equations must hold for all t in $[\tau, T]$.

The last equation in [15.17] remains an integral and can be written as

$$\int_\tau^T e^{r[T-t]}\{(H_c - 1)h_c + (H_b - 1)h_b + H_l h_l\} \, dt$$
$$= -\int_\tau^T e^{r[T-t]}\left\{\frac{r(T - t) + 1}{T - \tau}\right\} dA(\tau) \, dt \quad [15.18]$$

The consumer now chooses new functions $\hat{c}'(t)$, $\hat{b}'(t)$ and $\hat{l}'(t)$ such that the difference between the old optimal functions and the new ones satisfy equations [15.17]. That is, h_c, h_b, h_l in equations [15.17] are, respectively, equal to $\{\hat{c}'(t) - \hat{c}(t)\}$, $\{(\hat{b}'(t) - \hat{b}(t)\}$ and $\{\hat{l}'(t) - \hat{l}(t)\}$. These increments to the functions $\hat{c}(t)$, $\hat{b}(t)$, and $\hat{l}(t)$ are functions of the change in the capitalized value of income and assets available to the consumer since the maximum of our utility functional is a function of the capitalized value of income and wealth. Given that a unique maximum exists, we may express the integral of [15.18] in the following way:

$$e^{r(T-t)}\{(H_c - 1)h_c + (H_b - 1)h_b + H_l h_l\}$$
$$= -\Phi(t) \int_t^T e^{r(T-t)}\left\{\frac{r(T-t)+1}{T-\tau}\right\} dA(\tau)\, dt \quad [15.19]$$

for all t in $[\tau, T]$. The function $\Phi(t)$ is the proportion of the total change in capitalized initial assets that would be used up if the integrand of [15.18] were equal to the right-hand side of [15.19] for a unit of time. The increments in $\hat{c}(t)$, $\hat{b}(t)$ and $\hat{l}(t)$ {i.e., (h_c, h_b, h_l)} must be such that the new optimal functions $\hat{c}'(t)$, $\hat{b}'(t)$, and $\hat{l}'(t)$ satisfy the first order conditions for a maximum of the functional U. Thus, they must satisfy the first three equations in [15.17]; in addition, they satisfy [15.19] by construction. Therefore, the first three equations of [15.17] with [15.19] give us a system of four equations, in the four unknowns $h_c(t)$, $h_b(t)$, $h_l(t)$ and h_λ, that must be satisfied for all t in $[\tau, T]$. Noting that the coefficient matrix of this system of equations is equal to the matrix Q^* (the bordered matrix of the quadratic form [15.12]), we can express the solutions of system in terms of the determinant value of Q^* and its cofactors. The solutions in which we have an interest are

$$h_c(t) = -\Phi(t) \int_t^T e^{r(T-t)}\left\{\frac{r(T-t)+1}{T-\tau}\right\} dt\; \frac{Q_{41}^*(t)}{|Q^*(t)|}\, dA(\tau)$$

$$h_b(t) = -\Phi(t) \int_t^T e^{r(T-t)}\left\{\frac{r(T-t)+1}{T-\tau}\right\} dt\; \frac{Q_{42}^*(t)}{|Q^*(t)|}\, dA(\tau) \quad [15.20]$$

$$h_l(t) = -\Phi(t) \int_t^T e^{r(T-t)}\left\{\frac{r(T-t)+1}{T-\tau}\right\} dt\; \frac{Q_{43}^*(t)}{|Q^*(t)|}\, dA(\tau)$$

where $|Q^*(t)|$ is the determinant value of Q^* at time t and $Q_{ij}^*(t)$ is the cofactor of the (ij)th element in $Q^*(t)$.

We are now in a position to derive the effect on the optimal path of consumption, bequests, and leisure of a change in the value of initial assets $A(\tau)$; the reader will remember that in our model the value of these assets is the sum of the real value of bond holdings plus the stock of money. Thus,

$$A(\tau) = a(\tau) + m(\tau) \qquad [15.21]$$

so that

$$dA(\tau) = da(\tau) + dm(\tau) \qquad [15.22]$$

where $a(\tau)$ is the value of bond holdings at time τ. We can derive the partial derivatives in which we are interested by dividing equations [15.20] through by $dA(\tau)$:

$$\frac{h_c(t)}{dA(\tau)} = \frac{\partial c(t)}{\partial A(\tau)} = -\Phi(t) \int_\tau^T e^{r[T-t]} \left\{ \frac{r(T-t)+1}{T-\tau} \right\} dt \, \frac{Q_{41}^*(t)}{|Q^*(t)|}$$

$$\frac{h_b(t)}{dA(\tau)} = \frac{\partial b(t)}{\partial A(\tau)} = -\Phi(t) \int_\tau^T e^{r[T-t]} \left\{ \frac{r(T-t)+1}{T-\tau} \right\} dt \, \frac{Q_{42}^*(t)}{|Q^*(t)|}$$

$$\frac{h_l(t)}{dA(\tau)} = \frac{\partial l(t)}{\partial A(\tau)} = -\Phi(t) \int_\tau^T e^{r[T-t]} \left\{ \frac{r(T-t)+1}{T-\tau} \right\} dt \, \frac{Q_{43}^*(t)}{|Q^*(t)|}$$

$$[15.23]$$

for all t in $[\tau, T]$.

From the strong negativity requirement on [15.12] we know that $|Q^*(t)|$ must be negative for all t in $[\tau, T]$. Therefore, the determination of the signs of the asset effect requires that we determine the sign of the function Φ and the Q_{4i}^* $(i = 1, 2, 3)$. Let us then reflect for a moment on the function Φ. The unit of measure of Φ is the change in the capitalized value of assets, so that if Φ were equal to one for a unit of time, i.e., for an interval of length $[t - (t - 1)] = 1$, then the entire change in the capitalized value of assets would be accounted for. Thus, the sign of $\Phi(t)$ expresses the direction of the change in total expenditures on consumption, bequests, and leisure at any time t.[5] If we assume that expenditures during an interval are not inferior to expenditures during any other interval, then $\Phi(t)$ will be nonnegative for all t in $[\tau, T]$.[6] If, in addition, we assume diminishing marginal utility of consumption, bequests, and leisure (i.e., assume that μ_{cc}, μ_{bb}, μ_{ll} are negative for all t in $[\tau, T]$) and that consumption, bequests, and leisure bear a complementary relationship to one another (i.e., that the marginal utility of any one increases as more of either of the others is consumed, so that μ_{cb}, μ_{cl}, μ_{lb} are all positive for all t in $[\tau, T]$), we can determine the signs of the $Q_{4i}^*(t)$ ($i = 1, 2, 3$). In fact, for these assumptions, Q_{41}^*, Q_{42}^*, and Q_{43}^* are all positive, so that

$$\frac{\partial c(t)}{\partial A(\tau)} > 0, \qquad \frac{\partial b(t)}{\partial A(\tau)} > 0, \qquad \frac{\partial l(t)}{\partial A(\tau)} > 0 \qquad [15.24]$$

for each t in $[\tau, T]$ where μ_{cc}, μ_{bb}, $\mu_{ll} < 0$ and μ_{cb}, μ_{cl}, $\mu_{lb} > 0$. That is, an increase in initial assets will increase current levels of consumption, bequests, and leisure as well as all future levels as long as our assumptions concerning μ_{cc}, μ_{bb}, μ_{ll}, μ_{cb}, μ_{cl}, μ_{bl} remain valid.

There are several additional implications of the above results that bear mentioning before we go on to analyze the effect of changes in the rate of interest. First, the structure of initial assets (the portfolio) between money and bonds does not affect the signs in [15.24]. In particular, by applying [15.23] and setting the change in bonds at zero, we get the following effects of changes in money holdings:

$$\frac{\partial c(t)}{\partial m(\tau)} > 0, \qquad \frac{\partial b(t)}{\partial m(\tau)} > 0, \qquad \frac{\partial l(t)}{\partial m(\tau)} > 0 \qquad [15.25]$$

---

[5] Essentially $\Phi(t)$ is the first differential of the function relating utility to the capitalized value of income plus wealth, (C). That is,

$$\Phi(t) = U(C) = \int_\tau^T [\mu_c h_c + \mu_b h_b + \mu_l h_l]\, dt,$$

where h_c, h_b, and h_l, are defined as $\dfrac{\partial c(t)}{\partial C}$, $\dfrac{\partial b(t)}{\partial C}$, $\dfrac{\partial l(t)}{\partial C}$, respectively.

[6] This is a common assumption in analyses of this type.

Since the value of money holdings can change either by gifts of money to consumers or by changes in the value of money, either of these changes imply [15.25]. Thus, reductions in the price level known to be permanent (assuming that real income and real bond values remain constant) will increase the initial real asset holdings of the consumer and thus increase his current level of consumption, bequests, and leisure.[7] Therefore, for such price level changes we get

$$\frac{\partial c(t)}{\partial P} < 0, \qquad \frac{\partial b(t)}{\partial P} < 0, \qquad \frac{\partial l(t)}{\partial P} < 0 \qquad [15.26]$$

The Interest Rate Effect

The determination of the effect of changes in the rate of interest on the optimal path of consumption, bequests, and leisure is more complex than the initial asset effect, since such changes will have both a wealth effect and a price effect. The wealth effect will occur whether or not the value of the consumer's initial assets is affected by the change in the rate of interest, since the price of consumption, bequests, and leisure early in the horizon will have changed relative to later in the horizon, so that the capitalized value of the original optimal expenditure functions $\{\hat{c}(t), \hat{b}(t), \hat{l}(t)\}$ at the new rate of interest may exceed, be equal to, or fall below the value of the income function plus initial assets capitalized at the new rate of interest. If the new capitalized value of income plus initial assets exceeds the capitalized value of expenditures, then the consumer may enjoy more consumption, bequests, and leisure in every period. If the reverse is true, then there must exist an interval $[t_0, t_1]$ in $[\tau, T]$ such that at least one of the expenditure items is below the original optimal function throughout the interval. In particular, we evaluate the

---

[7] Reflection will indicate that this is true, *a fortiori*, for a price change not expected to be permanent.

following differential of the constraint [15.2]:

$$dC = \int_{\tau}^{T} \left\{ (T-t)e^{r[T-t]}\left[H(\hat{l}, \hat{c}, \hat{b}, G, t) + \frac{r(T-t)+1}{T-\tau} \right. \right.$$

$$\times A(\tau) - (\hat{c} + \hat{b} + rG) \Bigg]$$

$$+ \left. e^{r[T-t]}\left[\frac{(T-t)}{T-\tau} A(\tau) - G \right] \right\} dt \, dr \gtreqless 0 \quad [15.27]$$

If the integral in [15.27] is positive, then increases in the rate of interest will give the consumer an additional amount of wealth to dispose of, assuming the original optimal functions $\{\hat{c}(t), \hat{b}(t), \hat{l}(t)\}$ remain the same. However, it is unlikely that these original functions will remain the same, since, as the reader will recall, our necessary conditions require that

$$\frac{\mu_{c(t+k)}}{\mu_{c(t)}} = e^{-rk}\left\{ \frac{\{H_{c(t+k)} - 1\}}{\{H_{c(t)} - 1\}} \right\}$$

$$\frac{\mu_{b(t+k)}}{\mu_{b(t)}} = e^{-rk}\left\{ \frac{\{H_{b(t+k)} - 1\}}{\{H_{b(t)} - 1\}} \right\} \qquad [15.28]$$

$$\frac{\mu_{l(t+k)}}{\mu_{l(t)}} = e^{-rk}\left\{ \frac{H_{l(t+k)}}{H_{l(t)}} \right\}$$

so that a change in the rate of interest will require that the optimal $\{\hat{c}(t), \hat{b}(t), \hat{l}(t)\}$ change in such a way that the change in the relative marginal utilities satisfy

$$d\left\{ \frac{\mu_{c(t+k)}}{\mu_{c(t)}} \right\} = -ke^{rk}\left\{ \frac{\{H_{c(t+k)} - 1\}}{\{H_{c(t)} - 1\}} \right\} < 0$$

$$d\left\{ \frac{\mu_{b(t+k)}}{\mu_{b(t)}} \right\} = -ke^{rk}\left\{ \frac{\{H_{b(t+k)} - 1\}}{\{H_{b(t)} - 1\}} \right\} < 0 \qquad [15.29]$$

$$d\left\{ \frac{\mu_{l(t+k)}}{\mu_{l(t)}} \right\} = -ke^{rk}\left\{ \frac{H_{l(t+k)}}{H_{l(t)}} \right\} < 0$$

Thus, an increase in the rate of interest will require that the marginal rate of substitution of consumption, bequests, and leisure at time $(t + k)$ for consumption, bequests, and leisure at time (t) decrease. This implies that expenditures on consumption, bequests, and leisure must increase at time $(t + k)$ relative to time (t). In particular, if the sign of [15.27] is negative so that there must exist some interval such that at least one of the expenditure items is lower than the original optimal path, then [15.29] in conjunction with our assumptions concerning the second order partial derivatives of μ imply that this interval must contain the initial point in the horizon as an endpoint. In addition, it can be shown that if the sum of expenditures in an interval increases, then each of the three expenditure items must increase.

These results indicate that even if we assume that changes in the rate of interest do not affect the value of assets, the effect of changes in the rate of interest on initial consumption, bequests, and leisure is uncertain. Although we can determine the sign of the substitution effect from [15.29] and our assumptions concerning the function μ, we cannot *a priori* determine the effect of the change in the rate of interest on the capitalized value of income and wealth of the consumer. Thus, the direction of the wealth effect for an *individual* consumer is uncertain. Essentially, the direction of the wealth effect depends on whether or not the consumer's optimal plans make him a net borrower in the early years of his horizon. Early net borrowers are made better off by reductions in the rate of interest, since for the period where their planned expenditures exceed their income, the price of these expenditures relative to future expenditures will have fallen. The reverse is, of course, true for early net lenders.

Let us now consider the effect of relaxing our assumption that interest rate changes do not affect the value of initial assets. In this case we must add an additional term to the integrand of [15.27] reflecting the change in the value of initial assets resulting in

$$
\begin{aligned}
dc^* = \int_{\tau}^{T} \bigg\{ (T - t)e^{r(T-t)} \bigg[H(l, \hat{c}, \hat{b}, G, t) + \frac{r(T - t) + 1}{T - \tau} A(\tau) \\
- (\hat{c} + \hat{b} + rG) \bigg] \\
+ e^{r(T-t)} \bigg[\frac{(T - t)}{t - \tau} A(\tau) - G \bigg] \\
+ e^{r(T-t)} \bigg[\frac{r(T - t) + 1}{T - \tau} A'(\tau) \bigg] \bigg\} \, dt \, dr \quad [15.30]
\end{aligned}
$$

where $A'(\tau)$ is the partial derivative of A with respect to the rate of interest. In effect, we assume that the value of $A(\tau)$ is a function of the income flow from assets held relative to the rate of interest, the form of the function being determined by the distribution of maturities of assets in the portfolio. Thus, we assume

$$A(\tau) = \psi\left(\frac{y_A}{r}\right) \qquad [15.31]$$

where y_A is the income flow from the securities held and[8]

$$\frac{\partial \psi}{\partial r} < 0 \qquad \text{for all } y_A > 0$$

$$[15.32]$$

$$\frac{\partial \psi}{\partial r} > 0 \qquad \text{for all } y_A < 0$$

Assume that the rate of interest has increased. If our consumer previously had a positive $A(\tau)$ and had planned to be a net lender during the early years of his horizon, then he would have been made better off by the change in the rate of interest. Consideration of the effect of the change in the rate of interest on the value of his assets reduces the amount by which he is better off and may wipe out the increase in his wealth entirely. Thus, the consideration of the effect of changes in the rate of interest on asset valuations makes the final result more like the substitution effect for the case considered.

On the other hand, if our consumer had negative initial assets and planned on being a net borrower in the early years of his horizon, then an increase in the rate of interest would make him worse off. Consideration of the effect of interest rate changes on the valuation of his assets will make the extent to which he is worse off in this case smaller and may offset it entirely. Thus, just as in the previous case, allowing changes in the interest rate to affect asset valuations works to make the ultimate effect more like the pure substitution effect.

[8] For a consol this function is $A(\tau) = \dfrac{y_A}{r}.$

In those cases where negative assets are associated with planned lending early in the horizon or vice versa, the results are ambiguous and hence nothing can be said. But, since we have no *a priori* information concerning any consumer, this must be our general result. That is, considering the effect of changes in the rate of interest on the valuation of assets will not make the effect of interest rate changes on consumption, bequests, and leisure determinate for an *individual* consumer. However, the same statement is not true for the group of all consumers, as we shall show in Chapter 16.

The Effect of Changes in Human Wealth

While we have not considered the level of human wealth explicitly in the formulation, it is embodied in the income function. Thus, changes in human wealth must occur via shifts in the income function. That is, an increase in human wealth will increase the flow of income for any given $c(t)$, $b(t)$, $l(t)$, and $m(t)$. Thus, we may express the level of human wealth by introducing a shift parameter (σ) into our income function. Let us assume the following relationship:

$$y(t) = H[l, c, b, G, t, \sigma] \qquad [15.33]$$

where $H_\sigma = \dfrac{\partial H}{\partial \sigma} > 0$ for all t in $[\tau, T]$. Now determining the effect of changes in the income function amounts to finding the signs of $\dfrac{\partial c(t)}{\partial \sigma}, \dfrac{\partial b(t)}{\partial \sigma}, \dfrac{\partial l(t)}{\partial \sigma}$. However, there is a problem that must be handled before we can determine the signs of these partial derivatives; it results from the way in which changes in human wealth affect the income function. In particular, changes in human wealth usually do not result in parallel shifts in the income function but change the marginal return to work. Thus, changes in human wealth result in both wealth effects and substitution effects.

The case of parallel shifts is completely analogous to the asset effect just discussed. This type of change simply results in an increase in the capitalized value of assets and income, with no change in prices. As long as the assumptions we made concerning the non-inferiority of total expenditures in any interval relative to any other interval and concerning the second order partials of the function μ remain valid, the signs of $\dfrac{\partial c(t)}{\partial \sigma}$, $\dfrac{\partial b(t)}{\partial \sigma}$, and $\dfrac{\partial l(t)}{\partial \sigma}$ will all be positive.

However, once we allow the marginal return to work to be affected by changes in σ, the situation is markedly different. In this case the marginal cost of additional consumption, bequests, and leisure are also increased, and the marginal return to holding money is increased. Thus, we have both a substitution effect at each point in time and a wealth effect. Since it is possible for the wealth effect to more than offset the substitution effect, we again have some indeterminacy in the results. However, as long as we assume that consumption and bequests are not inferior to leisure in any interval in $[\tau, T]$, then it is easy to show that increases in σ will increase consumption and bequests for all t in $[\tau, T]$ and may increase leisure for some or all t in $[\tau, T]$.

Conclusion

The multiperiod analysis of consumer behavior contained in this chapter has revealed that an individual consumer will be made better off and increase his demand for all goods and services and for leisure if his nonhuman capital, monetary or nonmonetary, is increased, given the rate of interest, wage rate, and the price of money. Second, we also concluded that an individual consumer will be made better off and increase his demand for all goods and services and his demand for leisure if the price of money increases (if the general price level falls). Third, we have seen that a change in human wealth resulting from a change in the wage rate will make the consumer better off and, under normal assumptions, increase his demand for all goods and services; it may or may not increase his demand for leisure. Fourth, we have seen that a change in the rate of interest has complex results that lead to our inability to predict on *a priori* grounds whether the consumer will be made better off or worse off; consequently, it becomes impossible to predict on *a priori* grounds whether he will increase or decrease his demand for all goods and services and his demand for leisure. While such indeterminacy is unfortunate if the purpose of economic analysis is to make qualitative *a priori* predictions irrespective of empirical facts, it is not unusual: in the case of a change in the price of any specific product we also are unable to determine *a priori* whether the substitution effect will overcome the income effect or vice versa. Indeed, in the case of the rate of interest we are somewhat more fortunate, since our subsequent discussion of the application of the above results to a collection of individuals, to a society as a whole, will reveal that the above indeterminacy, as far as the changes in the rate of interest are concerned, disappears.

CHAPTER 16

Aggregation of Consumer Responses to Wealth Changes

In the previous three chapters we have considered the effect of changes in wealth, income, and interest rates on the individual consumer. However, if we are to incorporate this analysis into the macroeconomic discussion to follow, we shall have to show the relationship between the behavior of an individual consumer and the economy as a whole. As we know, what is true for the individual consumer (who can behave as if all supply functions were completely elastic) is not necessarily true of the economy as a whole. Thus, as a preface to our discussion of the macroeconomic relationship, we shall discuss the aggregation problem. In the course of this discussion, we shall relate the analytical results obtained to the permanent income hypothesis of Milton Friedman.[1] Also, this aggregation will prove to have important bearing on the issue of the relationship between consumption and the rate of interest. In Chapter 13, the reader will remember, we reported R. C. O. Matthews'

---

[1] Milton Friedman, *A Theory of the Consumption Function* (Princeton, N.J.: Princeton University Press, 1957).

analysis leading to an assertion of indeterminacy of this relationship and in Chapter 15 our own model confirmed this indeterminacy. We shall show in this chapter that this indeterminacy disappears once we discuss the economy as a whole.

Individual and Aggregate Consumption

From our discussion of the previous chapter we can derive a consumption function for an individual that expresses his current consumption as a function of his income function, his initial asset position, and the rate of interest. That is, we can write the level of consumption at any time τ for an individual consumer i as a function of the capitalized value of his income and initial assets, and the rate of interest. For simplicity let us assume that the optimal path of bequests is such that the function $b(t)$ equals zero for all t, except for a small interval around the termination of the consumer's life-span; that is, we assume that he reserves all bequests for terminal bequests. Or alternatively, that we include all bequests that occur during the consumer's lifetime in the consumption function and reserve the term bequests for its more normal usage as the disposition of the consumer's terminal assets. These assumptions result in the consumption function not containing the level of bequests as a separate argument. Thus, we write

$$C_{i\tau} = \gamma_i\left(\int_\tau^T e^{r[T-t]}H\,dt, A_\tau, r\right) \qquad [16.1]$$

where $C_{i\tau}$ is the real consumption of the i-th consumer for the τ-th period. From the previous chapter we know that

$$\frac{\partial C_{i\tau}}{\partial H} > 0; \qquad \frac{\partial C_{i\tau}}{\partial A_\tau} > 0 \qquad \text{and} \qquad \frac{\partial C_{i\tau}}{\partial r} < 0 \qquad [16.2]$$

where we assume that a change in the income function H is a parallel shift, so that the price of leisure does not change.

Unfortunately, most changes in the human income function in- volve changes in the price of leisure; that is, they are not parallel shifts in the H function, but involve rotational shifts as well. Hence, H_l, H_c, and thus H_m change. However, let us assume that if the income effect is larger than the substitution effect, this difference is never so large, so as to result in lower income in any period than existed before the change in the income function. In other words, we are assuming that consumption in any period is not an inferior good relative to leisure. (Note that this is not an additional restriction to those assumed in the previous chapter.) With these assumptions it can be shown that such a change in the income function will always result in an increase in the consumption function at every time in the consumer's horizon. Thus, for such a change in the function H the partial derivatives in [16.2] will hold. The reason for the determinacy of the sign of the partial derivative with respect to changes in the rate of interest is that we are holding constant the capitalized value of the income function plus initial assets. Of course, most changes in the rate of interest will also involve a change in this capitalized value, so that the total effect of the interest rate change is then ambiguous; this ambiguity will be discussed later in this chapter.

Consumer Behavior and the Permanent Income Hypothesis

Before we proceed with a discussion of the aggregation of the results derived in the previous chapter, we shall find it instructive to pause and relate the results obtained to Milton Friedman's permanent income hypothesis. We shall show below that our approach yields the permanent income hypothesis as a special case. Specifically, if we introduce into our basic model the assumption that the life-span of the consumers is infinite, we arrive at Friedman's result.[2]

Temporary Versus Permanent Income

Let us ignore initially the question of the finiteness of the consumer's life-span and consider any horizon that is longer than one period,

[2] See Milton Friedman, *ibid.*, pp. 7–19, for the theoretical underpinnings of Friedman's approach.

however defined. In this case, whether or not a shift in the consumer's
income function *H*, for a given period, is assumed by the consumer
to imply an equal shift for the remainder of his horizon is of para-
mount importance. In particular, if the consumer assumes that at
the end of the current period his income function will return to its
initial level, then the effect on the level of his consumption expenditures, leisure, and desired terminal assets will be smaller than if a
permanent shift had occurred. In fact, because of our assumption
of the noninferiority of consumption in any interval *vis à vis* any
other interval in the consumer's horizon, we know that a shift in the
income function, *H*, of a single period's duration will result in a
smaller change in consumption at any time *t* than an equal shift
for longer than, but including, the above period. Thus, if a given
shift in *H* occurs for, say, one year, the expectations of consumers
regarding the position of *H* in future years are crucial in determining
the effect of the known one-year shift in *H* on current consumption.
For example, if the shift in *H* results in the expectation that the
following year will see an opposite shift of equal capitalized value,
then no change will occur in current consumption, leisure, and desired
terminal assets so long as borrowing and lending rates are the same.
On the other hand, if the shift in the income function *H* in one year
is associated with the expectation that in the following year the function will merely return to its original level, there will be some increase in lifelong income and thus some increase in consumption in
any time interval *t*. Of course, for obvious reasons, this increase in
consumption will be smaller than if the *H* function were expected to
maintain its new position permanently. In terms of Friedman's
analysis, a shift of the *H* function for a short period of time and its
subsequent return give rise to what Friedman calls "transitory
income."[3] In terms of our analysis, a transitory increase in consumer's income represents a smaller addition to his wealth than a
permanent increase in his income.

In contrast to such transitory income, permanent income is

[3] Friedman, *ibid.*, pp. 21–22.

defined by Friedman as the maximum level of consumption expenditures per period consistent with a constant net asset position. In our model, we may express this definition by choosing the largest constant, $c(t) = \bar{c}$ for all t in the interval $[\tau, T]$ such that

$$\int_\tau^T e^{r[T-t]}[H\{\hat{l}(t), c(t), G, t\} - \{c(t) + rG\}]\,dt = e^{r[T-\tau]}A_\tau \quad [16.3]$$

where $\hat{l}(t)$ is the optimal path of leisure associated with H and A_τ. Let us denote the maximum value of $c(t)$ consistent with [16.3] as y_P. Since this concept is the equivalent of Friedman's concept of permanent income, we use his notation y_P.[4] Thus, it is possible for the consumer to consume his entire permanent income in every period for any number of periods; hence, the term *permanent* income. Now it is here that Friedman assumes that the utility function is homogeneous in its arguments (only consumption expenditures in this case) so that the marginal rate of substitution between consumption in any year relative to any other year depends only on the ratio of consumption in the two years and not on the absolute level of consumption.[5] From this result and from the assumption of an infinite horizon, Friedman derives his permanent income consumption function. That is, consumption in the interval I_0 is said to be some proportion k of the level of permanent income y_P in the interval I_0, where k depends on the rate of interest and the consumer's utility function but not on the level of permanent income.[6] However, these results do depend on the assumption of an infinite horizon and must be modified when a finite horizon is considered.

Finite and Infinite Life-span

Two problems arise concerning the compatibility of Friedman's results with the model we have developed in the previous three

[4] Friedman, *ibid.*, pp. 10–11.
[5] In our case we have a utility functional so that homogeneity would imply that proportionate shifts in $l(t)$, $c(t)$, and $b(t)$ would lead to proportionate shifts in utility.
[6] Friedman, *ibid.*, p. 14.

chapters, and both of these problems are partially the result of allowing for the fact that the lifetime of a consumer is finite. First, because the consumer has a finite life-span, he is interested in the value of his terminal assets and will respond to changes in the economic variables facing him in a manner that takes the desired level of terminal assets into account. Second, when terminal assets become relevant, the relative price of the acquisition of terminal assets becomes one of the economic variables facing the consumer; a change in this relative price may be expected to affect his decisions. Let us discuss these two issues in turn.

THE RELEVANCE OF TERMINAL ASSETS.   As we have indicated above, the fact that the consumer has a finite life-span makes the level of his assets at the termination of this life-span a relevant variable. First, the market will impose on him the constraint that these assets be nonnegative. Second, the human wealth component of his permanent income has a zero value at the termination of his life-span. Thus, the way in which permanent income changes makes a considerable difference on the extent to which the consumer's consumption reacts to this change:

1. If an increase in a consumer's *human* income function were to lead to a proportionate increase in his consumption in every period, the value of terminal assets will not have increased proportionately unless terminal assets were initially zero. But the assumption of homogeneity of the utility function will then imply that the marginal rates of substitution between consumption in any interval and terminal assets will have changed and thus the consumer will want to change the proportion of permanent income (k) he devotes to consumption. In fact, assuming the normal convex relationship between terminal assets and consumption in a given interval, the consumer will want to increase terminal assets resulting in lower consumption than would otherwise be the case. That is, the k in our consumption function [16.4] will be smaller than initially.

2. If the change in permanent income is the result of an increase in *nonhuman* assets, then a proportionate increase in consumption expenditures will result in a more than proportionate increase in terminal assets unless the human income function is identically zero. Thus, again the marginal rate of substitution will have changed and a readjustment in k will be required except that in this case the proportion of permanent income consumed, k, will be larger than initially.

3. If the change in permanent income is due to proportionate changes in both the human income function and the value of initial nonhuman assets, then a proportionate change in consumption in every interval is consistent with an equiproportionate change in terminal assets. The proportion of permanent income consumed, k, will remain constant.

Thus, when a finite horizon is assumed, the proportion of human to nonhuman income (and therefore wealth) is an important determinant of the level of consumption. This proportion is also considered important by Friedman but for another, perfectly valid, reason—uncertainty. He argues, "All forms of wealth are not, however, equally satisfactory as a reserve for emergencies." [7] This argument is essentially based on the nonmarketability of human capital and simply reinforces the result we have derived above.

RELATIVE PRICE OF TERMINAL ASSETS. There is still another consequence of making the assumption that the consumer's life-span is limited and that he is, therefore, interested in the value of his terminal assets. The distance of any specific time under consideration from the consumer's horizon affects the relative price of terminal assets. The closer the consumer is to the end of his life, the more expensive it becomes to purchase a terminal asset of a given value. As a result, the distance of any time point under consideration from the end of the consumer's time horizon will affect the proportion k of permanent income consumed.

[7] Friedman, *ibid.*, p. 16.

Conclusion of Comparison

It is now obvious that when our consumption function is recast in terms of permanent income, it yields results that are no different from Friedman's results except for the inclusion of $(T - \tau)$ as an argument of k. That is, under the conditions specified the consumption expenditures during a given interval will be some proportion k of the consumer's permanent income:

$$C_I = k y_P \tag{16.4}$$

where

$$k = k\left(\frac{e^{r[T-\tau]}A_\tau}{\displaystyle\int_\tau^T e^{r[T-t]}H\,dt}, r, T - \tau, \mu\right) \tag{16.5}$$

and where $I = [\tau, t_0]$.

As shown above, the ratio k depends on:

    (a) the rate of interest,

    (b) the time that is left to the consumer before he dies,

    (c) the consumer's utility functional,

    (d) the ratio of the capitalized value of nonhuman assets to the capitalized value of human wealth (that is, in turn, at any point of time the capitalized value of human income to be received from that time on). It may be pointed out, finally, that this ratio reduces to a ratio of human to non-human income provided that the capitalization rates applicable to these two incomes are the same.[8] To see that this is the case, consider a function H, which is a constant, say, y_h. Then the integral in the numerator of the fraction reduces to

$$\int_\tau^T e^{r[T-t]}y_h\,dt = e^{r[T-\tau]}\,\frac{y_h}{r} \tag{16.6}$$

so that the ratio in [16.4] becomes

$$\frac{e^{r[T-\tau]}A_\tau}{\displaystyle\int_\tau^T e^{r[T-t]}H\,dt} = \frac{A_\tau}{\dfrac{y_h}{r}} = \frac{y_n}{y_h} \tag{16.7}$$

---

[8] See Chapter 10 of the present book for reasons why these rates cannot be expected to be the same.

Thus, even if the capitalization rates applicable to human and non-human incomes were the same, the conclusion would follow that the larger the nonhuman income (or, by analogy, the larger taxes on human income) in proportion to human income (to taxes on nonhuman income), the larger the factor k: the bigger will be the consumption expenditures out of any given permanent income. This results from the fact that human wealth is not eligible for the task of becoming a legacy to others. But this inferiority is just a part of the general inferiority of human income. Therefore (cf. our discussion in Chapter 10), the capitalization rates applicable to human and nonhuman incomes will not be the same; the rate applicable to human income will be higher. But the higher this rate relative to the rate applicable to nonhuman income, the higher will be the factor k: the more will consumption expenditures out of any given permanent income increase as a result of a redistribution of the pretax income in favor of nonhuman income and as a result of a redistribution of the tax burden in the direction of human income.

Aggregation of Individual Consumption Functions

Let us now assume that the distribution of consumers by age, life-span, and income shares remains constant. Let us assume in addition that the distribution of consumers by the ratio of non-human income to human income relative to the ratio of nonhuman income to human income for the population also remains constant. For simplicity, we may let the human-nonhuman income ratio bear the entire burden of the inferiority of human income just discussed and assume that there is but one interest rate that is the same for all consumers. Then we can write the aggregate consumption function as

$$C^* = \gamma^* \left\{ Y_P^*, \left(\frac{y_n}{y_h}\right)^*, r \right\} \qquad [16.8]$$

where C^* is aggregate consumption, y_P^* is the community's permanent income, $\left(\frac{y_n}{y_h}\right)^*$ is the population proportion of nonhuman to human income, and r is the common rate of interest. If we had been willing to retain our assumptions used in the discussion of Friedman's permanent consumption function and additionally assumed that the distribution of consumers by permanent income share is independent of the other arguments of the consumption function, we could have written [16.8] as

$$C^* = k^* \left\{ \left(\frac{y_n}{y_h} \right)^*, r \right\} y_P^* \qquad [16.9]$$

However, for our purposes nothing is to be gained from having the consumption function in this particular form.[9]

From our discussion of the previous chapter we can infer the following signs to the partial derivatives of [16.8]:

$$\frac{\partial C^*}{\partial y_P^*} > 0, \qquad \frac{\partial C^*}{\partial \left(\frac{y_n}{y_h} \right)^*} > 0, \qquad \text{and} \qquad \frac{\partial C^*}{\partial r} < 0 \qquad [16.10]$$

Note that this last partial does not imply that the total effect of a change in the rate of interest is negative but only that if y_P^* and $\left(\frac{y_n}{y_h} \right)^*$ remain unaffected, then a change in the rate of interest will result in an opposite change in aggregate consumption. This result is consistent with our previous result, since, as we have indicated, the substitution effect of a change in the rate of interest is negative.

Since the y_P^* for the community can be determined by the levels of y_n^*, y_h^* and r, we can rewrite [16.8] as[10]

$$C^* = \delta^*(y_h^*, y_n^*, r) \qquad [16.11]$$

$$\frac{\partial C^*}{\partial y_n^*} > \frac{\partial C^*}{\partial y_h^*} > 0 \qquad \text{and} \qquad \frac{\partial C^*}{\partial r} < 0 \qquad [16.12]$$

---

[9] Since our observations seem to attest to the fact that the ratio of nonhuman to human income increases with age and that income itself increases with age, we would not expect the distribution of consumers by income share to be independent of their distribution by ratio of nonhuman to human income.

[10] The relationship between the first two partials follows from our discussion of the nonmarketability of human income.

Now, if a particular change in the rate of interest is due to a shift in the marginal efficiency of capital (so that with the same rate of investment as before the permanent income of society is raised), then such a change in the rate (a) may result in more or less present consumption than before the change, but (b) will certainly result in a greater level of saving. This result follows from the assumption that future consumption is not inferior to present consumption, so that at least some portion of the increase in permanent income will be put aside for future consumption.

Consumption and the Rate of Interest

Let us now turn our attention to the effect of aggregation on the conclusion reached in Chapter 15—that the effect of a change in the rate of interest on a consumer's consumption behavior is unpredictable on *a priori* grounds. This conclusion has also been reached by R. C. O. Matthews and has been applied by him to the economy as a whole. The key consideration here is that when we analyze the behavior of a single consumer, we are free to postulate a change in the rate of interest without inquiring into the source of this change. When we aggregate and consider the economy as a whole, this ceases to be possible, since in the economy as a whole a change in the rate of interest must have some specific cause. Consider, for example, the effect of a decision by all consumers to increase present consumption. Such a decision will reduce the level of aggregate saving and increase the rate of interest. But, at a reduced level of saving, capital accumulation will be reduced and thus the permanent income in future years will be reduced with no change in present aggregate permanent income. However, from the fact that present aggregate permanent income is unchanged, it does not follow that the permanent income of all consumers is unchanged. In fact, we expect the increase in the rate of interest to make net creditors worse off and net debtors better off, so that some consumers will experience increases in their permanent income and some reductions.

But this very discussion indicates that what is true, in this case, on the microeconomic level cannot be true on the macroeconomic level. True enough, a change in the rate of interest can be shown to make some consumers wealthier and some poorer; to use Matthews' terminology, the effect of this change depends on whether the consumer expects to be a "buyer" or a "seller"[11] of wealth. However, it is not feasible to extend this conclusion to society as a whole and to conclude either that the wealth of society does not change as a result of a change of the rate or that it changes in an unpredictable manner. Such a conclusion is impossible, since society as a whole *must* be a net wealth holder; again, using Matthews' terminology, society as a whole *must* be a net "seller." Since the value of these net wealth holdings was, before the change in the rate, the income of society divided by the rate of interest, given this income, a higher rate *must* result in a net reduction of society's wealth and thus *must* result in a reduction in the planned increase in total consumption. This conclusion is unaffected by the fate of individual consumers— fate that is, indeed, unpredictable *a priori*. What has occurred is simply that consumers' tastes have changed, so that at given rates of interest and levels of wealth they desired to consume more than previously. But since society as a whole cannot consume more without affecting the aggregate level of wealth, the reduction in the level of wealth informs the community of this fact of economic life and the increase in consumption is reduced. However, an increase still occurs.

Conclusion

In this chapter we have discussed very briefly some of the problems involved in the aggregation of individual consumption functions and

[11] R. C. O. Matthews, "Expenditure Plans and the Uncertainty Motive for Holding Money," *Journal of Political Economy*, *LXXI* (June, 1963), p. 205.

some of the pitfalls inherent in assuming that what is true for the individual is true for the society. In addition, we have shown the relationship between our analysis and the permanent income hypothesis of Milton Friedman. In the remaining chapters we will discuss the macroeconomic system, using the results of this chapter as a base.

PART V

WEALTH IN
MACROECONOMIC ANALYSIS

In Parts II and III of this book, we discussed the definition of wealth and specified the various elements that can cause an *initial* change in the level of wealth. However, as we have stressed throughout the analysis, the initial change will, in general, not be the *ultimate* change. The reason for this is that, as some components of the net wealth of the community change, the behavior of consumers will be affected in the manner discussed in Part IV of the book. This change in consumer behavior will disturb the equilibrium level of many or all variables and, especially, it will disturb the equilibrium levels of the two key variables that determine the level of wealth itself: the level of prices and the rate of interest. Thus, the initial change in wealth is not going to remain undisturbed. The economy will seek a new equilibrium. While each of us may be interested in the change in the level of some specific variable, it is most likely that we all are interested especially in one: the level of national income. Will the initial change in wealth, after disturbing the behavior of consumers, lead to a change in the equilibrium level of income enjoyed by society? It is the task of Part V of this book to answer this question.

CHAPTER 17

Diverse Issues in
Macroeconomic Analysis

In its basic structure, the model we shall use is the same as the one in general use today and the one we used in Chapter 1. However, there are a number of issues that were glossed over in Chapter 1 and that now merit discussion. First, we shall discuss briefly the reasons that lead most macroeconomic analyses, including ours, to concentrate on the flows of goods and services that pass through the market and to exclude nonmarket flows. Second, we shall discuss the reasons that lead most macroeconomic analyses, including ours, to separate the market for nonmoney goods and services from the market for money goods and services; that cause separation of demand for and supply of nonmoney goods and services from the demand for and supply of money goods and services. Third, we shall discuss in detail the economic links, the nexus, between the commodity market and the money market. Fourth, we shall briefly touch upon the traditional separation of governmentally produced goods and services. Fifth, we shall point out that there are certain differences between concepts as used in economic analysis and in national income accounting. With these issues out of the way, we shall in the next chapters restate the macroeconomic model and discuss the determinants of equilibrium within the structure of this model.

Exclusion of Nonmarket Incomes

It is customary to define the income variable in macroeconomic discussions so that it includes only market-produced incomes. The purpose is, mainly, to give the analysis empirical relevancy, since data for nonmarket incomes are, by and large, not available. However, we must bear in mind that we have made this exclusion because some of our results may now be affected by changes in the distribution of market versus nonmarket incomes. Specifically, an increase in total income (market plus nonmarket) will, under the conditions specified in Part IV, increase desired present consumption and desired future consumption, the latter being reflected in an increased demand for assets. However, an increase in nonmarket incomes, which from the standpoint of the analysis will also result in increased consumption and saving *in toto*, may show up in market terms as a decrease in saving because, if the consumer desires to increase both market and nonmarket consumption, this must, by the definition of market saving, reduce the level of market saving so long as market income remains constant. Thus, the results of an analysis that includes only market incomes must assume that the distribution of nonmarket to market incomes and consumption remains constant throughout the analysis.

Separation of the Money Market from the Commodity Market

The reasons for the separation of the money market, and thus of the contribution of the flow of services of money as either income to consumers or as factor services to firms, from the other determinants of aggregate supply and aggregate demand are manifold and merit discussion:

1. There is the problem of whether money should be considered a consumers' or producers' good. That is, should the flow of services from money be included in our measure of income or are these flows merely intermediate to the consumption and production of final goods and services? Our analysis in Chapter 14 treated money as an intermediate good, since money was demanded only because it increased income for any given amount of leisure consumed. However, this issue is not settled.[1]

2. The necessity of making a decision on this issue is obviated by the fact that there is a more pervasive reason for a separation of the money market from the other determinants of the aggregate demand for goods and services. In Chapters 3 through 5 we have shown that money has a technical property that is different from the technical properties of other goods: namely, money yields real income that changes equiproportionately with the price of money. Since in most macroeconomic models the price of money is permitted to fluctuate (the general price level is permitted to change), it becomes necessary to account separately for a good with this special technical property. This separation is accomplished, as has been shown in Chapter 1, by having a separate demand for goods and services other than money and a separate demand function for money. The first yields the Hicksian *IS* function, the second—along with the money supply—the Hicksian *LM* function; these two functions together determine the aggregate demand for nonmoney goods and services.

3. There is still another reason why, in modern economies, it is necessary to separate money from other goods. In economies making use of commodity money, all producers of goods would face a production function containing nonmonetary (human and nonhuman) wealth as a significant independent variable. As we have seen in Chapters 3 through 5, the special technical property of money has consequences not only for the users of money; it has consequences also for the producers of money. Specifically,

---

[1] For a detailed discussion of this issue, cf. pp. 52–55.

the fact that the real value of the services of money is independent of the price of money implies that this real value is also independent of the real costs of production of money. This is the reason why in modern economies commodity money is replaced by fiat money and bank money as soon as the monopolistic structure required for this replacement becomes feasible. Thus, in a model that assumes or permits, as one possibility, competitive markets everywhere but in the production of fiat and bank money (for competition would reduce fiat money to commodity money and bank money to bonds), it becomes necessary to separate these two types of markets, since their respective reactions to changes in the other parts of the system will differ significantly. It becomes necessary to have an aggregate supply of nonmoney goods and services and a separate supply of money goods.

Nexus Between the Money Market and the Commodity Market

However, a separation of the nonmoney commodity market from the money market makes it necessary to ask what is the economic nexus connecting these two markets. Formally, it is clear enough. The Hicksian *IS* function shows all the pairs of income and interest rates consistent with equilibrium in the commodity market; the Hicksian *LM* function shows all the pairs of income and interest rates consistent with equilibrium in the money market. Since we cannot have two different equilibrium pairs of income and the rate of interest, equilibrium requires a solution that satisfies, simultaneously, the requirements of both markets. If something in either market changes, one or the other function shifts and forces a change in the equilibrium values of income and interest. However, what is the economic mechanism that brings all this about? We can hardly rest satisfied with a solution based on geometry or mathematics. Unless we provide an economic rationale—describe the economic mechanism that leads to the results obtained—we have said very little or nothing.

Attempts to provide a full description of the linkages between the money market and the commodity markets, as Karl Brunner recently pointed out, have barely begun.[2] Since this problem has an important bearing on the main topic of this book—the exploration of the relationship between wealth and economic behavior—it appears desirable to discuss this issue in some detail. The economic nexus between the two markets that is most stressed and on which—in contrast with the neoclassical wealth-consumption effect—there seems to be general agreement today has been instructively summarized by Abba P. Lerner:

> However, it is unlikely that all or even a significant part of the surplus cash would be directed toward increasing current consumption.
>
> The public would regard the surplus cash as part of their wealth which it would be improvident to consume just because it was in a particular form—namely money—in which they preferred not to hold so much of their property. They would convert it into other forms by exchanging it for interest-yielding pieces of property such as land or mortgages or securities or promissory notes.[3]

This statement describes one of the important factors linking the money market with the commodity market—a linkage that is based on the hypothesis that the consumers desire to hold a balanced wealth portfolio. In the monetary-nonmonetary wealth dichotomy the causality must be expected to go, of course, both ways. While Lerner in the above quotation concentrates on the causality going from monetary wealth to nonmonetary wealth, Lloyd A. Metzler, in an article that we discussed in Chapter 13,[4] concentrated on the causality going from nonmonetary wealth to monetary wealth. Clearly, Lerner and Metzler describe the opposite sides of the same

---

[2] Karl Brunner, "Some Major Problems in Monetary Theory," *American Economic Review, LI* (May, 1961), p. 47.

[3] Abba P. Lerner, *The Economics of Control* (New York: The Macmillan Co., 1952), p. 280.

[4] Lloyd A. Metzler, "Wealth, Saving, and the Rate of Interest," *Journal of Political Economy, LIX* (April, 1951), p. 113.

372   *Wealth in Macroeconomic Analysis*

coin. Upon dichotomizing total wealth into money wealth and non-money wealth, Lerner further dichotomizes nonmoney wealth into real wealth and financial wealth and points out that the consumers, stimulated by an increase in their money wealth, will buy (a) real wealth, such as land, and (b) financial wealth, such as securities or mortgages or promissory notes. However, this analysis cannot be made to fit the Procrustean bed of the "Keynesian"[5] accounting identity according to which consumers either consume (i.e., demand goods and services) or save (i.e., fail to demand goods and services and, perhaps, demand nonmoney financial wealth). Instead of abandoning the dichotomy, since it conflicts with analysis, Lerner abandons his analysis by making it fit the consumption-saving dichotomy. He decides to call *both* the purchases of real wealth[6] and the purchases of financial wealth "lending":

> They would convert it into other forms by exchanging it for interest-yielding pieces of property such as land or mortgages or securities or promissory notes. *All of these are included in the alternative way of decreasing cash holdings which we called "lending."* [Emphasis ours.][7]

Next, we are offered economic analysis of the consequences of lending in its original meaning of "making loans":

> When individuals *lend* [emphasis Lerner's] their surplus cash, this lowers the rate of interest. . . . The rate of interest . . . determines the rate of investment. The rate of investment . . . determines the level of employment.[8]

---

[5] We are enclosing this word in quotation marks for reasons that will become obvious shortly.

[6] We may note that if the consumer buys real wealth out of current output. these purchases are "investment purchases"; if he buys real wealth out of the stock that existed at the start of the period, they are not. However, in the latter case the consumer merely shifts the portfolio disturbance to somebody else and this somebody else will now enter the act. This makes it clear that equilibrium of the economy as a whole can be restored solely through investment purchases.

[7] Abba P. Lerner, *op. cit.*, p. 280.

[8] Abba P. Lerner, *ibid.*, p. 281.

The roundaboutness of this nexus, the many stages through which money must pass before it can be converted into a change in aggregate demand, is well suited for an argument stressing the uncertainty of this process. In the work just quoted, Lerner devotes the entire next chapter to showing that "at each step in the automatic elimination of unemployment (and inflation) the machinery is likely to stall."[9] Elsewhere, he summarized more succinctly the familiar argument that one can pull on a string but not push it, that there is many a slip 'twixt the cup and the lip:

> But even this third order of price flexibility would fail to restore full employment if a very high elasticity of liquidity (the liquidity trap) prevented the rate of interest from falling or if a low elasticity of investment (collapse of confidence) made the fall in interest ineffective. In that case the alternative . . . (an increase in the stock of money to yield the same increase in liquidity without putting the economy through the wringer) would also fail. This is a variant of the Keynesian Special Case where fiscal policy has to bail out monetary policy. The fiscal measures might involve an increase in the money stock, but that would be "mere window dressing."[10]

These sweeping and basic conclusions (that monetary wealth in the consumer's wealth portfolio is mere window dressing, that less-than-full-employment equilibrium even in a fully competitive system is possible, and that monetary policy is ineffective for the task of restoring a full-employment equilibrium) hang on a startlingly slender thread. Let us catch our breath and retrace the steps just taken in a more leisurely fashion. There are five basic links through which the money market may be connected with the aggregate demand for goods and services other than money:

1. Changes in household consumption.
2. Changes in household investment.

[9] Abba P. Lerner, *ibid.*, p. 285 and chapter 23.
[10] Abba P. Lerner, "The *General Theory* After Twenty-Five Years: Discussion," *American Economic Review*, LI (May, 1961), p. 21.

3. Making loans for consumption purposes.[11]
4. Making loans for household and business investment purposes.
5. Making loans that lead to the refinancing of existing obligations.

In the analysis just discussed, the first link between the money market and aggregate demand is dismissed as inconsequential, so that only items 2 through 5 remain for consideration. Since the consumption-saving dichotomy does not permit investment by households, these four items are given the common name of *lending*. In subsequent analysis, the original meaning of the word *lending* (i.e., making loans) is restored so that item 2 disappears and only items 3 through 5 are left for consideration. Since by the saving-investment dichotomy households only lend and businesses only borrow, consumer credit cannot be accommodated and thus only items 4 and 5 remain for consideration. Since, as already stated, the consumption-saving dichotomy does not permit household investment, lending for these purposes cannot by definition occur either. What is now left for analysis is only the latter part of item 4 and item 5. After this drastic pruning of the links between the money market and aggregate

---

[11] In discussions of lending operations attention seems to be most frequently focused on lending to finance business investment; lending to finance household investment or consumption is frequently neglected. Even if not neglected, it is at times handled in a manner that is not analytically adequate. For instance, the often quoted study by Thomas Mayer concluded that lending to households responds to changes in monetary policy within a month or two; lending to businesses was discovered to be much less flexible. From all this the conclusion has been drawn that monetary policy takes seven months to be half effective and twenty-two months to be fully effective. (Cf., Thomas Mayer, "The Inflexibility of Monetary Policy," *Review of Economics and Statistics*, XL (November, 1958), pp. 358–374.

However, the entire study rests on, and we believe is vitiated by, implicit and crucial assumptions (cf. Mayer's Table 7 and its application) according to which bankers (a) establish the fraction by which each sector participates in total credit, (b) earmark newly acquired loanable funds to each sector in accordance (or roughly in accordance) with that fraction, and (c) hold these earmarked funds idle until the "proper" sector makes use of them. It is surely superfluous to point out that this assumed mode of bankers' behavior is inexplicable by value theory and that it is contradicted by the post-war levels of excess reserves.

demand, a case is postulated in which either the liquidity trap, or the immovable and inelastic investment function, or both, exist. The liquidity trap argument denies that any of the above five responses to changes in money obtains. The investment function argument points out that, under the conditions specified by it, the response in the second half of item 4 will fail to obtain and only the response in item 5 will obtain. In view of the attention that the last two arguments received in the literature, let us look at them in greater detail:

1. The liquidity trap argument asserts that the consumers will hold any quantity of money at the going interest rate. It is, therefore, a geometric representation of a situation in which the consumers desire neither an income-consumption equilibrium nor a portfolio equilibrium; it is a geometric representation of corner solutions for both of these cases. In terms of the above enumeration of the links between the money market and aggregate demand for nonmoney goods, the "liquidity trap" represents merely a denial that any one of the responses outlined in items 1 through 5 above will occur. But to say then that the liquidity trap will block money from having economic consequences is tantamount to saying that attempts to restore income-consumption and portfolio equilibria will be blocked if there is no attempt to restore these equilibria. What appears to be an analytical conclusion is actually a restatement of an initial assumption.

2. The second argument, based on the immovable and inelastic investment function, is no less circular, because it contains an internal contradiction. According to this argument, increases in money cause increases in "lending" that, however, fail to increase aggregate demand, since they do not lead to increases in investing. We have seen above that the name "lending" is the sum of two components: making loans for a number of purposes (items 3, 4, and 5 above) *and* direct investing (item 2 above). Let us therefore restate the above proposition not in terms of the sum ("lending") but in terms of the two main components of the sum: making loans and investing. It then reads: increases in money

cause increases in making loans plus increases in investing that, however, fail to increase aggregate demand because they do not lead to increases in investing.

Both current economic analysis and empirical evidence[12] fail to lend support to the notion that the consumers do not desire an income-consumption equilibrium and a wealth-portfolio equilibrium. Unless and until this changes, there seems to be no point in allowing for the possible existence of the liquidity trap in micro- or macroeconomic analysis. As far as the argument based on the immovable and inelastic investment function is concerned, all that needs to be done to dispose of it is to focus attention on the terminological sleight of hand inherent in calling a direct increase in aggregate demand "lending." Once this is done, the two major analytical findings based on it—the fully competitive unemployment equilibrium and the ineffectiveness of monetary policy associated with it—go out not with a bang of clashing theories but with a whimper of terminological confusion. It is not without irony to observe the complete reversal of the fate of these two findings from Chapter 2 to this chapter:

1. In Chapter 2 (cf. equation [2.3]) we have shown that existing economic theory made it possible to stipulate—merely for the sake of argument—the existence of a strong wealth-consumption relationship and still uphold the less-than-full-employment competitive equilibrium and ineffectiveness of monetary policy.
2. The above discussion of the nexus between the money market and the commodity market makes it, in turn, possible to stipulate— merely for the sake of the argument—the nonexistence of the wealth-consumption relationship and still reject the less-than-full-employment competitive equilibrium and the ineffectiveness of monetary policy.

---

[12] One cannot prove a negative. All we can say is that we are not aware of any body of empirical evidence indicating that the consumers do not maintain an income-consumption equilibrium and a wealth portfolio equilibrium. Note that correlations of time series on the money supply and the rate of interest have little, even though some, bearing on the two basic issues stated above.

In other words, the neoclassical wealth-consumption relationship is not needed to reject these two findings because the rejection can be based solely on a rethinking of the "strictly Keynesian" macroeconomic model. All that needs to be done is to remove the arbitrary and simplifying assumption that only households consume, save, and lend, whereas only business enterprises invest and borrow.

We use the word "Keynesian" because this term is so firmly ingrained in economic discussions that a failure to use it may simply block understanding of what is being said. Yet, we use that word with extreme reluctance because space limitations prevent an adequate inquiry into the problem of whether, and to what extent, Keynes was a "Keynesian." In the few instances in which such an inquiry was necessary (Chapters 1, 11, and 14) we concluded that the connection is tenuous indeed; it may well prove to be questionable in this case as well. The present macroeconomic analysis in the literature commonly called "Keynesian" employs the following identities:

$$y = c + i \qquad\qquad [17.1]$$

$$y = c + s \qquad\qquad [17.2]$$

$$i = w_{t_2} - w_{t_1}; \qquad\qquad [17.3]$$

where w_{t_1} and w_{t_2} are the level of wealth at time t_2 and t_1, respectively, and y is the level of income produced between the point of time t_1 and the point of time t_2. Equations [17.1] and [17.3], in conjunction, indicate a definition of consumption that is consistent with the analysis of consumption by the theory of value: it is the consumers' use of a certain quantity of resources during a certain period of time for their personal enjoyment and in a manner that leaves no resource left at the end of that period. Similarly, investment is simply the quantity of resources produced but not used up for consumption during that time period and that, consequently, becomes an increment to society's wealth endowment. If we now add to the above the assumptions that the community consists of two groups, businesses and consumers, and that consumers receive all the income produced and only consume and save but do not invest (equation [17.2]), it then follows that only businesses invest. Thus, the only way in which saving and investment are linked is through lending (in the *bona fide* meaning of "making loans"). While analytically rigorous, this does not happen to be the way in which Keynes used the word "consumption." He attached to this word the popular meaning of next to any purchase made by the households:

> Expenditure on consumption during any period must mean the value of goods sold to the consumer during that period, which throws us back to the question of what is meant by a consumer-purchaser. Any reasonable definition of the line between consumer-purchasers and investor-purchasers will serve us equally well, provided that it is consistently applied. Such problem as there is, e.g., whether it is right to regard the purchase of a motor-car as a consumer purchase and the purchase of a house as an investor-purchase, has been frequently discussed and I have nothing material to add to the discussion.[13]

If the current rigorous definition of the key variables entering the macroeconomic model is "Keynesian," Keynes clearly is not a Keynesian. His "consumption" contains consumption, as rigorously defined, and investment, as rigorously defined. Since history of economic analysis is not our concern, we made no attempt to establish whether this discrepancy between the rigorous and Keynes' definition of the key variables affected his own analysis or merely the subsequent interpretations of it.

Let us now close this section with the expression of our belief that this reconsideration of the nexus between the commodity market and the money market has proved useful because it has revealed what strictly mathematical or geometric analysis cannot reveal: that there are at least two basic links between these two markets based on the balanced wealth portfolio analysis—one, linking the money market with the commodity market through consumers' demand for real wealth (such as consumer durables) and thus through the demand for consumers' investment; the other, less direct, linking these two

[13] John Maynard Keynes, *The General Theory of Employment Interest and Money* (New York: Harcourt, Brace & World, 1936), p. 61.

markets through the consumers' demand for financial wealth and thus through lending. Of course, the neoclassical wealth effect adds a third link that, by relating any wealth to consumption, as rigorously defined, links the monetary wealth market to consumption.

Separation of the Private Markets from the Government "Market"

Consumers may find that there are a number of activities that can be performed more efficiently if carried out by collective activity rather than individually. It then becomes essential to account *separately* for that part of income (supplied and demanded) that is affected. The reason for this is, of course, that many of the rules of value theory become inapplicable. The consumer is not free, as far as these incomes are concerned, to purchase more or less of these goods in accordance with his utility function and in accordance with the determinants of his demand for other things. Frequently, he has no other choice except for the "all or nothing" type, with the "nothing" choice requiring exile. In other cases, he may purchase more privately if he so chooses but may not purchase less (he may hire a bodyguard but not a negative policeman). This has several implications for macroeconomic analysis. First of all, the theory of collective decision making is so imperfect that hardly anything more can be done but to treat these flows of incomes as exogenously determined. Second, even the issue of whether these governmentally controlled flows are or are not additive to the remaining flows (the fact that both are measured in dollars notwithstanding) poses some difficulties as long as the purpose of national income accounts is to measure not merely resources used up but useful outputs produced. These two incomes would be additive only if the marginal utility of a dollar privately spent and the marginal utility of a dollar publicly spent were the same;[14] but everybody agrees that this is not the case and everybody disagrees as to the sign and the size of the deviation.

[14] For a more detailed discussion of this issue, cf. pp. 259 ff.

But then, there is an economic case not only for a separation of these two income flows but even for a refusal to add them up. They are being added, nevertheless, on the basis of an assumption that we all say we know to be a false one and that is being made nevertheless for lack of a better one. Since our interest is solely analytical, there was no purpose in including in our model the government purchases of goods and the taxes necessary to finance these purchases. By including them and making them, as is customary, exogenously determined we would add nothing substantive to the analysis.

Relation of Analytical Concepts to Empirical Evidence

Before we start to discuss the model, let us make the usual caveat found in most macroeconomic books. The concepts used in this purely analytical book are related to but are not identical with the concepts that one finds in empirical works. For instance, "consumption" in our terminology means what it says; in terms of national income accounts it means all purchases of wealth made by the consumer directly, with the exception of residential construction. Thus, it contains a sizable component of goods that are not consumed within the time period covered by the accounts. On the other hand, it excludes all consumption of income yielded by wealth that the consumer purchased in the past, again with the exception of income yielded by residential construction. Casual empiricism fails to give us any indication of whether the theoretical concept of consumption is much or little related to the national income concept of "consumption."[15] Needless to say, from this it follows that the concepts of "savings" and "investment," being merely the complements of consumption, suffer from the same shortcoming. In the case of

---

[15] The reader may best judge the importance of this item by estimating the compensating increase in his annual income that he would require were he asked to vacate his household right now, taking with himself nothing but the clothes he is wearing, or were he asked to purchase all services he now provides for himself (assuming that he would have no more leisure time).

another major item, money, the relationship between the analytical concept and empirical definition is much closer. The current definition of money by the Federal Reserve System coincides with the definition arrived at in Part II of this book with the exception of travelers' checks (minus the reserves held by the producers of these checks); casual empiricism based on reading of the financial sections of the daily press suggests that this missing component is a relatively minor one. On the other hand, there are substantial differences in the definition of money for past periods. At some time, demand deposits paid interest and thus were partly money and partly bonds; time deposits were transferable by check and thus were partly bonds and partly money (cf. Chapters 4 and 5). Thus time series on money may be used in empirical analyses of macroeconomic theories only with great caution. Finally, most of the accounts cover only the incomes that pass through the market and some minor imputed items; but economic analysis must consider the entire range of income enjoyed by the consumer. Casual empiricism suggests that there may be a consistent bias here, since in a growing society, wealth owned by consumers is increasing, so that a greater and greater volume of their income is not passing through the market at any one time. Let us not multiply examples but merely close by saying that there is many a slip between the pen and the lip.

CHAPTER 18

Simple Macroeconomic Model of Income Determination

Currently, macroeconomic models run the gamut from the very naïve to the very complex. On the one extreme, there are the simple one-equation models that make the dependent variable, national income, depend on one or several independent variables.[1] On the other hand, models with dozens of equations—such as the Ta-Chung Liu[2] model—dealing with but one part of the total economy are not uncommon these days. Indeed, models containing several hundred equations[3] are now in use. There is no *a priori* presumption that a one-equation model is better than a hundred-equation model or *vice versa*. To paraphrase Gilbert and Sullivan, we must make the

[1] Cf., e.g., Milton Friedman and David Meiselman, "The Relative Stability of Monetary Velocity and the Investment Multiplier in the United States, 1897–1958," in Bertrand Fox and Eli Shapiro (ed.), *Stabilization Policies* (Englewood Cliffs, N.J.: Prentice-Hall, 1963), pp. 165–268.

[2] Ta-Chung Liu, "An Exploratory Quarterly Econometric Model of Effective Demand in the Postwar U.S. Economy," *Econometrica, 31* (July, 1963), pp. 301–348.

[3] James S. Duesenberry *et al., The Brookings Quarterly Econometric Model of the United States* (Chicago: Rand McNally, 1965).

complexity fit the task; as in all scientific endeavors, economy of means is imperative. It is this principle that shall guide us in what follows.

Basic Model

Let us now revise the macroeconomic model of Chapter 1 so as to take account, in the simplest possible manner, of all the analytical conclusions reached in this book. The aggregate demand for non-monetary market goods and services is simply the sum of the demand for consumption purposes and the demand for investment purposes:

$$y_h + y_n = c + i \qquad [18.1]$$

Thus, the aggregate demand must be such that the total of goods and services demanded equals the total consumed plus the total saved and invested:

$$c = y_n + y_n - s \qquad [18.2]$$

This relationship may be summarized with the familiar condition

$$s = i \qquad [18.3]$$

where s is the level of saving and i is the level of investment. As we have shown in Part IV, the level of saving depends on the level of human income, the level of nonhuman income, and the rate of interest. However, these income variables were taken to be the sum of market plus nonmarket incomes. Thus, as pointed out above, we must assume that the proportion of market to nonmarket income remains constant for both human and nonhuman income, but not for the sum of human and nonhuman income. In other words, we allow the proportion of market to nonmarket to be different for human and nonhuman income. In addition, there is one imputed income stream that we shall consider separately from those we are assuming to move proportionally with nonhuman income: the flow of services of money. Thus, we write our saving function as

$$s = s(y_h, y_n, r, m) \qquad [18.4]$$

where y_h is real human income, y_n is real nonhuman income, r is a weighted average of the rate of interest relevant for human capital and the rate relevant for nonhuman capital, and m is the real stock of money. Note here that [18.4] can be written as a function of real nonhuman wealth (w_n) as follows:

$$s = s(y_h, r, w_n) \qquad [18.5]$$

where

$$w_n = \frac{M_d}{P} + \left(\frac{M_p}{P} - \rho\frac{M_p}{P}\right) + \frac{y_n}{r_n} \qquad [18.6]$$

We assume that the rate of interest on human capital relative to the rate on nonhuman capital remains constant.

The demand for investment goods is made to depend, for simplicity, only on the rate of interest. Incorporation of capital stocks and aggregate levels of income would merely reinforce the effect that these variables have through the saving function. Thus, we assume that

$$i = i(r_n) \qquad [18.7]$$

Note that investment in human capital is not considered as investment in the national income accounts and hence we have excluded it in our definition of investment. This accounts for the neglect of the rate of interest on human capital as a determinant of investment. Needless to say, from the standpoint of empirical relevance, the investment function above is simplified to an heroic extent.

From our discussion of Chapter 14, we can construct a demand for real money balances as a function of total expenditures and the rate of interest. In addition, if we allow for uncertainty so that some money balances may be held for portfolio reasons, then the level and composition of wealth, both human and nonhuman, will affect the level of money balances desired. Since the level of total expenditures is essentially determined by the level of income and assets, we write our demand for money as

$$m_d = m(y_h, y_n, r) \qquad [18.8]$$

or

$$m_d = m(y_h, r, w_{nm}) \qquad [18.9]$$

where w_{nm} is the nonmonetary nonhuman wealth held by consumers. The supply of the nominal stock of money is assumed, again for simplicity, to be fixed exogenously—i.e., we assume that the producer of dominant (fiat) money takes whatever actions necessary to maintain a constant stock of nominal money:

$$\overline{M}_s = M_d + (M_p - \rho M_p) \qquad [18.10]$$

Equilibrium in the money market then requires

$$\frac{\overline{M}_s}{P} = m_d \qquad [18.11]$$

The aggregate demand function for market-produced goods and services (by definition the national income) is then defined as the locus of price levels (P) and income ($y_n + y_h$) that are consistent with the simultaneous satisfaction of [18.11] and [18.3].

Finally, we reach the aggregate supply of market-produced income. In general, it will be a function of human capital (labor) and of all nonhuman capital. However, in the short run the quantity of the nonhuman nonmonetary capital that is available to the employer for use is fixed. Also, it appears quite likely that the very existence of money makes a drastic difference for the production function, but empirical evidence as to whether changes in the quantity of money make much difference is lacking. In any case, for simplicity, we shall exclude all nonhuman wealth and we shall write merely

$$y_s = y(N) \qquad [18.12]$$

where N stands for employment. The demand for labor in a fully competitive economy will be given by the marginal product of labor; in a noncompetitive economy it will be merely a function of the real wage:

$$N_d = N_d(b) \qquad [18.13]$$

The supply of labor, as shown in Part IV, will be a function of the real wage of labor, the rate of interest, the level of nonhuman income, and the real stock of money that the laboring class holds:

$$N_s = N_s(b, w_n) \qquad [18.14]$$

Equilibrium in the labor market requires, of course, that the supply of labor be equal to the demand for labor:

$$N_s = N_d \qquad [18.15]$$

Finally, general equilibrium requires that the aggregate demand for market-produced incomes be equal to the aggregate supply of market-produced incomes:

$$y_h + y_n = y_s \qquad [18.16]$$

Summary of the Model

Let us review the model that we have developed up to this point.

(a) The Commodity Market

$$s = s(y_h, y_n, r, m)$$
$$i = i(r)$$

(b) The Money Market

$$m_d = m(y_h, r, y_n)$$
$$\overline{M}_s = M_d + (M_p - \rho M_p)$$

(c) The Labor Market

$$N_d = N_d(b)$$
$$N_s = N_s(b, y_n, r, m)$$

(d) Aggregate Demand

$$y_h + y_n = c + i$$

(e) Aggregate Supply

$$y_s = y(N)$$

(f) Equilibrium Conditions

$$i = s$$
$$m_d = \frac{\overline{M}_s}{P}$$
$$N_s = N_d$$
$$y_h = y_n = y(N)$$

(g) Definitional Equations

$$c = y_n + y_h - s$$
$$w_n = \frac{M_d}{P} + \frac{(M_p - \rho M_p)}{P} + \frac{y_n}{r_n}$$
$$w_{nm} = \frac{y_n}{r_n}$$

Relevant Partial Derivatives

Since we are interested in deriving the effect on the equilibrium levels of income and prices of various changes in the exogenous variables, we shall need to know the various partial derivatives of the functional relationship of our model. Let us first note the various partials and then discuss their derivation.

(a) The Commodity Market

$$0 < \frac{\partial s}{\partial y_h} > \frac{\partial s}{\partial y_n} \gtreqless 0, \qquad \frac{\partial s}{\partial r} > 0, \qquad \frac{\partial s}{\partial m} < 0, \qquad \frac{\partial i}{\partial r} < 0$$

(b) The Money Market

$$\frac{\partial m_d}{\partial y_h} > 0, \qquad \frac{\partial m_d}{\partial r} < 0, \qquad \frac{\partial m_d}{\partial y_n} > 0$$

(c) The Labor Market

$$\frac{\partial N_d}{\partial b} < 0$$

$$\frac{\partial N_s}{\partial b} > 0, \qquad \frac{\partial N_s}{\partial y_n} < 0, \qquad \frac{\partial N_s}{\partial r} > 0, \qquad \frac{\partial N_s}{\partial m} < 0$$

We shall discuss each market's partial derivatives in the order presented.

THE COMMODITY MARKET. First, as our discussion of Chapters 15 and 16 has shown, an increase in human income will increase desired future consumption and the desired level of terminal assets and thus increase saving. On the other hand, a similar increase in the level of nonhuman income increases the level of current assets, and thus any given desired levels of future consumption and of terminal assets will require a lower level of saving than in the human income case. In fact, the level of current assets could have increased enough, so that current saving could be reduced and still reach the desired increase in future consumption and terminal assets. Thus, a given increase in income will result in a larger increase in the saving function if it is human rather than if it is nonhuman. From this it follows that a redistribution of income away from human income and in favor of nonhuman income will decrease the level of saving and increase the level of present consumption. As we have shown in

Chapter 15, an increase in the rate of interest that is not accompanied by any change in present or future incomes will result in a redistribution of consumption from the present to the future and thus increase present saving. Lastly, an increase in real money holdings will increase current assets and desired terminal assets, but the increase in the latter must be smaller than the former, due to our assumption of the noninferiority of consumption in any period to terminal assets, and thus will decrease saving. Lastly, we arrive at the negative sign for the effect of interest rate changes on the level of investment by assuming the traditional diminishing marginal efficiency of investment.

THE MONEY MARKET.   Here the discussion of Chapter 14 comes to the fore. There we showed the relationship between total expenditures and the desirability of holding money. Since total expenditures are determined by human income and assets, i.e., the capitalized value of nonhuman income, increases in human income and increases in nonmonetary wealth will increase the demand for real money. In addition, if money balances are included in an optimal portfolio, then increases in nonmonetary wealth will also increase money holdings. Lastly, increases in the cost of holding money will reduce desired cash holdings, so that increases in the rate of interest will decrease cash balances. As we have pointed out, we are assuming that the monetary authorities behave so as to keep the nominal stock of money constant, with the result that the partials of this function are all zero.

THE LABOR MARKET.   The negative effect of increases in the real wage rate on the demand for labor follows from the negative slope of the marginal revenue product schedule for each firm in the industry. As we have shown in Chapter 15, changes in the wage rate may increase or decrease the hours worked. However, we assume here that the entry of new laborers into the market more than offsets any decline in hours worked by existing members of the labor force. Lastly, the analysis in Chapter 15 indicates that increases in nonhuman wealth will reduce the supply of work, hence our negative sign for the partial of labor supply with respect to nonhuman income and with respect to real money holdings. The positive sign for changes in the rate of interest reflects the substitution effect and the effect of changes in the rate of interest on the value of current assets. We assume that these two effects more than offset any reverse effect of a change in the capitalized value of planned income plus current assets.

Conclusion

In the next chapter, we shall use this model to construct the aggregate demand function for market-produced income and the aggregate supply function of market-produced income.

CHAPTER 19

Equilibrium in the Macroeconomic Model

In Chapter 1 we have outlined the consequences of the neglect of wealth in a simple model of income determination. We showed that this neglect leads to the conclusion that even in a fully competitive model a less-than-full-employment equilibrium is possible. Also, we have shown that the very same forces block the effectiveness of monetary policy and make it necessary for the policy maker to raise aggregate demand for goods and services by making direct expenditures on goods and services—to employ fiscal policy. In Chapter 17 we have shown that these conclusions are predicated on a more thorough neglect of wealth than has been realized: that the above conclusions are not only due to a denial that wealth and changes in it may affect consumption but are also due to a fragmentary consideration of the links that connect the commodity market with the money market. The time has now come to incorporate the conclusions reached in this book about wealth and its effect on economic behavior in the macroeconomic model of income determination for the purpose of checking the manner in which these analytical conclusions affect some of the basic issues discussed in Chapter 1. We shall, once again, proceed along traditional lines and divide the forces that determine income, employment, and the level of prices into demand and supply: we shall derive the aggregate supply function and the aggregate demand function and then use them to discuss the characteristics of the final equilibrium.

The Aggregate Supply Function

As we have pointed out in the preceding chapter, the aggregate supply function is assumed to be simply a function of the level of employment; that is, we assume that the rates at which all other factors are used are fixed or that their supply functions are fixed. The demand for labor is assumed to depend only on the production function and the supply functions of the other factors, all of which are fixed, and thus, since we assume that the labor market is competitive, this demand depends only on the marginal product of labor. The supply of labor depends on the real wage rate, the level of nonhuman income, the rate of interest, and the public's real money holdings. Thus, our aggregate supply subset consists of the following equations:

$$y_n + y_h = y(N) \qquad\qquad [19.1]$$

$$N_d = N_d(b) \qquad\qquad [19.2]$$

$$N_s = N_s(b, y_n, r, m) \qquad\qquad [19.3]$$

Our task is then to solve the labor market for the equilibrium rate of employment and substitute this into [19.1] to determine the equilibrium supply of goods and services. This task is complicated somewhat by the fact that the aggregate supply of goods and services affects the supply of labor through its effect on the level of nonhuman income. Since we assumed that supply functions of all nonhuman factors are fixed, we can specify these supply functions and the aggregate production function and then determine the equilibrium proportion of nonhuman income in total income for any given aggregate supply of total goods and services. For simplicity let us assume that this proportion is a constant k_{y_n} and add this equation to our system of equations for the aggregate supply subset:

$$y_n = k_{y_n}(y_s) \qquad [19.4]$$

where

$$y_s = y_n + y_h \qquad [19.5]$$

With these relationships in mind let us derive the aggregate supply function; that is, let us derive the relationship between the price level and the aggregate supply of goods and services.

We shall find this task simplified if we first derive a relationship between the level of nonhuman income and equilibrium in the labor market (full employment in the labor market). In Chapter 15 we showed that an increase in the level of wealth increased the consumption of leisure, goods and services, and terminal assets and hence it reduces the supply of labor for any specific wage rate. This effect on the labor supply function, combined with the assumption of a negatively sloping demand for labor function, yields a negative relationship between the level of nonhuman income and the equilibrium utilization of labor. In the upper left-hand quadrant of Figure 19–1, we show a set of such negative relationships. For reasons that will become obvious presently, this set *EE* is constructed for one specific rate of interest, r_0, and for various quantities of real monetary wealth *m*. The upper right-hand quadrant contains the relationship between the level of aggregate supply and the level of nonhuman income as it is expressed in equation [19.4]; the lower right-hand quadrant contains the production function (equation [19.1]); the lower left-hand quadrant contains a 45° line that enables us to find on each function in the upper quadrant a point yielding employment along the horizontal axis that is the same as employment shown along the vertical axis.

The Aggregate Supply Function with a Constant Interest Rate

Let us now use Figure 19–1 for the purpose of constructing the aggregate supply function. At the start, we make the simplifying

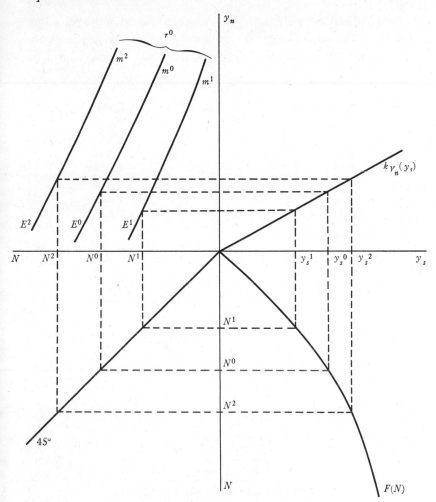

Figure 19–1

The Aggregate Supply Subset

assumption that the rate of interest is constant at r_0 (on which the set EE is based), and that the real quantity of money is m^0. As a result, we can read from Figure 19–1 that full employment will exist at employment level N^0 and that the aggregate supply of goods and services will be y_s^0. Since, as we explained in the preceding chapter, the nominal quantity of money is assumed to be given, this conclusion is equivalent to one stating that income y_s^0 will be supplied if the level of prices is such as to make m^0 equal to $\dfrac{\overline{M}_s}{P}$; let us assume that this level of prices is P^0. This information can be

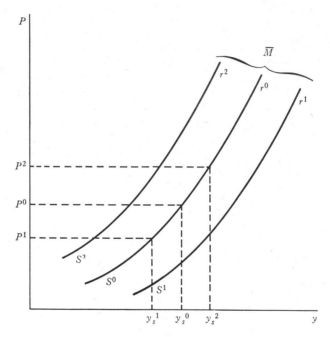

Figure 19–2

Projection of the Supply Surface

now plotted in Figure 19–2, giving us the point (P^0, y_s^0). Now, suppose that the price level decreases, to, say, P^1. This increases the level of real balances and thus increases the consumption of leisure for every given level of nonhuman income. The function relating the level of nonhuman income to the equilibrium quantity of labor shifts, so that at a given level of nonhuman income the equilibrium quantity of labor will be smaller; that is, the function relating the level of nonhuman income to the equilibrium quantity of labor has shifted to the right in Figure 19–1. This shift to the right of the labor market equilibrium function *EE* results in a reduction in the aggregate supply of goods and services to y_s^1. On the other hand, an increase in the price level to, say, P^2 will shift the labor market equilibrium function to the left and will result in an increase in the supply of goods and services. Function S^0 in Figure 19–2 summarizes these results.

The Family of Aggregate Supply Functions

The r^0 notation on the function S^0 in Figure 19–2 is a reminder that throughout the derivation of it we have held the rate of interest constant. Should the rate of interest increase to r^1, the aggregate supply function will shift to the right to S^1. This shift in the aggregate supply function is caused by a leftward shift in the family of labor market equilibrium functions *EE* depicted in Figure 19–1, which, in turn, is due to an upward shift in the supply function for labor. Where does this upward shift come from? Essentially, an increase in the rate of interest has three effects on the supply of labor. First, there is a substitution effect. Since leisure in the future has become cheaper relative to present leisure, future leisure will be substituted for present leisure, and this increases the supply of labor. Second, the increase in the rate of interest may change the capitalized value of income plus assets, and thus there may be an income effect. As we have pointed out in Chapter 15, the direction of this effect is uncertain. Third, to the extent that the consumers hold fixed income securities there will be a wealth effect—that is, the current value of their assets will be reduced by an increase in the rate of interest, and this will also increase the supply of labor. Thus, the direction of the shifts in the labor market equilibrium functions reflects our assumption that the substitution plus the wealth effect will more than offset any net income effect. This seems reasonable, since the substitution and the wealth effects work in the same direction for all consumers, whereas the income effect does not, so that aggregation will tend to cancel the income effect. Everything we have said above for an increase in the rate of interest works in reverse for a decrease to, say, r^2, and thus such a change in the rate of interest will result in a leftward shift in the aggregate supply of goods and services (function S^2 in Figure 19–2).

There are three important differences between the results just obtained and those usually presented in discussions of macroeconomic models. First, any specific supply function above has a positive slope even though it is constructed without assuming any downward wage rigidities in the labor market; consequently, each positively sloping aggregate supply function is based on full employment. The different levels of income and, implicitly, of employment shown by each function are not due to unemployment but are due to the fact that the changing level of monetary wealth causes changes in the quantity of labor that will be supplied at any given real wage. Of course, downward wage rigidities in the labor market could be introduced, as we have done in Chapter 1, and the model would then lead to a less-than-full-employment solution. Such rigidities would, in terms of our Figure 19–2, cause the aggregate supply functions to lie above the functions shown at any income to the left of the original equilibrium. Second, instead of having one single aggregate supply function, Figure 19–2 shows a family of supply functions, each member being drawn for one specific rate of interest. The reason for this is, again, the presence of wealth in the labor market; as the rate of interest changes, so does the level of nonmonetary wealth and the relative price of future as compared with the present leisure. Both these factors change (in the same direction) the supply of labor at any given wage rate. Third, the family of supply curves shown in Figure 19–2 is constructed for one specific nominal money supply. As the nominal money supply increases, the real money supply increases at any given level of prices and thus increases the real wealth owned by the suppliers of labor who respond to such changes by decreasing the quantity of labor offered at any given wage rate.[1] There are as many families of aggregate supply curves as there are possible nominal money supplies.

The Aggregate Demand Function

Our aggregate demand subset consists of two markets: the commodity market (so called because it embodies the consumption function and the investment function, the sum of which determines the total demand for goods and services) and the money market. Thus, our aggregate demand subset consists of the following equations:

$$i = i(r) \qquad\qquad [19.6]$$

$$s = s(y_h, y_n, r, m) \qquad\qquad [19.7]$$

$$m_d = m(y_h, y_n, r) \qquad\qquad [19.8]$$

$$m_s = \frac{\overline{M}}{P} \qquad\qquad [19.9]$$

In addition, we retain our assumption that the proportion of non-human income in total goods and services produced is a constant: equation [19.4] above. Let us stress again that for the sake of geometric simplicity we have eliminated money from the investment function even though the effect of a change in wealth on household investment purchases is, as we argued in Chapter 17, an important link between the money market and the commodity market. However, analysis

---

[1] It is probably superfluous to point out that the fact that we have one function for each nominal money supply has no relationship to the case of "the money illusion in the labor market" that is sometimes discussed in the literature; e.g., Jacob Marschak, *Income, Employment, and the Price Level* (New York: Augustus M. Kelley, 1951), pp. 71–77. In the money illusion case, workers are assumed to respond to money wages and not to real wages. In our case, workers are responding to changes in their real wealth; specifically, to changes in monetary wealth. For any given price level, shown on the vertical axis in Figure 19–2, an increase in nominal money supply represents an increase in the real money supply and thus in wealth.

of the determinants of the aggregate demand function—and that is our sole purpose now—remains unaffected if for simplicity, but analytically incorrectly, household investment purchases are classified as household consumption purchases.

Let us proceed as we did in Chapter 1 by constructing the Hicksian *IS* and *LM* functions that summarize conditions consistent with equilibrium in the commodity market and the money market. However, since we have shown in Chapter 14 that the demand for money cannot be separated into a transactions and asset demand— one being determined by income and one determined by the rate of interest—we will not use the graphical technique used in Chapter 1 because it is analytically misleading. Instead, we make use of a slightly less direct approach.

The right-hand quadrant of Figure 19–3 contains the money market. We show there the demand for money functions $m^1 < m^0 < m^2$, each drawn for a different level of income $y^1 < y^0 < y^2$; we also show there several money supply functions $\frac{\overline{M}}{P^1} < \frac{\overline{M}}{P^0} < \frac{\overline{M}}{P^2}$, each drawn for a given nominal money supply, and various price levels $P^1 > P^0 > P^2$. Choosing any one of these money supply functions, say, $\frac{\overline{M}}{P^0}$, we obtain a number of intersections of the various money demand functions with this money supply function. By transferring the information yielded by these interesections to the center quadrant, we obtain one Hicksian *LM* function, LM^0. It shows all the pairs of the rate of interest and income consistent with equilibrium in the money market, given the nominal money supply $\overline{M}$ and the price level P^0. In the left-hand quadrant we show the investment function *ii* and a set of saving functions $s^2 > s^0 > s^1$, each constructed for a different level of income $y^2 > y^0 > y^1$ and for a given real money stock, say, $\frac{\overline{M}}{P^0}$. We obtain a number of intersections of the saving functions with the investment function; by transferring the information yielded by these intersections to the center quadrant, we obtain one Hicksian *IS* function, IS^0. It shows all the pairs of the rate of

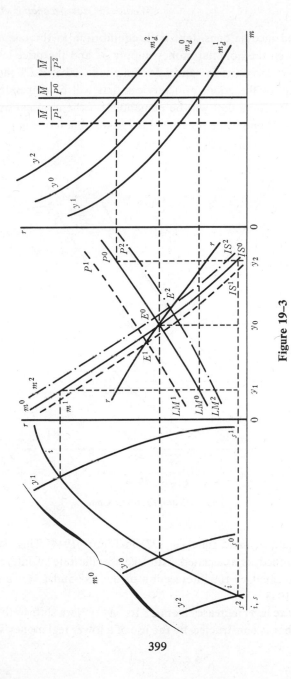

Figure 19-3

The Aggregate Demand Subset

interest and income consistent with equilibrium in the commodity market, given the nominal money supply $\overline{M}$ and the price level P^0. The intersection of the IS^0 and LM^0 functions, labeled E^0, indicates the quantity of the goods and services that will be demanded (the quantity of income that will be demanded) if the nominal quantity of money is $\overline{M}$ and if the price level is P^0; we obtain one point along

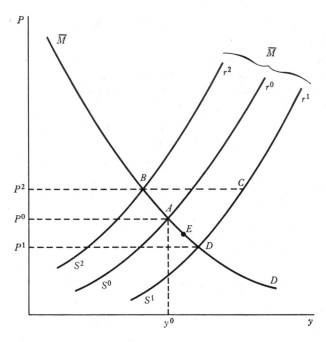

Figure 19–4

The Full-employment Case

the aggregate demand function DD in Figure 19–4. This point, it might be added, is associated with one specific rate of interest, the rate r^0, indicated by the intersection of the IS^0 and LM^0 functions in Figure 19–3.

If the price level increases from P^0 to, say, P^1, we shift to the LM^1 function that is constructed by the use of a lower real money supply,

$\dfrac{\overline{M}}{P^1}$. In the commodity market, this increase in the price level reduces the real quantity of money held by the consumers to m^1, and since income has not changed, such a change in monetary wealth results in an increase in saving. The family of saving functions s^1s^1 shifts leftwards and causes the resulting locus of equilibrium rates of interest and incomes to shift to IS^1. Thus the new higher price level P^1 changes the equilibrium point at which both markets are in equilibrium to the point E^1 in the center quadrant in Figure 19–3. Since both the IS and the LM functions shifted leftwards, this new equilibrium must result in a reduction of the quantity of goods and services demanded; it must result in a decrease in the quantity of income demanded. It might be pointed out that in Figure 19–3 we show the new equilibrium resulting in a higher rate of interest. (This, however, is not necessary on *a priori* grounds; we shall return to the discussion of the meaning of it shortly.) If the price level were reduced to, say, P^2 instead of increased, the reverse of the process just discussed would occur. Both the IS^0 and LM^0 functions would shift downward to IS^2 and LM^2, intersect at point E^2, and indicate an increase in income demanded and a decrease in the rate of interest.

In this manner we are able to derive, in Figure 19–4, the aggregate demand function for goods and services. We might point out that in deriving this demand function we held the nominal quantity of money constant. It can easily be established that increases in this quantity will shift the aggregate demand function to the right because they will increase the real quantity of money at any given price level. Also, it may be borne in mind that each point along this function is consistent with only one value of the rate of interest. Thus, the function is a curve in the three-dimensional space (y, r, P). As far as the income-price relationship is concerned, the function will have a negative slope throughout, reflecting the fact that a fall in the general price level increases aggregate demand both through the money market and through the commodity market. In the case of the former, this increase results from attempts made by the money holders to lend the additional real money held—in the case of the latter, from increased purchases of goods and services both for the purposes of current consumption and for the purposes of household investment.

The Final Equilibrium

Figure 19–4 contains the aggregate demand function just constructed. We may now transfer to this figure the family of the aggregate supply functions from Figure 19–2; we are also transferring the notation attached to this family of curves, reminding us that while each curve in the family is drawn for one specific rate of interest, the family as a whole is drawn for one specific nominal money supply. Increases in the nominal quantity of money increase, for any given price level, the stock of real money and thus shift the labor market equilibrium functions in Figure 19–1 to the right; hence, such increases shift the family of the aggregate supply functions, shown in Figure 19–2 and now also in Figure 19–4, to the left.

The final equilibrium level of prices and income are not immediately apparent from Figure 19–4 because the relationship between the rate of interest and the level of aggregate demand is not made explicit in the figure. This is the result of the aggregate demand function being shown as a curve rather than a line in three-dimensional space. The relationship between income and rates of interest along the aggregate demand function may be taken from the locus of equilibrium points shown by function *rr* in the center quadrant of Figure 19–3. As can be seen from this function, the interest rate falls as the equilibrium level of income increases. However, this relationship is the result of an assumption that the effect of price changes on the stock of real money affects the money market more than the commodity market. If, on the other hand, changes in the real stock of money affect the commodity market more than the money market, the slope of the function *rr* in Figure 19–3 would be positive rather than negative. Let us assume for the moment the negative slope of the *rr* function and determine the equilibrium price level and income. Essentially, the solution to this problem is given by the intersection of the aggregate demand function, which is a curve in three-dimensional space, and the aggregate supply function, which is a surface in three-dimensional space. As long as the aggregate demand function is not parallel to the aggregate supply surface, this intersection will exist; as long as the aggregate demand function does not bend back on itself, the solution will be unique.

Returning to our summary of the model contained in Figure 19–4, the solution amounts to finding among the family of aggregate supply functions the one that intersects the aggregate demand function at a point at which the rate of interest on the aggregate demand function is the same as the rate of interest consistent with the aggregate supply function. Let us assume that the equilibrium is at point A, so that the equilibrium price level is P^0, the equilibrium income is y^0, and the equilibrium interest rate is r^0. To show that this equilibrium is a stable one let us assume that the rate of interest is accidentally disturbed and rises from r^0 to r^1. At this higher rate of interest, the aggregate supply function shifts rightward to S^1. However, the point on the aggregate demand function consistent with this higher rate of interest occurs at a higher price level P^2 and a lower income shown by, say, point B. At this higher price level, excess supply BC will exist and the price level will fall. Thus the equilibrium is stable. If, however, the rr function in Figure 19–3 was positively sloped, then the stability of the equilibrium is in doubt. In fact, in this case it is necessary that the increase in the rate of interest as the level of income increases along the aggregate demand function occur more slowly than along the aggregate supply function. That is, the shift in the aggregate supply function depicted in Figure 19–4 must exceed the movement along the aggregate demand function. To show the validity of this condition, assume that this is not the case. Then the point on the aggregate demand function consistent with the higher rate of interest r^1 will lie above the aggregate supply function consistent with r^1, so that excess supply will exist (see point E in Figure 19–4).[2] But excess supply will cause

[2] Notice that we are now discussing the behavior of the aggregate demand function and of the aggregate supply function in the third dimension and

a reduction in the price level; that is, the opposite of the adjustment required to return to equilibrium. If, on the other hand, the increase in the rate of interest along the aggregate demand function occurred more slowly than along the aggregate supply function, then point E would have been below the aggregate supply function consistent with r^1 and excess demand would have existed, thus forcing an increase in the price level and a return to the original equilibrium.

ALTERNATIVE THREE-DIMENSIONAL REPRESENTATION.   A reader who does not find it confusing to be faced with a representation of three dimensions on a flat surface may find it useful to review the arguments presented in this chapter by the use of Figure 19–5. In this figure, the income-interest plane contains all the functions that were shown in the center panel of Figure 19–3: the set of IS functions, the set of LM functions, and the rr function. However, Figure 19–5 draws our attention to the fact that these functions are merely projections of one single IS surface and one single LM surface which intersects in space and yield the aggregate demand function DD. When the points on this function are projected on the income-interest plane, we obtain the rr curve of Figure 19–3; when the very same points are projected on the price-income plane, we obtain the aggregate demand function $D'D'$ of Figure 19–4. The aggregate supply function is shown in Figure 19–5 as a surface. When this surface is cut at various rates of interest, by the planes labeled in Figure 19–5 r^2, r^0, and r^1, the edges of the aggregate supply surface at the point of cut yield, when projected on the price-income plane, the set of aggregate supply functions S^iS^i of Figure 19–4. Equilibrium of the

----

that projections of this third dimension on our horizontal plane in Figure 19–4 might cause confusion. The fact that point E, representing the rate of interest r^1 on the DD functions, shifted from the original equilibrium point A by *less* than the SS function for the rate r^1 indicates that the increases in the rate of interest along the DD function occur *faster* than the increases along the SS function. The steeper the DD function with respect to the rate of interest, the closer will be a point such as E to the original equilibrium point A. The DD function will be less interest elastic than the SS function if the point E on the DD function lies below the point D on the SS function.

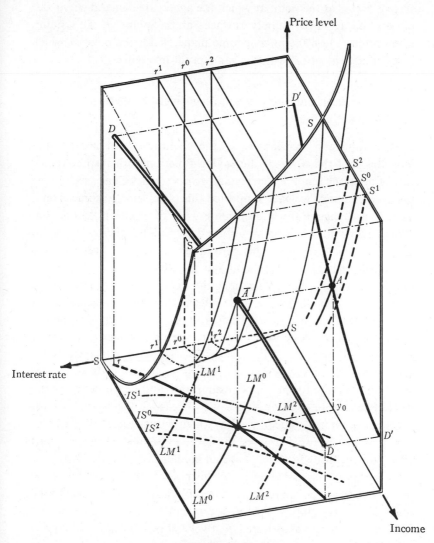

Figure 19–5

*Aggregate Demand Function
and Aggregate Supply Surface*

system occurs at the point at which the aggregate demand curve DD pierces the aggregate supply surface: at the point $\overline{A}$. This point, when projected on the price-income plane, yields the point A which is, of course, identical with the same point in Figure 19–4.

A Digression on the Subject of a Negatively Sloped Saving Function

There appears occasionally in the literature a discussion that indicates that the slope of the saving function with respect to the rate of interest cannot be determined *a priori*.[3] As we have seen in the previous chapters, we have supported this conclusion to some extent. That is, a change in the rate of interest has three effects on the consumer. First, there is a substitution effect. Second, there is a wealth effect—that is, the value of his current assets may be affected by the rate of interest. Third, there is an income effect—that is, the capitalized value of his planned income and wealth may be increased or decreased. The first two of these effects have a determinate effect on the level of saving *a priori*. They both result in the saving function having a positive slope with respect to the rate of interest. That is, an increase in the rate of interest decreases the price of future consumption relative to present consumption, hence leads to a substitution of future for present consumption, and hence increases the level of saving. In addition, this same increase in the rate of interest reduces the current value of wealth, which reduces current consumption and hence also increases the level of saving. Only the third effect, the income effect, may have an indeterminant sign. Therefore, what we have been assuming up to this point is that the effect of the first two is large enough to more than offset any opposite effect of the third. However, suppose that this were not true, so that the saving functions in Figure 19–3 were negatively sloped instead of the positive slope that we have depicted. This situation is shown in Figure 19–6 which follows. Here the saving functions are drawn so that they

[3] Cf., e.g., Lawrence R. Klein, *The Keynesian Revolution* (New York: The Macmillan Co., 1950), p. 59.

are steeper than the investment function which is the requirement for stability in the commodity market. Also by comparing Figure 19–6 with Figure 19–3, it can be seen that the negative slope for the saving functions does not change the slope of the *IS* functions, since

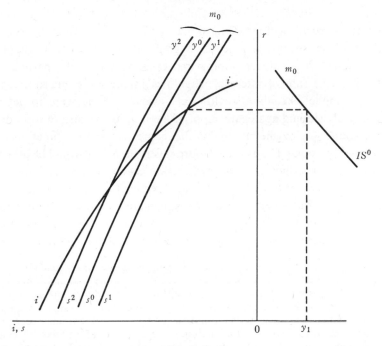

Figure 19–6

Revised West Panel of Figure 19–3

higher incomes are still associated with lower interest rates. In addition, the effect of reductions in the price level still results in shifting the saving functions leftward, and this shift makes each rate of interest consistent with a higher income and thus the *IS* function shifts to the right. Therefore, nothing we have said is dependent on the assumed relationship between the rate of interest and the level of saving.

Conclusion

The introduction of wealth into the macroeconomic model affects several of the conclusions reached on a basis of a model that excludes wealth. In the case of the aggregate supply function, we lose the single-valued sharpness of the full-employment level of income and obtain, instead, a three-dimensional surface which, when projected on a plane, results in a set of aggregate full-employment supply functions, all positively sloping and each based on one particular level of the rate of interest.[4] Rigidities in the labor market, that in the model excluding wealth were essential if we were to get a positively sloping aggregate supply function, in the case of a model including wealth merely make the aggregate supply functions— positively sloping in any case—more elastic than they would be otherwise. Also, the aggregate supply function becomes dependent on the rate of interest both indirectly and directly. In a model excluding wealth, the rate of interest affects aggregate supply only indirectly and in the long run by affecting the level of investment and thus the size of increments to the capital endowment of the community on

---

[4] Note that the existence of an upward sloping aggregate supply function does not impair the neoclassical position that changes in the quantity of money, other things constant, will simply result in a proportionate change in the price level with no change in the level of output or in the rate of interest. To see this point, assume that a doubling of the quantity of money occurs. This change causes (1) the *EE* functions in Figure 19–1 to shift right reducing aggregate supply for any given price level and rate of interest, and (2) the *IS* and *LM* functions in Figure 19–3 to shift right resulting in an increase in the level of aggregate demand for any given price level. If no money illusion exists, then the shift in the aggregate demand function must be such that at the original rate of interest and double the original price level aggregate demand must be at its original level. Again with no money illusion the *EE* functions in Figure 19–1 will return to their original positions if the price level doubles so that aggregate supply will, at the original rate of interest, be the same as before the change in the quantity of money. Thus, the original rate of interest and double the original price level must be a point of equilibrium for the economy. By applying the stability conditions outlined in the latter part of this chapter it is easy to see that any other price level will result in either excess demand or excess supply depending on whether that price level is less than or more than double the original price level.

which the production function is based. In a model including wealth, another underlying relationship determining aggregate supply, the supply of labor, becomes directly dependent on the rate of interest. The lower the rate, the higher the level of nonhuman wealth, and the lower is the supply of labor. In other words, the higher the rate of interest, the smaller is the willingness of the owners of human capital to offer it for productive uses. In addition, the lower the rate, the cheaper present leisure becomes in terms of future leisure, and hence the lower is the supply of labor.

Similar complexities appear in the case of the aggregate demand for goods and services. In a model excluding wealth from the determination of consumption expenditures by households and in a model excluding monetary wealth from determination of the investment expenditures by households, the aggregate demand function may acquire under certain circumstances a perfectly inelastic segment— these circumstances being described, of course, by the terms "liquidity trap" and "immovable and perfectly inelastic investment function." Realization that monetary wealth affects the aggregate demand for goods and services not only through lending of monetary wealth to others (either for investment or consumption purchases) but also, and more directly, through household purchases of investment goods is sufficient to remove the possibility of a perfectly inelastic aggregate demand function. Next, incorporation of wealth in the determination of consumption purchases by households further strengthens this conclusion. As a result, the aggregate demand function becomes asymptotic to the income axis, and the possibility of an inelastic segment, on which the less-than-full-employment fully competitive case rests, is eliminated. Changes in nonmonetary wealth caused by changes in the rate of interest may make the slope of the aggregate demand function less or more steep, but they cannot affect the basic conclusion that the function does have a negative slope throughout. The elimination of the inelastic segment of the aggregate demand function also precludes the argument that, because of this inelastic segment, changes in the aggregate demand for goods and services may be brought about only through changes in fiscal policy and cannot be brought about by changes in monetary policy. Both policies are, once again, eligible for the task of affecting the level of the aggregate demand for goods and services.

We believe we have demonstrated that the decision to include wealth in the micro- and macroeconomic model of consumer behavior is a sound one. At the same time, we believe that the implications of our analysis have an intuitive appeal that simplifies both understanding and exposition of the basic ideas presented here. It appears intuitively obvious that the supply of labor should depend not only on the real wage offered to the laboring class but also on the level of wealth owned by this class. Purely intuitively, we would surely expect that the wealthier the individual, the less willing will he be, *ceteris paribus*, to offer the human capital that he owns for productive uses. Once this is granted, the conclusions reached about the aggregate supply surface—determined by the price level, the nominal money supply, and the rate of interest—follow. Similarly, it appears intuitively attractive to conclude that when consumers are faced with an increase in their monetary wealth they will do all three of the following things: they will consume more, they will purchase more real wealth, and they will purchase more financial wealth. Or, to state it differently, they will consume more, invest more, and lend more to others either for consumption or for investment purposes. Again, once this is granted, the conclusion follows that the aggregate demand function is negatively sloping throughout and that it is asymptotic to the income-interest rate plane.

PART VI

CONCLUSION

A book is supposed to have a concluding chapter, which may be either a summary of the work that has been done or of the work that has not been done. Our chapter contains both. We summarize, very briefly, the main analytical results obtained, not so much to refresh the reader's memory but rather to break ground for an outline of unfinished business. In a book of reasonable internal unity and of reasonable length, many implications of the analysis presented could not be pursued.

One topic of great current importance is banking theory. Once it is shown that competitive production of commodity money substitutes is impossible, it follows that a banking industry that is permitted (or forced) to be competitive internally must have its output regulated from outside. Effective regulation of this output, as we have shown, requires a price restraint and this restraint, in turn, rests on two main pillars: the instant repurchase clause and the no-interest-payment clause. However, in a book devoted purely to theory we ignored the fact that effective enforcement of these two clauses necessitates a whole galaxy of detailed rules governing the banks' investment policies. This subject deserves very careful consideration in view of the current tendency to dismiss the merits of these rules as just another example of an industry misusing the government for the purpose of elimination of competition or of government's meddling with free enterprise. Once it is shown that competition in the industry producing money substitutes would not maximize welfare, anti-competitive measures turn out to be not inimical to the maximization of society's output but essential for it. However, this topic is so delicate and so broad that all we can do now is to touch upon it; we offer a more formal treatment of it in our soon-to-appear book on the *Economics of the Money and Banking Industry*.

However, there are many other issues in this book that were pursued only as far as it was essential for our own purpose but which merit further detailed scrutiny, both analytical and empirical. In the chapter that follows, we attempt to state them in a systematic fashion.

CHAPTER 20

Epilogue and Prologue

We are now at the end of our inquiry. At the outset, we outlined the challenge that the Keynesian argument of a fully competitive less-than-full-employment equilibrium posed to those interested mainly in general economic theory and that the Keynesian argument or ineffectiveness of monetary policy for righting a noncompetitive less-than-full-employment equilibrium posed to those interested mainly in economic policy. For the pure theoretician, an apparent proof that one may obtain a fully competitive "equilibrium" in which one market is out of equilibrium is a serious challenge indeed, and not merely an esthetic one. If competition can be shown to fail to yield equilibrium in one case, who is to say that next year it will not be shown to fail in another case; one crack thus raises questions about the entire structure. For the policy maker, the conclusion that one of the major traditional tools of policy might be—even conceptually—ineffective is no less disturbing. Since, in the real world, those who are subjects of any policy expend a great deal of ingenuity in developing shock absorbers that isolate them from the scope of it, any attempt to use a policy that, even conceptually, in pure frictionless economy can be shown to be ineffective is to

413

engage in an exercise in futility. We have seen that the answer to the Keynesian argument was not long in coming and that the cornerstone of the answer was the argument that Keynes' interpretation of his analysis and especially the analysis of Keynes' followers neglected the role that wealth plays in the economic decisions of the individual spending units. Indeed, Keynes himself, before he plunged into the attempt to demonstrate that the classical answer to the Great Depression is inadequate, outlined clearly all that was necessary to deny the major conclusions drawn from his work: he outlined, with great clarity, the price-induced and the interest rate-induced wealth effect.

The Keynesian theory became so thoroughly dominant, or rather its mathematical version did, that those who offered amendments to it did so—with the exception of Gottfried Haberler—in a very apologetic manner. They explained that their amendments have no chance of being posed on the checkerboard of real life and that one should not attach much practical importance to them. It is puzzling why a suggestion that wealth does play a role in an analysis of the manner in which the economy enables individuals to acquire wealth in the least disagreeable way and to dispose of wealth in the most agreeable way should produce—even now—such an unmistakable air of heresy. After all, this suggestion is, if anything, trite and obvious. One of the first books a graduate student is asked to pay obeisance to is called *The Wealth of Nations*; he can hardly hope to complete his studies without reading another book called *Value and Capital*.

Yet, attempts to dispatch wealth, monetary and nonmonetary, from macroeconomic analysis are almost too numerous to count. Some merit little attention, such as the widespread view that mere assertion of downward rigidities of prices and wages is sufficient to eliminate wealth from consideration. Besides being irrelevant for a discussion of a competitive economy—and surely we do not want to give up that benchmark—it enhances rather than diminishes the policy relevance of wealth in a model that does contain these rigidities. Other arguments against the incorporation of wealth into economic analysis are much more intricate and weighty. Without repeating them in detail let us merely state that they rest on three major arguments: (1) monetary wealth of some is a liability of others; (2) government bonds are an asset of some that is offset by a capitalized tax liability of others; (3) changes in the value of nonmonetary wealth benefit some and harm others. Thus, in all three cases, if there are effects of changes in wealth, they are merely due to distribution effects and are thus of second order of importance.

These arguments appeared so incontrovertible that it probably did not seem worthwhile to formalize this set of negations by subjecting the issue of wealth and its role in the economy to systematic analysis. In this book we attempted to bridge this lacuna and in the course of our investigation we discovered that none of the arguments favoring the elimination of wealth from analysis can stand scrutiny. Ignoring details, we can summarize our results by saying that our analysis revealed three major items that affect the level of wealth and three major channels through which wealth affects economic behavior and, by doing so, the equilibrium of the system as a whole. First, monetary wealth has been shown to be an independent part of the net wealth of the community, wealth of some that is not offset by debts of others. Second, government bonds have been shown to be a part of the total wealth of the community, net of the capitalized value of taxes; it has also been shown that even in a society with perfect knowledge these bonds will not be fully offset by the capitalized taxes. Third, it has been shown that the structure of human and nonhuman incomes affects the level of wealth in the community. As far as the effects of changes in wealth on the behavior of an individual consumer are concerned, we concluded that changes in monetary wealth, nonmonetary capital, government bonds, and taxes have effects that are predictable *a priori* and that changes in the level of nonmonetary wealth caused by changes in the rate of interest have effects that are not predictable *a priori*. However, we have also shown that the latter indeterminacy disappears when we shift analysis from an individual consumer to the community as a whole; the assertion that the indeterminacy of the responses of an individual consumer to a change in the rate of interest applies to the community as a whole is revealed as a fallacy of composition.

Changes in wealth induce the consumer to revise a number of his economic decisions. By affecting the level of his wealth, they cause the consumer to revise his consumption and saving decision, thus changing the aggregate demand for currently produced goods and services. By affecting the structure of the consumer's wealth portfolio, they cause him to take measures to restore portfolio equilibrium. While each consumer may attempt to accomplish this goal merely by purchasing already existing wealth, the community as a whole may do so only by changing its aggregate demand for currently produced goods and services—specifically, by changing the investment part of this demand. Finally, even a balanced change in all the wealth items disequilibrates the wealth portfolio in which the capitalized value of the opportunity cost of leisure is included. Thus, changes in one component will, again, lead to changes in the desired level of the other component. Since changes in the quantity of leisure taken have their mirror image in the quantity of labor supplied, the aggregate supply of currently produced goods and service changes whenever wealth changes.

As a result, monetary wealth net of reserves and warranties and nonmonetary wealth (both real and financial) net of warranties and other liabilities must be incorporated into the economic analysis of forces that govern production and consumption of wealth: into the micro- and macroanalysis of the consumer and of the economy in which he lives. Obvious and trite when stated as baldly as we have just done, we believe these conclusions to be significant, if for no other reason than because they have been denied with such great vigor and persistency by many distinguished members of our profession. Although the above conclusions are significant as such, the analysis leading to them yields numerous by-products and fringe benefits that are also important: (1) As far as we know, this book is the first which has subjected the common assumption of homogeneity of all capital, and especially of human and nonhuman capital, in the long run and in a static society with perfect knowledge, to careful analysis. (2) The inquiry into the problem of whether money is or is not net wealth forced us to reconsider many important issues in monetary theory and in value theory. Let us recapitulate both of these two major issues in each area in turn.

In the past, economic theorists have accepted the proposition that there will be a tendency, in a static economy, towards the equalization of all rates of return and that, in the long run, all these rates of return will be equalized. This conclusion has been reached by considering solely nonhuman capital; after it has been realized that the productive power of human capital is also capital, it has been extended by the way of analogy to human capital without any inquiry as to whether this is a permissible procedure. Specifically, it was extended without any inquiry as to whether these two types of capital, human and nonhuman, may be considered to be homogeneous. We have analyzed this issue and concluded that they cannot be considered homogeneous, barring some major technological breakthrough, the nature of which we are unable to foresee. The reason for this is that human capital, even in a static society with perfect knowledge and in the long run, suffers from the inferiority of not being separable from its owner. If human capital is inferior to nonhuman capital, then income yielded by human capital is inferior to income of the same size yielded by nonhuman capital; but then the capitalization rate applicable to human income must be higher than the capitalization rate applicable to nonhuman income. Finally, we strengthened this conclusion by pointing out the neglected fact that, conceptually and empirically, it appears impossible to divide gross human income into net human income and operating costs. Several consequences of this conclusion were of direct interest to us and were discussed in detail. Let us merely mention that one consequence is that government bonds become a part of the net wealth of the community; the structure of taxes on human and nonhuman wealth affects the level of wealth; the structure of pretax human and nonhuman income affects the level of wealth. Other consequences of this conclusion had to be barely touched upon, since we did not want to range too far afield. Let us mention a few interesting related issues. First, recent empirical studies indicate that the rate of return on investment in human capital is higher than the rate of return on investment in nonhuman capital. This has been widely interpreted as signifying that there is underinvestment in human capital. The above analysis suggests that these empirical results, interesting and important as such, have no bearing on the decision whether there is overinvestment, equilibrium investment, or underinvestment into human capital, since they are consistent with any one of these three possibilities. But then—however advantageous it might be to the teaching profession—they cannot be used in support of public policies aimed at an increase in investment in human capital. Second, this conclusion reopens the consideration of the question of whether the capital market performs satisfactorily when it allocates resources into human and nonhuman capital. Whatever the actual performance, it is better than the above-mentioned empirical results would have led us to believe, because they cannot be interpreted to mean that disequilibrium exists. Third, it also follows that regardless of whether or not government intervention is justified at present, any public policy that would cause equalization of rates of return on human and nonhuman capital would not, if our analysis asserting inferiority of human capital holds, improve the allocation of resources. Rather, an equalization of returns would be a *prima facie* evidence that any such public policy caused a misallocation of resources.

A major part of this book was devoted to the examination of money. Of immediate importance for use was the conclusion that money is net wealth and that, at the present time and in the United States, money must be defined as currency in circulation plus demand deposits plus travelers' checks. To reach this conclusion it was necessary to undertake a detailed analysis of current monetary and banking theory. In the course of this analysis, we concluded that there is but one economic theory that is equally applicable to all economic problems and that is simply given a different name whenever applied to a different problem. It receives the name of

- —"value theory" when applied to capital that has the technical property of yielding real income, the level of which is independent of the price per unit of this capital (nonmoney capital).
- —"monetary theory" when applied to capital that has the technical property of yielding real income the level of which is proportionate to the price per unit of this capital (money capital).
- —"production theory" when used to analyze the behavior of firms or industries (producing nonmoney *or* money capital) that face the orthodox production function in which nonmoney capital is a significant input variable.
- —"banking theory" when used to analyze the behavior of firms or industries producing money-substitute capital and facing a production function in which the dominant money capital is the only significant input variable.
- —"theory of fiat money" when used to analyze the behavior of noncommodity dominant money producer who faces a production function containing no significant input variable.

This difference in names notwithstanding, all of the above problems can be solved by the use of just one theory, *the general economic theory*. This theory is able to explain the existence and the different technical properties of both money capital and nonmoney capital and account for these differences in the analysis. It is also able to explain why the technical property of money makes it possible to shift production away from commodity money and toward commodity money's substitutes. Finally, it is also able to explain and account for the production functions that make the above shift of production economically advantageous and that become the relevant production functions to consider after this shift occurs. When the various "theories" listed above are viewed in this manner, it becomes obvious that they are not theories in the general meaning of the word; that they are not independent and unrelated to each other. Rather, they are merely names that we give to the various application of general economic theory to specific problems under consideration. From this follows that to speak about an "integration" of the various "theories" listed above is not a meaningful way of describing a problem for the simple reason that, as our analysis shows, there is nothing to integrate. "Value theory" can be integrated with, say, "monetary theory" no more meaningfully than can "value theory" be integrated with, say, "production theory"; or than can, say, a theory of the soft drink industry be integrated with a theory of the beer industry. They are all part and parcel of the same thing—of general economic theory.

There are more ramifications of this conclusion than we could hope to enumerate—or even think of. To start on the lowest level of generality and highest level of policy-making relevance, it becomes easy to show that public control (and the restrictions that stem from it) upon the industry producing commodity money substitutes violates no criteria of welfare economics, since without such controls competition would deprive the money industry of the two production functions described above and make this industry face the "orthodox" market situation; it would destroy money substitutes and force society to waste resources by the production of commodity money. On the other hand, public control of firms engaging in intermediations (and that includes the savings deposit departments of commercial banks) can be shown to violate criteria of welfare economics in the same manner as does public control of any other intermediating or producing competitive industry. On a somewhat more abstract level, it becomes conceptually easy to distinguish between nonmoney wealth, money wealth, and mere debts and to determine the proportions that these three items have in any specific joint product: in the money-good, good-debt, money-debt, and—conceivably—money-good-debt. The world around us actually makes it easy to apply these conceptual distinctions, since our society, partly by choice and partly by legal restraints, avoids the use of money-goods and money-debts and prefers to assign the task of money to a specialized resource—money. This contrasts sharply with nonmoney goods and debts that frequently exist in specialized forms and no less frequently are found in the hybrid form of a good-debt. On a still more abstract plane, it might be pointed out that the analysis outlined here reduces the great complexities found in those parts of literature devoted to a discussion of "the determinacy of the general price level." It becomes easy to show that by "the general price level" is simply meant the reciprocal of the average relative price of any base good chosen and that, in addition, money is the only base good given consideration. Obviously, then, this reciprocal does not exist—is indeterminate or, more precisely, undefined—if the base good either does not exist or has a zero price. Similarly, it becomes easy to determine that competition in the industry producing this base good would lead to a zero price of the base good and thus would lead to a general price level that is indeterminate as long as computed on the basis of this base good. This brief sampler of the implications of our analysis indicates that there are substantial gains to be realized in terms of clarity, simplicity of exposition, and correctness both of analysis and of policy recommendations stemming from it if we follow the approach to the various theories outlined in this book.

Provided that the theoretical foundations of this book are able to withstand scrutiny—and we can but hope that this will be the case—two tasks become pressing. First, it will become necessary to apply this theory rigorously to the numerous related issues, only some of which were outlined above, and to undertake empirical investigations of the implications of this theory. Such investigations have, as always, the twofold task of testing a theory itself by a discovery of supporting and no contradictory evidence and of quantifying the important coefficients so as to enable the policy maker to make not just qualitative judgments but quantitative judgments as well. Only then can an abstract theory acquire the practical significance that is, after all, the sole justification for the existence of our profession. As we end this book, we can only hope that it has opened one more path for the quest of our profession to determine the best ways of increasing the wealth of nations.

List of Symbols Used

a	real value of bonds
A	real value of assets
b	real wage rate
$b(t)$	time path of bequests
B	nominal wage rate
$B(t)$	time path of bartering
c_h	cost of production of human capital
$c(t)$	time path of consumption of goods and services
C_B	base capital good
C_I	consumption during interval I
C_i	capital good i
C_k	a specific capital good
C_w	consumption measured in wage units
C^*	aggregate consumption
D	nominal debt
g	government real interest payments
h	durability of human capital
i	real investment
I	time interval
k	proportion of tax liabilities not discounted (Patinkin)
k	proportion of permanent income consumed by a consumer (Friedman)
k^*	proportion of aggregate permanent income consumed

422

$l(t)$	time path of consumption of leisure
L_I	consumption of leisure during an interval
m	real quantity of money
m_a	real quantity of money demanded for asset purposes
m_d	real quantity of money demanded
m_s	real quantity of money supplied
m_t	real quantity of money demanded for transaction purposes
$m(t)$	time path of money holdings
M_b	nominal quantity of bank money
M_c	nominal quantity of commodity money
M_d	nominal quantity of dominant money
M_D	nominal quantity of credit money
M_p	nominal quantity of privately produced money
M_s	nominal quantity of money supplied
MD	nominal quantity of money-debt
n	durability of nonhuman capital
N	employment
N_d	quantity of labor demanded
N_s	quantity of labor supplied
o_h	operating costs of human capital
p_i	price of y_i in terms of C_B
P	price level
P_a^n	probability of human resource of age a of being alive at age n
P_B	price of C_B in terms of C_i
$\bar{P}_B$	Average price of C_B in terms of all C_i
P_i	price of C_i in terms of C_B
P_k	price of C_k in terms of C_B
r	rate of interest
r_h	capitalization rate applicable to human income
r'_h	proxy capitalization rate applicable to y'_h or to y''_h
r_g	capitalization rate applicable to government interest payments

r_n	capitalization rate applicable to nonhuman income
r_p	interest rate paid on private money-debt
r_{t_h}	capitalization rate applicable to taxes on human income
r_{t_n}	capitalization rate applicable to taxes on nonhuman income
r_t	time path of interest rate
R	government reserves of commodities
s	real saving
t	time
t	real taxes
t_h	real taxes on human income
t_n	real taxes on nonhuman income
T	end of consumer's time horizon
u	real subsidies
w	wealth
w_h	human wealth
w_n	nonhuman wealth
w_{nm}	nonhuman nonmonetary wealth
$w(t)$	time path of work
w^*	economically relevant (gross) wealth
W	wealth in nominal terms
y	real income
y_a	real income yielded by foreign securities
y_b	real income yielded by bank securities
y_A	real income from assets
y_B	perpetual flow of services of C_B
y_g	real income produced by the government
y_h	real human income
y'_h	real human income plus operating costs
y''_h	impermanent real human income
y_i	perpetual flow of services of C_i
y_n	real income yielded by nonhuman wealth
y_p	permanent real income
y_p^*	permanent aggregate real income

y_s	real nonmonetary income supplied
Y	income in nominal terms
Y_f	nominal income foregone because of the necessity to hold inventories of dominant money
Y_i	money interest payments
Y_w	income measured in wage units
β_I	bequests made during an interval
π	proportion of money in money-debt
ρ	reserve ratio
γ	ratio of M_d to M_p desired by the consumers
τ	present time
χ	marginal propensity to consume

Bibliography of Works Cited

Ahmad, Syed. "The Saving-Wealth Relation and the Measure of Real Value of Assets," *Journal of Political Economy*, *LXX* (1962), pp. 287–293.

Alhadeff, David A., and Charlotte P. Alhadeff. "A Note on Bank Earnings and Savings Deposit Rate Policy," *Journal of Finance*, *XIV* (1959), pp. 403–410.

Ando, Albert K. (See Bach, George L., and Albert K. Ando.)

———. (See Modigliani, Franco, and Albert K. Ando.)

Archibald, G. C., and R. G. Lipsey. "Monetary and Value Theory: A Critique of Lange and Patinkin," *Review of Economic Studies*, *XXVI* (1958), pp. 1–22.

Arena, John J. "The Wealth Effect and Consumption: A Statistical Inquiry," *Yale Economic Essays*, *3* (1963), pp. 251–303.

Ashheim, Joseph. "Commercial Banks and Financial Intermediaries: Some Fallacies and Policy Implications," *Journal of Political Economy*, *LXVII* (1959), pp. 59–71.

Bach, George L., and Albert K. Ando. "The Redistributional Effects of Inflation," *Review of Economics and Statistics*, *XXXIX* (1959), pp. 1–13.

Bailey, Martin. "Saving and the Rate of Interest," *Landmarks in Political Economy*, ed. Earl J. Hamilton, Albert Rees, and Harry G. Johnson. Chicago: The University of Chicago Press, 1962, pp. 583–622.

———. "The Welfare Cost of Inflationary Finance." *Journal of Political Economy*, *LXIV* (1956), pp. 93–110.

Becker, Gary S. *Human Capital*. New York: National Bureau of Economic Research, 1964.

———. *A Theory of the Allocation of Time*, IBM Research, 1964.

Boulding, Kenneth E. *Economic Analysis: Macroeconomics*. New York: Harper and Row, 1966.

Brainard, William C. (See Tobin, James, and William C. Brainard.)

Brumberg, R. (See Modigliani, Franco, and R. Brumberg.)

Brunner, Karl. "Some Major Problems in Monetary Theory," *American Economic Review, LI* (1961), p. 47.

Burstein, M. L. *Money.* Cambridge: Schenkman Publishing Co., 1963.

———. (See Clower, R. W., and M. L. Burstein.)

Carson, Deane. "Bank Earnings and Competition for Savings Deposits," *Journal of Political Economy, LXVII* (1959), pp. 580–588.

Champernowne, D. C. "Expectations and the Links Between the Economic Future and the Present," *Keynes' General Theory,* ed. Robert Lekachman. New York: St. Martin's Press, 1964, pp. 174–202.

Chandler, Lester V. "Should Commercial Banks Accept Savings Deposits?", *Readings in Financial Institutions,* ed. Marshall Ketchum and Leon T. Kendall. Boston: Houghton Mifflin Company, 1965, pp. 65–73.

Chiang, Alpha C. "Instalment Credit Control: A Theoretical Analysis," *Journal of Political Economy, LXVII* (1959), pp. 363–376.

Clower, R. W., and M. L. Burstein. "On the Invariance of Demand for Cash and Other Assets," *Review of Economic Studies, XXVIII* (October, 1960), pp. 32–36.

Collery, Arnold, "A Note on the Saving-Wealth Relation," *Journal of Political Economy, LXVIII* (1960), pp. 509–510.

Committee on the Working of Monetary System, *Report.* London: Her Majesty's Stationery Office, 1959.

Conard, Joseph W. "The Causes and Consequences of Inflation," in Commission on Money and Credit, *Inflation, Growth, and Employment.* Englewood Cliffs, N.J.: Prentice-Hall, 1964, pp. 1–144.

Culbertson, J. M. "Intermediaries and Monetary Theory," *American Economic Review, XLVIII* (1958), pp. 119–131.

Duesenberry, James S., *et al. The Brookings Quarterly Econometric Model of the United States.* Chicago: Rand McNally, 1965.

Edwards, Edward E. "Should Commercial Banks Accept Savings Deposits?", *Readings in Financial Institutions,* ed. Marshall D. Ketchum and Leon T. Kendall. Boston: Houghton Mifflin Company, 1965, pp. 55–64.

Fisher, Irving. *The Purchasing Power of Money.* New York: Augustus M. Kelley, 1963.

Fomin, S. V. (See Gelfand, I. M., and S. V. Fomin.)

Friedman, Milton. *A Theory of Consumption Function.* Princeton, N.J.: Princeton University Press, 1957.

———. *Price Theory.* Chicago: Aldine Publishing Company, 1962.

———. "Windfalls, the 'Horizon,' and Related Concepts in the Permanent Income Hypothesis," in *Measurement in Economics,* ed. Carl F. Christ *et al.* Stanford: Stanford University Press, 1963, pp. 3–28.

———, and David Meiselman. "The Relative Stability of Monetary Velocity and the Investment Multiplier in the United States, 1897–1958," in *Stabilization Policies,* ed. Bertrand Fox and Eli Shapiro. Englewood Cliffs, N.J.: Prentice-Hall, 1963, pp. 165–268.

———, and Anna Jacobson Schwartz, *A Monetary History of the United States 1867–1960.* Princeton, N.J.: Princeton University Press, 1964.

Gelfand, I. M., and S. V. Fomin. *Calculus of Variations.* Englewood Cliffs, N.J.: Prentice-Hall, 1963.

Goldsmith, R. W. *Financial Intermediaries in the American Economy Since 1900.* Princeton, N.J.: Princeton University Press, 1958.

Gurley, John G., and Edward S. Shaw. *Money in a Theory of Finance.* Washington, D.C.: The Brookings Institution, 1960.

Haberler, Gottfried. *Prosperity and Depression.* Geneva: League of Nations, 1941.

———. "The General Theory After Ten Years," in *Keynes' General Theory,* ed. Robert Lekachman. New York: St. Martin's Press, 1964, pp. 269–288.

———. "The Pigou Effect Once More," *Journal of Political Economy,* *LX* (1952), pp. 240–246.

Hansen, Alvin. *Guide to Keynes.* New York: McGraw-Hill, 1953.

———. "The General Theory (2)," in *The New Economics,* ed. Seymour E. Harris. New York: Alfred A. Knopf, 1948, pp. 133–144.

Hart, Albert G., N. Kaldor, and J. Tinbergen, "International Commodity Problems," United Nations Conference on Trade and Development paper E/CONF.46P/7, February 17, 1964.

Hashimi, R. M. H. *Studies in Functional Income Distribution.* East Lansing, Mich.: Michigan State University Press, 1960.

Hicks, J. R. *Value and Capital.* London: Oxford University Press, 1948.

———. *Capital and Growth.* New York: Oxford University Press, 1965.

———. "A Suggestion for Simplifying the Theory of Money," in *Readings in Monetary Theory,* ed. Friedrich A. Lutz and Lloyd W. Mints. New York: The Blakiston Company, 1951, pp. 13–32.

Horwich, George. *Money, Capital, and Prices.* Homewood: Richard D. Irwin, Inc., 1964.

Hough, Louis. "An Asset Influence in the Labor Market," *Journal of Political Economy, LXIII* (1955), pp. 202–215.

Johnson, Harry G. "The General Theory After Twenty-Five Years," *American Economic Review, LI* (1961), pp. 1–17.

———. "Monetary Theory and Policy," *American Economic Review, LII* (1962), pp. 335–384.

Kaldor, Nicholas (See Hart, Albert G.)

Keynes, John Maynard. *The General Theory of Employment Interest and Money.* New York: Harcourt, Brace & World, 1936.

———. *A Treatise on Money,* Vol. 1. London: The Macmillan Co., 1958.

Klein, Lawrence R. *The Keynesian Revolution.* New York: The Macmillan Co., 1950.

———. "A Postwar Quarterly Model: Description and Application," in *Studies in Income and Wealth,* Vol. 28. Princeton, N.J.: Princeton University Press, 1964, pp. 11–36.

Knight, Frank H. *The Ethics of Competition.* New York: Augustus M. Kelley, 1951.

———. *On The History and Method of Economics.* Chicago: The University of Chicago Press, 1956.

———. "Diminishing Returns from Investment," *Journal of Political Economy, LII* (1944), pp. 26–47.

Lamale, Helen H. "Changes in the Concepts of Income Adequacy over the Last Century," *American Economic Review, XLVIII* (1958), pp. 291–304.

Lerner, Abba P. *The Economics of Control.* New York: The Macmillan Co., 1952.

———. "A Program for Monetary Stability," in *Conference on Savings and Residential Financing,* ed. Marshall D. Ketchum and Leon T. Kendall. Chicago: The United States Savings and Loan League, 1962, pp. 33–47.

———. "Consumption-Loan Interest and Money," *Journal of Political Economy, LXVII* (1959), pp. 512–518; and "Rejoinder," same, pp. 523–525.

———. "The General Theory After Twenty-Five Years: Discussion," *American Economic Review, LI* (1961), pp. 20–23.

———. "Financial Institutions and Monetary Policy: Discussion," *American Economic Review, LIII* (1963), pp. 401–407.

Lipsey, R. G. (See Archibald, G. C. and R. G. Lipsey.)

Liu, Ta-Chung. "An Exploratory Quarterly Econometric Model of Effective Demand in the Postwar U.S. Economy," *Econometrica, 31* (1963), pp. 310–348.

Liviatan, N. "On the Long-Run Theory of Consumption and Real Balances," *Oxford Economic Papers, 17* (1965), pp. 205–218.

Marschak, Jacob. *Income, Employment, and the Price Level.* New York: Augustus M. Kelley, 1951.

Marshall, Alfred. *Principles of Economics.* New York: The Macmillan Co., 1949.

Matthews, R. C. O. "Expenditure Plans and the Uncertainty Motive for Holding Money," *Journal of Political Economy, LXXI* (1963), pp. 201–218.

Mayer, Thomas. "The Inflexibility of Monetary Policy," *Review of Economics and Statistics, XL* (1958), pp. 358–374.

——. "The Empirical Significance of the Real Balance Effect," *Quarterly Journal of Economics, LXXIII* (1959), pp. 275–291.

Meckling, W. H. "An Exact Consumption-Loan Model of Interest: A Comment," and "Rejoinder," *Journal of Political Economy, LXVIII* (1960), pp. 72–76 and 83–84.

Meiselman, David. (See Friedman, Milton and David Meiselman.)

Meltzer, Allan H. "Demand for Money: Evidence From the Time Series," *Journal of Political Economy, LXXI* (1963), pp. 219–246.

Menger, Carl. *Principles of Economics.* New York: Free Press of Glencoe, 1950.

Metzler, Lloyd A. "Wealth, Saving, and the Rate of Interest," *Journal of Political Economy, LIX* (1951), pp. 93–116.

Mints, Lloyd W. *A History of Banking Theory.* Chicago: The University of Chicago Press, 1945.

Mises, Ludwig von. *The Theory of Money and Credit.* New Haven: Yale University Press, 1953.

Mitchell, W. C. *A History of the Greenbacks.* Chicago: University of Chicago Press, 1903.

Modigliani, Franco. "Liquidity Preference and the Theory of Interest and Money," in *Readings in Monetary Theory*, ed. Friedrich A. Lutz and Lloyd W. Mints. New York: The Blakiston Co., 1951, pp. 186–240.

——. "How to Make a Burden of the Public Debt: A Reply to Mishan," *Journal of Political Economy, LXXII* (1964), pp. 483–485.

——, and Albert K. Ando. "The 'Life Cycle' Hypothesis of Saving," *American Economic Review, LIII* (1963), pp. 55–84.

——, and R. Brumberg. "Utility Analysis and the Consumption Function: An Interpretation of Cross-Section Data," in *Post-Keynesian Economics*, ed. K. K. Kurihara. New Brunswick, N.J.: Rutgers University Press, 1954, pp. 388–436.

Mundell, Robert A. "The Public Debt, Corporate Taxes, and the Rate of Interest," *Journal of Political Economy, LXVIII* (1960), pp. 622–627.

Patinkin, Don. *Money, Interest, and Prices*, First Edition. New York: Harper & Row, 1956.

———. *Money, Interest, and Prices*, Second Edition. New York: Harper & Row, 1956, 1965.

Pesek, Boris. "A Comparison of the Distributional Effects of Inflation and Taxation," *American Economic Review, L* (1960), pp. 147–153.

Pigou, A. C. "The Value of Money," in *Readings in Monetary Theory*, ed. Friedrich A. Lutz and Lloyd W. Mints. New York: The Blakiston Co., 1951, pp. 162–183.

———. "Economic Progress in a Stable Environment," in *Readings in Monetary Theory*, ed. F. A. Lutz and Lloyd W. Mints. New York: The Blakiston Co., 1951, pp. 241–251.

Pritchard, Leland J. "Should Commercial Banks Accept Savings Deposits?", in *Readings in Financial Institutions*, ed. Marshall D. Ketchum and Leon T. Kendall. Boston: Houghton Mifflin Co., 1965, pp. 37–54.

Samuelson, Paul A. *Economics*. New York: McGraw-Hill Co., 1955.

———. *Foundations of Economic Analysis*. New York: Atheneum, 1965.

———. "A Brief Survey of Post-Keynesian Developments," in *Keynes' General Theory*, ed. Robert Lekachman. New York: St. Martin's Press, 1964, pp. 331–347.

———. "An Exact Consumption-Loan Model of Interest With or Without the Social Contrivance of Money," *Journal of Political Economy, LXVI* (1958), pp. 467–482.

———. "Consumption-Loan Interest and Money; Reply," *Journal of Political Economy, LXVII* (1959), pp. 518–522.

———. "An Exact Consumption—Loan Model of Interest, Reply," *Journal of Political Economy, LXVIII* (1960), pp 72–84.

Sayers, R. S. "Monetary Thought and Monetary Policy in England," *Economic Journal, LXX* (1960), pp. 710–724.

Schumpeter, Joseph A. *History of Economic Analysis*. New York: Oxford University Press, 1954.

Schwartz, Anna Jacobson. (See Friedman, Milton, and Anna Jacobson Schwartz.)

Secrist, Horace. *Banking Ratios*. Stanford, Calif.: Stanford University Press, 1930.

Shaw, Edward S. "Money Supply and Stable Economic Growth," in *United States Monetary Policy*, ed. Neil H. Jacoby. New York: Fredrick A. Praeger, 1964, pp. 73–93.

———. (See Gurley, John G., and Edward S. Shaw.)

Smith, Adam. *The Wealth of Nations*. New York: Random House, 1937.

Solomon, Ezra. "Financial Institutions in the Saving-Investment Process II," in *Readings in Financial Institutions*, ed. Marshall D. Ketchum and Leon T. Kendall. Boston: Houghton Mifflin Co., 1965, pp. 22–33.

Stigler, George. "The Cost of Subsistence," *Journal of Farm Economics*, *XXVII* (1945), pp. 303–314.

———. "The Economist and the State," *American Economic Review*, *LV* (1965), pp. 1–18.

Strotz, R. H. "Myopia and Inconsistency in Dynamic Utility Maximization," *Review of Economic Studies*, *XXIII* (1956), pp. 165–176.

Tinbergen, Jan. (See Hart, Albert G.)

Tobin, James. "Commercial Banks as Creators of 'Money'," in *Banking and Monetary Studies*, ed. Deane Carson. Homewood, Ill.: Richard D. Irwin, 1963, pp. 408–419.

———. "Money, Capital, and Other Stores of Value," *American Economic Review*, *LI* (1961), pp. 26–37.

———. "Money and Economic Growth," *Econometrica*, *33* (1965), pp. 671–684.

———, and William C. Brainard. "Financial Intermediaries and the Effectiveness of Monetary Controls," *American Economic Review*, *LIII* (1963), pp. 383–400.

Weisbrod, Burton A. "The Valuation of Human Capital," *Journal of Political Economy*, *LXIX* (1961), pp. 425–436.

Yaari, Menahem E. "On the Consumer's Lifetime Allocation Process," *International Economic Review*, *5* (1964), pp. 304–317.

———. "Uncertain Lifetime, Life Insurance, and the Theory of the Consumer, *Review of Economic Studies*, *32* (1965), pp. 137–150.

Index of Names

433

homogeneous utility function, 355
horizon of consumers, 280
infinite horizon, 355, 356
interest elasticity of demand for money, 328, 329
interest rate restrictions, 120, 131
money as store of value, 170
permanent-transitory income, 307, 353, 354, 355
slave society, 265, 266
value of money, 246
wealth as emergency reserve, 357
Gelfand, I. M., 335
Goldsmith, R. W.
banks as intermediaries, 205
Gurley, John G.
bank money as debt, 143
control of banks discriminatory, 165
distribution effect, 212, 241
gross money concept, 228
inside money, 221, 222
money as veil, 174
net money concept, 228
outside money, 210
Outside Money Case I, 210
Outside Money Case II, 214
Outside Money Case III, 215
Outside Money Case IV, 219
Outside Money Case V, 224
price determinacy, 128, 130
subsidies in kind, 215
Haberler, Gottfried, 2, 204
bank and commodity money, 206
Pigou effect, 224
real balance effect, 276
"the system would collapse," 11

wealth effect, 12
Hansen, Alvin, 20
Hart, Albert G.
state theory of money, 225
Hashimi, R. M. H.
operating costs of humans, 270
Hicks, J. R., 2
bank money as debt, 229
practical insignificance of wealth, 15
uncertainty and money, 178
value and monetary theory, 235
wealth effect of hard money, 207
Horwich, George
on price determinacy, 58
Hough, Louis
wealth and leisure, 304
Johnson, Harry G., 204
basis for monetary theory, 41, 240, 245
capitalization rates, 261
commodity money as debt, 175, 207
equality of capitalization rates, 281
on Haberler, 224
importance of money, 23
money as debt, 49, 176, 207
money as limiting case, 176
Kaldor, Nicholas
state theory of money, 225
Keynes, John Maynard, 2
aggregate supply, 7
basic model, 3
definition of consumption, 378
demand for money, 333, 334, 335
empirical significance of wealth, 19
flow-stock relationship, 28

Index of Subjects

439

Liquidity trap, 10, 375
LM Curve, Hicks', 5 ff., 10, 398 ff.
Loans
  consumption, 330
  interest-free, 240
  investment, *see* Investment
    loans

Marginal cost of money, 315 ff.,
  328
Marginal productivity
  of capital, 177
  of labor, 385
Marginal propensity to consume,
  17, 34
Marginal utility, diminishing, 343
Market rate of interest, 113, 119,
  177
Maximization
  intertemporal, 308 ff., 335 ff.
  of income, 313 ff.
  of utility, 308 ff., 333 ff.
M-Branch of banks, 123, 132, 231
Medium of exchange, 48, 106,
  181, 183 ff.
Monetary economy, 47
Monetary policy, 11, 14, 23, 370
  ff., 375
Monetary reforms, 211
Monetary theory
  defined, 135
  and value theory, 243, 246,
    253, 419
Monetization of debts, 176
Money
  for asset purposes, 4, 323
  bank, 79 ff., 127 ff., 227 ff.
  commodity, 47 ff.
    deferred expenditure on,
      192 ff., 196
    full bodied, 190 ff., 196

competitive, 70, 99, 116, 128,
  129, 136, 137, 250
consumer's good, 52, 369
credit, 36, 49, 79, 165
demand
  asset, 4, 323
  comparative statics of, 316 ff.
  and price of money, 320
  speculative, 323 ff.
  time path of, 315
  total, 4, 313 ff., 384
  transaction, 4, 6, 313 ff.,
    333 ff.
  and uncertainty (Keynes),
    325
demand deposits, 97, 107, 131,
  149 ff., 151 ff., 184
  accounting interpretation of,
    149 ff.
dominant, defined, 80
effects of changes in quantity,
  46, 63, 81
equilibrium output of
  bank money, 82, 128, 129
  commodity money, 62
  fiat money, 69
  money-debt, 114, 128, 129
fiat money, 68 ff.
  accounting interpretation of,
    158 ff.
final services of, 52, 369
industry, theory of, 419
"in the limit," 176 ff.
inside, 221, 222, 223, 229
market, 5, 368 ff., 370 ff.,
  384 ff., 397 ff.
monopolistic, 70, 99, 116, 128,
  129, 136, 137, 250
in national income accounts, 52,
  243
output restrictions